OXFORD POLITICAL THEORY

Series Editors: David Miller and Alan Ryan

───

A TREATISE ON SOCIAL JUSTICE
VOLUME II

JUSTICE AS IMPARTIALITY

OXFORD POLITICAL THEORY

Oxford Political Theory presents the best new work in contemporary
political theory. It is intended to be broad in scope, including original contributions to political philosophy, and also work in applied political theory.
The series will contain works of outstanding quality with no restriction as
to approach or subject matter.

OTHER TITLES IN THIS SERIES

Multicultural Citizenship: A Liberal Theory of Minority Rights
Will Kymlicka

Real Freedom for All: What (if Anything) Can Justify Capitalism?
Philippe Van Parijs

A TREATISE ON SOCIAL JUSTICE
VOLUME II

JUSTICE AS IMPARTIALITY

BRIAN BARRY

CLARENDON PRESS · OXFORD

1995

Oxford University Press, Walton Street, Oxford OX2 6DP
Oxford New York
Athens Auckland Bangkok Bombay
Calcutta Cape Town Dar es Salaam Delhi
Florence Hong Kong Istanbul Karachi
Kuala Lumpur Madras Madrid Melbourne
Mexico City Nairobi Paris Singapore
Taipei Tokyo Toronto
and associated companies in
Berlin Ibadan

Oxford is a trade mark of Oxford University Press

Published in the United States
by Oxford University Press Inc., New York

British Library Cataloguing in Publication Data
Data available

Library of Congress Cataloging in Publication Data
Barry, Brian M.
Justice as impartiality / Brian Barry.
(Oxford political theory) (A treatise on social justice; v. 2)
Includes bibliographical references and index.
1. Justice. 2. Fairness. I. Title. II. Series.
III. Series: Barry, Brian M. Treatise on social justice; v. 2.
JC578.B37 1989 vol. 2 320.01'1 s—dc20 [320.01'1] 94-29637
ISBN 0-19-827913-2

Set by Hope Services (Abingdon) Ltd.
Printed in Great Britain
on acid-free paper by
Biddles Ltd.
Guildford & King's Lynn

This book is dedicated
to the memory of
Alan Donagan
10 February 1925–29 May 1991

[I]f a dispute arises, then this means that those more constructive emotions and passions which might in principle help to get over it, reverence, love, devotion to a common cause, etc., have shown themselves incapable of solving the problem. . . . There are only two solutions; one is the use of emotion, and ultimately of violence, and the other is the use of reason, of impartiality, of reasonable compromise.

Karl Popper, The Open Society and Its Enemies

CONTENTS

PREFACE

Although it is designed to be self-contained, *Justice as Impartiality* forms part of a larger project going under the general title of *A Treatise on Social Justice*. The first volume of this was published in 1989 as *Theories of Justice*.[1] This is the second. The analysis of social justice in *Theories of Justice* turned round a contrast between justice as impartiality and a rival which I called justice as mutual advantage. This latter is, in broad terms, the Hobbesian notion of justice as a device for securing civil peace and cooperation by finding rules from whose observance everyone stands to benefit. This is an obviously attractive idea, and it seemed to me (and still does) the only other serious contender for the status of a general theory of social justice.

In *Theories of Justice*, I ended with an assertion of the superiority of justice as impartiality over justice as mutual advantage. This argument is restated in Part I of the present book. At a number of points I refer readers back to *Theories of Justice* for fuller exposition; at the same time, I believe that there is enough that is new in what I say here to warrant the attention of those who have already read *Theories of Justice*. Part II presents what I see as the central argument for justice as impartiality, and in particular for one highly controversial feature: the claim that it is in some sense neutral between different conceptions of the good, and thus offers a fair basis for agreement among those who hold different conceptions of the good. Part III consists of responses to a variety of criticisms that have been made of justice as impartiality. I seek to show here that these criticisms largely depend on a misunderstanding of the role that impartiality plays within the theory of justice as impartiality. At the same time, these defensive manœuvres allow me to develop and apply the theory itself in a number of ways.

In the Preface to *Theories of Justice* I gave hostages to fortune by announcing the plan for the rest of the *Treatise*. Volume II, I said, would be 'devoted to defending justice as impartiality, to laying out the theory in more detail, and to drawing attention to some of its implications for the distribution of benefits and burdens in a society'.[2] The third and final volume would aim 'to arrive at specific conclusions about what justice entails for economic institutions, both within countries and between them'.[3] Being of a cautious disposition, I was prepared to say this only because I was secure in the knowledge that I already had a complete draft of the second volume, which covered all the topics listed, and also a draft of a large chunk of Volume III. When I returned to the manuscript of Volume II after the publication of *Theories of Justice*, however, I recognized that the reply to critics (the forerunner of Part III of this book) needed to be preceded by a more extensive development of the theory of justice as impartiality, and this has gradually grown into Parts I and II.

There have been two driving forces behind this departure from the earlier plan. The first is that, in the years since 1986 (when the original draft was completed), it has become clearer what are the points at which the theory of justice as impartiality is most vulnerable to criticism. This has set the stage for a defence in greater depth than I had earlier thought necessary. The second point is that reviewers of *Theories of Justice*, who were almost without exception very kind, at the same time all agreed that more needed to be said about the version of justice as impartiality that I espouse. They may, of course, feel that in the event they have got rather more than they bargained for. However, given the importance of the topic, I do not feel called upon to apologize for breaching the limits imposed by the earlier plan for the *Treatise*.

The upshot is that much of what was originally promised for Volume II will now appear in Volume III, under the title *Principles of Justice*. The primary object of that book will be to develop and explore some Principles of Justice within the framework developed here.[4] I shall also raise some issues about the psychology of justice and take up the question of how far and in what sense justice is a universal value. I dismiss in the first section of the present book some answers that seem to me definitely misguided. But that still leaves the need for a good deal of further discussion. The tasks originally assigned to Volume III will remain to be done. I have already published an essay covering a part of the ground, to the extent that this can be done in advance of the development of Principles of Justice.[5] Since there are a number of disparate topics to be taken up, I envisage a series of essays published separately and then collected to make up Volume IV.

It is customary, and proper, to thank those individuals and institutions that have provided help in the preparation of a book. Before I do that, however, I feel that I should make an acknowledgement of the crucial importance of John Rawls. Without the stimulus and inspiration provided by *A Theory of Justice*,[6] I find it hard to imagine that this *Treatise* could have been conceived. The best known, and by far the best worked out, exemplar of what I am calling justice as impartiality is Rawlsian 'justice as fairness'. It should therefore scarcely be surprising if I sometimes find that the best way into some issue is to start by taking a critical look at what Rawls has had to say about it.

I must insist, however, that my primary object in this *Treatise* is to develop some ideas of my own, and that I discuss those of others only as a means to that end. Perhaps entitling the first volume *Theories of Justice* appeared to hold out the promise of some sort of even-handed general survey. If so, I do not see how any such expectation could have survived the first section, in which I tried to make it as clear as was humanly possible that my concern was with two *Theories of Justice*: justice as mutual advantage and justice as impartiality.[7] In spite of this, even some reviewers who were generally well disposed towards the book complained that there was not enough about natural rights or utilitarianism—complaints that could only, it seems to me, stem from a misconception of the point of the whole exercise. As it happens, there is rather more about both in this volume. But this comes about not out of any belated attempt to ensure 'coverage'. It simply reflects the way in which the argument develops. Since the focus here is on impartiality, utilitarianism enters in as an impartialist theory—though not one of justice as impartiality. (See Section 3 and Chapters 6 and 9.) And the defence of justice as impartiality requires me at one point to demonstrate that it does not rest on idiotically individualistic premises of the kind assumed by Robert Nozick in *Anarchy, State, and Utopia*[8] (see section 19). I shall also (in Section 33) show that a Nozickean society could not be compatible with justice as impartiality.

I have drawn attention to the importance of Rawls for my undertaking. Several reviewers of *A Theory of Justice* built upon this an expectation akin to that of those who expected a general survey of theories of justice, complaining that I had not offered an exegesis of Rawls's theory. I must again emphasize, however, that my primary concern in this *Treatise* is to develop my own ideas. I focus only, therefore, on those aspects of Rawls's theory that are relevant to the pursuit of that end. *A Theory of Justice* is an enormously rich book, and I believe that some parts of it are in tension with others. I have picked out those parts that contribute to the creation of a Rawlsian theory of justice as impartiality. I have not in general felt obliged to draw attention to the existence of other passages in *A Theory of Justice*.

I should perhaps take up separately a matter that was raised by almost all of the reviewers of *Theories of Justice*. They noted that, when I talked about Rawls, I referred almost entirely to *A Theory of Justice*, and suggested that I should have taken account of Rawls's subsequent changes of mind. One reviewer carried this line of criticism to the point of self-parody by suggesting that my discussion of Rawls must be worthless because it was based on the English text of *A Theory of Justice* rather than the German translation! Since I have the authority of

Rawls's own practice for referring to the original text, and in any case the points affected by the translation are fully dealt with in articles by Rawls (as he himself has said), I need hardly say that I dismiss this complaint as lacking in merit.[9] However, that still leaves the general issue. It seems to me that there is a hidden premise underlying the complaint that I neglected Rawls's later views in *Theories of Justice*, and it is worth dragging it into the light and confronting it. This is the assumption that later Rawls must *ipso facto* be better Rawls. It is sometimes assumed that an author must be regarded as the final authority on the relative value of the ideas he has held at different times.[10] But I can see no reason for this. Naturally, an author will think that his more recent ideas are better than his earlier ones on the same subject. But it is open to others to take a different view.[11] My own view is that the articles that Rawls wrote in the first few years after the publication of *A Theory of Justice* defending and extending the theory (especially 'The Basic Structure as Subject')[12] form a valuable addition to the canon, but that everything since then has tended to weaken the theory. Since the main points involve the psychology of justice and the scope of justice, I shall discuss the later development of Rawls's ideas in Volume III of this *Treatise*.

Prudence would no doubt dictate that I leave the question there, but I shall throw caution to the winds and add that what matters ultimately is whether my arguments are good or bad. In the course of developing these arguments I refer to other positions and attach names to them. But, strictly speaking, the cogency of my arguments would not be affected even if the person I refer to as 'Rawls' were a figment of my imagination. (Stanislaw Lem has, after all, written books consisting entirely of reviews of non-existent works.)[13] For my own purposes, I wish to be able to refer to a position that I have constructed out of *A Theory of Justice*. I believe that it is a legitimate reading of it. But what really matters is that it should be clear what I mean when I refer to the Rawlsian theory of justice.

It is now, at last, my pleasant duty to thank those who have in different ways helped along the protracted process of bringing this volume into the light of day. I mentioned at the beginning of this Preface that a forerunner of Part III of this book was completed back in 1986. All the acknowledgements made in the Preface to *Theories of Justice* are therefore also relevant for this one. I should only like to add to them a few words about the person to whose memory this book is dedicated, Alan Donagan. I was fortunate enough to have him as a friend and colleague at three institutions during the ten-year period I spent in the United States: at the Center for Advanced Study in the Behavioral Sciences, the

University of Chicago, and the California Institute of Technology. Without being in the least forbidding, he was a man of rock-solid integrity, and his death has brought home to me how few people one gets to know in a lifetime whose judgement can be trusted implicitly.

The European University Institute did not have the opportunity of impeding work on this book, since the 1986 draft was already complete when I went there for the academic year 1986–7, and by the time I returned to it in 1988 I had moved to the London School of Economics. I have to concede that the view from my window (into an office block a few feet away across the street) is a sad come-down from the Tuscan vista I enjoyed at the Badia, but I can think of no other respect (even the food) in which the London School of Economics is not a more congenial environment. However, it promotes the delightful idea that it is possible to run a business with a turnover of more than a million pounds a year (the salary bill of the Government department), at the same time teaching and supervising Ph.D. students, while also continuing to write books. Unfortunately, this is not quite true, and my excuse for this book appearing later than I would have hoped has to be that I have had very little chance to do even the relatively modest amount of work needed to finish it since I became convener (chairman) of the Government department almost two years ago.

The LSE provided me with several opportunities to try out work in progress in the form of lectures and seminar papers among various gatherings. I have also benefited from the chance to circulate some chapters for discussion by the Government department's Political Theory Workshop for Ph.D. students. I must offer a special word of thanks to the students in my M.Sc. course on contemporary *Theories of Justice* in 1992–3 and 1993–4, who acted as guinea-pigs for drafts of this book. I am grateful to them for perceptive criticism and also for showing me where the exposition needed to be made clearer. I must especially thank Rachel Harmon for forcing me to rethink some central ideas in Chapter 3.

Elsewhere in London, I have had the opportunity to present some of my ideas to the Philosophy Society at University College and Heythrop College. I have also benefited from discussion of work in progress by the Rational Choice Group of the Political Studies Association. Outside London, I am grateful to Jerry Cohen, Ernesto Laclau, and Peter Nicholson for invitations to speak at the Universities of Oxford, Essex, and York respectively. Further afield, I have presented some of the material in this book to members of the Faculty of Law at the University of Valencia, the Social Science Faculty at the University of Seoul, the Political Science department at the University of Oslo, and to the Program in Ethics and the Professions at the Kennedy School of Government of Harvard University. I am grateful to my hosts, Professors Ballasteros, Rhee, Lane, and Thompson respectively and to the audiences for their questions. I must also thank Tim Scanlon and Stephen Macedo for their written comments on the lecture at Harvard.

I feel very fortunate in that a number of people have with great generosity given their time to reading and providing comments on successive drafts of this book. Russell Hardin and Jerry Cohen both made detailed comments on the 1986 draft, which helped propel me towards the present expanded version. Derek Parfit read an early version of the current book, and the questions he raised about it were a valuable spur to improving the arguments. I am also grateful for written comments and suggestions from Keith Dowding and Vittorio Bufacchi. The editors of the series in which the book appears, David Miller and Alan Ryan, both supplied me with comments on the draft completed in April 1993 that were an ideal mix of encouragement and criticism. My attempts to answer David Miller's many probing questions have improved the clarity of every chapter. John Horton and Albert Weale also read the manuscript for OUP, and their detailed comments have led to a number of changes—though not always of an accommodating kind! The draft of November 1993 that incorporated responses to these comments and second thoughts was kindly read by Percy Lehning. His numerous detailed comments, in addition to more general ones, have ensured that the final revision has amounted to a good deal more than simply tidying up.

As far as I am aware, nobody saw the manuscript of *Leviathan* before it was delivered to the printer. But for those of us who lack the powers of a Hobbes, it is hard to underestimate the importance of comments in suggesting where the argument has to be developed or reformulated. (Even Hobbes might have benefited from some hard questions about certain points in *Leviathan*.) Although none of the people mentioned above can, of course, be held responsible for what appears here, I am nevertheless happy to think of the book as a collaborative enterprise.

I was fortunate to hold a Leverhulme Senior Research Fellowship (administered by the British Academy) for the academic year 1991-2 and it was only this that made it possible within that period to complete a draft of what became an almost new book. The grant also provided funds for typing and editorial assistance, which made the year more productive. Vanessa Sulch typed much of the first draft, but the rest and the seemingly endless rounds of revision have been undertaken with great fortitude and immense competence by Claire Wilkinson. Matt Matravers has checked all the quotations, ruthlessly suppressing my tendency to improve the punctuation and grammar in quotations from Rawls, and has also performed a variety of other editorial tasks conscientiously and even cheerfully. This is also an appropriate place in which to acknowledge that he was the first person to spot an error in the example on pages 18–19 of *Theories of Justice*, and worked out how to fix it up in the same length for a reprint in 1993.

Part II of the book was substantially rewritten and expanded during March 1992, while I was a guest of the Rockefeller Foundation at its Study and Conference Center in Bellagio. I am especially grateful to Pasquale Pesce, Gianna Celli, and Elena Ongania for making my stay at the Villa Serbelloni so pleasant and productive, and to Vittorio Gilardoni for mixing a Bloody Mary guaranteed to banish any trace of writer's cramp (or anything else that might ail one) at the end of a day's work. After a long weekend spent at Randolph Hearst's estate in California, George Bernard Shaw was asked for his impressions. It was, he said, how God would live if he had the money. If I were God, and had the money, I might well opt for life at the Villa Serbelloni. The final round of revision was carried out while I was a guest of the Centre for Advanced Studies and the Centre for the Study of Rationality and Decision Theory at the Hebrew University, Jerusalem. I am grateful to my hosts, especially Avner de-Shalit and Alon Harel, for looking after me and for discussing with me some of the themes of the book. The British Council contributed to travel expenses.

In the Preface to *Theories of Justice* I paid tribute to the classical music stations in Chicago and Los Angeles for their part in helping to keep me going during the laborious process of writing. I had expected that in this Preface I would say the same for the BBC's music programme, Radio 3, but I found that in my absence it had (in common with all other public services) deteriorated, becoming infected with the kind of inane chatter previously segregated (and hence easily avoided) on Radio 4. It took a further lurch downward with the accession of a new Controller in 1992, and much of its output now appears to be aimed at people listening with half an ear while driving a car. (This is especially odd since it is broadcast only on FM and hence inaudible a great deal of the time on a car radio.) My thanks therefore go instead to whoever invented a machine that plays six compact discs one after another. That Preface also acknowledged the important role played in alleviating the loneliness of the long-distance writer by my canine and feline companions. (The term is not only politically correct but also in this case accurate.)[14] Henry and then Gertie played the same role for this book, and I can truthfully say that there is scarcely a page of manuscript that does not show signs of having been thoroughly trampled by a feline paw. Anni Parker also contributed to the writing process but by the opposite method of keeping out of the way. If she had not been around the rest of the time, however, it is anybody's guess whether there would be a book at all.

Bloomsbury, May 1994

PART I

IMPARTIALITY AND JUSTICE

CHAPTER 1

Impartiality

1. Introduction

My choice of an epigraph drawn from Karl Popper's *The Open Society and Its Enemies*[1] is not a casual one. Looking back later at the writing of that book, which was completed in 1943 (though only published later), Popper wrote: 'My own voice began to sound to me as if it came from the distant past—like the voice of one of the hopeful social reformers of the eighteenth or even the seventeenth century.'[2] Those words were written in 1950, and Popper added that his mood of depression had by then passed.[3] Fifty years later, I find the state of mind that Popper recalled having been in during 1943 only too familiar.

This may at first sight seem eccentric. Undoubtedly, the kind of liberal constitutionalism advanced by Popper is better established now than it was in 1943. It is true that the defeat of Hitler and Mussolini in 1945 and the subsequent collapse of Fascist regimes in Spain and Portugal have not led to the disappearance of appeals to blood and soil or of regimes based on religious authoritarianism: far from it. But against that must be set the existence of many more liberal democratic states than in 1943. Moreover, the basic ideas of liberal constitutionalism have proved to be attractive in varying degrees within almost every country, including those with no history of liberal institutions.

If all this is so, how am I to account for my sense of affinity with Popper's feelings of archaism fifty years ago? My answer is that I continue to believe in the possibility of putting forward a universally valid case in favour of liberal egalitarian principles. This appears to be a deeply unfashionable view among contemporary anglophone political philosophers. From a number of premises, including Burkean conservatism, concern for 'stability', worries about 'cultural imperialism' and postmodernist 'irony', they have tended to converge on the conclusion that the so-called 'Enlightenment project' of addressing the reason of every human being of sound mind was a gigantic error and that all we can aspire to is articulating the shared beliefs of members of our own society.

If this were true, it would have devastating implications for movements dedicated to securing human rights in countries where they are not respected and never have been. The government would be able to point to a long tradition of repression and cite my philosophical colleagues to show the absurdity of counterposing mere abstract principles to the dense network of lived morality. Needless to say, would-be reformers in illiberal countries would not be able to look for help to foreign governments or bodies such as Amnesty International. For this would be to invite outsiders to impose their ideas on the local shared understandings.[a]

Within a society marked by widespread support for liberal institutions, a process of interpreting shared understandings would (truistically) support liberal institutions. But it would lack any resources for arguing with those who rejected these shared understandings and instead, say, espoused the view that some particular religious doctrine should form the basis of its institutions. From within the existing orthodoxy, the new idea could be said to be wrong; but that would be no more than to affirm the existing orthodoxy. Suppose that by some combination of immigration, outbreeding, and conversion the new idea became the dominant one. Then the shared understandings articulated by the society's political philosophers would condemn the old one. The point is that there is no perspective from which this abandonment of liberalism could be characterized as a deterioration. In essence, the idea that there is no appeal capable of transcending the shared ideas of the inhabitants of some territory is an updating of the doctrine of the Peace of Augsburg. *Cuius regio, eius religio* was a rotten idea in 1555, compared with universal religious toleration; and its successor is no better.

The picture of the world that sustains the anti-universalist programme is one of different societies each of which has a distinct, homogeneous, and coherent set of political beliefs. Some societies are close enough together in beliefs to allow for some transferability of arguments from one to another; others are so remote that the debates in one

---

[a] I do not wish to suggest that this view is held only by political philosophers. In Britain it often comes out when people who write newspaper columns or appear on the radio wax indignant about threats to Salman Rushdie's life while he is protected by British law, the implicit suggestion being that if he were executed under the laws of Iran as an apostate and blasphemer that would be perfectly all right. As far as I am concerned, killing Salman Rushdie for publishing *The Satanic Verses* would be equally obnoxious whether it was carried out by a bounty-hunting hit-squad in Britain or under the auspices of an Islamic state such as those of Iran, Pakistan, the Sudan or Saudi Arabia.

are literally unintelligible in the others. Of course, it is not usually put quite as crudely as that, but the legacy of nineteenth-century romantic nationalists such as Herder, who articulated precisely such ideas, is unmistakable in contemporary anti-universalism. The picture was never an accurate one. Today it requires an extraordinary act of will to build a political philosophy on it. Neither of its presuppositions—the homogeneity of belief-systems within societies and the mutual incomprehensibility of belief-systems between societies—holds good.

To take the first point first, let us consider as an example the way in which political philosophers in the United States are currently engaged in a struggle for the soul (if it has one) of the American body politic. Remarkably, political philosophers spanning a range from democratic socialism to libertarianism all claim that they are not just putting forward their own views but are also articulating the deepest political commitments of Americans. This may be dismissed as armchair empiricism, but turning to genuine empirical studies does not help as much as one might expect. Attempts to reconstruct in some detail the beliefs about fairness of individual Americans tend to reveal a good deal of confusion, suggesting that not only do different people have different ideas but that different and incompatible ideas jostle one another within a single psyche, one coming out on top in one context and another in a different context.[4] This conclusion is reinforced by national election results, which display a persistent majority among those who vote supporting Republican presidents and Democratic congressmen. Mass opinion surveys give the same impression of ambivalence. Responses are extremely labile, and minor variants in the form in which questions are asked characteristically elicit large variations in the answers.

Faced with the phenomenon of a number of political philosophers all maintaining that they are offering the most faithful interpretation of common American values, we might naturally conclude that all except one must be mistaken. I think, however, that the conclusion to be drawn is that all of them without exception are mistaken. For they are arguing about the whereabouts of something that does not exist. There is no such thing as a set of underlying values waiting to be discovered. Perhaps some societies might be found to be less culturally diverse than the United States; others are surely more divided. Two things can be said with confidence. One is that no contemporary society is really homogeneous. The other is that claims to derive conclusions from the allegedly shared values of one's society are always tendentious. If they were not, it would have to be regarded as a remarkable coincidence that the shared values a political philosopher says he has detected always happen to lead to conclusions that he already supports.

Why, it might reasonably be asked, do these political philosophers engage in such grotesque manoeuvres? They could, after all, avoid doing so easily enough by admitting (what is obvious anyway) that they are extracting from the common store of ideas available within their society those that fit together to lead to the conclusions that they wish to recommend. Their reluctance to do so stems, I surmise, from the recognition that they would then have to answer the question 'Why this selection and not a different one that would lead to different conclusions?' Trying to answer that question would inevitably lead to an attempt to show that these are the *right* ideas to start from. But it is hard to see how that could be done without raising the spectre of universalism. For any attempt to explain why you start from here rather than there—once you abandon the idea that you start from the shared presuppositions of your society—must get you into making general statements about what makes for a good starting point. Thus, a theory of justice cannot simply be a theory about what justice demands in this particular society but must be a theory about what justice is in any society.

I have spoken of the common stock of ideas available within one society. I am supposing that, though heterogeneous, this is not normally so heterogeneous as to make an argument drawn from a selection among these ideas unintelligible to anyone in the society. This brings me to the second defect in the anti-universalist picture of the world, its tendency to exaggerate the incommensurability of the ideas prevalent in different societies. In particular, the family of ideas drawn upon in this book forms part of the stock of ideas available in virtually every society in the world. There can scarcely be a country in which such ideas do not have adherents. In very many countries these people are a minority; but their existence is sufficient to demonstrate that the ideas are accessible and make sense within the (invariably fragmented) local culture.

Long before the post-revolutionary French state showed its appetite for territorial expansion by military means, the other European powers feared and detested it because of the contagiousness of its ideas. They have continued to spread to every corner of the world, and this is quite explicable if I am correct in maintaining that such ideas are the only ones capable of forming a basis of reasonable agreement. The theory of justice developed here is in many ways a reformulation of those basic ideas. It starts from the premise that Burke perciently attacked as fundamental: the denial of the authority of prescription. Once we ask for some justification of social and political institutions that can be presented for the approval of each person's reason, we are launched on a journey that must, I contend, proceed along the lines of the argument of this book.

The standard response of the anti-universalists is to offer an account of the universalists' method that makes it sound so quixotic that the 'interpretative' approach seems quite sensible in comparison. Universalists are said to aspire to be like 'men from Mars' who regard all existing ideas with contempt. They either purport to bring news of some supersensible intellectual realm inaccessible to ordinary mortals or to deduce an entire political philosophy from the bare notion of rationality.[6]

While it may be possible to attach the names of real people to these positions, the prime exemplar of the extreme rationalist variant is always taken to be the Rawls of *A Theory of Justice*.[7] I must insist, however, that it is a travesty of Rawls's approach and that of those inspired by his work.[b] Anything claiming to be a theory of justice must articulate with common modes of thinking about justice: otherwise there is no basis for calling it a theory of justice rather than a theory of, say, hurricanes. Rawls and those who (like myself) follow in his footsteps meet this requirement in virtue of the connection we establish between the content of justice and the terms of reasonable agreement. For I believe that it would widely be acknowledged as a sign of an unjust arrangement that those who do badly under it could reasonably reject it.

As far as the appeal to reason is concerned, this is completely misconstrued if it is understood as referring purely to logical deduction. Historically, reason has been contrasted with authority, prescription, revelation, or coercion as a basis for the justification of institutions. In this context 'reason' means reasoned argument, from premises that are in principle open to everyone to accept. We can add a contemporary gloss to this by saying that these are premises which reasonable people, seeking to reach free, uncoerced agreement with others, would accept.

A theory of justice which makes it turn on the terms of reasonable agreement I call a theory of justice as impartiality. Principles of justice that satisfy its conditions are impartial because they capture a certain kind of equality: all those affected have to be able to feel that they have done as well as they could reasonably hope to. Thus, principles of justice are inconsistent with any claims to special privilege based on

[b] It is in my view an open question how far Rawls puts forward a universalist position in *A Theory of Justice*; what is certain is that he has subsequently repudiated any universalist aspirations explicitly. For my own analytical purposes, I attribute to the Rawls of *A Theory of Justice* a universalist theory when I set it out in Chapter 3. I believe that this is a legitimate reading of *A Theory of Justice*, though it is probably not one with which Rawls would now wish to associate himself. The relevance of this for the current topic is simply that, if *A Theory of Justice* is not universalist, the criticisms I cite are even more off the point than otherwise. Since, however, I am interested in defending universalism, what is important to my exposition is that a universalist reading of *A Theory of Justice* still does not expose it to the charges made against it.

grounds that cannot be made freely acceptable to others. This still leaves it open that inequalities may be legitimated; but it rules out immediate claims to advantage based on, for example, high birth, ethnicity, or race. For although you would benefit from a principle establishing your skin colour (say) as a basis for privileged treatment, you cannot reasonably expect this to be accepted by those who stand to lose from the operation of such a principle.

Clearly, I have introduced substantive moral ideas in the course of talking about what could reasonably be rejected. Since I have already said that nothing can be expected from the bare notion of rationality itself, I am not in the least embarrassed by recognizing that this is so. The underlying assumption here is that claims to special advantages based simply upon membership of a certain bloodline, ethnic group or race are too transparently self-serving to form a basis of agreement that others can seriously be asked to assent to. More deeply, the whole idea that we should seek the agreement of everybody rests upon a fundamental commitment to the equality of all human beings. This kind of equality is what is appealed to by the French Declaration of the Rights of Man and of the Citizen and by the American Declaration of Independence. Only on this basis can we defend the claim that the interests and viewpoints of everybody concerned must be accommodated. There is nothing inevitable about such a claim: it would be denied by anybody who maintains that the interests of members of different races or ethnic groups are not to be weighed in the same scales. The criterion of reasonable acceptability of principles gives some substance to the idea of fundamental equality while at the same time flowing from it. This is, if you like, a circle—but not a vicious one. Both are expressions of the same moral idea.

An obvious problem with the formulation of a criterion of justice put forward here is that it leaves a lot of work to be done by the concept of reasonableness. It is therefore quite natural that we should look for some more powerful machinery with which to generate terms of reasonable agreement. This was what Rawls claimed to be offering in *A Theory of Justice*, and the boldness of the claim had a lot to do with the excitement with which the book was greeted, not only among philosophers but in many other disciplines as well. Rawls describes his own theory by using the expression 'justice as fairness'. I shall follow him in this, treating his theory of 'justice as fairness' as the best-known, the most influential, and the most fully developed variant of justice as impartiality.

Rawls's distinctive piece of machinery is an 'original position' designed in such a way that the principles chosen in it are guaranteed to be principles of justice. The underlying idea may be appreciated by imagining two people arguing about reasonableness of some principle proposed by one of them. The other might quite naturally frame an objection in the words: 'You wouldn't advocate that if you didn't know how it would work to your advantage.' Kant's formulation of the Categorical Imperative that asks us to see if we could will the maxim of our act as a general law may be seen to build on the familiar question: 'What if everybody did that?' In a similar way, the construction of Rawls's original position systematizes a move that is already common in moral argument. Admittedly, it is an *ad hominem* argument rather than a substantive one; but, since the object is to reduce the pressure on substantive moral argument, a generalized *ad hominem* argument is exactly the right kind of thing. The charge of gratuitous abstraction levelled against Rawls by the 'interpretative' school ignores the way in which his conception of an original position is developed from a kind of counterfactual hypothesis that is not in the least esoteric. (I shall expand on this in Section 9.)

The Rawlsian original position is, then, intended to exclude information that might bias the process of deliberation about principles of justice. The 'veil of ignorance' that conceals from the parties features of themselves that would contaminate their reasoning is specified on the basis of inescapably moral arguments about what constitutes an irrelevant factor. The hope is, as Rawls makes clear, not to eliminate substantive moral argument but to locate it in the arguments about the appropriate specification of the original position. The rest of the theory can then take a more or less strictly deductive form by asking what rational agents in the original position would choose as principles to govern their life together. The loop back to terms of reasonable agreement can then be made by saying that the pedigree of the principles chosen in a correctly specified original position gives them a strong claim on everybody's allegiance.

Rawls deserves great credit for the ingenuity with which he has developed the idea of an original position and the persistence with which he has tried to make it work. In the end, however, I believe that it fails. Moreover, the fault is a fundamental one, and there is no chance of salvaging the Rawlsian original position by tinkering with the specifications. (Rawls himself has gone in for a good deal of tinkering.) I shall set out my reasons for saying this in Section 9, and will not attempt to summarize them here. Let us suppose for now that I am right. The question that then arises is: where does this leave the project of founding justice on reasonable agreement?

It may be that somebody will come up with a new piece of machinery

that will accomplish what the Rawlsian original position was intended
to achieve. I am very doubtful but I cannot see any way of ruling out
the possibility. What I do feel confident about is that nobody has done
so yet. I cannot therefore see any alternative to returning to the idea of
reasonable agreement itself and trying to elaborate it. The most useful
proposal along these lines has been made by T. M. Scanlon, who in
effect stipulates an alternative original position to that of Rawls—one in
which well-informed people in a situation of equal power (guaranteed
by each having a veto) seek to reach agreement with others who are
similarly motivated on terms that cannot reasonably be rejected.[8]

I shall explain this idea more fully in Section 11. For the present purpose, I simply want to observe that the charge of gratuitous abstraction
has even less basis in relation to the Scanlonian choosing situation than
it has in relation to the Rawlsian one. The people who are arguing about
principles of justice are not deprived of information; on the contrary
they are well informed. And there is nothing recondite about the motivation attributed to them: they are actuated solely by a motive that has
force with almost all of us to some degree, the desire to act in ways that
can be defended to others.

Earlier in this section, I criticized the 'interpretative' approach to
political philosophy. Starting from the Scanlonian construction, however, I believe that actually existing moral beliefs can be given an important place in a theory of justice. We want to know what people *would*
agree to under certain hypothetical conditions. The closer that actual
conditions approximate to those stipulated by Scanlon, the more we can
call upon them as evidence of what would be agreed upon under ideal
conditions. The crucial difference between this method and the 'interpretative' one is that I draw upon ordinary beliefs critically and selec-
tively, employing a general theory of justice as a touchstone. Since
everyday practices and beliefs reflect unequal power relationships, the
theory tells us to be especially wary of the deliverances of common
sense morality where we may most expect them to express a bias arising
from an inequality of power. Thus, for example, it is very plausible that
much of what common-sense morality has to say about relations
between the sexes will be suspect: putting this in terms of the theory, we
may surmise that it could reasonably be rejected by women.

By the same token, evidence from some countries will carry far more
weight than evidence from others: those that come closest to satisfying
the conditions of equal power and the articulation of all major interests
will provide the best evidence for what would be agreed upon in a
Scanlonian original position. This clearly differentiates the approach
that I am outlining here from the 'interpretative' one that I began by

criticizing, since that has no higher standpoint from which the beliefs prevalent in a society can be assessed. I shall reserve until later a full exposition and defence of the approach that I advocate, which I call the 'empirical method' of studying social justice (see Sections 32 and 34). My present purpose in bringing it up is to make it clear that rejecting the methodological premises of the 'interpretative' school does not commit one to an approach that fails to articulate with ordinary beliefs.

So far I have tried to give an idea of the nature of the theory to be developed in this book. I am aware, however, that I have said little to give a clue to its content. I want to remedy that in the remainder of this section by setting out two themes that run through the book and tracing their recurrence. The first theme is the way in which the concept of impartiality plays two distinct roles within the theory. My contention is, indeed, that resistance to the theory arises partly from a failure to distinguish between these two ways in which the standard of impartiality can be invoked.

What the theory of justice as impartiality calls for are principles and rules that are capable of forming the basis of free agreement among people seeking agreement on reasonable terms. If we call impartiality in this context second-order impartiality, we can contrast it with first-order impartiality, which is a requirement of impartial behaviour incorporated into a precept. Roughly speaking, behaving impartially here means not being motivated by private considerations. This is often cashed out by claiming that to be impartial you must not do for one person what you would not do for anybody else in a similar situation— where your being a friend or relative of one but not the other is excluded from counting as a relevant difference.

What is the relation between first-order and second-order impartiality? The two levels are often illegitimately conflated by critics of impartiality. The effect is to assume without argument that any principles which can be impartially justified must of necessity be principles that mandate universal impartiality. However, the relation between impartiality at the second-order level and impartiality at the first-order level has to be established within the theory of second-order impartiality itself. Thus, the question to be asked is: what would rules and principles capable of attracting general agreement require in the way of impartial behaviour?

What kind of answer should we expect? The section following this one is devoted to an analysis of the common-sense idea of impartiality. I take this to have a tripartite structure: some matters call for strict impartiality; some are completely discretionary; and others fall somewhere between. In Chapter 8, I argue that this tripartite structure would be endorsed in an appropriately constituted choosing situation. The implication is, therefore, that second-order impartiality does not entail universal first-order impartiality.

One form of universal first-order impartiality is introduced in the last two sections of the present chapter and discussed further in Section 37. This is the kind that arises from the notion that everybody has at all times a duty to attempt to maximize the amount of good in the universe. Another form is introduced in Section 38. This is a sort of bastardized Kantianism which rests upon a hypertrophied conception of what equal treatment requires. I argue in Chapter 9 that neither version of universal first-order impartiality is worthy of acceptance. And in Chapter 10 I suggest that a characteristic feminist line of criticism of impartiality arises from the perfectly justifiable rejection of the ideas of Lawrence Kohlberg, who identified the two highest stages of moral development with crude versions of utilitarianism and Kantianism that entail universal first-order impartiality.

The second theme that runs through the book is that of the relation between justice and the good. As it is developed in this book, a crucial task of justice as impartiality is to mediate between conflicting conceptions of the good. This theme is already sounded in the last section of the present chapter, where I argue that a fatal objection to the idea of a duty to pursue the good is the existence of unresolvable dispute about what the good consists in.

The simplest response to this is to see justice as a device for resolving these conflicts by drawing up rules that reflect the balance of power. I discuss this in Chapter 2, rejecting it in both of the forms in which it has been proposed, which I call justice as mutual advantage and justice as reciprocity. This clears the way for the theory of justice as impartiality, which is presented in Chapter 3. The aspect that is relevant here is that impartial justice is fair between conflicting conceptions of the good in virtue of its maintaining a certain kind of neutrality between them. The final section of Chapter 3 puts the theory of justice as impartiality through its paces by showing how it has a distinctive approach to the justification of rules of justice and contrasting this with the way in which rules of justice are derived within conceptions of the good. 'Rules of justice' are defined here as rules of the kind that any society requires if it is to avoid conflict. Chapter 4 then pursues the contrast between the two approaches in one very important matter: the devising of a constitution and a political system. Most of the chapter is taken up with an exposition of the political implications of justice as impartiality, and it provides an illustration of the way in which the pursuit of neutrality can be applied to practical issues of institutional design.

The theme of justice and the good runs through the whole of Part II of the book. Chapter 5 addresses a challenge to the integrity of justice as impartiality that has been mounted by a number of people: I focus on the version advanced by Alasdair MacIntyre, though I range more widely in the course of the discussion. The charge is that the claim to neutrality on the part of the theory of justice as impartiality is fraudulent, and that this conception of justice unavoidably rests on a conception of the good of its own. MacIntyre's candidate is a conception of the good as want-satisfaction (in other words preference-utilitarianism). I argue in Chapter 6 that this does indeed generate a kind of neutrality, but not the same kind as that intrinsic to justice as impartiality. Chapter 7, which completes Part II, analyses several recent arguments in favour of neutrality of the form that I advocate. I suggest here that the only line of argument that is adequate is one that appeals to the unresolvability of disputes about the good. The case for neutrality is then that it is the only fair, and thus generally acceptable, way of dealing with this fact.

2. *The Common-sense Idea of Impartiality*

If we try to think of a role in which impartial conduct is demanded, we shall most likely come up with that of a judge. As Jeremy Bentham asked rhetorically: 'Where is the cause in which any the slightest departure from the rule of impartiality is, in the eye of justice and reason, anything less than criminal on the part of the judge?'[9] Judges are supposed to be unmoved by personal interests or the congeniality or otherwise of those who appear before them. Because we recognize the force of partiality, we ask judges to disqualify themselves from hearing a case if they have financial interests in it or if they have personal connections with any of those involved in it. Partiality—what Hobbes called 'accerption of persons'[10]—is the introduction of private considerations into a judgement that should be made on public grounds.

Max Weber's well-known analysis of bureaucracy also emphasized impartiality as one of the prime virtues of public officials. Bureaucracy is, he said, marked by 'the dominance of a spirit of formalistic impersonality: "*Sine ira et studio*", without hatred or passion, and hence without affection or enthusiasm. The dominant norms are concepts of straightforward duty without regard to personal considerations. Everyone is subject to formal equality of treatment; that is, everyone in the same empirical situation. This is the spirit in which the ideal official conducts his office.'[11] Later on, in *Economy and Society*, he expressed

the same idea even more strongly: 'Bureaucracy develops the more perfectly, the more it is "dehumanized", the more completely it succeeds in
eliminating from official business love, hatred, and all purely personal,
irrational, and emotional elements which escape calculation.'[12]

The dispassionate impartiality that is the stock-in-trade of the ideal
judge or bureaucrat may be demanded of the rest of us on special occasions such as refereeing a game, judging the entries in a show, or examining a candidate. The exclusion of personal considerations from the
work of show judges or examiners is often assured, where this is feasible, by making the entrants or examinees anonymous. It would be an
error, however, to suppose that impartiality makes its home only in
such chilly surroundings. Teachers, for example, are liable to be accused
of 'favouritism'. And playing favourites—the creation of 'teachers'
pets'—is nothing other than a deviation from the kind of impartiality
appropriate to a teacher. Impartiality is relatively easy to achieve if a
teacher maintains a distance from all the students and treats them all
alike. What is very much harder to pull off is engaging with the pupils
as individuals and creating a personal relationship with them while at
the same time steering clear of favouritism. Nevertheless, I think that
common-sense morality—among both pupils and teachers—holds up
impartiality of the right kind as a virtue.

All the same considerations are valid with redoubled force in the case
of relations between parents and their children. There are sentimental-
ists (including some contemporary philosophers) who believe that
notions of fairness have no part to play within families. It is clear, however, that siblings normally have a well-developed sense of unfair treatment. Parents, too, worry about it—and not simply in the quest of a
quiet life. They try to check tendencies towards favouritism, and if they
actually prefer one child to another they often make strenuous efforts
to prevent this from showing. Needless to say, the behaviour of good
parents is far from the affectless and rigid impartiality of the ideal judge
or civil servant when engaged in their official duties. Impartiality
between children is consistent with the development of different relations with different ones according to their personalities. And, although
young children are liable to demand a mechanical equality of treatment,
it is a sign of maturity to recognize that impartiality within a family
does not require this. What is ultimately most important is that children
should have a sense of being equally valued by their parents.
Combining spontaneous affection with impartiality is difficult, as
numerous works of fiction in addition to personal experience attest.
(We have the authority of Henry Fielding for the observation that 'it is
almost impossible for the best Parent to observe an exact Impartiality to

his Children.')[13] But I suggest that common-sense morality would condemn at any rate gross departures from impartiality within families.

Contrary to a misconception frequently found among philosophers (and no doubt others), we cannot say that impartiality rules in the public sphere while partiality has free reign in the private sphere. Nevertheless, it does have to be emphasized that the scope of impartiality is bounded. Common-sense morality holds up a standard of impartiality to parents in respect of their own children but does not ask them to be impartial between their own children and those of other people. (This does not license them, however, to pursue their children's interests at all costs, a point to which I shall return in at the end of this book (Section 42). Similarly, common-sense morality does not ask a man faced with a choice between rescuing his wife or rescuing somebody else from a burning building to make the decision impartially, taking account of the rival claims of the candidates for rescue and leaving out of consideration the fact that one of them is his wife. (This well-worn philosophical example will figure largely in Chapter 9.)

Some choices, according to common-sense morality, may legitimately be based on precisely the kinds of factor that judges and bureaucrats are supposed to exclude from their deliberations. A good example here is the choice of friends. We become friends with people not because they score higher on some list of objective characteristics than other people we meet but simply because for some reason or other we like their company and want to be associated with them. Nobody who was not in the grip of a system would imagine that there was anything untoward in that. This is not to say that common-sense morality is without resources that will enable a criticism to be mounted of somebody's choice of friends. We could say that he has fallen in with people who are leading him astray, or that his choice of friends betrays an unpleasant taste for social climbing or expresses racial or ethnic prejudices. But we still would not suggest that the fault was one of deficient impartiality. He has not failed in some obligation; rather, he has a moral right to make any choice he likes, but the use he actually made of that right reflects poorly on his character. (For more on such 'moral rights', see the end of Section 12.)

Common-sense morality is clear that there are some matters where impartiality is relevant and other matters where impartiality is out of place, the choice of friends being paradigmatic. The boundaries are, however, not fixed and at any given time there is likely to be an area that is in dispute. It used to be taken as axiomatic that the choice of club members was to be assimilated for moral purposes to the choice of friends. A club that excluded Jews, blacks, or women might be criticized on much the same basis as a person's choice of friends might be—as being indicative of racial or sexual prejudice. But no issue of fairness was seen to arise, any more than it could in the choice of friends. This view of the matter is open to challenge, however, and has been challenged.

The kind of case that most straightforwardly lends itself to analysis in terms of fairness is one where a private club can be looked upon as controlling a scarce resource. Suppose the club numbers among its members most of the city's top executives, and is known to be a place where a lot of business gets done informally. If it has a policy of excluding women from membership, it is open to moral and in some places legal pressure. In effect, the club is thought of as controlling a special kind of scarce resource in the form of access under favourable conditions to its members. And because of the significance of this resource for success in business life, the blanket exclusion of women raises questions of equity. The case is even more straightforward where a club controls access to a scarce tangible resource such as a golf course. If the only golf club in an area excludes Jews or blacks from membership, or if there are several clubs but all of them have the same policy, the relevance of fairness is patent. The value of freedom of association here conflicts with the principle that people should not be put at a material disadvantage on the basis of belonging to a certain ethnic or racial group.

Some clubs do not exercise any discretion in the choice of members except to operate a blanket exclusion of, say, Jews or women. Subject to not being in a prohibited category, anybody may join, or go on to a waiting list if the maximum number of members has already been reached. Such clubs have a relatively weak claim based upon the value of freedom of association: the analogy with the choice of friends is not at all close. The demand that they should choose their members impartially, by removing the blanket exclusion, is therefore quite well grounded. Many clubs, however, have some process of election which allows otherwise eligible candidates to be rejected on purely personal grounds—perhaps because of the intense antipathy of a few of the existing members towards them. Here the claims of freedom of association are stronger, yet it may be argued that a club should be able to retain the rejection of candidates on idiosyncratic grounds but should not be able to operate a policy of excluding people automatically on the basis of such characteristics as race or sex. This may seem perverse but I suggest that it has a certain logic to it. Being excluded from a club arbitrarily is a possibility that anybody has to face, and is inherent in the power of clubs to elect their own members at all. But being excluded on the basis of race or sex gives the members of the excluded group a legitimate grievance of a kind that somebody excluded on a personal basis does not have. Since the grievance is based simply on the policy of exclusion—its stigmatizing effect on a whole group—it does not make any difference here whether the club controls a scarce resource or not. (The point is clear in the case of, for example, restaurants. A restaurant that refuses to serve, say, blacks cannot get itself off the hook by saying that there is an equally good restaurant round the corner that does.) If this line of reasoning is followed, it will be seen that it demands impartiality in one way but not another. This again illustrates the way in which impartiality can set certain constraints on conduct while leaving choice open in other directions.

I have said that the relevance of impartiality to the membership policies of private associations is a matter on which common-sense morality does not speak with a single voice. I should add, of course, that what is widely agreed upon within a society changes over time and also differs from one country to another. Thus, in spite of the greater penetration of social democratic ideas in Western Europe than in the USA, Americans have carried much further the practice of legal intervention in what would in earlier times have universally been regarded as the private affairs of associations. This can be accounted for by the far greater seriousness with which Americans have from the 1950s onward deployed the legal system to attack racial discrimination. The legal instruments developed in this context have subsequently been picked up and used to strengthen the position of other groups such as women and (in some places) gays. Even where legal intervention is not available—and perhaps not even considered desirable—moral criticism of the way in which associations conduct their business is quite common in America wherever 'private' decisions have an impact on the relative standing of different groups in the society.

Although it would be possible to go on indefinitely adding further examples, those already given are sufficient for my present purpose, which is to draw some broad conclusions about the common-sense idea of impartiality. What emerges is that impartiality is not a strong organizing concept within common-sense morality. I mean by this that it is not a primary moral notion generating subsidiary ones. Rather, impartiality features in a number of different contexts, and in each context there is some other—and deeper—way of characterizing what is at issue. Thus, impartiality in a judge is obviously important; but if we ask why this is so we shall see that its significance is derivative. Judicial impartiality is one of the elements (though only one) in a fair trial. Similarly, in so far as the impartiality of a Weberian bureaucrat is a virtue—a matter on which Weber himself was notoriously ambivalent—

it is a virtue because it assures fair treatment. Like cases will be treated alike without regard to any characteristics of the parties other than those defined in advance as relevant: their economic circumstances, say, and not their clothing, manners, or ethnicity.

The point is, then, that impartiality in the conduct of judges and bureaucrats is significant as an aspect of procedural fairness. We might initially have expected it to be the other way round—that impartiality would be the general concept and fairness an aspect of it. But this is not so. It is perhaps worth adding that the value of this kind of fairness is itself dependent upon the justice of the rules that are being applied. For it amounts to the correct application of the rules. A well-run bureaucracy is, as Weber emphasized, an efficient piece of machinery; but it is a machine that can be directed to evil ends as easily as to good ones. Given an order to round up all Jews for deportation, an ideal Weberian bureaucrat will do so, whereas a bureaucrat who permitted human feelings to enter into his work might respond to emotional appeals, and a venal one would be prepared to take bribes for neglecting his duty.[c]

Fairness may be said to lie at the root of impartiality in my other examples as well, though there are in these cases other and more precise ways of expressing the point. Consider again the prescription that teachers and parents should be impartial. Not showing favouritism might be described as a requirement of fair dealing. But we could spell this out more fully by presenting the cases as ones where a presumptive equality of status (as pupils or as siblings) gives rise to a presumption of equal treatment. If impartiality has more content here, this arises simply because the context creates a presumption that pupils or siblings are to be treated as equals, in contrast to the impartiality of judges and bureaucrats, which calls only for the discriminations built into the rules to be adhered to without fear or favour.

As I have already pointed out, treatment of children as equals leaves a good deal of latitude for doing different things with or for different children in the same family. For example, upper class parents in earlier days would have felt that they were doing equally well by all their children if they sent the sons to public school and university while giving the daughters a governess and a London 'season'. But the notion of treatment as equals is still not devoid of content. Under contemporary conditions, parents can hardly be said to have done well by their daughters if all they have done is create the conditions for a 'good marriage'.

---

[c] István Deák, having spoken of 'a long tradition of bureaucratic laxness and corruption' that Romania inherited from the Ottoman Empire, adds that 'bribery of officials helped to save thousands of Jewish lives during World War II'. István Deák, 'Survivors,' *The New York Review of Books*, 5 March 1992, pp. 43–51, quotations from p. 43.

Victorian novels usually ended with a marriage; contemporary novels often begin with a divorce. There is not really a lot of room for doubt that today denying a good education to a daughter while ensuring one for a son is treating her disadvantageously. Moreover, there are many practices common in non-Western cultures that quite unequivocally establish the second-class status of females within the family, such as the custom of their serving food to the males first and eating what is left, or the convention that any male (of whatever age) can order about any female (of any age).

The case of blanket exclusions from club membership also exhibits clearly the way in which impartiality is not a central organizing concept in common-sense thinking. We can, if we wish, bring the case under the umbrella of impartiality. I have suggested that the exclusion of whole groups on the basis of, for example, race or gender is an evil of a different order from that of arbitrary exclusions of individuals and that this is because blanket exclusions have the effect of stigmatizing whole groups of the population. We can say that what is at issue here is fairness, in that it is unfair to be a victim of stigmatization. And I think this is indeed the right thing to say. But it is clear that if we go on to say that the exclusion of a category of people offends against impartiality, we are not adding anything and perhaps subtracting something, since the same may equally well be said of individual exclusions.

To sum up, the notion of impartiality is certainly not foreign to common-sense moral thinking. But it does not play a central role, and it is indeed dispensable in that there is always some concept available that would carry the moral burden equally well if not better. What is to be especially observed, since it will be crucially important in the rest of this book, is that it would be possible for anyone to satisfy all the requirements of impartiality, as they are understood in common-sense morality, and still be left with a lot of discretion. Some matters are not covered by impartiality at all. For the rest, impartiality operates most of the time to set the outer limits on acceptable behaviour. Very often it takes a conditional form: it says that if you do x you cannot also do y, but it does not tell you whether or not to do x. Even in the judicial or bureaucratic contexts with which I began, what does the work of constraining the decision tightly is the requirement of rule-following. To say that the rule should be followed impartially is simply to say that it should be followed faithfully. To be more precise, it is to say that the rule should not be departed from in the specific ways constituted by exhibiting partiality.

3. Impartial Conceptions of the Good

My focus in this chapter is upon ideas about impartial conduct. However, in order to introduce the second of the two conceptions of impartial conduct that I want to discuss, I must first shift to a different level and talk about an impartial conception of the good. By this I mean a conception of the good that does not give any special weight to the interests or concerns of the agent but treats all interests or concerns in the same way. By contrast, a partial conception of the good is one that attributes more weight to the interests and concerns of the agent or of those connected to him in some way (his family, his ethnic group, or his fellow-countrymen, for example) than to those of others. I should make it clear that an impartialist theory does not have to confine its concern to the interests and concerns of human beings. The requirement can therefore be stated more generally by saying that, to the extent that a conception of the good takes account of the interests and concerns of human beings, it must treat them all on the same footing if it is to count as an impartial conception.

I want to follow up these remarks by distinguishing three broad categories of impartialist theory, each of which is capable of generating more than one conception of the good. I shall call them the anthropocentric, the zoocentric, and the ecocentric. By an anthropocentric conception of the good I mean one that attributes value only to the states of human beings. It is possible for different people to assent to the general proposition that the good of human beings is the only thing that counts and that the good of all human beings counts equally while disagreeing about what constitutes the good for a human being. (Candidates have included happiness, pleasure, want-satisfaction, and self-realization). Even among those with a common view of what constitutes the good for a human being, there can still be disagreements about the way in which the good of different people is to be brought together to form an assessment of the goodness of a state of affairs. This is not settled by the constraint that everybody's good is in some sense to count equally. The simplest answer is that all good is to count equally however it is distributed among people, but it is important to recognize that this is only one possible answer. It would also satisfy the requirement of impartiality to say that a given amount of good has more value the more equally it is distributed, or that special significance is to be attached to how well those with the smallest amount of good are faring, for example. If we combine four conceptions of the good for a human being and three ways of relating the good of different people, we arrive at a dozen specific conceptions of the good, and these do not exhaust the possibilities.

The idea underlying the ecocentric approach is 'that nature, as an object of reverence, love and respect, itself has a moral worth and therefore should be protected for its own sake and not simply for the "satisfactions" or "benefits" it offers human beings'.[14] Inanimate nature and plant life as well as animals are thus assigned value by this view: 'the good of the biotic *community* is the ultimate measure of the moral value, the rightness or wrongness, of actions.'[15] The value to be maximized is 'the integrity, stability, and beauty of the biotic community'.[16] It is easy to imagine that even a society all of whose members adhered to this objective might well disagree a good deal about what exactly it called for in a given situation. A similar problem of indeterminacy afflicts the zoocentric approach, more familiarly known now as 'animal liberation'. Peter Singer suggests that it is the only way of implementing the slogan 'All animals are equal'.[17] But an equal weighting for the interests of all sentient beings turns out to mean only that *arbitrary* distinctions are ruled out, which leaves us with an ill-defined problem comparing the interests of cockroaches and cats to those of human beings.

Each of the three ethics finds room for the others, but only on its own terms. Thus, if we care for the ecosystem, this will presumably contribute to the well-being of non-human animals and human beings. If we put the aggregate welfare of all animals at the center, then the health of the ecosystem will have instrumental value (on the same assumptions as before) and the welfare of human beings is obviously a constituent in the aggregate. Finally, from an anthropocentric viewpoint the ecosystem will again have instrumental value on the assumption that the health of the ecosystem contributes to human wellbeing. By the same token, animals pressed into serving human purposes will tend to do so better (at any rate up to some point) if they are well looked after. In addition, the ecosystem and the welfare of animals can also enter in as elements in human utility functions: if some people care about the state of the environment or about the sufferings of non-human animals, then catering to the interests of human beings will necessarily entail doing a certain amount to meet the environmental or humane concerns of these people.[d]

---

[d] Thus, the so-called 'green theory of value' proposed by Robert Goodin is in fact a form of utilitarianism that simply draws attention to a possible source of utility that might otherwise be overlooked. He summarizes the theory in the following three propositions: '(1) People want to see some sense and pattern to their lives. (2) That requires, in turn, that their lives be set in some larger context. (3) The products of natural processes, untouched as they are by human hands, provides precisely that desired context', Robert E. Goodin, *Green Political Theory* (Cambridge: Polity Press, 1992), 37. Goodin

We should not, however, underestimate the degree to which the three perspectives lead to conflicting prescriptions. It is perhaps apparent enough that an exclusive concern with human interests is liable to violate the conditions required by the maximization of value on ecocentric or zoocentric criteria. But the potential for a clash between those two perspectives is also ever-present. For example, 'to preserve the healthy functioning and integrity of an ecosystem, it might be necessary . . . to let many individual creatures perish—deer, for example—that might easily be saved from starvation by human intervention or might even prosper in a managed environment.'[18] Again, from an ecological perspective the survival of the last members of a species would be valued far above the survival of an equal number of some closely related but common species. But this judgement would be incomprehensible on an animal welfare ethic.[19]

It may be said that in reality the conflict is less stark than might be anticipated from my presentation of the problem, because people normally acknowledge multiple sources of value. It is, perhaps, true enough that few would utterly deny any independent value to the ecosphere, the interests of non-human animals and the interests of human beings. But it seems equally clear that different people give very different relative weights to these sources of good, so that when they come into conflict the trade-offs between them are made differently. This is enough to entail that there will still be disagreements arising from the three approaches I have outlined.

acknowledges that as a theory of value this 'runs contrary to the self-conception of most greens' (ibid., 43) because 'it traces the value of nature to its value to human beings and the place it occupies in their lives' (ibid., 42–3). Anyone attached to an ecocentric conception of the good is, in my view, quite right to reject Goodin's proposed substitute for the quite straightforward reason that it makes the case for the preservation of the natural environment depend upon what people actually want. Suppose somebody says that, after carefully considering the matter, he has concluded that his desire for a 'larger context' to his life (in as far as he has one) is adequately catered for by his work or his family and that he therefore prefers cheap hamburgers to the preservation of the Brazilian rain forest, uncrowded new ski slopes to virgin mountainside, and so on. There is absolutely nothing that an adherent of the Goodin theory of value can say to him, except that he is in a minority—which may or may not be true in any given instance. The same point can be made about attempts to derive a case for animal welfare from human wants. If the only reason for prohibiting fox-hunting, stag-hunting, or hare-coursing is that it offends the sensibilities of a number of people, their distaste for the cruelty involved simply has to be put into the utilitarian calculus alongside the pleasure (claimed by those who take part to be intense) of those who enjoy the sport. There is no room for the obvious objection based directly on the suffering of the foxes, stags, and hares.

4. Consequentialist Impartiality

Most of us carry around with us a conception of the good of some sort. It will almost certainly not be fully articulated. But, to the extent that we are prepared to say that one state of affairs is better than another, we presumably have some implicit notion of what it is that makes outcomes better or worse. However, if we adhere to the kind of common-sense morality discussed in the first section, we shall not believe that there is any general duty to bring about the best possible state of affairs. Suppose we think that there would be a net gain in happiness if we were to make friends with somebody whose company we (in common perhaps with most other people) find uncongenial, because the gain to this person would more than balance the loss to us. We may well accept that this constitutes *a* reason for doing it, but we shall not think that we have a duty to do so.

I said in Section 2 that 'nobody who was not in the grip of a system' would think we were failing in a duty however we chose our friends. There is, however, a system according to which duty extends to all areas of life, even including the choice of friends. This is consequentialism, understood here as the doctrine that everyone has a duty to perform at each moment the action that will, in his estimation, maximize the total amount of good in the universe. If we start from an impartial conception of the good, the addition of consequentialism gives us an account of the demands of impartial conduct that is sharply at odds with that which I attributed to common sense in Section 2. For, except in the trivial case where two alternative acts have identically good consequences, there is always in principle one act that is required, namely, the one that stands to create the best state of affairs. It is true that within a consequentialist calculus based on preferences our own preferences will be factored in. If I prefer the company of A to that of B, that preference counts as heavily as anybody else's preference of the same strength. But if, after that has been duly allowed for, the answer comes out that utility would be maximized if I befriended B, the implication of consequentialism is that I must do so.

This is, in effect, to extend to the whole of conduct the requirements of impartiality that on the common-sense view are restricted to judges and bureaucrats acting in their official capacities. It is thus an extremely stringent doctrine, as its first and still most eloquent exponent, William Godwin, pointed out. In Godwin's scheme, every human being of sound mind is enrolled willy-nilly in a kind of secular priesthood dedicated to the service of humanity at large: 'In the same manner as my property, I hold my person as a trust in behalf of mankind. I am bound to employ my talents, my understanding, my strength and my time, for the production of the greatest quantity of general good. Such are the declarations of justice, so great is the extent of my duty.'[20] The Godwinian doctrine still finds support. A recent book by Shelly Kagan opens with the words: 'Morality requires that you perform—of those acts not otherwise forbidden—that act which can be reasonably expected to lead to the best consequences overall.'[21] And Kagan goes on a little later to say that, if this were accepted, 'in a sense, neither my time, nor my goods, nor my plans would be my own. On this view, the demands of morality pervade every aspect and moment of our lives— and we all fail to meet its standards.'[22] If the demands of morality are derived from zoocentric consequentialism, we fall even further short.[e]

This rigoristic notion of what the demands of morality amount to has always been open to mockery. Max Beerbohm wrote a parody, savage and also very funny, of a Utopian novel by H. G. Wells in which labour is so attractive that there has to be a law compelling people to take their allotted day off (one in every ten day week). 'But I don't suppose there will often be need to put this law in motion. The children of the Dawn, remember, will not be the puny self-ridden creatures that we are. They will not say, "Is this what I want to do?" but "Shall I, by doing this, be (*a*) harming or (*b*) benefiting—no matter in how infinitesimal a degree—the Future of the Race?"'[23] Kagan himself concedes that the doctrine of strict consequentialism is 'deeply counterintuitive'.[24] But then why should we accept it?

It appears to me that there are three lines along which an argument in favour of the doctrine may be constructed. But none of them is in my view adequate to the task. One quite popular path has been that of sim-

---

[e] Peter Singer argues for such a position in *Animal Liberation*. However, his argument trades heavily upon the thought that we have obligations toward non-human animals for whom we have acquired responsibility by domesticating them, raising them for food, using them in tests and experiments, and encroaching on their habitats. But these sentiments are not plausibly derived from an open-ended duty to maximize total animal welfare, which might for all I know turn out to require flying vets for caribou or shelters for penguins. Singer addresses this issue briefly in *Animal Liberation* (pp. 225–6) and, in customary utilitarian fashion, helps himself to a convenient factual assumption—that efforts to help are likely to do more harm than good—in order to block off the dangerously expansive implications of his general principle. Singer's own conclusion is that 'except in a few very limited cases, we cannot and should not try to police all of nature. We do enough if we eliminate our own unnecessary killing and cruelty toward other animals' (p. 226). This conclusion seems to me perfectly sound, but it is I suggest more aptly understood as following from a view about the inherent limits to our responsibilities than as an *ad hoc* restriction on the potentially unlimited implications of a duty to maximize aggregate animal welfare. (Part of the case for an ecocentric ethic is that it would make sense of such a thought, as Callicott points out in the book cited in n.15.)

ply defining 'duty' so that consequentialism becomes a necessary truth. This was the route taken by Godwin himself[25] and was picked up again at the beginning of this century by G. E. Moore.[26] However, considered as an analysis of existing moral language this is plainly wrong; and considered as a proposed reform it begs the question, since we shall want some substantive argument in favour of consequentialism as a moral doctrine before taking the proposed definition seriously. A second line of argument is simply that it cannot be rational to put up with less good than might be achieved. This runs into the objection that the concept of rationality is too weak to bear the burden of supporting an intrinsically implausible substantive moral theory.[27]

The third strategy is that pursued by Kagan. He argues as follows.[28] Common-sense morality holds it to be wrong not to rescue a drowning child if one could do so without danger to oneself. The best explanation of this is that common-sense morality implicitly regards the promotion of the maximum good as always *a* (moral) reason for acting. This becomes a decisive reason for acting only in the absence of (moral) countervailing reasons, but it is always a *pro tanto* reason. It is easy to see how this argument sets things up for Kagan's conclusion, since he has no great difficulty in establishing that, for example, the agent's merely preferring to do something other than promote the good can scarcely count as an overriding moral reason for doing something else. A duty to pursue the good therefore follows.

It is on the face of it highly implausible that we could all be so wrong about the structure of common-sense morality. Kagan's strategy is a high-risk one in that it collapses if anyone can produce a rationale for the duty to rescue a child without danger to oneself other than the one proposed by Kagan. I do not think that this task is particularly difficult to achieve. An obvious alternative to a duty to maximize the good that would generate a duty in the case as stated is a duty to prevent harm. If common-sense morality holds that there is a duty to prevent harm but not a duty to promote the good (let alone maximize it), this will explain why there is a duty to rescue the child but not a duty to buy it an ice-cream.

It might be objected that this is too quick. If common-sense morality makes a distinction between preventing harm and promoting good, is this coherent? Showing that it is requires that we give some reason for making the distinction. But this can be done. The reason is, I suggest, that there is a great deal of disagreement about what the good consists in, whereas people with a wide variety of conceptions of the good can agree on the badness of harm. (Indeed, as I shall argue in Chapter 4, 'harm' might be defined as what can be widely agreed on to be bad—see Section 14.)

I have argued that nobody has produced a good argument in favour of consequentialism. But the point just made about the diversity of conceptions of the good forms the basis of a strong argument against it. I showed in the previous section that the three types of impartialist conception of the good I examined gave rise to a variety of very diverse practical implications. An injunction to maximize the good is therefore bound to lead people to pursue incompatible aims. It is thus a formula for mutual frustration and conflict. Of course, there is no incoherence in an injunction to everybody to maximize some specific conception of the good. But the question is: how can people be persuaded to accept the same conception of the good?

If, as G. E. Moore believed, goodness is a non-natural property that can be perceived by a process analogous to sense-perception, we should have reason to hope that there would be widespread agreement about the good.[29] But it is apparent that there is in fact persistent disagreement. This might be accounted for by saying that some people are better at the process of intuiting goodness than the rest of us. But in the absence of any independent and generally acceptable criteria for superior ability, this leaves the dispute unresolved and unresolvable. 'In practice,' as Keynes wrote of arguments among the members of Moore's circle, 'victory was with those who could speak with the greatest appearance of clear, undoubting conviction and could best use the accents of infallibility.'[30]

The failure of Moore's theory should not leave us in complete despair. For we are not completely baffled by disagreements about the good, as we would be by disagreements about whether a certain post-box was red or blue when seen in daylight. There is in fact nothing particularly mysterious about the way in which we go about trying to persuade one another to adopt one conception of the good and reject another. For example, we attempt to make vivid the implication of any conception that gives no independent weight to the sufferings of non-human animals, and argue from similarities of physiology to similarities of experience. Or we may make an effort to inspire a sense of wonder and awe at the workings of nature, and suggest on the basis of this that any satisfactory conception of the good must give independent value to the integrity of ecological systems. Nevertheless, I think it has to be accepted that there is no reasonable prospect of closure in these arguments. It is true, of course, that many people have claimed to be able to prove the correctness of their own view to the satisfaction of all rational beings. But the perpetual failure of such claims to achieve any semblance of universal conviction has to cast very serious doubts on the plausibility of any claim of this sort. (See Section 27 for a more extended discussion.)

We must therefore anticipate that the normal state of affairs will be one in which there is no consensus on the nature of the good. That being so, we cannot take seriously the possibility of a society all of whose members are united in pursuing the maximization of a shared conception of the good. Rather, we have to anticipate that a society in which everybody accepted a duty to maximize the good would be one in which a lot of people were pursuing mutually inconsistent ends. Morality, instead of providing a basis on which the members of a society could live together in harmony, would be a recipe for deadlock and frustration, conflict, and (as history all too often attests) civil war.

If there is no hope of consensus based on everyone's pursuing the same conception of the good, does any alternative hold out any more promising prospects? This is the question that I shall take up in the next two chapters.

CHAPTER 2

Justice as mutual advantage and justice as reciprocity

5. The Problem

'Mere altruism, surprisingly enough, does not provide a common stand-point from which everyone can reach the same conclusions . . . Altruism by itself generates as many conflicting standpoints as there are conceptions of the good.'[1] Drawn from a recent book by Thomas Nagel, this may be taken as a succinct summary of the conclusion arrived at by the end of the previous chapter. However, the conceptions of the good discussed by Nagel differ from those that I have given: his central example of a person acting on a conception of the good is that of somebody who 'believes that by restricting freedom of worship he is saving innocent people from the risks of eternal damnation to which they are exposed by deviation from the true faith'.[2] Such a belief is, he suggests, a recipe for unresolvable conflict unless the issue can be shifted to a higher level.

Now, it may be said that the conception of good that is being invoked here is not in itself controversial. Nagel himself says that 'those who wish to limit my religious freedom are doing so, in the case under consideration, with my own best interests in mind. They believe that eternal salvation has priority in any person's good even over basic personal autonomy, and if I shared their views I would have to agree with them.'[3] The point can be put even more strongly. Suppose that I do not believe that there is any such thing as an afterlife, at any rate in any form that gives us any reason now for taking an interest in it. Or suppose that I do agree with the people who wish to impose their views on me that there is an afterlife worth caring about, but I differ from them as to what actions in this life lead to salvation rather than damnation. On either supposition, I am not precluded from accepting the general proposition that posthumous felicity would be a good and posthumous torment a bad, and that if they extended over eternity their goodness and badness would outweigh any goodness and badness we could experience in this life.

Nagel describes different ideas about the reality of or the means to salvation as different conceptions of the good, even though we might all agree on the superiority of salvation to damnation. Where one person believes in an afterlife and another does not, it seems straightforward that they have different conceptions of the good. For the second one does not think that the good believed in by the first actually exists. In the case of two people who both believe in posthumous survival but disagree about the kind of conduct required for salvation (say, because one is a Christian and the other a Muslim), it might appear that we should describe the situation as one of disagreement about the means of attaining a good that both conceive of in the same way. However, disagreements about the means to salvation differ from disagreements about the means to a good to be found on earth in that there is no way in which they could ever be settled by the accumulation of evidence or by any process of rational argument. Since disagreements of this kind about the means to the good have the same interminable character as disagreements about the good itself, it will be convenient for my purposes to bring them both under the heading of conflicting conceptions of the good. For what can be said about the one can equally well be said about the other, and a solution to one kind of disagreement will be a solution to the other.

Religions are, of course, concerned with much more than individual salvation, and in some it plays no part at all. We may nevertheless say that religions compete with secular conceptions of the good in that they all offer some answer to the questions of the meaning of life. What makes religious views distinctive is the belief that 'the meaning of human life is grounded in the fact that it is sacred because God is its origin and its destiny'.[4] I do not of course intend to deny that many religions include within them peremptory demands and prohibitions such as those comprised by the Ten Commandments. The reason for paying heed to these demands and prohibitions is, however, their divine origin. They will have no authority with those who do not accept the religious account of the meaning of life in which they are embedded.

I suggested above that different ideas about the means to a given end, salvation, should be treated as different conceptions of the good, because there was no way in which the conflicts between adherents of different views could be resolved. I now suggest that for the same reason we should follow the usage established by Rawls in *A Theory of*

Justice[5] and include all religiously-derived views about the right thing to do within the scope of conceptions of the good.[a] Any classification worth making must be informed by some purpose, and my purpose in this book is to explore the possibility of arriving at a consensual basis for the ground rules of social life. Secular conceptions of the good and religious views are to be assimilated, I propose, because they create the same problems for the project: they give rise to conflicting practical implications and these conflicts cannot be resolved by rational argument.

What I am doing is, if you like, offering an invitation to look at religious beliefs in a certain way. An analogy is the invitation that utilitarians offer to look at religious beliefs as giving rise to preferences, which are to be factored in with other preferences in the utilitarian calculus. The difference between these two invitations is (as I shall argue at length in Chapter 6) that the utilitarian invitation can reasonably be rejected, whereas there are good grounds for accepting mine. I must acknowledge, however, that the case for accepting it includes the claim that religious beliefs are not susceptible to rational proof or disproof. I have so far stated it but not supported it. I shall not get around to putting forward my argument on this until Chapter 7, where it forms part of a larger discussion (see Section 27). I must therefore beg the reader's indulgence in granting that premise provisionally until then.

Following this prolegomenon, the problem that arose in the previous Chapter can now be restated. In its most general form it is simply that a society in which people accept no guide to conduct except their own conception of the good (in the broad sense now defined) is one doomed to mutual frustration and conflict. For if nobody recognizes any court of appeal with an authority superior to that of his own conception of the good, there is no basis on which conflicts stemming from diverse conceptions of the good can be resolved. Wars of religion illustrate how ferocious and devastating can be the conflicts arising from religious differences. Partial conceptions of the good—the exaltation of the interests of one ethnic group over those of others, for example—can lead to equally unrestrained conflicts, including attempts to exterminate whole

---

[a] Rawls has subsequently taken to describing the same phenomena as 'comprehensive views.' He has not, as far as I am aware, explained this change of usage. It may well be, however, that he has been moved to make the change in order to accommodate the objection that religious ideas (which appear to be increasingly the focus of his attention) include more than conceptions of the good understood literally. (See, for example, Rawls, *Political Liberalism* (New York: Columbia University Press, 1993), esp. pp. 13 and 175.) I prefer to talk about conceptions of the good, with a gloss on the meaning to be given to that expression, rather than resort to something as vague as 'comprehensive view'.

peoples perceived as threats to the purity or hegemony of a dominant ethnic group. The effort to discover some mutually acceptable basis for the accommodation of different conceptions of the good is thus a matter of the utmost practical importance.

Since the seventeenth century, finding a solution to this problem has been a major preoccupation of political philosophers. Bearing in mind that conflicting conceptions of the good are what create the problem, we may pose it by asking what might provide a form of argument capable of moving people to forgo or at any rate limit their pursuit of the good as they conceive it. The answers that I shall examine in this Chapter and the next can all be (though they do not have to be) cast in the form of social contract theory. This is natural because the essence of a contract is that each of the contracting parties voluntarily accepts constraints on the pursuit of his own ends. And that is precisely what we are looking for: a mutually acceptable basis for restraint in the pursuit of one's conception of the good.

I curtailed the first sentence of the quotation from Nagel with which I began this Chapter. Let me conclude the section, then, by supplying the missing words. It will be recalled that, because 'altruism by itself generates as many conflicting standpoints as there are conceptions of the good', it follows that altruism 'does not provide a common standpoint from which everyone can reach the same conclusion'. But Nagel adds that the aim of supplying such a common standpoint 'is the essence of the contractarian or Kantian idea of legitimacy'.[6] It is that idea, in different forms, that I shall be exploring here.

6. *Justice as Mutual Advantage*

I shall begin by taking up the most simple approach, which will for ever be associated with the name of its greatest expositor, Thomas Hobbes. Hobbes took it for granted that people would pursue their own good. But he suggested that they might all be brought to see that the unconstrained pursuit of their own ends was bound to lead to conflict. (In his own terms, 'the state that men naturally are in' is 'a state of war'.) The recognition of this result of each person independently pursuing his own ends formed the basis of Hobbes's next move, which was to argue that by taking counsel people could hope to do better for themselves. 'Reason suggesteth convenient Articles of peace, upon which men may be drawn to agreement.'[7]

Hobbes helped himself to the assumption that all human beings have a single dominant end, which is the desire to avoid violent death. This entails that it is rational for everybody to agree to any arrangement that stands to minimize the chance of suffering violent death, whatever the costs that this arrangement imposes by curtailing the opportunity of achieving other ends. If we value plausibility in a theory, we must refuse to follow Hobbes in assuming that everybody gives an absolute priority to avoiding violent death, with the implication that even a small improvement in the prospects of avoiding it outweighs any loss of other things. But the general Hobbesian idea will withstand the withdrawal of the assumption. The problem of finding a *modus vivendi* becomes more complex but not necessarily insoluble if we drop the Hobbesian postulate that, even if there is no *summum bonum*, there is a *summum malum*.

The project we are to examine has the following shape: we are to imagine people with different conceptions of the good seeking a set of ground rules that holds out to each person the prospect of doing better (on each person's conception of what 'doing better' consists of) than any of them could expect from pursuing the good individually without constraints. The version of this project that has been the most often discussed assumes (as did Hobbes) that people pursue their own good or at most that of their families. In *Theories of Justice*, I called this the theory of justice as mutual advantage. However, the upshot of the previous section is that exactly the same incentive for agreeing to a set of mutually restraining rules will arise where each person is pursuing a conception of the good, whatever its content. (The only exception would occur if everyone shared the same conception of the good and its implications.) Since the structure is the same whatever the scope of the conceptions of the good being pursued, I shall let 'justice as mutual advantage' cover the project in all its varieties. Except where otherwise specified, 'advantage' is to be construed broadly in what follows, so that anything that conduces to the realization of somebody's conception of the good counts as being to that person's advantage.

It may be objected that to extend the notion of advantage in this way entails departing drastically from normal usage. I reply that, where rival conceptions of the good (whatever their nature) come into conflict, we quite naturally find ourselves using words such as 'advantage'. Let us stipulate for the purpose of the present discussion that the divisions on policy (e.g. the ordination of women) within the Church of England are based entirely on differences about what line the Church should take in order to carry out its mission and that no thought of personal interest enters into the decision to support one faction rather than another. It is nevertheless quite unexceptionable to say that, for example, a change in the voting rules that makes some proposed reform more difficult to get through works to the advantage of those opposed to the reform and to the disadvantage of its supporters. On the basis of this, it seems reasonable enough to suggest that a plan with a prospect of advancing the (divergent) ideal interests of two people or groups, in comparison with the outcome of their fighting it out, might properly be said to be mutually advantageous.

I believe that justice as mutual advantage is a radically defective theory. In this section I want to focus on a defect internal to the theory. I shall argue, in other words, that it cannot even succeed in its own terms. I shall not question here the feasibility of coming up with a set of rules that, if they were generally observed, would hold out to everybody a better prospect of achieving the good as they conceive it than a state of nature could offer. The drawbacks of a free-for-all are so manifest that it should not be impossible to suggest ways of improving on it. The problem is one that emerges once the rules are agreed on. Suppose you accept that some set of rules would advance everybody's conception of the good (including yours) if generally complied with, in comparison with a situation in which each person pursued his conception of the good independently. The question is: why does that give you a reason for complying with the rules on an occasion when you believe that you could advance your conception of the good more effectively by breaking the rules?

An answer that may naturally occur to us is to say that by breaking the rules you are exploiting those who keep them—taking advantage of their forbearance while refusing to show the same forbearance yourself. They are permitting their own pursuit of the good (as they conceive it) to be constrained by the rules, while your own pursuit of the good (as you conceive it) is not similarly constrained. This is, we may say unfair. Indeed, John Rawls's 'principle of fairness' is based on the idea that we must contribute our 'fair share' to the maintenance of a benefit that we enjoy as a result of 'the cooperative efforts of others'. More formally, 'the intuitive idea' of the principle of fairness 'is that when a number of persons engage in a mutually advantageous cooperative venture according to certain rules and thus voluntarily restrict their liberty, those who have submitted to these restrictions have a right to a similar acquiescence on the part of those who have benefited from their submission'.[8]

The trouble with this move is that it is not available within the theory of justice as mutual advantage as I have defined it here. For it introduces a new motive: a concern to behave fairly. But no such motive can be accommodated by the theory, which presupposes that people are still motivated solely by the wish to advance their own conception of the good. They agree to be bound by rules because they foresee that this will be a means (so long as others do likewise) of advancing their own ends, whatever these ends may be. The question therefore remains: why should they adhere to the rules if on some occasion some other course of action holds out a better prospect of advancing their conception of the good? In the absence of a satisfactory answer, the theory of justice as mutual advantage collapses because there is no point in agreeing on rules unless they have some restraining effect.

Answers have been offered that stay within the confines of the theory of justice as mutual advantage. I shall now examine these. The most convenient way of proceeding will be to divide the discussion into two stages. In the first stage I shall revert to the narrow construal of 'advantage' and aim to show that people pursuing partial goods would not have an adequate motive for compliance with the rules. Then in the second stage I shall extend the conclusions reached in the first stage and argue that they apply equally well to justice as mutual advantage in the broad construal of 'advantage'.

What kinds of rules would be agreed on by parties concerned to advance their personal interests more effectively? The rules would, I suggest, fall into two broad classes, legal and moral. First, then, there would be formal rules with a specialized enforcement apparatus able to call upon coercion where necessary. These rules would obviously have to prohibit people from harming others. They would also have to raise the funds necessary for financing public services, and provide a reliable basis for civil transactions such as contracts, wills, and marriages. Behind these rules would have to lie a set of constitutional rules specifying how the authority to make and implement the first-order legal rules was to be acquired.

No society has ever got by with only legal rules. Some simple societies have managed without a specialized agency of law enforcement and hence without any need for separating out legal from moral norms, though it is hard to see how societies of any complexity could get by without having some areas of life subject to definitive regulation and specialized enforcement. But what is surely true is that every society needs in addition a system that may be called 'positive morality' on analogy with 'positive law'—that is to say a common system of guidance operating on the members of the society by internalization, the pressure of others' opinions, and diffuse sanctions (in contrast with the centralized ones of law).[9] To a large extent, the rules making up positive morality cover much the same areas as those making up positive law but go beyond them, so that contracts are extended by promises, the legal duties of spouses or parents are supplemented by norms specifying morally required conduct, and so on.

Given that the only motive that can be appealed to is self-interest, how can things be arranged so as to make it in everybody's self-interest to comply? Obviously, there are legal sanctions, which attach a penalty to non-compliance if it is detected and proved in a court of law. However, sanctions are effective only if the great majority of the population are prepared to accept the existence of the law as itself a reason for complying with it. Sanctions can then have some effect in deterring the minority for whom obedience to the law turns on where the balance of advantage lies. But in urban societies the chances of being convicted for most offences (especially profitable ones such as burglary or car theft) are so low that the deterrent effect of punitive sanctions is also low.

When we turn to the realm of morality that falls outside the law, the inadequacy of sanctions is even more apparent. There are, of course, moral sanctions in the form of the disapproval of other people. But only bad behaviour that has a definite victim is liable to incur such sanctions, because antisocial behaviour that does not have a definite victim is likely to go undetected. Moreover, the diffusion of information about people normally operates through personal networks. Moral sanctions are therefore relatively effective in closed communities but not in societies where relationships are compartmentalized and there is a lot of mobility, so that somebody can leave a bad reputation behind in one place and start afresh in another.[10]

There is, however, a further problem about moral sanctions which does not have an analogue with any problem about legal sanctions. The problem may be explained as follows. If we understand the positive morality of a society as 'the morality actually accepted and shared by a given social group',[11] it is surely clear that this is a collective good in the technical sense that it provides diffuse benefits to the members of the society—benefits which in the nature of the case cannot be confined to those who contribute to the supply of the good. Now, maintaining the fabric of a society's positive morality requires constant effort: people have to take the trouble to form judgements about the conduct and character of others, and then undertake the sometimes unpleasant task of communicating their conclusions to those concerned. But this creates the familiar problem of collective action, that there is no self-interested incentive to contribute to a public good. In the calculus of any given individual, the benefits to be expected from adding to the supply of the public good are far less than the cost of the contribution because by definition the benefits are spread over the whole society. With legal sanctions, this problem can be overcome because taxes can be raised to support specialized agencies whose job is the enforcement of the law (including, of course, enforcing the obligation to pay taxes), and there is a collective interest in setting up and maintaining this system. But there is nothing analogous that can be done to overcome the collective action problem posed by moral sanctions.

What I have said casts doubt on the feasibility of operating a system of moral sanctions in a society of self-interested people. But behind that problem lies a deeper one that goes to the nature of moral sanctions themselves. Is it even intelligible that there could be such a thing as moral sanctions in a society of self-interested people, at any rate so long as they were rational? Think again of a case in which I express moral condemnation of someone for acting in a certain way. The idea is supposed to be that this will help to deter this person and others from acting wrongly in future. But how exactly does this deterrence work? Criticizing somebody's conduct on moral grounds is not simply giving that person a hard time in a general kind of way. It is giving the person the specific kind of hard time that consists in being told that what one had done is morally wrong. But what sort of a hard time is that in a world of self-interested individuals?

According to the analysis we are investigating, to say that something is wrong is to say that it is in breach of a system of rules and principles that would have formed the subject of a hypothetical contract. But why should you, as a self-interested person, be distressed by having it pointed out to you that you have behaved wrongly in that sense? It is no good saying 'I am trying to give you a hard time because we shall all be better off if conduct like yours is discouraged.' Unless my moral condemnation cuts some ice with you, it will not cause your sense of what is in your interests to shift in the desired direction.

In real life, moral sanctions work because other people are able to activate an appropriate internal response, so that criticism (if we recognize its validity) triggers off feelings of guilt or self-reproach. But why should anybody in a world of self-interested people have such feelings? It is true that others (e.g. parents or teachers) might have a self-interested reason for attempting to inculcate such feelings. But anyone who reached the age of reason would presumably see through this indoctrination—while hoping that it still worked for other people. If such a person broke a rule and was found out, the consequences might be deleterious enough to make him regret having done it. (For example, he might find out that he was no longer trusted after getting bad publicity for having broken a promise.) But this would be the same kind of sentiment that he might feel about having put money on a horse that turned out in the event to be a loser. Regret is not remorse.

Attempts have been made to deal with these difficulties. I am confident that all such attempts are bound to fail. The typical strategies consist in pushing up the costs imputed to being found out in a way that strains credulity, as in Hobbes's reply to 'the foole' who 'hath sayd in his heart, there is no such thing as Justice'.[12] A recent variant is to suggest that a disposition to violate moral norms is visible to others, and when detected is disadvantageous, so that it pays to cultivate a disposition to comply with such norms unconditionally.[13] But there simply seems to be no reason for thinking that human beings have the ability postulated to distinguish between unconditional conformists and those who conform only after calculating that it will pay to do so in the case in hand, bearing in mind the risks of detection and the loss from being detected. Moreover, neither of these strategies, even if successful, would do anything to cope with the fundamental incoherence that I have claimed to lie at the heart of morality based on self-interest.

It would be easy to imagine that all these difficulties arise simply in virtue of reliance on self-interest as the sole motivation to be appealed to. But strictly analogous problems arise if we replace self-interest by the pursuit of any conception of the good. The essence of justice as mutual advantage in all its forms is that people do not give up the single-minded pursuit of their ends, be they self-interested or otherwise. The only significance they attach to whatever agreement they make is that it will, they hope, offer a more effective way of achieving their ends than is provided by their unconstrained pursuit of those ends. If we assume that the end is self-interested, we can say that there is no reason for adhering to the rules agreed upon whenever self-interest would be advanced by not doing so. If we drop that limitation, the same point can simply be restated at a higher level of generality: adherence to the rules is rational only to the extent that it can be anticipated to advance the good as that is conceived by the agent. Even where that good is defined by an impartial secular conception of the good or a universal religion, it is still true that the rules are to be adhered to only to the extent that doing so will further the good so defined.

The fragility of rules based on nothing but mutual advantage can be illustrated by taking the example of rival religions within a single territory. Suppose that a *modus vivendi* is agreed upon in the form of a secular state—one that does not give a special status to any religion. Unless the institution of the secular state attracts support on some other basis so that it is regarded as right in principle rather than as a compromise reflecting the balance of forces, the prognosis cannot be encouraging. For the adherents of each faith will constantly be seeking ways of breaching the provisions if they think they can get away with it. Moreover, the adherents of one religion may at any time challenge the existing settlement if they ever come to feel that the balance of forces has tilted in their favour, so that they can reasonably hope for some new deal more advantageous to their ideal interests.

To illustrate this, let me call attention to the relevance of the Indian experience since Independence. The generation of the founders—Jawaharlal Nehru and those around him—were self-conscious heirs of the Enlightenment, and believed that a secular state was the right response to the religious divisions within India rather than a merely expedient response to the balance of forces between Hindus and Muslims. (There are also, of course, large numbers of adherents of other religions as well, but over the country as a whole Hindus and Muslims account for the bulk of the population.) However, the idea that the state should be secular never became well established as an unbreachable principle. The most overt breach occurred in 1986, when the government of Rajiv Gandhi used its parliamentary majority to enact a law 'declaring that Muslim personal law was superior to the country's civil law in matters of marriage and divorce, and no Muslim woman could opt out of it without leaving the faith itself'.[14] The case that triggered this was brought by a Muslim woman, Shah Bano, who filed for maintenance after having been divorced by her husband. The husband argued that the provision of maintenance was inconsistent with Islamic law. The Supreme Court upheld the claim of Shah Bano under the civil law, but this was overridden under pressure from Muslim communal leaders, thus denying Muslim women the possibility of maintenance.

With extraordinary cynicism, Gandhi claimed that this move was called for by the principle of secularism, as a way of creating greater emotional security for Muslims. (It is hard to see that it improved the security of Muslim women!) Scarcely surprisingly, however, it created a Hindu backlash, and played straight into the hands of the Hindu nationalists (the Bharatiya Janata Party), who were able to use it as the springboard for their own religious demand, that the mosque at Ayoda reputed to be the birthplace of the popular deity Ram should be converted to a temple.

If once it is established that the state is merely an instrument for whichever religious group pushes hardest, it is easy to see why the BJP, with its project of making India a Hindu state, should gain adherents. However, it is clear that the prospect of officially sponsored marginalization in such a Hindu state would be totally unacceptable to all the religious minorities in the country. We can therefore predict that any moves towards the creation of a Hindu India will provoke bloodshed on a scale that will make the communal violence of recent years pale into insignificance and compare rather with carnage that accompanied partition in 1947.

Settlements underwritten by justice as mutual agreement are no more than truces. As soon as one side or the other feels it can improve its position, there is nothing to restrain it so long as (measured within its own conception of the good) the prospective gains outweigh the anticipated costs. This is true if the conception of the good calls for the advancement of religious values as well as if the conception of the good is the most crass self-interest.

I would not wish to deny that, even when the battle-lines are drawn up with the opposing parties defined by religion, much of the dispute may well turn around the distribution of scarce goods that are recognized as goods by all the communities involved: such things as places in universities and jobs in the public service. My point is, however, that even demands that are motivated purely by religious ends are liable to create deep conflicts. Justice as mutual advantage in such cases simply invites a struggle for positional advantage. Recalling the passage from Nagel with which I began this chapter, the author of the study of India from which I have quoted has offered the following reflection: 'Given contrasting conceptions of truth, religiously driven men may also be intolerant and violent, notwithstanding the morality of each religious system. Moral men do not necessarily make a tolerant society if there are multiple and exclusive conceptions of morality.'[15] The problem that I identified in the first section of this chapter is of momentous practical importance. Literally millions of lives in India alone depend on getting the answer right.

7. Is it Justice?

Is justice as mutual advantage really a variety of justice at all? The assertion put into the mouth of Thrasymachus in Plato's *Republic* that 'justice is nothing but the advantage of the stronger' has always had a paradoxical air about it.[16] For we surely think of the appeal to justice as one that must be open to the weak. Yet the whole point of justice as mutual advantage is to translate strength into advantage as smoothly as possible.

As my remarks at the end of the previous section suggested, actually arriving at an equilibrium, or moving from one to another, may not take place smoothly. For even if the parties agree that there are terms of agreement that are better for all than perpetual conflict, there will normally be a multiplicity of alternative settlements all of which are superior to perpetual conflict. The problem is how to settle on one. The theory of justice as mutual advantage prescribes that the amount received by the parties under the settlement must reflect their relative bargaining power. For any party that gets less than this will have an incentive to try to upset the settlement and attempt to bring about another on more advantageous terms. But how is relative bargaining strength to be determined? The answer is that all the parties can indulge in 'sabre-rattling.' But at some point the sabre may have to be drawn to back up its owner's claims to prowess.

The assumption underlying justice as mutual advantage is that the parties will arrive at the same conclusions about their relative bargaining power and hence agree on the appropriate terms. The ideal would be the apocryphal South American wars in the nineteenth century in which the opposing armies drew up facing one another, the rival generals counted the men, horses, and weapons, and they then agreed upon which side should be deemed to have won, according appropriate booty to the putative winner. But in real life, as we know very well, there are strikes and there are wars. Information is often not good enough to enable both sides to arrive at a common prediction of the outcome of conflict. In particular, what neither side usually knows about the other (or indeed quite often about its own) is their degree of determination and their consequent willingness to accept losses.

It is worth taking a moment to reflect on the significance of this. It is commonly said that, whatever else may be wrong with the idea of justice as mutual advantage, it does at any rate have one thing going for it: it produces determinate answers. The contrast is then drawn with the alternative proposal that we should be looking for a fair basis for resolving conflicts. This, it is pointed out, will serve to settle disputes only to the extent that the parties can be brought to share a single view of what fairness implies. The latter point is perfectly valid, and I accept the burden of dealing with it in this *Treatise*. But it is important to recognize that the problem of indeterminacy is one that dogs the theory of justice as mutual advantage as well. The partisans of fairness have been too quick to concede the virtue of determinacy to justice as mutual advantage.

The theory of justice as mutual advantage is, as I have already argued, internally inconsistent. I shall go on in the rest of this section to argue that it offends against our most elementary ideas of what justice requires. But the upshot of what I have now said is that these severe defects in justice as mutual advantage do not have to be offset against superiority in terms of preventing violent or economically destructive conflict. For the pursuit of a settlement conforming to the requirements of justice as mutual advantage may lead straight to such conflict.

Let me return to the question with which I began this section.

Assume away, if you like, the problem of actually arriving at an equilibrium reflecting the balance of forces. Is it plausible to say that the terms must necessarily be just? Incredulity is most easily aroused where the relative power of the parties is very unequal. A striking example of this inequality is given by the relations between Europeans and indigenous inhabitants in the New World and Australasia. I shall focus on the well-documented process by which free-living Indians were eradicated from the territory of the United States, which began in the seventeenth century and ended in the nineteenth. This was punctuated by treaties, sometimes grandiosely called treaties of perpetual peace. Indians were driven into signing these treaties by the destruction of villages, crops, and game as well as by the indiscriminate killing of men and very often women and children too. As Ouray, the chief of the Utes, put it when invited to sign such a treaty in 1868, 'The agreement an Indian makes to a United States treaty . . . is like the agreement a buffalo makes with his hunters when pierced with arrows. All he can do is lie down and give in.'[17]

Plainly, this was not a process of frictionless adjustment. The Indians had to be convinced of the greed, ruthlessness, and superior firepower of the whites by bitter experience before becoming sufficiently resigned to the hopelessness of their position to sign treaties. Let us imagine, however, a counterfactual history in which the experience of the Indians in Massachusetts convinced all the rest of the hopelessness of resistance, so that their dispossession from their land took place without bloodshed. Would this entail that the process was morally unproblematic? Suppose that there were, in this counterfactual world, treaties reflecting the (very unequal) balance of power between whites and Indians. A theorist of justice as mutual advantage would have to say that any treaty was just so long as it was better for both parties than the alternative of fighting. He would also have to say that, since the only motive either side could have for adhering to the terms of the treaty was a sense of the gains to both sides if both sides observed it, it would also be just for the whites to tear up the treaty (however permanent a settlement it purported to represent) as soon as they reached a position in which it would be more advantageous to drive the Indians by force from the territory that they had been granted.[b]

[b] The war in Bosnia following the breakdown of Yugoslavia offers a contemporary illustration of the same points. The Muslims have protested at each of the proposed 'peace plans' that they are 'unjust and that they legitimise Serbian control of ethnically cleansed territories'. (Edward Luce, 'Crucial concessions fail to impress Muslims', *Guardian*, 21 August 1993, p. 8.) However, since the only rationale of these proposals has been that of justice as mutual advantage, there is no way of saying that any proposal is unjust so long as it reflects the balance of military advantage. The inability of the

As I pointed out in *Theories of Justice* (p. 162), David Hume was prepared to accept that this was the implication of justice as mutual advantage. David Gauthier, the contemporary champion of justice as mutual advantage, is more squeamish and says that on his version of the theory 'what actually occurred' was not 'free from injustice'.[18] However, he can say this only on the basis of a theory of original acquisition (see *Theories of Justice*, pp. 300–4) that violates his own insistence that no motive except that of self-interest can be appealed to. Even then, Gauthier does not think that driving the Indians off their land by force was unjust. The only questionable aspect of the business was confining them to reservations instead of giving them the opportunity to join the American labour force. Oddly for someone who operates with a subjective (preference-based) conception of advantage, Gauthier claims that the Indians didn't know what was good for them, so that it would have been legitimate to force them to change their nomadic ways.[19]

Suppose we allow Gauthier the constraints that he artificially imposes, the range of justice is still by ordinary standards very impoverished. In particular, the 'congenitally handicapped and defective' fall outside its protection, because 'the disposition to comply with moral constraints . . . may be rationally defended only within the scope of expected benefit,' and nobody can expect any benefits in return for maintaining them.[20] This point is expanded in a sinister footnote, which tells us that life-extending therapies are all right for the aged, 'who have paid for their benefits by earlier productive activity' but that 'care for the handicapped' creates a 'problem' with 'ominous redistributive potential'. Gauthier interprets talk of 'enabling them to live productive lives' as a way of 'euphemistically' attempting to make care for the handicapped look as if it will pay for itself. Yet, as he says 'the services required exceed any possible products', and this is 'an issue which, understandably, no one wants to face'.[21] I do not believe, however, that when we talk about enabling seriously handicapped people to lead productive lives we mean anything except enabling them to lead lives that are worthwhile to themselves. We are not suggesting that caring for them can be made to show a profit. That Gauthier thinks we must be claiming this simply shows that he seriously believes other people to occupy his own morally pathological universe.

It would be a mistake to think that the obnoxious implications of jus-

formula to generate peace is also apparent: all the various cease-fires and agreements have broken down as soon as any of the parties has perceived an advantage in violating its terms. In particular, the Serbian forces, analogously to the whites in the American west, had no incentive for keeping agreements that stabilized the *status quo* while they could see a prospect of further military gains.

tice as mutual advantage would disappear if people had conceptions of the good that were not based upon material self-interest. For it will remain true that the ability to impose one's conception of the good will be proportional to one's power. Those without power may be the incidental beneficiaries of somebody else's pursuit of his own conception of the good. But they cannot hope to make any headway in the pursuit of the good as they themselves conceive it. Those written off by Gauthier as unproductive members of society may be kept alive if there are enough well-organized utilitarians around in their society to have an impact on public policy. But it will remain true that the views of the congenitally handicapped themselves (either about what should happen to them or about anything else) will not be taken account of if they have no power. Similarly, even if American whites had been more concerned for the welfare of the native population than they were, this concern would have been for the welfare of the Indians as conceived by the whites, since the Indians would still have lacked the power to assert their own conception of the good. Gauthier's paternalistic conception of Indian welfare would no doubt have been typical, and we have seen that it would have been compatible with driving them off their lands.

Religiously based conceptions of the good, when imposed on the weak by the strong, are even less likely than impartialist secular conceptions to be genuinely beneficial to all. Zeal to convert everybody in the society to the true faith leads straight to the *auto-da-fé*. And in the United States naked rapacity was cloaked in the doctrine of 'Manifest Destiny'—a teleological conception with the delightful feature of being totally immune to any form of rational refutation. Thus, the manifesto of the Big Horn Association claimed that the valleys of Wyoming were 'destined for the occupancy and sustenance of the Anglo-Saxon race', while the wealth in its mountains had 'been placed there by Providence to reward the brave spirits whose lot it is to compose the advance-guard of civilization'. It concluded that 'the destiny of the aborigines is written in characters not to be mistaken. The same inscrutable Arbiter that decreed the downfall of Rome has pronounced the doom of extinction upon the red men of America'—presumably with a little help from its human instruments, the 'Anglo-Saxon race'.[22]

If this is the nature of justice as mutual advantage, the question with which I began this section poses itself with redoubled force. Is justice as mutual advantage really a variety of justice at all? One way of presenting it as a genuine theory of justice is to tie the notion of justice to some social institution and then say that the form taken by that institution depends on the balance of power and hence reflects mutual advantage. The claim by Thrasymachus that justice is the advantage of the stronger turns out to be an example of this strategy. For when challenged by Socrates to back up his assertion he assumes 'justice' to be obedience to the established laws of a polity.[23] 'Each government frames laws for its own advantage.' And since 'the government in each [city] has the power', it follows that 'justice is the same thing everywhere—the advantage of the stronger'.[24] Hume was following a parallel tack in identifying 'justice' with the observance of property rules, arguing that the origin of justice so understood was an appreciation of the mutual advantage of having stable rules governing possession.[25]

It is clear that 'justice' is doing no real work here. We could equally well drop the word altogether and simply let Thrasymachus say that obedience to law is to the advantage of the stronger (i.e. the rulers) and Hume that observance of property rules is mutually advantageous in comparison with a free-for-all. There is, of course, a hidden agenda lying behind these definitions of 'justice'. Thrasymachus is a debunker, who is seeking to show that what is ordinarily regarded as justice is a façade behind which rulers operate for their own profit. Hume, as a conservative, has precisely the opposite end in view. By defining justice as observance of property rules, he hopes to make it impossible even to raise the question of the justice of property rules. However, both of these manœuvres rely for their effectiveness on our retaining some sense of the commendatory force of 'justice'. Otherwise Thrasymachus would not be able to create a *frisson* or Hume defend the *status quo*.

A more promising line, which can also be extracted from Hume, is that justice as mutual advantage counts as justice because it has at any rate one feature in common with what is normally thought of as justice: it calls for constraints on the pursuit of self-interest. Of course, the driving force behind rules of justice, on this conception of justice, is still self-interest. 'There is no passion', Hume says, 'capable of controlling the interested affection, but the very affection itself, by an alteration of its direction. Now this alteration must necessarily take place upon the least reflection; since 'tis evident, that the passion is much better satisfy'd by its restraint, than by its liberty. . .'[26] But restraint motivated by mutual recognition of the advantage to all of complying with the rules of justice is still restraint.

The same idea underlies Gauthier's claim to be setting forth a theory of morality. As I have said, his theory is that of what I am calling justice as mutual advantage: morality is a set of restraints that are advantageous to all if generally observed. Echoing Hume, he says that 'rational constraints on the pursuit of interest have themselves a foundation in the interest they constrain'.[27] In virtue of the restraining element, Gauthier feels justified in claiming that he will 'defend the traditional conception of morality as a rational constraint on the pursuit of individual interest'.[28] This makes it explicit that morality is to be identified with constraint; and the same move might, as I have suggested, be made in connection with justice.

This is, we may say, a definition of justice in terms of function rather than content. But content can be rescued, at least to a certain extent. For it can be pointed out that, so long as even very rough equality of strength obtains among the parties to rules of justice, the rules recommended by justice as mutual advantage will tend to correspond to those that we would ordinarily think just. Within a society, the rules covering able-bodied adults would be of the kind we would think of as just, prohibiting harm and enjoining the practice of contributing to collective benefits. Where this rough equality fails to obtain, the correspondence will break down, as in the case of the congenitally disabled or the relations between Europeans and indigenous inhabitants in the Americas and Australasia. But there will still be a core area in which the prescriptions of justice as mutual advantage and what is ordinarily thought of as justice will overlap.[c]

I shall take it that these considerations are adequate to warrant our calling justice as mutual advantage a kind of justice. But it suffers from two immense drawbacks that I have spelt out in this Chapter. One is that there is a gap between acknowledging that some rule, universally adhered to, would advance one's conception of the good and having a motive (based on nothing but the pursuit of one's conception of the good) for adhering to the rule. The other is that, even if we can establish

[c] In *Theories of Justice* this overlap was the only reason I gave for accepting justice as mutual advantage as a theory of justice. The more comprehensive discussion here is, I hope, an improvement on my treatment of a key point in the rationale of the book. Even on the issue of overlap, I now think that my discussion was defective. I said in *Theories of Justice* (p. 163) that 'justice as mutual advantage will coincide with common views over a large core area (namely, where the circumstances of justice do obtain)' but I would now say that Hume's 'circumstances of justice' comprise a necessary but not sufficient condition, since they require only that there should be *some* advantage to the stronger in reaching a settlement with the weaker. I would now therefore wish to say that rough equality of strength (as specified in the text above) must be insisted upon. Thus, the American Indians were not in the same position as the 'race of creatures' imagined by Hume who were 'incapable of all resistance' (see *Theories of Justice*, pp. 161–2). Their capacity to resist was never negligible: they could always raid a settlement, harass a wagon train, or derail a locomotive, for example. This was precisely what led whites to regard it as worth making treaties: so long as very little had to be given up, it was advantageous to aim for peace. However, the inequality in power was such that it appeared advantageous to the whites to break these treaties whenever the cost of renewed fighting was outweighed by the benefits to land-hungry migrants or gold-hungry prospectors of seizing more land. Thus, we may say that the circumstances of justice obtained (weakly), but that, because of the unequal bargaining power, justice as mutual advantage failed to generate anything ordinarily recognizable as justice.

some connection between justice as mutual advantage and justice as ordinarily understood, justice as mutual advantage fails egregiously to do one thing that we normally expect a conception of justice to do, and that is provide some moral basis for the claims of the relatively powerless.

8. Justice as Reciprocity

In this section I want to discuss the idea that I canvassed in Section 6: that we might combine mutual advantage as the criterion for rules with a motive for keeping them that I described as a sense of fair play. I shall call this hybrid theory 'justice as reciprocity'. As a way of introducing it, I shall offer some reflections on what has gone on so far in this Chapter. Let me suggest, then, that a theory of justice may be characterized by its answers to three questions. First, what is the motive (are the motives) for behaving justly? Secondly, what is the criterion (are the criteria) for a just set of rules? And thirdly, how are the answers to the first two questions connected? We want to know exactly how somebody with the stipulated motive(s) for behaving justly would be led to comply with rules that are just according to the stipulated criterion or criteria. A theory of justice that cannot answer the third question satisfactorily fails on the ground of internal inconsistency.

Of course, a theory may be internally consistent and still be objectionable in other ways. But I believe that we can get a long way without having to appeal to anything beyond the test of internal consistency. I can illustrate this by reanalysing justice as mutual advantage in terms of its answers to the three questions. This theory of justice answers the first question by saying that the motive for complying with the constraints imposed by rules of justice is that this is, taking a long view, a more effective way of advancing one's conception of the good than is not complying with these rules. The answer to the second question is that a set of rules is just if general compliance with the rules would be more advantageous to everybody (in terms of each person's conception of the good) than the alternative of a 'state of nature' in which everybody pursued their conceptions of the good without any constraints.[d]

---

[d] It is common nowadays to describe the situation brought about by unconstrained maximization as a 'state of nature'. There can be no objection to this. However, it should at the same time be recognized that, although the terminology is borrowed from the classic social contract theorists, neither Hobbes nor Locke would have accepted this characterization of a state of nature. That Locke's state of nature had 'a law of nature to govern it' is familiar enough. But what should be observed is that Hobbes elaborated a large number of rules for 'the conservation of men in multitudes', which he called 'laws

The answer to the third question has to show how the motive stipulated by the answer to the first question will necessarily be activated by rules meeting the criterion set out in the answer to the question. And the burden of Section 6 is that there is no adequate answer to the third question. There is, on the face of it, an obvious gap between saying that universal compliance with a certain set of rules would be more advantageous to everybody than a 'state of nature' and demonstrating that compliance is advantageous to each person on every occasion. For the two alternative states of affairs canvassed do not exhaust the possibilities. It may be possible to 'free ride' on the compliance of others, and that may be more advantageous than complying oneself. I shall not rehearse here the attempts that have been made to show that, appearances notwithstanding, the gap can be plugged. These all rely on the notion that, once the anticipated reactions of other people are taken into account, it really is the most advantageous course of conduct to comply with rules of justice. I believe that I have been able to establish, however, that none of the moves that have been made along these lines is successful, and it seems to me extraordinarily unlikely that any better move along the same lines is waiting to be discovered. The conclusion to be drawn is therefore that the theory of justice as mutual advantage is internally inconsistent.

There are two ways in which we might try to preserve something of the theory. One would be to change the criterion of a set of just rules so as to require that it should be advantageous to each person that he should find it more advantageous on each occasion to comply with them than not to. This is manifestly a far more stringent requirement than the original one, which said only that *general* compliance should be more advantageous to everybody than the condition of general noncompliance referred to as a 'state of nature'. It would certainly provide a good answer to the third question, since there would now be no gap between motive and criterion. But the arguments adduced already against the original version can be adapted to show that there is no set of rules satisfying the new requirements. For there is no general rule setting up constraints on the pursuit of one's conception of the good that it might not on some occasion be more advantageous to break than to keep, taking always as the measure the prospects of advancing one's conception of the good. Obviously, there is nothing to be said for a

---

of nature'. Admittedly, Hobbes thought that they could be only of limited value in securing peace (and hence preservation) in the absence of the security provided by a sovereign. But it remains true that Hobbes's state of nature already incorporates elements of justice as mutual advantage.

theory of justice which has the implication that there can be no rules of justice. We may therefore abandon that direction of development.

The other direction in which we can go is to retain the criterion that a just set of rules is one that is agreed on as mutually advantageous if complied with, but to change the motivation for compliance with the agreed-upon rules. We now say that a sense of fairness leads to compliance. The name 'justice as reciprocity' is well established for this theory,[29] which has recently been defended by Allan Gibbard in a book and in a review of my *Theories of Justice*.[30] What are we to make of it?[e]

I have so far identified an external objection to justice as mutual advantage and two internal ones. The external objection is simply that the criteria for just outcomes generated by justice as mutual advantage can fail to correspond in crucial respects to what is normally considered to be just. I shall return to this, because it is in my view the Achilles heel of justice as reciprocity, becoming an internal objection. The two internal objections to justice as mutual advantage can be restated briefly as follows. The first is that the pursuit of advantage does not provide an adequate motive for compliance with rules that would be mutually advantageous if generally observed. The other is that the claim of justice as mutual advantage to provide a basis for peaceful interaction is undermined by its necessarily encouraging a constant struggle for positional advantage.

In his book, *Wise Choices, Apt Feelings*, Allan Gibbard argues that reciprocity solves both of these problems. I have already outlined the solution to the first problem. Suppose we have an innate 'sense of fair dealing'. (Gibbard speculates that this can be explained in evolutionary terms, since it smooths the path of cooperation, which has survival value.)[31] Then we will have a motive for behaving in accordance with the demands of reciprocity even in cases where it is contrary to our advantage to do so. Gibbard speculates that reciprocity solves (or at any rate eases) the second problem because 'judgments of fairness stabilize bargaining. . . . Gains from cooperation and restraint could be distributed in many different ways. Common expectations are stabilized by

---

[e] For the benefit of readers of *Theories of Justice*, I should point out that I there used 'justice as mutual advantage' for any theory according to which the rules of justice are those that would be advantageous to all if generally adhered to. In retrospect, I recognize that this was pushing conceptual parsimony too far. Even so astute a critic as Allan Gibbard, in the review referred to in the text, takes 'justice as mutual advantage' to rule out any motive for compliance except the pursuit of advantage. However, my account in *Theories of Justice* (see esp. ch. 4) of the aspect of Rawls's theory that I claimed to fall under the theory of justice as mutual advantage was intended to fit in with the idea that the motive for compliance would be a sense of justice as 'fair play,' i.e. a duty to do one's part to sustain a mutually advantageous institution. I regret not making this more explicit and as a result leaving my readers to do too much of the work themselves.

common standards of fairness, with their potential for anger and retaliation if the standards are violated.'[32]

In Gibbard's conception of justice as reciprocity, the criterion of justice is indeed mutual advantage; but the suggestion is that a notion of 'fair dealing' may pick out a unique outcome from the range of outcomes that would all be mutually advantageous (compared with the baseline of non-cooperation or conflict), thus avoiding a fight over the division of the spoils. Gibbard takes (here as elsewhere) a line reminiscent of Hume: the judgements of fairness that we make appeal to the imagination. 'We latch onto symmetries, favoring equal division or proportionality. We identify entitlements and protect them.'[33] Gibbard thus admits that these conceptions of fairness are pretty arbitrary, depending on what people locally regard as salient, but this does not concern him because he is interested only in the possibility of securing agreement on mutually advantageous terms. The terms themselves are of no significance to him.

What this means is that Gibbard as a theorist is adopting a different perspective from that of his subjects. They are strongly attached to some idea about what fairness requires, and are strongly motivated to pursue it. Provided the ideas of the parties mesh together, this will save them from having to fight it out to determine the point of mutually advantageous equilibrium.[f] Gibbard, however, does not have a substantive theory of what fair dealing requires. Thus, contrary to superficial appearances, his theory corresponds to my original definition of justice as reciprocity. That is to say, the criterion of justice is that any mutually advantageous deal that is agreed on is to be deemed just—exactly as in the theory of justice as mutual advantage. What is different from that theory is that, if the parties believe the deal to be fair, that in itself gives them a motive for upholding it.

Gibbard thus suggests a source of motivation for adhering to mutually advantageous agreements that is independent of advantage. But there is a price to be paid for this gain. Let me go back to the analysis with which I began this Section. A theory of justice must, I said, tell us what is the motive for behaving justly and what is the criterion for a just set of rules. Then it must explain how the two fit together. Justice as

---

[f] The downside of this is, of course, that the conflict is liable to be exacerbated if the parties have incompatible ideas about what fairness calls for. Fuelled by a sense of outrage at the prospect of what they see as an unfair outcome, the conflict between the parties may well be more intense than it would be if they saw the issue in more neutral terms as one of establishing an agreement in accord with the balance of forces. Since Gibbard believes that a shared idea of what is fair arises from shared experience, it would seem to follow that his proposed solution to the problem of conflict over the point to be picked is liable to backfire unless the parties do respond to the same cues.

reciprocity fails to meet the third requirement satisfactorily, and that is its downfall. Even if it did not in the end work, justice as mutual advantage had a certain brutal consistency between criterion and motive. If the American Indians asked why they should adhere to some treaty extorted by superior firepower, they could be told that it was in their interest to adhere to it, just as it had been in their interest to sign it in the first place. But can we seriously say to them that they have a good motive for compliance arising from the fairness of the deal?g When we endorse the notion that reciprocity is a form of fairness (and I accept that we do), we surely have in mind something different from this. Implicitly, we assume a starting point from which gain is to be calculated that is itself fair—or at any rate not grossly unfair.

We can, if we wish, reformulate the theory of justice as reciprocity so that it has built into it a stipulation that the baseline from which advantage is to be reckoned must not be established by coercion. Notice, however, that it is then explicit that justice as reciprocity is an incomplete theory, since we have to import a broader notion of fairness to get it started. Even modified in this way, moreover, the theory of justice as reciprocity still has all the other distasteful features of justice as mutual advantage, as Gibbard himself acknowledges. For it still allows for the exclusion of those who cannot provide benefits for others, such as the congenitally handicapped.[34]

Rather than build the case up step by step any further, let me state the generalization to which we should be led by further analysis along the same lines. This is that we have to turn things around and start from a generic conception of fairness. Within this, mutually advantageous deals will count as fair only under highly restrictive conditions. The baseline must itself be fair, and the parties must be well informed and well matched. Thus, for example, we may be prepared to say that the standard baseline in contracts, where either party can maintain the *status quo* in the absence of an agreement, is fair. Yet it will often be the case that the bargaining power of the parties is so unequal as to render sus-

g Fairness *à la* Gibbard does nothing to alleviate the situation. We are assuming that, because of the weak bargaining position of the Indians, any deal advantageous to both sides will have to be very bad for them. All that Gibbard's story adds is that not every conceivable division of land will be considered, but only those with certain salient features, e.g. those following the line of a river or the ridge along the top of a mountain range. (Notice how often frontiers between countries follow one or the other.) The *locus classicus* for the analysis of salient solutions is Thomas C. Schelling, *The Strategy of Conflict* (Cambridge, Mass.: Harvard University Press, 1960), esp. chs. 4 and 6. This gives the flavour: 'One cannot expect to satisfy an aggressor by letting him have a few square miles on this side of a boundary; he knows that we both know that we both expect our side to retreat until we find some persuasive new boundary that can be rationalized' (p. 111).

pect any contract between the parties. For example, both by legislation and judicial interpretation many kinds of onerous conditions and limitations of liability in the small print of contracts that firms ask their customers to sign have been invalidated—and many more should be.[35]

We can already begin to discern from this the outlines of the generic conception of fairness for which we now need to look. It will make fairness what can freely be agreed on by equally well-placed parties. Justice as impartiality—the theory of justice we arrive at by pursuing this idea—can offer a satisfactory answer to the three questions with which I began this section. In rough terms, the criterion of just rules and institutions is that they should be fair, and the motive appealed to is the desire to behave fairly. The answer to the third question is that the two fit together perfectly.

How do we know this? We cannot read it off from the mere fact that the motive has the same name as the criterion. For that is equally true of justice as mutual advantage. We have to dig deeper, into the game structure underlying the two theories.[36] Justice as mutual advantage is unstable because it has the structure of a prisoner's dilemma. What is in my interest is that everybody else cooperates and I defect—in other words, that everybody else adheres to rules that are mutually advantageous if generally adhered to and I break them whenever it is to my advantage to do so. Justice as impartiality, however, has the structure of an assurance game. If I am motivated by a desire to behave fairly, I will want to do what the rules mandated by justice as impartiality require so long as enough other people are doing the same. Thus, people motivated by fairness reinforce one another's motives.

CHAPTER 3

Justice as impartiality

9. The Rawlsian Construction

If justice as reciprocity is no more than a fragment of a more comprehensive theory of justice, then it behoves us to identify this theory of justice. The present chapter will be devoted to the task of setting out the theory, which I shall call justice as impartiality. This shares with justice as reciprocity its answer to the first question: it says that the motive for complying with the demands of just rules is the desire to behave fairly. But it departs from the criterion for just rules that justice as reciprocity retains from justice as mutual advantage. In place of mutual advantage, it proposes a criterion that is intended to articulate more directly with the motive of behaving fairly. The basic idea here is that just rules are those that can be freely endorsed by people on a footing of equality.

It is natural to look for some machinery capable of giving more precision to that basic idea, and the most familiar example is John Rawls's theory of 'justice as fairness'. As promised in Section 1, I shall expound it here and argue that Rawls's construction of an 'original position' fails to capture the underlying idea of fairness adequately. In the next section, I shall take up Rawls's attempt to support his principles of justice by arguing that they avoid excessive 'strains of commitment'. I shall suggest that, in spite of appearances, this is actually an alternative moral argument for the principles of justice, and one of a more satisfactory nature. If we attempt to systematize it, we get a different idea of the way in which agreement on principles is to be conceived. In the following section (Section 11), I shall expound the version of justice as impartiality put forward by Thomas Scanlon, which may be seen as the kind of systematization that is called for. It has the advantage that the motive that it ascribes to people for complying with rules of justice fits the criteria that it puts forward for rules of justice. It thus provides a satisfactory response to the third of the questions that I said (in Section 8) every theory of justice must be able to answer. The final section illustrates the workings of justice as impartiality by showing how it gives rise to rules for living together and contrasting this with the way in which social rules are derived from a conception of the good.

The object that Rawls wished to achieve with his conception of choice in a suitably characterized original position has been well set out by H. L. A. Hart as follows:

Though any rational person must know in order to live even a minimally tolerable life he must live within a political society with an ordered government, no rational person bargaining with others on a footing of equality could agree to regard himself as bound to obey the laws of any government if his freedom and basic interests, what Mill called 'the groundwork of human existence', were not given protection and treated as having priority over mere increases in aggregate welfare, even if the protection could not be absolute.[1]

I want to argue that Rawls's construction of an 'original position' fails to capture that central idea and instead drives towards precisely the kind of aggregation that he is so anxious to avoid. Before doing so, however, I want to defend it briefly against some criticisms that are still being made. For unless the misconceptions underlying these criticisms are cleared away it is impossible to get any grasp on the nature of the theory.

The most serious error is to regard the derivation of principles of justice from rational choice in the original position as if it were the whole theory. This leads to the preposterous claim that Rawls aspired in *A Theory of Justice* to deduce principles of justice from the bare concept of rationality and nothing else. (For an example, see the discussion of Alasdair MacIntyre in Section 18.) Now, it is quite true that Rawls says that 'the argument aims eventually to be strictly deductive. . . . We should strive for a kind of moral geometry with all the rigor which this name connotes.'[2] But we must take note of the context of these remarks. Rawls introduces them by saying that 'the acceptance of these principles is not conjectured as a psychological law or probability. Ideally anyway, I should like to show that their acknowledgment is the only choice consistent with the full description of the original position.'[3] And whenever in *A Theory of Justice* Rawls talks about the relevance of rational choice theory, it is always plain that its relevance is confined to the attempt to show deductively what principles would be chosen in the original position.

Thus, what 'connects the theory of justice with the theory of rational choice' is that 'we have to ascertain which principles it would be rational to adopt given the contractual situation'.[4] But the specification of the contractual situation that is given does not form part of the theory of rational choice. Rather, 'the original position is the appropriate initial status quo which insures that the fundamental agreements reached in it are fair. This fact yields the name "justice as fairness"'[5] As Rawls has said in a subsequent comment on *A Theory of Justice*: 'There is no thought of trying to derive the content of justice within a framework that uses an idea of the rational as the sole normative idea.'[6]

It is, in my view, only by coming to *A Theory of Justice* with a preconceived notion of its style of argument, and maintaining a wilful indifference to everything that Rawls actually says, that anybody could emerge from reading it with 'an idea of the rational as the sole normative idea'. As in other respects, Rawls has given too much ground to his critics in recent years. Thus, he has said that 'it was an error in *Theory* (and a very misleading one) to describe a theory of justice as part of the theory of rational choice'.[7] But the two page numbers that he gives as sources of this error do not actually support such a reading: both quite clearly show that the context is the choice made by the parties in the original position.[8]

What Rawls now tells us he 'should have said' is what he in fact did say—repeatedly, as with all key statements in *A Theory of Justice*. Thus, just before the 'moral geometry' passage that is so often taken out of context, Rawls says that 'the philosophically favoured interpretation of the initial situation incorporates conditions which it is thought reasonable to impose on the choice of principles. . . . It is a state of affairs in which the parties are equally represented as moral persons and the outcome is not conditioned by arbitary contingencies or the relative balance of social forces.'[9] This does not differ in any material respect from what Rawls now claims he 'should have said', which is 'that the conception of justice as fairness uses an account of rational choice subject to reasonable conditions to characterize the deliberations of the parties as representatives of free and equal persons; and all of this within a political conception of justice, which is, of course, a moral conception'.[10]

Rawls is quite clear then, that the constitution of the original position has to be justified by arguments that are not themselves deductions from the idea of rationality. Rather, as he puts it, 'the idea here is simply to make vivid to ourselves the restrictions that it seems reasonable to impose on arguments for principles of justice, and therefore on these principles themselves'.[11] The first example that Rawls gives of a reasonable restriction is enough to show how full of substantive content these restrictions are. 'Thus,' he says, 'it seems reasonable and generally acceptable that no one should be advantaged or disadvantaged by natural fortune or social circumstances in the choice of principles.'[12] Once

we unpack this assertion, we shall soon come to see that it entails a
frontal assault on all forms of inequality arising from either fortunate
genetic endowment or favourable family background. (See *Theories of
Justice*, Section 27.) Again, Rawls says that 'we should insure . . . that
particular inclinations and aspirations, and persons' conception of their
good do not affect the principles adopted'.[13] This, too, clearly embodies
a fundamental moral commitment: a distinctively liberal idea about the
way in which conflicts between conceptions of the good should be
treated.

Rawls's construction of the original position is anchored in substantive moral considerations at both ends. I have shown how the features
of the original position are supposed to embody reasonable constraints.
But Rawls acknowledges that there may well be more than one way of
specifying an original position so as to satisfy the general requirements
of a fair choosing situation. How are we to proceed? Suppose we work
out one specification that satisfies the requirements. We then see what
principles would be chosen in it. If 'these principles match our considered convictions of justice, then so far well and good'. But if not, we
'can either modify the account of the initial situation or we can revise
our existing judgments'.[14] We may well, Rawls suggests, do some of
each until 'eventually we shall find a description of the initial situation
that both expresses reasonable conditions and yields principles which
match our considered judgments duly pruned and adjusted'.[15]

This is not necessarily a final resting place. 'It is liable to be upset by
further examination of the conditions which should be imposed on the
contractual situation and by particular cases which may lead us to revise
our judgments. Yet for the time being we have done what we can to
render coherent and to justify our convictions of social justice.'[16] Rawls
defines this state of rest as one of 'reflective equilibrium'.[17] The version
of the original position put forward by Rawls is his contribution to the
search for reflective equilibrium: 'It represents the attempt to accommodate within one scheme both reasonable philosophical conditions on
principles as well as our considered judgments of justice.'[18] It would be
hard to imagine a more explicit statement of Rawls's intentions, or one
that made it clearer how wide of the mark is the depiction of him as a
pure rationalist.

A second line of criticism that is sometimes made of Rawls's construction of an original position is that it is objectionable in principle
simply because it is hypothetical. But there is nothing wrong with the
idea that we can throw light on what is fair by asking questions about
what we might think in hypothetical situations. Even people entirely
innocent of academic moral philosophy can be found asking 'How

would you like it if someone did that to you?' or saying 'You wouldn't
think that if you were one of the victims'. It is only because recourse to
hypotheticals of this kind constitutes a commonplace mode of argument that a story Kingsley Amis tells about his fellow-novelist John
Braine is worth telling. Braine and Amis both belonged to a right-wing
lunch club, and on one occasion Braine regaled its members with an
account of his triumph over the left-wing Methodist divine, Lord Soper.
According to Braine, he had been singing the praises of the United
States, from which he had recently returned, to Soper. ' "Soper said,
H'm all right if you're not black, and I said, But you stupid bugger, I'm
not black." '[19]

It is surprising how often Braine's incapacity to appreciate the force
of hypotheticals surfaces in critics of Rawls. An excellent—because very
clear—illustration is provided by Henry Phelps Brown, a distinguished
economist whose book *Egalitarianism and the Generation of Inequality*,
contains an extensive discussion of Rawls's theory.[20] He writes: 'It is
hard to see why an engagement that appears rational, and binding, to a
person of one kind, allowed very limited information should continue
to be acceptable or to be binding upon that person when he and all others like him have been greatly changed and are altogether better
informed.'[21] Phelps Brown concedes that 'at one point Rawls does
speak as if the principles adopted by the hypothetical persons would
commend themselves to the actual persons of ordinary life'[22] but he
does not appear to understand why Rawls thinks that they should. It is,
of course, in any case odd to say that Rawls suggests only 'at one point'
that the conclusions reached in the original position are intended to
make demands on real people since that is for Rawls the only point of
the original position, as he emphasizes throughout *A Theory of Justice*.
Let that pass. What is relevant here is that Phelps Brown is apparently
incapable of recognizing that Rawls invites people to put themselves in
others' shoes in order to concentrate their minds on what they should
think is fair while wearing their own shoes.

A related blunder, which Phelps Brown also falls into and which is
again surprisingly common in the critical literature, is to confuse the
motivations of people in Rawls's original position with the motivations
that Rawls supposes people to have in real life. In *A Theory of Justice*,
the parties in the original position are concerned to advance not exactly
their self-interest but at any rate their (presumptively conflicting) conceptions of the good. Real people are also concerned to do so. But if
they have what Rawls describes as an 'effective sense of justice', they
will be constrained by the overriding claims of justice. Phelps Brown,
however, assumes that real people have the psychology he attributes

(rather crudely) to Rawls's people in the original position. So, according to him, 'the view of human nature that informs Rawls's approach' is 'that people are actuated solely by self-interest. On that limiting assumption, he sets out to show how it is rational for them none the less to be egalitarian.'[23] Naturally, if people are self-interested in real life the conclusions reached in the original position will cease to attract them once they know their real situation. But Rawls's conclusions are intended to appeal to his readers' sense of justice, not their self-interest. What they would think when pursuing their self-interest (or more precisely their conception of the good) within the constraints of the original position is supposed to guide their thinking when they consult their sense of justice in real life.[a]

Having dismissed three misdirected criticisms of Rawls's original position, I now want to mount my own criticism of it. The crucial problem lies in the lack of fit between the specification of Rawls's original position and his objectives in constructing it. The people in the original position are to pursue their conception of the good. But if we were to leave things there, we would have justice as reciprocity: the motive for compliance with the principles would be fairness but the principles themselves would arise from mutual advantage and thus reflect the bargaining power of the parties. The outcome would thus fail to meet the requirement that the principles of justice should be capable of earning free assent.

---

[a] I am here finessing a tricky point in *A Theory of Justice* by assuming that if people have an 'effective sense of justice' it will constrain their pursuit of their conception of the good. Rawls does at one point say that, in accepting the principles of justice, people 'implicitly agree . . . to conform their conceptions of their good to what the principles of justice require, or at least not to press claims which directly violate them' (p. 31). But the second option drops out in the rest of his analysis, so that the standard idea of the way in which somebody's sense of justice becomes operative is by his conception of the good being brought into line with the requirements of justice. Thus, the picture is not one of justice constraining the pursuit of the good but rather one of 'congruence' between the two. (See esp. section 86, 'The Good of the Sense of Justice', pp. 567–77.) I believe, and I shall try to show in the next volume of this *Treatise*, that this idea is the origin of the progressive unravelling of Rawls's theory in his subsequent restatements. However, it does not play any part in *A Theory of Justice* (or, indeed, subsequently) in the argument for the principles of justice. I therefore simply note that I am departing from Rawls's idea of the relation between justice and the good to this extent: for Rawls, justice constrains the *content* of the good; in the version I am propounding, justice constrains the *pursuit* of the good. On the account offered here I may, for example, think it would be for my good to have a larger income than the principles of justice yield me, but my acceptance of the principles of justice commits me to accepting my fair share. On Rawls's account, I can 'affirm my sense of justice' only if I see my having no more than my fair share as for my good. In *A Theory of Justice*, the required 'congruence' is underwritten by the 'Kantian interpretation' according to which each person's highest good lies in acting justly. It is scarcely surprising that Rawls has subsequently concluded that this is too controversial a notion to form the basis of general compliance with the demands of justice.

Where, in that case, does fairness get into the picture? Rawls believes that the fairness of the original position can be rescued by stipulating a 'veil of ignorance' which temporarily denies the parties in the original position the knowledge of who they are. This, of course, entails that people cannot pursue their own ends, in any ordinary sense of 'their own'. For if you do not know who you are—only that you may be any member of your society—you cannot assess proposed sets of principles in the light of your own particular situation, personal characteristics, or conception of the good. It would therefore appear that you must take account of the way in which everybody will be affected by alternative principles, because you may turn out to be anyone. But, while this guarantees that everybody's concerns will in some way be figured into the solution that emerges, it does not thereby ensure that they will be taken account of in the way envisaged by Rawls.

The nature of the problem is highlighted by Hart's statement that within Rawls's system we are concerned with what 'no rational person bargaining with others on a footing of equality could agree to'. For the trouble is that Rawls's original position does not have any room for bargaining with others—on a footing of equality or any other footing. There can be no bargaining among people who, even though they actually have conflicting ends, do not know what those ends are. The whole idea of bargaining thus becomes inapplicable and the choice of principles reduces to a choice by anyone in the original position picked at random. Of course, we may still say that the people in the original position reach an agreement, but this is entirely trivial since they are clones. All we are saying is that, faced with identical information and reasoning in an identical fashion, they arrive at identical conclusions. We might as well talk of computers having the same program and fed the same input reaching an agreement.

This shift from collective agreement to individual computation has serious repercussions, because it means that the whole idea of an outcome protecting the vital interests of each of the parties is jeopardized. An individual choosing under conditions of uncertainty may well decide that rational maximizing of his prospects entails that he maximizes the average prospect of all the people he may turn out to be.[24] It is controversial whether individual rational maximization does entail exactly this, but what can at any rate be said with confidence is that it is rational to take some risks to secure a higher expectation, reckoning that the prospective gains if one turns out to be one person outweigh the prospective losses if one turns out to be another.

Rawls himself says that 'from the standpoint of contract theory one cannot arrive at a principle of social choice merely by extending the principle of rational prudence to the system of desires constructed by the impartial spectator. To do this is not to take seriously the plurality and distinctness of individuals, nor to recognize as the basis of justice that to which men would consent.'[25] Rawls's own theory does not involve an ideally sympathetic impartial spectator (on the lines laid out in Adam Smith's moral theory), but it does in practice operate by 'extending the principle of rational prudence' to the calculations of a single individual who is attempting to maximize the prospects of all the people he might turn out to be when the 'veil of ignorance' is removed. Rawls is thus open to precisely the charges that he levels against 'impartial spectator' theories of ethics: he 'does not take seriously the plurality or distinctiveness of individuals' (what he elsewhere calls the 'separateness of persons') nor does he 'recognize as the basis of justice that to which men would consent'. For it is perfectly open to someone to say 'I accept that if I were making the kind of decision stipulated in the original position I would have chosen *x*; but that has no relevance to what I can reasonably be asked to agree to here and now.'

Rawls does not do much in *A Theory of Justice* to explain why he starts from an original position in which the parties are single-mindedly pursuing their own conceptions of the good. He does say that this enables us to deploy the resources of rational decision theory and also that it enables a determinate result to be achieved. But even if these claims are valid (and I do not in fact believe that the concept of rationality is strong enough to generate a unique solution), they are plainly inadequate. What we need is not an assurance that this is the way to get *an* answer but rather some reason for thinking that this is the way to get the *right* answer. A clue may be found, I believe, in Rawls's response to the review of *Theories of Justice* by Allan Gibbard that I discussed in Section 8. Rawls follows Gibbard's suggestion that his own theory is best viewed as one of justice as reciprocity.[26] Apart from the terminology, there is nothing new here, since *A Theory of Justice* is replete with references to a society as a 'cooperative scheme for mutual advantage.' Justice is therefore, according to Rawls, about the sharing out of the gains from cooperation. However, the baseline from which gains are to be calculated must itself be fair, and Rawls takes a fair baseline to be an equal one.[27] Thus, the theory cannot be a self-contained theory of justice as reciprocity, because it requires the importation of an ethically driven baseline, and the rationale for that cannot (as I argued in Section 8) come from the idea of reciprocity itself.

Rawls distorts the logic of reciprocity even further. For his view of the fair way of dividing the gains from cooperation is the difference principle, which says that all social and economic inequalities are justifiable only to the extent that they maximize the position of the worst off group. And this flows from the premise that I have already mentioned as being expressed in the original position: that the natural and social advantages that make people more or less productive are a matter of good fortune and hence do not constitute ground-floor claims to receive more or less of the social product. This notion, however, clearly implies that the congenitally disabled cannot be held responsible for lack of productivity and should therefore have a valid claim on a share of their society's resources. Yet Rawls at the same time accepts that the grim logic of justice as reciprocity excludes them from its scope.[28]

For the purpose of this book, I shall simply excise from Rawls's theory any reference to justice as reciprocity. If we do this we get a coherent theory of justice as impartiality.[b] My reason for bringing up reciprocity here is, as I have said, that I believe it illuminates Rawls's specification of the original position. For the criterion of justice within the theory of justice as reciprocity is mutual advantage over some baseline. And this is, clearly, represented within Rawls's specification of his original position by the provision that the parties are to pursue their own conceptions of the good unconstrained by any considerations of fairness. Of course, the addition of the veil of ignorance means that this pursuit of advantage fails to take off, so that we finish up with a prudential calculation by one person under conditions of radical uncertainty. I suggest, though, that it is the misguided importation of justice as reciprocity that leads Rawls towards the motivational postulate that he puts into the original position.

---

[b] In his discussion of Gibbard's review of *Theories of Justice*, Rawls says that his theory is one of justice as reciprocity (as I have already noted) and also that it is not one of justice as mutual advantage or justice as impartiality (Rawls, *Political Liberalism*, 16–18). I agree that Rawls's theory is not one of justice as mutual advantage, because in the usage I am adopting here (which follows that proposed by Gibbard) justice as mutual advantage has built into it the idea that the motive for compliance with the terms of agreement is that of self-interest, or more generally the advancement of one's good. (This is not the reason offered by Rawls, which equates mutual advantage with Pareto improvement, so that *any* move from *any* status quo that benefits all parties is just. I take justice as mutual advantage, following the Hobbesian tradition, to have a baseline in which the parties fight it out.) Rawls's rejection of the depiction of his theory as one of justice as impartiality also rests on a misunderstanding. He speaks (p. 16) of 'the idea of impartiality, which is altruistic (being moved by the general good)'. Although there is a reference to my *Theories of Justice* in this context, it should be clear that Rawls is here identifying impartiality with the kind of consequentialist utilitarianism that I discussed in Section 4. (See also Part III *passim*.) On my definition of justice as impartiality, Rawls does subscribe to the theory. It is true that he at the same time subscribes to certain elements of justice as reciprocity, which renders his theory incoherent. (See chapter 4 of *Theories of Justice* for a development of this claim, which is there presented as a clash between justice as impartiality and justice as mutual advantage, since I did not distinguish in that book between mutual advantage and reciprocity.)

I offer this speculation for what it is worth, since it does at any rate provide an answer to a question that has always puzzled me and that I have not seen answered by anybody else. (I did not attempt to answer it myself in *Theories of Justice*.) Nothing turns on its correctness, however, for my overall argument. Whatever the reason for Rawls's setting up the original position in the way that he does, it remains true that it fails to instantiate the 'separateness of persons'. It cannot therefore naturally accommodate Rawls's fundamental egalitarian idea that principles of justice have to be acceptable above all to those who stand to do least well under them. Within the framework of the original position, this idea can be worked in only by attributing to the parties in it a maximin decision rule. This has the effect of making them concerned exclusively with the worst that could happen to them under any proposed rule of justice. It gets the results that Rawls wants, but only in a highly artificial way. For, in spite of all Rawls's attempts to justify the use of this decision rule, there is no way in which it can be presented as an appropriate rule of decision-making in the context of the original position. Its justification must come from its being the only way of producing the desired outcome. But then the redundancy of the whole construction is patent.[29]

10. *'The Strains of Commitment'*

What I have said so far is not the whole story about Rawls's original position. It is in fact only half the story. According to Rawls, when the parties in the original position have made their choice of principles, they have to proceed to a second stage. For, he says, they 'cannot enter into agreements that may have consequences they cannot accept. They will avoid those that they can adhere to only with great difficulty'. Rawls makes it clear that what he calls the 'strains of commitment' are assumed to be especially acute for those who turn out to do badly under whatever principles are implemented. Thus, he says that 'when we enter an agreement we must be able to honor it even should the worst possibilities prove to be the case. Otherwise we have not acted in good faith. Thus the parties must weigh with care whether they will be able to stick by their commitment in all circumstances.'[30]

Why should we (or the people in the original position) be concerned with this problem? Suppose we are convinced that the specification of Rawls's original position accurately captures the constraints that are relevant to a fair choosing situation, and that Rawls's principles are what would be chosen in an original position so specified. Should we not then simply be concerned that those who reject the principles because they do badly from their operation will not be able to cause too much trouble? We shall (as Rawls acknowledges) have to have mechanisms of enforcement anyway, to prevent backsliding and to provide those who accept the principles with assurance that others will play their part by, for example, paying their taxes.[31] So why should we not rely on the same mechanisms to keep in line those who do not accept the principles, provided they constitute a small and disorganized minority?[c]

In *Political Liberalism* Rawls makes it plain that, in seeking stability, he is not interested in finding 'means of persuasion or enforcement' to ensure that just institutions can be maintained by compliance 'if need be prompted by penalties enforced by state power'[32] And in *A Theory of Justice* it is equally clear that the drive for stability is moral rather than practical. That is to say, Rawls starts from the deep conviction that principles of justice for a society should be freely acceptable to all the members of that society. Thus, although Rawls is keen to guard against the charge that stability is to be viewed 'as a purely practical matter',[33] he is nevertheless concerned with the practical question of finding a basis of agreement. 'The kind of stability required of justice as fairness is based, then, on its being a liberal political view, one that aims at being acceptable to citizens as reasonable and rational, as well as free and equal, and so as addressed to their public reason.'[34]

What are we to make of the quest for stability, understood in this way? I have always thought there was something puzzling about it. For, if the original position had really been drawn up to incorporate 'what we are prepared to regard as limits on the fair terms of social cooperation', why would not the principles derived from it be 'acceptable to citizens as reasonable and rational'? Why, in other words, should there be any need for a separate stage?

It would be understandable if Rawls were to be worried about people being too selfish to fit into a just society and to ask if it were possible to set up just institutions that could rely on self-interest to maintain them. This is a familiar line of enquiry within Benthamite utilitarianism: how to make the pursuit of self-interest coincide with the pursuit of the

---

[c] The stability of societies such as those of Britain and the USA which make no pretence to provide a decent standard of living to everybody in them seems to depend on the fact that the losers—the long-term unemployed and one-parent families for example—are too marginalized, too demoralized, and too busy trying to cope with life to be in a position to threaten a breach of civil order. (Discontent that mobilizes ethnic or racial groups is much more of a danger.) I am not suggesting that justice as impartiality (in its Rawlsian form or any other) would endorse principles from which the institutions of Britain or the USA would emerge as just. The question remains, however, why *realpolitik* calculations of this kind should not be relevant when the stability of justice as impartiality is in question.

greatest happiness of the greatest number. And the same underlying idea—designing institutions so that people with private motives nevertheless produce public benefits—underlies a great deal of work in the field of public choice. But this is clearly not Rawls's project. He specifically disclaims the Hobbesian ambition of creating stability among egoists.[35] And his central notion of 'a well-ordered society' is of one whose 'members have a strong and normally effective desire to act as the principles of justice require'.[36]

Rawls considers the possibility that this 'criterion of stability' might be 'flouted' and mentions Bentham in this context. If there is a fundamental divergence between the principles underlying institutions and the motives of the members of the society, he says 'the best that the ideal legislator can do is to design social arrangements so that from self- or group-interested motives citizens are persuaded to act in ways that maximize the sum of well-being'.[37] In contrast with this, a society that was well-ordered by the utilitarian criterion would be a society whose members acknowledged it and were motivated by the pursuit of aggregate utility to comply with the demands of utility-maximizing institutions.[38] Similarly, a society well-ordered by Rawls's two principles of justice would be one in which just institutions were supported in virtue of their being recognized as just. This is the condition of stability with which Rawls is concerned.

The people in the original position, then, are to be told that they have the capacity for an effective sense of justice. This does not, of course, mean that they know the content of their conception of justice: that is what they are in the original position to determine. 'Rather, it means that the parties can rely on each other to understand and to act in accordance with whatever principles are finally agreed to. Once principles are acknowledged the parties can depend on one another to conform to them.'[39] But then, to repeat, why do we need the second stage?

Rawls's answer is that 'the assumption only says that the parties have a capacity for justice in a purely formal sense: taking everything relevant into account, including the general facts of moral psychology, the parties will adhere to the principles eventually chosen. They are rational in that they will not enter into agreements they know they cannot keep, or can do so only with great difficulty.'[40] This reply calls for some thought. Suppose that the principles that emerge as the rational choice in an appropriately constituted original position turn out to fail the 'strains of commitment' test. It may be tempting to think that the response of the parties should be: 'Too bad: it turns out that just principles aren't stable enough, so we'd better find some others that are less just but more stable.' But Rawls does not endorse this kind of reaction.

Rather, he insists that whatever principles are finally chosen by the parties in the original position are to be accounted principles of justice. Hence, if they change their minds about the principles they endorse, it is their final choice that creates principles of justice.

But should they change their minds? Rawls moves too quickly to the conclusion that they should. If, as his talk of psychological facts suggests, it is simply a matter of brute fact that some people will be reluctant to do what there are good independent reasons for saying justice demands, perhaps the right conclusion to be drawn is that the people in the original position should be content if the principles they arrived at could be expected to be stable in the sense that Rawls has rejected: that they could be maintained by coercing those who do not accept them freely. In fact, right towards the end of *A Theory of Justice* Rawls concedes that this might prove to be necessary anyway. Thus, in saying that the parties in the original position would agree to 'penalties that stabilize a scheme of cooperation', he adds that 'those who find that being disposed to act justly is not a good for them cannot deny' that 'it is rational to authorize the measures needed to maintain just institutions'.[41]

When we look at Rawls's actual discussion of the 'strains of commitment', however, we find that the impression of the problem as constituted by brute psychological facts is highly misleading. It is not, for example, as if Rawls takes there to be some level of well-being below which nobody can be expected to fall voluntarily, and that that sets the limits to what justice can demand. This is indeed a possible view. (I shall discuss Bernard Williams's version of it in the next volume of this *Treatise*.) But it is not Rawls's view: 'a just person,' he says, 'is not prepared to do certain things, and so in the face of evil circumstances he may decide to chance death rather than to act unjustly. Yet although it is true enough that for the sake of justice a man may lose his life where another would live to a later day, the just man does what all things considered he most wants; in this sense he is not defeated by ill fortune the possibility of which he foresaw.'[42]

We can see how the argument concerning the 'strains of commitment' works within Rawls's theory by seeing how Rawls uses it to promote his two principles of justice at the expense of the utilitarian criterion. Rawls himself makes it clear in the Preface to *A Theory of Justice* that he takes utilitarianism as the theory to beat,[43] and it is perhaps surprising how often the case in favour of the principles of justice turns on demonstrating their superiority to the utilitarian criterion. 'The problem of relative stability' is throughout taken by Rawls to be the problem of showing that the principles of justice are more capable of generating support than is the utilitarian criterion (whether understood to enjoin the maximizing of average or total utility).[44] Indeed, Rawls says at the end of his discussion of 'the strains of commitment' that the characterization of the original position could lead to the endorsement of utilitarianism instead of Rawls's principles of justice were it not for the introduction of 'the strains of commitment' into the reasoning of the parties: 'the restrictions on valid undertakings . . . are an essential part of the argument for the two principles'.[45]

The argument in favour of Rawls's principles of justice is, then, that it avoids 'a sacrifice of [life] prospects'. But, as we have seen, Rawls concedes that the absolute level of well-being arising from the application of his principles may be very low, even to the point at which people have to give up their lives for the principles. What Rawls is talking about, then, is the unacceptable *reasons* for making sacrifices that are inherent in utilitarianism. Thus, he goes on: 'We are to accept [in a society ordered by utilitarianism] the greater advantages of others as a sufficient reason for lower expectations over the whole course of our life. This is surely an extreme demand. In fact, when society is conceived as a system of cooperation designed to advance the good of its members, it seems quite incredible that some citizens should be expected, on the basis of political principles, to accept lower prospects of life for the sake of others.'[46]

The essence of Rawls's argument here is that the utilitarian principle—averaging the average expectation—might seem to be an attractive gamble from the point of view of the original position. But once people emerge from behind the veil of ignorance someone who finds that he has lost out from the application of the utilitarian criterion 'is bound to remind himself that he had the two principles of justice as an alternative' so he 'may have difficulty abiding by his undertaking'.[47] This information about reactions in the real world is to be available to the people in the original position, and Rawls argues that it should make them abandon utilitarianism even if they were previously inclined to endorse it as a rational gamble.

This is a perfectly sound argument. But it is clearly a moral argument and not one about psychological propensities. What is says is that the inequalities that arise under the Rawlsian principles of justice can be justified to those who fare least well under their application, whereas those that arise under the application of utilitarianism cannot be justified to those who do least well. How exactly is the case to be made, in Rawls's view? The nub is the difference principle. Why should the worst off accept their lot in a society governed by it? We have to be careful to state the principle correctly. Otherwise we are liable to get the argument wrong.[48] Suppose the institutions in some society satisfy the demands of the difference principle. We can express this condition loosely by saying that the worst off people in the society will then be as well off as they can be made. However, the term 'the worst off' in this sentence is not to be understood as a rigid designator. All it means is that the worst off (whatever their identities) could not be made any better off: any institutional change would have the effect of making the worst off (whatever their identities) worse off.

What then can we say to the actual worst-off people in a society where the difference principle is instantiated? We cannot say that *they* could not be made better off.[d] But we can say that the currently worst-off people could be made better off only if some other people were made worse off than the currently worst-off people are now. The minimum level, in other words, would have to become lower. This necessarily follows from the stipulation that it is currently as high as it can be. Now, there is nothing to stop the members of the worst-off group saying 'Fine: make us better off at the expense of these others.' But this cannot be a *moral* demand. For the only moral basis for their being as well off as they are now is that the worst off (whatever their identities) should be as well off as possible.

Rawls's argument against utilitarianism is in essence that it fails as a theory of justice because it is liable to place unfair burdens on some people. The inequalities in well-being that it can give rise to cannot be justified to those who are at the losing end of them. Hence, those who lose from the application of the utilitarian criterion can reasonably reject it. Now, if this is so, it is irrelevant whether or not utilitarianism

---

[d] More precisely: it does not follow from the difference principle's being satisfied that the actual worst-off group could not be made better off. Nevertheless, it is quite plausible that as a matter of fact there would be no way of making the actual worst-off group better off *in a society that satisfied the other principles of justice as well*. If we violate this proviso, we can easily enough make up an example in which different designated groups (distinguished by race or ethnicity, say) are arbitrarily assigned a privileged socio-economic status or subjected to arbitrary deprivations. For example, we can imagine that all the best-paying jobs are reserved for the members of one group and the members of the other group are subjected to special taxes and denied benefits available to the others. (South Africa and Israel are examples that come to mind.) Call the two groups the blues and the greens. We can simply stipulate that in one state of affairs the blues are arbitrarily privileged and in an alternative state of affairs this is true for the greens. In the first case, obviously, the greens could be made better off than they are and in the second case the blues could be. (This is the essence of the example produced by John Broome in his 'guest appearance' in Appendix H of Derek Parfit's *Reasons and Persons* (Oxford: Clarendon Press, 1984), 490–3.) But the point is that this whole scenario could occur only by blatantly violating Rawls's first principle (equal civil and political rights) and the first part of his second principle (equal opportunity for all to achieve advantageous positions). And both of these, it should be borne in mind, have lexicographic priority over the difference principle in Rawls's theory.

would be chosen in an original position characterized by agents pursuing their own interests from behind a veil of ignorance. If utilitarianism does indeed emerge as the choice under those conditions, all that goes to show is that those conditions have nothing to tell us about justice.

I suggested in the previous section that utilitarianism is very plausibly the outcome of a self-interested choice made from behind a veil of ignorance. The point of appealing to the strains of commitment is that it gives Rawls the basis for saying that, if that is the answer that emerges from an original position specified along these lines, that does not matter because the principles that are finally chosen must satisfy the test presented by the strains of commitment. But what this really shows is that the rest of the specification of the original position is doing no work. For we have to recognize that the implicit criteria determining what principles are consistent with the 'strains of commitment' test are actually the criteria for principles of justice. What Rawls is asking is whether or not a principle could reasonably be rejected by someone aware of its impact on him. If we try to fill out the idea of reasonableness here, I believe that we shall arrive at the specification of a Scanlonian choice situation. Thus, the Scanlonian construction can helpfully be seen as a more effective realization of Rawls's objectives than his own original position could ever be.

11. The Scanlonian Alternative

The construction proposed by T. M. Scanlon departs from that of Rawls in two fundamental ways. The first is that the parties are aware of their identities and hence of their own interests. The second is that they are not motivated simply by the wish to advance their interests. Rather, we are to conceive of them as motivated by 'the desire for reasonable agreement'.[49] They are not, however, to be conceived of as solely motivated by this desire. Rather, the approach 'takes the fundamental question to be whether a principle could reasonably be rejected (for application in our imperfect world) by parties who, in addition to their own personal aims, were moved by a desire to find principles that others similarly motivated could also accept.'[50] Scanlon's full statement of his 'contractualist account of the nature of moral wrongness' runs as follows: 'An act is wrong if its performance under the circumstances would be disallowed by any system of rules for the general regulation of behaviour which no one could reasonably reject as a basis for informed, unforced general agreement.'[51] Let me offer a gloss on some of the key clauses in this statement.

First, then, it will be observed that Scanlon talks about rules whose violation is wrong whereas I have been talking about rules whose violation is unjust. I do not believe that there is any difference of substance here. As the applications of his account that he offers show, what he is mainly interested in are (*a*) laws and institutions, including political institutions and (*b*) rules forming the positive morality of a society. He proposes his account as a way of explaining what we are doing when we say that it is wrong to execute convicted murderers or to fail to keep one's promises. I concede that in many contexts 'wrong' would be more idiomatic than 'unjust'. But I shall stick to my own terminology because I want to keep it clear that the sphere of morality is wider than the sphere of rules that would satisfy Scanlon's conditions. (I shall return to this point in the next section.)

Secondly, it may be asked why the formulation talks about '*any* system of rules . . . which no one could reasonably reject'. The reason for putting the matter this way is to allow that there may well be alternative sets of rules that meet the standard. Thus, there may be alternative sets of moral rules which would pass the test. It is a matter of convention which one is established in a given society, and whichever one is established is the one that it would be wrong not to follow.[52] Similarly, there may be alternative laws that could not, on substantive grounds, be reasonably rejected. If one of them is actually enacted (especially if it was enacted by a procedure that itself could not reasonably be rejected) then that is the one that it would be wrong not to keep. I shall take up these points below, in Chapters 4 and 8. My present purpose is simply to explain the terms of Scanlon's construction.

The requirement that the agreement should be 'unforced'—the third point for comment—reflects considerations about the nature of a fair basis for agreement that were raised above in Chapter 2. An unforced agreement is, of course, incompatible with the parties in the original position attempting to coerce one another. But the stipulation is also intended, as Scanlon emphasizes, to rule out the translation of superior bargaining power into an advantageous outcome. 'The only relevant pressure for agreement comes from the desire to find and agree on principles which no one who had this desire could reasonably reject.'[53] That failure to agree would plunge the parties into a 'state of nature' holding out a more dire prospect to some than to others is thus not relevant, as it would be if justice were conceived of as a matter of drawing up an agreement on mutually advantageous terms.

Fourthly, something should be said about the requirement that the agreement should be 'informed'. It seems fairly clear that some such stipulation must be included in the conditions if there is to be any hope of deriving any specific answers about the requirements of morality from the construction. If someone believes that God will visit the fate of Sodom and Gomorrah on any society that fails to forbid a certain kind of conduct, he will surely be quite reasonable in rejecting any proposed rule that allows such conduct. But others who do not share his belief and regard the conduct in question as entirely harmless will surely be reasonable in refusing to agree that it should be forbidden. The result must be deadlock. This means that the construction has broken down, since it has failed to produce a principle capable of adjudicating a conflict.

While there is a patent necessity for some requirement about informed agreement, there is some room for disquiet about the extremely strong form that the requirement assumes in Scanlon's hands. He devotes only one sentence to explaining what he means by it, which runs as follows: 'The idea of "informed agreement" is meant to exclude agreement based on superstition or false belief about the consequences of actions, even if these beliefs are ones which it would be reasonable for the person in question to have.'[54] The trouble with this is that one person's superstition is another's belief. Must the disposition of moral questions wait on the final settlement of all conflicts on that score? If so it seems that it will have to wait a long time.

Again, the truth about the consequences of actions may be very hard to come by, especially where we are talking about the long-run social effects of actions of some kind. Much of the disagreement that there is about the justice of institutions stems from differing assessments of consequences. Should not a contractarian theory have something to say about the way to proceed in the face of disagreements about consequences rather than wiping out the problem by fiat? I believe that this is where proceduralism has a part to play, and I shall say something about that in the next chapter (see Section 16). All I want to do now is to indicate that some sort of information condition is certainly needed to get the construction off the ground, but at the same time to flag the difficulties that arise in any attempt to specify the condition in detail.

The fifth and final point worthy of discussion is that the relevant rules are said to be ones that 'no one could reasonably reject'. One point in favour of this negative way round of putting the criterion is that it emphasizes the continuity with the social contract tradition in insisting that each person has a veto on all proposed principles for regulating social life. However, the point upon which Scanlon lays stress is not so much this but the following: that we could imagine a situation in which under some proposed rule some people would suffer burdens that under an alternative feasible rule nobody need bear. These people could reasonably reject the first rule because of the availability of the second. But if under the first rule their sacrifice yielded large gains for others, they might be willing to accept it altruistically, and we should not necessarily wish to say that they were acting unreasonably in doing so. Scanlon concludes that 'the principle imposing these burdens is put in doubt',[55] but as I understand it the conclusion to which he should tend is that the rule imposing the burdens ought to be disallowed because it could reasonably be rejected.

Although I believe that Scanlon is on to something here, I do not think that it is very perspicuously captured by the distinction between acceptance and non-rejection. The underlying idea is, I suggest, that it is unfair for the generous to be exploited by the hard-hearted at the point at which general rules are being laid down. The conclusion that should be drawn is that nobody should accept a rule that would require a uni-lateral sacrifice of their interests. It is true that it is not unreasonable to be generous. But it is one thing to be praised for behaving generously against a background norm which leaves the act optional and quite another to be led by generosity to accept a rule that would expose one to moral condemnation unless one were to sacrifice oneself unilaterally. It would not be reasonable to accept the latter.

The upshot is that I do not think anything crucial turns on the distinction between a formulation of the criterion in terms of non-rejectability and a formulation in terms of acceptability. I shall therefore employ them interchangeably, though I shall use the negative formula-tion whenever I want to emphasize the point that in justifying a princi-ple special attention must be given to the problem of justifying it to those who stand to do least well out of its operation. For prima facie (even if not in the last analysis) they have the best reasons for rejecting it.

I believe that the Scanlonian approach which I have just outlined achieves Rawls's objectives better than does the construction proposed by Rawls himself. Let me illustrate this by taking up one point: the derivation of equal basic rights within the two alternative frameworks. By 'basic rights' I mean here the kind of rights that must, according to Rawls's first principle of justice, bear equally on all the members of a society: rights such as freedom of speech and freedom of religious wor-ship, an equal legal status before the courts, and so on. Now the Scanlonian construction leads directly to a very strong presumption in favour of equality here, since it invites us to ask why anybody should freely consent to being treated less well in respect of rights than any-body else in his society. It does not rule out in advance the possibility that an adequate answer might be forthcoming in certain cases.

(Otherwise, its reaching egalitarian conclusions would be of no interest.) But it insists, as it should, that a mere balance of overall advantage should not count as a justification for a system of unequal rights. Rather, the necessity for truncating the rights of some (compared with those of others) must be so compelling that even the victims should not be able reasonably to withhold their consent. Only some dire emergency, in which the whole system of liberty was at stake, could with any plausibility satisfy this condition.

Rawls quite plainly wants to make the same moves. Thus, he says that 'these rights are assigned to fulfill the principles of cooperation that citizens would acknowledge when each is fairly represented as a moral person'.[56] And, when discussing the possibility of granting less political liberty to some citizens than to others, he tells us that 'we must now reason from the perspective of those who have the lesser political liberty [under the proposed constitutional arrangements]. An inequality in the basic structure must always be justified to those in the disadvantaged position. This holds whatever the primary social good and especially for liberty. Therefore the priority rule requires us to show that the inequality of right would be accepted by the less favoured in return for the greater protection of their other liberties that results from this restriction.'[57]

The idea that any inequality must be accepted by all, including those who finish up with less under the proposed rule, is obviously pure Scanlonism. The trouble is, however, that this line of analysis simply does not fit in with Rawls's official story about the way in which principles are to be derived from the original position as he conceives it.[e] Talking about citizens acknowledging principles of cooperation when

[e] To avoid any charge of misrepresenting Rawls, I should make it clear that the decision about equality or inequality of political rights does not take place in the original position where the two principles of justice are arrived at. Rather, it occurs at a second stage, which is conceived of as an ideal constitutional convention. This point, while it is worth making to keep the record clear, is not of any significance in the present context, because the choice is still to be made by a single individual typical of all—here a 'representative citizen' instead of a 'representative person'. The members of this constitutional convention are to be told some things concealed from the people in the original position: 'the relevant general facts about their society, that is, its natural circumstances and resources, its level of economic advance and political culture, and so on.' But what matters here is that they still 'do not know their own social position, their place in the distribution of natural attributes, or their conception of the good', (Rawls, *A Theory of Justice*, 197). It is, clearly, precisely this aspect of the 'veil of ignorance' that boils down the choice to that made by a single representative individual. Incidentally, the term 'representative' is somewhat misleading in this context, since it suggests a range of variation from which we pick the central tendency, whereas the truth is that the individuals are completely interchangeable because they are reasoning with identical information from identical motives.

fairly represented sounds as if individual points of view are to be retained in the original position, yet (as we saw earlier in this section) Rawls's construction reduces to a choice made by a single person trying to advance his conception of the good in ignorance of his personal identity. Similarly, Rawls's official doctrine is explicitly affirmed when he says that in thinking about unequal political liberty 'one takes up the position of the representative citizen in the constitutional convention and assesses the total system of freedom as it looks to him'.[58] But it seems impossible to legitimize the immediate shift from that to his claim that 'the perspective of those who have the less political liberty' is to be taken as decisive here. For the 'representative citizen' must surely give equal weight to all the prospects that face him. And this is, as I have argued, quite compatible with—indeed would appear rationally to require—some trading off between good prospects and poor ones.

12. Justice and Morality

In the last section of this chapter, I want to show how justice as impartiality works and to contrast it with the pursuit of any one conception of the good. The context in which I shall do so is that of the relation between justice and morality. I shall try to show how justice as impartiality proposes to deal with the existence of differing and sometimes conflicting systems of morality. The conclusion towards which I shall move is that the rules endorsed by impartial justice are of great importance, but that they leave a great deal of scope for people to live within them according to their own moral ideas.

My subject, then, is rules of justice. I define these as the kind of rules that every society needs if it is to avoid conflict—on any scale from mutual frustration up to civil war. Ideally, rules of justice assign rights and duties to people in their personal and official capacities in such a way that, in any situation, it is clear what each person is entitled or required to do. These entitlements and requirements should fit together harmoniously: we should not find, for example, that A is entitled to demand a certain thing from B but that B is not under a duty to supply it to A.

It is worth emphasizing the point that *every* society needs what I am calling rules of justice. Consider a society of utilitarians who all shared a common conception of the 'utility' to be maximized. Jeremy Bentham was clear that such a society would need a constitutional code setting out the powers of public officials and their mode of appointment (e.g. the election of a parliament). Within this constitution there would have to be provision for laws creating the basic economic and social institutions and for a system of adjudication and enforcement. 'The principle of utility . . . requires individuals to act in accordance with rights and legal norms which direct action toward the end of the maximum of social well-being. . . . This . . . explains how Bentham was able to reconcile the motto of the good citizen *"To obey punctually; to censure freely"* with the requirements of a utilitarian morality.'[59] John Stuart Mill, in chapter 5 of *Utilitarianism*, filled out the picture by including non-legal rules enforced by social sentiment and conscience: 'Justice is the name for certain classes of moral rules which concern the essentials of human well-being more nearly, and are therefore of more absolute obligation, than any other rules for the guidance of life.'[60] Keeping promises, telling the truth, and not inflicting harm on other people are obvious examples of general obligations that in a utilitarian society would be part of the common moral code.

Any comprehensive conception of the good—not simply one that, like utilitarianism, assumes a single homogeneous good to be maximized —can be brought within the same analytical framework. To illustrate this, let us take the doctrines of St Thomas Aquinas about the human good in this life and the next. This example is especially interesting because of the place it plays in the recent work of Alasdair MacIntyre. I shall look in Chapter 5 at MacIntyre's negative claim: that the aim of creating agreement about justice in the absence of a shared substantive conception of the good is doomed to inevitable failure. For the moment, I am more concerned with the positive part of MacIntyre's argument. In *Whose Justice? Which Rationality?* he studies a number of Western traditions of thought and announces at the end an 'emerging Thomistic conclusion'.[61] Thomists, MacIntyre tells us, 'have every reason at least so far to hold that the rationality of their tradition has been confirmed in its encounters with other traditions' and that 'the task of characterizing and accounting for the achievements and successes, as well as the frustrations and failures, of the Thomistic tradition in the terms afforded by rival traditions of enquiry, may, even from the point of view of the adherents of those traditions, be a more demanding task than has sometimes been supposed.'[62]

MacIntyre heaps a fair amount of scorn and contempt on the attempts of liberal theorists to devise a basis of rules of justice that will be independent of substantive conceptions such as that embodied in Thomism. But this attitude can be justified only if he really believes—in spite of the cautious wording of his claim—that there are considerations in favor of Thomism that are in principle capable of appealing to adherents of all traditions. For, unless it is feasible to establish the superiority of one tradition over all others according to some standard that is not simply the criterion of rationality interior to that tradition, there would seem to be nothing for it but to make the best of 'modernity', with its plurality of conceptions of the good.[f]

Let us, for the sake of the argument, lay aside any incredulity we may feel about the prospect of Thomism becoming the consensual basis of a contemporary Western society's institutions. If it did happen, what would this imply about rules of justice? This question is not easy to answer because, as MacIntyre himself emphasizes, traditions evolve as social conditions change. Materially and intellectually, our world is so different from that of the thirteenth century that it is hard to imagine that substantial adaptations would not have to be made to the doctrines of Aquinas before they could be applied. Yet MacIntyre is studiously silent in *Whose Justice? Which Rationality?* about neo-Thomism—the fruit of efforts by clerical and lay Roman Catholics over the past century to work out the possible implications of Thomism for contemporary societies. And he does not make up for this silence by advancing any thoughts on the subject on his own account.[g] Let us, simply in order to fix our thoughts, postulate that unreconstructed Thomism as

    [f] It has to be conceded that, if MacIntyre is committed to claiming that it is possible to obtain a vantage point from which the overall superiority of Thomism can be discerned, this creates something of a puzzle. For it would seem to contradict the official thesis of *Whose Justice? Which Rationality?* This is, precisely, that there are no 'tradition-independent standards' for assessing traditions. According to MacIntyre, the 'Enlightenment project' (as he calls it) of discovering an ahistorical, contextless conception of rationality is chimerical. But if he held fast to that line, it is difficult to see how he could escape the kind of radical relativism enunciated some years ago by Paul Feyerabend, when he wrote that 'a tradition ... is neither good nor bad, it simply is ... [T]raditions ... become good or bad (rational/irrational; pious/impious; advanced/'primitive'; humanitarian/vicious; etc.) only when looked at from the point of view of some other tradition. "Objectively" there is not much to choose between anti-semitism and humanitarianism. But racism will appear vicious to a humanitarian while humanitarianism will appear vapid to a racist', Paul Feyerabend, *Science in a Free Society* (London: New Left Books, 1978), 8–9. Since there is no sign that MacIntyre is prepared to accept this kind of pure perspectivism, the best interpretation seems to me to be the one offered in the text.
    [g] More light is thrown on MacIntyre's opinion of neo-Thomism in his Gifford Lectures, *Three Rival Versions of Moral Enquiry* (London: Duckworth, 1990). Here he criticizes attempts to 'modernize' the thought of Aquinas as taking on board too much Kantianism (see pp. 71 and 146). The only writers in the last century for whom MacIntyre has any time are those who 'in retrieving stage by scholarly stage the historical understanding of what Aquinas himself said, wrote, and did, recovered for us an understanding of what is distinctive about the mode of enquiry elaborated in its classical and most adequate form by Aquinas' (p. 77). This is all deeply ironical, since MacIntyre maintains that the only way in which anyone can acquire moral knowledge is by attaching himself as an apprentice to a practising master and learn it as a craft (see pp. 60–6 and 125–30). But, in repudiating the actual living tradition of Thomism, MacIntyre makes becoming a Thomist into a desperate act of individual will of a kind that is, according to his own theory, an impossibility.

portrayed by MacIntyre in his exposition becomes the universally accepted basis of belief and conduct at some future time.

The point that I now want to make is that a Thomistic world would require rules covering much the same matters as the rules in a world of utilitarians, though the content of those rules would of course be different. Thus, in each society there would have to be a constitution specifying the source and scope of political authority, though in a Thomistic world all authority would be subject to the ultimate temporal supremacy of the Pope.[63] There would have to be a system of laws, which in a Thomistic world would be drawn up in accordance with Thomistic doctrine. And there would have to be rules outside positive law defining conduct as wrong. The Church would, of course, offer its teachings on this matter, but the sanctions would still have to be conscience and public opinion.

We have so far been looking at rules of justice for a utilitarian or a Thomist society. Does it make sense to think of these rules as being derived from principles of justice? We can indeed talk about principles of justice in this context, but only so long as we are clear that they have no independent status. That is to say, they will be nothing other than theorems within the overall moral system. Thus, turning back for a moment to utilitarianism, we can say that there can be principles of utilitarian justice in so far as it is possible to formulate general guidelines for the creation of rules of justice. Bentham did precisely that in his writings on the civil law, arguing that the utilitarian legislator should be guided by four 'subordinate objects'—subordinate, that is, to the ultimate object of 'the happiness of the body politic'.[64] These objects are subsistence, abundance, equality, and security. Spelling those out gives us the principle that everyone should have enough to live on, the principle that greater overall prosperity is better than less, the principle that a given amount is better the more equally it is distributed, and the principle that people should be able to form and act upon stable expectations.[65] We can if we like call these principles of distributive justice, but we should be clear that their status is that of theorems: their validity depends upon the truth of the claim that their fulfilment is a means to the advancement of the utilitarian end.

Thomism likewise has room for principles of justice. These will, as in the utilitarian case, be derived from the overarching conception of the good, though their relation to it will be different. Utilitarianism prescribes that the amount of something ('utility', however understood) is to be maximized, so principles of justice can figure only as general means to the attainment of that simple homogeneous end. In contrast, Thomistic principles of justice emerge from a grasp of God's plan for the world and of the place that mankind has in that plan. If we again follow MacIntyre's account, we shall find that the system generates principles to govern the rules about distribution. Thus, distributive justice requires that 'each person receives in proportion to his or her contribution, that is, receives what is due in respect of their status, office, and function and how well they fill it and so contribute to the good of all'.[66] In economic dealings, 'deception and exorbitant pricing are prohibited unconditionally, and so is usury'.[67] These principles would presumably be implemented in the social and economic institutions of a Thomistic society.

Although utilitarianism and Thomism differ substantively at almost every point, they agree that justice and morality are cut from the same cloth. By this I mean that, within these theories, the relation between justice and morality is a simple one. In both cases, we start with a conception of the good that is to be achieved, as far as possible. We then assess potential rules of justice by their conduciveness to the achievement of that good. Principles of justice have a purely derivative status: they function as guides to the selection of appropriate rules. Thus, for example, within the utilitarian system, the best regime is the one that holds out the best prospect of advancing the utilitarian end of maximizing utility. Within the Thomistic system, according to MacIntyre, 'the best regime is that whose order best conduces to education into the virtues in the interest of the good of all'.[68] To generalize the point: utilitarians and Thomists can both endorse the idea that 'to be practically rational . . . is to act in such a way as to achieve the ultimate and true good of human beings'.[69] There is, needless to say, a vast gulf between the conception of ultimate and true good as utility and the conception of it as loving God and serving Him. But beneath this difference we can discern a common structure. There is no need to invoke a special motive for behaving in accordance with the demands of justice. Apprehension of the good will underwrite observance of the rules of justice in as far as observance of them can be seen to contribute to the attainment of the good.

Impartial justice has to be conceived of as having a radically different status from this. We are looking here for a free-standing notion of justice: one that is not subordinate to any one conception of the good, and must therefore call upon a distinctive motive for observing its requirements. Within the utilitarian and Thomist systems, impartiality figures as an aspect of the conception of the good to be advanced. But in justice as impartiality, as I am defining it, the role of impartiality is far more central than that. Precisely because we cannot say now that the value of justice is that it tends to the achievement of some good, justice must stand or fall on its intrinsic merits. Its claim to be respected must lie in its impartial adjudication of conflicting claims arising from differing interests, perspectives, and conceptions of the good.

Let me now repeat the question I have already asked in relation to utilitarianism and Thomism. Within the theory of justice as impartiality, how are justice and morality connected? Justice is, of course, a moral concept: it is wrong to behave unjustly because that is to breach the terms of a fair agreement for mutual constraint. But justice as impartiality provides the ground rules that set the legitimate limits to the pursuit of any particular moral system's precepts. It is thus a great mistake (and a source of much misdirected criticism) to suppose that justice as impartiality is intended to constitute a complete, self-sufficient moral system in itself. Thus, if we say with Bernard Williams that what really matters is to answer the Socratic question of 'how one should live',[70] nothing will be easier than to demonstrate its inadequacy.[71] For justice as impartiality is not designed to tell us how to live. It addresses itself to a different but equally important question: how are we to live *together*, given that we have different ideas about how to live?[h]

To illustrate, consider again the case of a committed utilitarian. Subject to the constraints imposed by a set of rules consistent with justice as impartiality, such a person may—and indeed should, given his beliefs—pursue the maximization of aggregate utility both in his private actions and in his efforts to influence public policy. Similarly, we may say that, within the same constraints, a Thomist will seek to live his own life in accordance with the teachings of Aquinas, will associate together with others for the same purpose, and will seek to influence public policy in a Thomistic direction. It must be conceded that justice as impartiality may leave very little scope for action by a Thomist under the third head. But that does not constitute a valid objection, since it is no part of the case for justice as impartiality that all positions are equally well accommodated by it. Those who start by making the most oppressive demands must naturally expect to have them cut back the furthest.

[h] The best way of making this point is to observe that, until he came across Man Friday, Robinson Crusoe would have no reason for concerning himself with justice as impartiality. Yet there is no moral system that would not give rise to relevant prescriptions. Consider, for example, the three forms of simple value-maximizing theory discussed in Chapter 1. The ecocentric version would bid him to treat the ecology of his island with respect; the zoocentric version would bid him take due account of the welfare of all sentient creatures that his behaviour affected or could affect; and the anthropocentric version would tell him that, as the only human being in the picture, he should maximize his own happiness (or whatever the maximand is taken to be). And it is surely clear that Thomistic doctrine would have much relevance in that it would prescribe duties to God.

In asking how justice as impartiality is related to morality, we should cast our net widely for examples of moral thinking. Utilitarianism and Thomism, though opposed on issues of substance at almost every point, have in common that they are both universalistic moral systems: they both have a conception of the good for all human beings and a view of the way in which the good of each person should be brought into relation with the good of others. They subject every moral agent to an identical set of prescriptions once his situation has been adequately described. It is important, however, to recognize that by no means all moral notions take this universalistic form. An orthodox Jew believes that Jews should observe the laws of kosher and keep the Sabbath holy. But he does not believe that these injunctions apply to anybody who is not a Jew. The whole point of the injunctions is that they arise from a covenant between God and the Jewish people.[72] Again, someone may have a personal ideal—a notion of the right way to conduct himself or a moral purpose to which he is committed, for example—and feel guilty about failing to live up to it. But he may well not believe that others should feel guilty if they act in ways that fall short of this ideal.

No doubt, religious injunctions and personal ideals could be fitted into a universalistic framework with sufficient determination and ingenuity. Thus, we might perhaps say that any people that has a covenant with any god should observe its conditions. Similarly, we might say that anyone with a personal ideal should attempt to live up to it and should feel guilty if he or she fails to do so. But these generalizations are quite artificial and may even result in misrepresenting the actual beliefs of the people concerned, who may repudiate the claim that what they ought to do is derivable from some claim about what everybody ought to do. A Jew may have no views at all about what non-Jews should do or even take a strongly negative view (as the ancient Israelites seem to have done) about other covenants with other gods. And, in much the same way, someone with a certain moral ideal may think that it is none of his affair what other people do about their personal ideals or he may think that whether or not people ought to attempt to live up to their personal ideal depends on the nature of the ideal (without committing himself to the claim that everybody ought to share his own ideal). It would, of course, be possible to rule out a priori any non-universal moral ideas and say that they are not really moral. But I can see no sense in this.

The crucial point to be made about all this in the context of justice as impartiality is that in general no problem arises from the existence of religious injunctions or personal ideals that differ among the groups or individuals making up a society (or *a fortiori* the world as a whole). Suppose I believe that I ought to do *x* under certain conditions while you believe that under the same conditions you ought not to do x. (Let us stipulate that 'conditions' here do not include anybody's beliefs about what ought to be done.) There may be no disagreement at all between us. We may both agree, say, that I am under an obligation to abstain from the eating of pork and that you are not. Or we may both be indifferent to each other's diet. In that case, although we do not agree on what each of us ought to do, we do not disagree either: it simply is not an issue between us.

Now consider a case in which there is a real moral disagreement. Perhaps, for example, while not believing that everybody ought to share my personal ideal (which leads to the conclusion that I ought to do x under certain conditions), I do nevertheless believe that your personal ideal (which leads to the conclusion that you ought to do y under the same conditions) is misguided. We may still agree that each of us has a perfect right, within both the positive law and the positive morality of our society, to do either x or y. And we may furthermore agree that in this respect the positive law and positive morality of our society satisfy the requirements of justice as impartiality.

What I have just offered is, needless to say, a philosophically loaded account of what is supposed to be an everyday occurrence: I do not wish to claim that people actually go around talking about justice as impartiality. But people do say things like 'I think you ought not to do such-and-such but I concede that you have a right to do it.' And when they talk like this they are not usually intending to refer (solely or at all) to the legal position. What, then, do people ordinarily understand by employing a vocabulary that implies the existence of 'moral rights'? My suggestion is that they are saying that the action in question is permitted by the moral rules actually prevailing in the society and that they are not disposed to think that the relevant rule is radically defective. Justice as impartiality fits into the picture as a proposed basis for assessing the moral rules of a society.

CHAPTER 4

The political theory of impartial justice

13. Two Approaches to Constitution-Making

In this chapter, I shall pursue two related aims. In the present section, I shall continue the theme of the last section of the previous chapter by contrasting the utilitarian approach to constitution-making with that implicit in justice as impartiality. The rest of the chapter will focus on justice as impartiality, showing how it bears on a variety of issues in the appraisal and design of political institutions. I hope that this discussion will give some substance to the idea of justice as impartiality, making clearer its practical potential.

Let me begin, then, with the utilitarian approach to constitution-making. Utilitarianism follows a consistent bottom-up strategy. What I mean by this is that everything is in the last analysis a matter of what happens to people—how much pleasure they get, how far their wants are satisfied, and so on. Yet utilitarian legislation and rules of positive morality are defined not over outcomes but over actions. That is to say, utilitarianism employs a vocabulary of permissions, prohibitions, and requirements for setting out its concrete implications. Nevertheless, any proposed structure of rights and duties is to be assessed by the utilitarian criterion. This means that an attempt will have to be made to guess what use people will make of the opportunities that the legal and moral rules offer them. These outcomes will then have to be attributed a value according to the amount of aggregate want-satisfaction they can be expected to give rise to. This value is then to be read back into the laws and the moral rules themselves.

Constitutions are a stage further up from want-satisfaction but are ultimately to be judged by their effects on it. Thus, proposed constitutions will be assessed instrumentally by making a guess about the kinds of laws and government policies that they can be anticipated to lead to. This means once again that the subject-matter is a set of rules—this time rules governing the behaviour of political actors—but that the assessment of these rules turns on the amount of utility generated by the outcomes to be expected when people work within them in predictable ways (or predictably breach them in certain ways).

It is scarcely necessary to observe that any attempt to follow out this programme fully would overtax the predictive capacity of any conceivable social science. We should have to go from constitutional rules back to legislation and government policy then back from there to outcomes (what happens to people) and finally back to utility. To assess a constitution, every link in the chain would have to be secure. Yet it is apparent that each link could be established only by drawing upon bodies of knowledge that do not exist and quite possibly could not in principle exist. It is hardly surprising therefore that drastic short-cuts have been found inescapable. Thus, Bentham and James Mill postulated that, in countries such as Britain, the legislation and policies that were in the interests of a majority would produce outcomes satisfying the utilitarian criterion.[1] The constitutional problem now reduced itself to one of ensuring that voters are well informed and able to make legislation and governments accountable. Bentham therefore exhausted (as John Stuart Mill said) 'all the resources of ingenuity in devising means for riveting the yoke of public opinion closer and closer round the necks of all public functionaries.'[2]

This approach is controversial even within utilitarianism. For there seems on the face of it to be no reason for being so confident that the interests of the majority will coincide with the deliverances of the utilitarian criterion. Suppose, for example, that we attribute value to want-satisfaction, taking due account of the intensity of the wants that are satisfied and frustrated by any given outcome. Then it might well be that there were majorities with weak wants for suppressing kinds of behaviour that a minority very strongly wanted to engage in. The conclusion to be drawn from this might be that the utilitarian criterion would be better served by a constitution which included in it limitations on what majorities could do in the way of ordinary legislation. There is no need for present purposes, however, to enter into these intramural disputes. The essential point is that the process of constitutional design within utilitarianism works upwards from outcomes to constitutional rules.

If we now compare the utilitarian approach with that characteristic of justice as impartiality, we can see that they must be different because there is nothing corresponding to the utilitarian *summum bonum*. The bottom-up method inherent in the attempt to maximize the amount of good must therefore be abandoned. The whole point of justice as impartiality is that there is no single end that can be taken as authoritative for a whole society as the basis of its institutions. Rather, there are conflicting conceptions of the good and the object of justice as impartiality is to find some way of adjudicating between them that can be generally accepted as fair.

The method of justice as impartiality is top-down, to at any rate this extent: it does not have any systematic way of evaluating outcomes. To illustrate this, let me take the example of freedom of religious worship. From the point of view of virtually any conception of the good, the possibility of practising the form of religious worship in which one believes (or practising none if one's beliefs lead in that direction) will be regarded as an important component of the good life. Freedom of religious worship for only some members of a society cannot plausibly be put forward as a proposal intended to elicit general agreement, since those excluded can reasonably reject the proposal. A rule permitting religious worship on the same terms to everybody is therefore one of the rules of justice that emerges from the theory of justice as impartiality. (See Section 11 *ad fin.*)

Now, the outcome of such a rule in any given society will depend on the use its members make of their freedom to worship (or not) as they please. This outcome can be evaluated independently from the point of view of each conception of the good. Thus, somebody who thinks that all religion is an illusion will presumably value any form of religious worship negatively : a society will count as better the less religious worship goes on in it. A Muslim will presumably value the outcome according to the number of members of the society who follow the precepts of Islam, and so on for the adherents of any other religion. Someone with a conception of the good as autonomy will not care what religion (if any) people practise, but he will value the outcome according to the number of people who have arrived at their religious beliefs by a process that makes those beliefs genuinely their own and act on those beliefs. The point is, I hope, sufficiently made by these examples: justice as impartiality cannot and does not aspire to create a superordinate evaluation of the outcome. It is thus quite different from utilitarianism, which has a single calculus to cover all cases.

Whereas utilitarianism values rules only derivatively, in the light of their tendency to promote want-satisfying outcomes, justice as impartiality has as its subject the rules of justice themselves. It is these which are pronounced to be a fair resolution of conflicts between different conceptions of the good. The outcome of a rule is simply the outcome. People may evaluate it, each from the point of view of their own conception of the good, but the theory of justice as impartiality has nothing to say about the outcome. The fairness of the rule is a property of the rule itself, and can be established without any need to predict what the outcome of it will be at any particular time and place.

Freedom of religious worship is a well-established component of liberal democratic constitutions and is indeed (in a sweeping form) the subject of the first of the ten amendments that collectively constitute the Bill of Rights of the United States. Freedom for consensual sexual relations does not form an element in any of the older bills of rights, though the European Court of Human Rights has ruled that the European Convention on Human Rights prohibits the criminalization of homosexual acts.[3] A wide range of consensual sexual practices are still banned in many American states (though most of these laws are not enforced), and the Supreme Court has declined to extend the 'constitutional right to privacy' to cover private homosexual acts.[4] I wish to press the case that the arguments for both kinds of freedom being constitutionally guaranteed are strictly parallel. This will, I hope, throw light on the nature of the argument itself.

Let me begin by restating the rationale of a constitutionally guaranteed right of religious freedom. There were, let me recall, two stages to the argument. In the first stage, we picked out a practice—religious worship—central to most people's lives. (This is true for non-believers as well as believers so long as we recognize that freedom of religious worship includes the freedom not to worship.) The importance of getting the category right—'religion' rather than 'true religion'—has been emphasized by Thomas Nagel. 'Since there is more than one true description of every action, the selection of the morally operative one is crucial.' Thus, if we ask the question 'How would you like it if someone did that to you?' the answer turns on the way in which we describe what is being done. If we describe it as 'being saved from eternal damnation' then this is something we would all like to have done to us—but that description depends upon the prior identification of the true religion. As Nagel says, 'under the description "restricting freedom of worship"' somebody who was proposing to restrict others' freedom 'wouldn't want others to do it to him'.[5]

The second stage invokes the thrust of justice as impartiality towards equal treatment to derive the conclusion that the only generally acceptable basis for freedom of worship is equal freedom for everybody. The way in which this is worked out depends, of course, on the form in which the theory of justice as impartiality is cast. Thus, within Rawls's version, people in the original position do not know what their religious views are and can best protect themselves by supporting freedom of religion. Within the Scanlonian construction, we argue that anybody could reasonably reject a proposal that would put him at a relative disadvantage by excluding him from a rule of religious freedom, so the only terms on which agreement can be reached are ones that treat everybody in the same way.

Let me now draw the parallel. At the first stage, we again have to get the category right. The equivalent of 'religious worship' is 'sexual activity'. Restricting protection to 'natural' sexual activity (according to some teleological conception of nature) or sexual activity approved of by some religion would be similar to restricting freedom of religious worship to the 'true religion'. We argue as before that the category we have picked out is one that is central to people's lives. The expression of their sexual nature is crucial to most people's conception of the good life for them. Like religious belief, sexual orientation is at the core of self-identity, and if its expression is denied it leaves a gap in life that cannot be filled in any alternative way. The second stage of the argument is, as before, that the only generally acceptable way of meeting the commitment to equal treatment inherent in justice as impartiality is to legalize homosexual as well as heterosexual acts.

The argument from justice as impartiality is one that urges the fairness of moving from your own particular conception of the good to a higher level of generality. If freedom to worship in the way you think right is of great importance to your own ability to live what you regard as a good life, then you are asked to accept that it is important to others too. Similarly, if the expression of your sexual nature is important to your living a good life, as you see it, then again you are asked to accept that is equally important to those with a different sexual orientation from yours.[a]

Religious and sexual tolerance can, of course, be derived from some conceptions of the good. If you value autonomy, you will presumably conclude that it is good that people should choose a way of life (religion and sex being two highly significant areas) and be able to act on their

---

[a] What if some homosexuals accept (on the basis of a certain set of religious precepts, for example) that homosexual behaviour is wrong, and welcome laws prohibiting it? The question is: can homosexuals, any more than heterosexuals, legitimately deploy the criminal law in order to advance their conception of the good in this way? My answer is that, so long as there are some homosexuals who will defy such a law (and there always have been, however ferocious the penalties), they can reasonably reject the proposal that they should be subject to the sanctions of the criminal law. Even if those who wish to abstain from homosexual activity have this wish made harder to fulfil if such acts are legally permitted, they are still not prevented from living according to their conception of the good. But those whose conception of the good is centrally bound up with homosexual activity have to choose between abstinence and the risk of prosecution. This is clearly a far more serious invasion of their opportunity to pursue their conception of the good. Their claims therefore trump those of the others in the choosing situation.

choices. (See Section 20.) Or you might have a substantive conception of the good according to which religious worship is valuable whatever its object; more plausibly, perhaps, you might believe that 'friendship, care, affection, intimate society, all of these goods and more are promoted through homosexual as well as heterosexual relationships'.[6] Suppose, as a third possibility, that you have a conception of the good as want-satisfaction. Then you may conclude that on balance religious and sexual toleration do more good than harm. (I shall follow up this idea in Section 21.)

What has to be emphasized is that justice as impartiality is a distinctive approach, which appeals to fairness rather than goodness. People with conceptions of the good other than those canvassed above are not asked to shift to a more encompassing conception of the good. They can keep their existing conception of the good, according to which (say) only one cult or one form of sexual activity has value. Therefore, different people can accept the justice of religious and sexual freedom while evaluating differently the use made of it. There is a disanalogy between the religious and sexual cases only to this extent: homosexuals do not think that heterosexual acts are sinful or unnatural *per se* (though some profess to find the thought of them repugnant in the same way as some heterosexuals claim to find the thought of homosexual acts). But this incomplete symmetry does not seem to me to change the point that outcomes will be valued differently and that justice as impartiality has no way of creating a superordinate valuation.

There are other rules that are suitable for incorporation into a constitution. Thus, it is easy to see how, in an appropriately constituted original position, there would be agreement on the desirability of the usual guarantees against detention without trial, torture of suspects, and so on. Constitutions also need to lay down the basic rules defining the workings of the political system so as to remove them from the reach of governments and legislative majorities, which have an obvious interest in manipulating the rules in order to perpetuate their own tenure. Freedom of speech and freedom of political organization are also best thought of as an aspect of a satisfactory political decision-making process. I shall explain the rationale within the theory of justice as impartiality later in this chapter (Section 16). I mention it here, however, simply to make it clear that freedom of religious worship and consensual sexual expression do not exhaust the scope of rules suitable for incorporation into a constitution derivable from the theory of justice as impartiality.

I wish to resist, however, a couple of moves that are made by a number of other writers who endorse the general notion of justice as impartiality.

One is that justice as impartiality has as a theorem the 'harm principle' put forward by John Stuart Mill in *On Liberty* that restricts state action to the prohibition of actions harmful to those other than the actor. The other has been called the 'preclusion principle'. It may be stated as follows: wherever it is not absolutely necessary for there to be a single binding rule of conduct that applies to everybody in a society, issues that raise moral controversy should always be settled by leaving the decision to the individual. I shall take up these ideas in the next section.

14. The Harm Principle and the Preclusion Principle

In the previous section I made an argument for freedom of speech and freedom of consensual sexual expression that derived them directly from justice as impartiality. I suspect that a number of readers will have found themselves becoming impatient with this procedure and wondering why I did not instead argue that the 'harm principle' is a theorem of justice as impartiality and then derive these conclusions and a great many others from it. (In this context, it is worth recalling that the authority of Mill's 'harm principle' was relied on heavily by the committee whose report led to the legalization of homosexual acts between consenting adults in Britain.)[7] The reason is that I do not believe the 'harm principle' to be a theorem of justice as impartiality.

Let me begin the discussion by quoting Mill's canonical formulation of the principle: 'that the sole end for which mankind are warranted, individually or collectively, in interfering with the liberty of action of any of their number, is self-protection. That the only purpose for which power can be rightfully exercised over any member of a civilized community, against his will, is to prevent harm to others.'[8] This would as it stands entail the illegitimacy of any kind of legislation for the protection of the interests of non-human animals. For Mill makes it clear throughout *On Liberty* that the 'others' whose harm is the only justification for coercive intervention are to be understood as other human beings. Yet it seems absurd to suggest that all animal welfare legislation is inherently unjust. Mill's principle would also rule out the prohibition of a great variety of activities that affect others adversely but could not by any stretch of the imagination be said to harm them. Public nuisances that are not health risks would fall in this category as would the destruction of ancient trees and buildings and the erection of buildings that are out of keeping with their surroundings (including the case where *any* building would spoil the area aesthetically). I cannot conceive of any grounds for suggesting that in a Scanlonian original position the proposition that matters such as these should be left to the course of ordinary legislation could reasonably be rejected.

Much more discussed (especially by Americans, who seem quite obsessed by it) is the relatively trivial issue of so-called paternalism. Mill's harm principle is explicitly aimed at outlawing any intervention for a person's own good. However, I cannot see why, where there is a clear disproportion between the harm risked by an activity (e.g. not wearing a seat belt or motorcycle helmet) and the good forgone—on virtually any substantive conception of the good—the activity should not be prohibited. The point is that, in sharp contrast with bans on certain forms of religious worship or on homosexual activities, it is not plausible for people to say that their lives are going to be blighted—in relation to their own conception of the good—if they cannot travel in a car without wearing a seat belt or ride on a motorcycle without protective headgear. Nobody therefore has any reasonable basis for rejecting the proposition that laws about the wearing of seat belts and helmets should be left to be settled by the ordinary political process.

Within that political process, there is nothing to prevent those who place a very high value on individual liberty from making their arguments based on that and trying to prevent legislation contrary to Mill's harm principle from being enacted. Mill, it may be recalled, declined to claim 'any advantage which could be derived to [his] argument from the idea of abstract right':[9] he appealed ultimately to 'utility in the largest sense, grounded on the permanent interests of man as a progressive being',[10] and proximately to the 'greater good of human freedom'.[11] Mill's contemporary followers can similarly defend the 'harm principle' on the basis of a conception of the good which gives a high value to individual liberty. What they cannot demand, without inviting reasonable rejection of their demand by others with different priorities, is that the harm principle be assigned a privileged position.

What is usually called Mill's harm principle takes a negative form: it denies that there can be any valid reason for preventing an act except its harmful consequences. However, Mill also enunciated what we may call a positive form of the harm principle: that it is a *sufficient* condition for preventing an act that it has harmful consequences. 'If any one does an act hurtful to others, there is a *primâ facie* case for punishing him, by law, or, where legal penalties are not safely applicable, by general disapprobation. . . . In all things which regard the external relations of the individual, he is *de jure* amenable to those whose interests are concerned, and if need be, to society as their protector.'[12] The case for a positive harm principle on these lines is, I suggest, rooted in the concept of harm itself. For the point of describing an outcome as harmful is to say that it is deleterious from the point of view of a very wide range of conceptions of the good.[13] The paradigm of harm is physical injury, and on virtually any conception of the good life goes better in the absence of physical injury. A rule of justice prohibiting the injuring of other people is therefore something that can be easily agreed upon by people with a wide diversity of overall conceptions of the good.

I should amplify this so as to forestall abuses of the positive harm principle. What justice requires, it has to be emphasized, is the prohibition of acts that themselves cause harm directly to others. With the exception of incitement to violence, the positive harm principle does not underwrite the prohibition of acts that are liable to result in *other* people causing harm. Unless this qualification is added to the scope of the principle, it will entail that any group capable of mounting a plausible threat of creating a state of public disorder will be able to bring any behaviour they dislike under the principle. Thus, civic officials in towns in the southern United States have in the past invoked the positive harm principle to defend ordinances prohibiting interracial couples from walking down the street; and the Indian government's precipitate ban on the publication of Salman Rushdie's *The Satanic Verses* was justified by it (and has been defended by some political theorists) on similar grounds. Of course, it can happen that a government has lost the ability to deter or prevent riots against activities legitimated by impartial justice. What this shows is, however, that the conditions under which impartial justice can be realized do not exist. It does not show that impartial justice legitimizes the criminalization (in response to unjust threats of behaviour) of actions that should be protected in any just society.[b]

I want to take up now another general principle that purports to pre-empt a large range of political decisions by suggesting that where issues turn on 'controversial moral or religious conceptions' they can justly be disposed of only in one way: by allowing people to follow their own judgement or conscience.[14] Thomas Nagel, who espouses this principle, admits that there is abroad 'the suspicion that the escalation to a higher

---

[b] It need hardly be said that a just society cannot be maintained if a large enough minority is prepared to use violence against just provisions such as religious toleration, freedom of speech, or the elimination of grossly unjust socioeconomic privileges (slavery, apartheid, or the caste system, for example). Under these conditions, Mill's introductory remarks in *On Liberty* pointing out the limited scope of the theory are to the point. (See Mill, p. 224.) Liberal democracy can subsist only if liberty is not used by one group to organize attacks on another group and democracy is not turned into an instrument for the exploitation of minorities by majorities. In the absence of these conditions some kind of authoritarian regime is in the long run inevitable to avoid anarchy or civil war. The best that can be hoped for is that the regime will attempt to create the conditions under which liberal democracy may eventually be possible—as Mill himself argued.

level of impartiality is a sham'[15] because it is equivalent 'to the public adoption of an individualistic conception of the good'.[16] My view is that such a suspicion is wholly justified, when the move takes this form.

Stated more precisely, the idea is that, except where 'everyone recognizes that some unified policy is absolutely necessary, . . . legitimacy requires that individuals be left free, consistent with the equal freedom of others, to follow their own paths'.[17] Thus, subject to the proviso about necessity, controversies about what should be prohibited and what permitted have to be settled by coming down on the side of those who want to perform acts of the controversial kind. As with Mill's harm principle in its negative form, this undeniably gets the right answer in the cases of freedom of worship and the legality of homosexual relations. But it is far too sweeping to suggest that justice as impartiality requires all controversies to be resolved in favour of liberty. Those who place a high value on individual autonomy can press this principle in public debate, and if they succeed then it will not be unjust to enact laws in accordance with it. But we cannot say that it would always be unjust to enact laws that contravene the principle.

The affinity of this 'principle of preclusion,' as it has been called,[18] with the harm principle becomes apparent if we ask how the proviso concerning 'necessity' is to be filled in. When does everyone recognize that some unified policy is absolutely necessary? Obvious candidates would be harmful activities such as killing, injuring, raping, robbing and so on. Nagel offers the example of 'national defence' as one where 'everyone recognizes that some unified policy is absolutely necessary, and we all have to take the risk that the actual policy decided on will be abhorrent to us'.[19] And it may be observed that Mill, in his statement of the positive 'harm principle', accepted that consistently with it anyone could 'rightfully be compelled to perform' acts for 'the benefit of others' such as 'to bear his fair share in the common defence'.[20]

The principle of preclusion is, however, even more restrictive in its scope than the negative form of the harm principle. It is true that not all religiously motivated objections to public coercion would go through: Macaulay claimed in 1843 that 'it is by the command, and under the special protection of the most powerful goddesses that the Thugs join themselves to the unsuspecting traveller, make friends with him, slip the noose round his neck, plunge their knives in his eyes, hide him in the earth, and divide his money and baggage'.[21] Pretty clearly no society could reasonably tolerate predation of this kind, whatever its motivation. As a later Victorian writer remarked: 'If a Thug makes strangling of travellers a part of his religion, we do not allow him the free exercise of it.'[22] However, the Roman republic proved that there was no necessity to prohibit a *paterfamilias* from having a life and death power over his children, so a religious sect claiming this as a part of its cult would be in a strong position. Again, public order would necessarily be disturbed by the immolation of widows on their funeral pyres, even unwillingly. Similarly, female genital mutilation is something that does not have to be prohibited and in some societies is not. Even where it is prohibited it is often widely practised, with no breakdown of social order. If these practices are to be prohibited it is not because there has to be a public policy taking the decisions out of private hands but simply because they cause harm.[23]

In these cases I believe that justice as impartiality leads to the endorsement of the positive harm principle and thus to the conclusion that harmful acts such as these are unjust. Even if that claim is not accepted, can it be denied that such practices can without injustice be prohibited under the criminal law following the ordinary legislative procedures? Even that modest conclusion is sufficient to explode the preclusion principle, which seeks to remove them from the sphere of legislation—'take them out of politics'.

The preclusion principle is deployed very commonly, and with great confidence, in the debate about the legalization of abortion. The argument is made that, since the status of the foetus is controversial, there is only one just solution, which is to permit abortions. For there is no necessity for a law mandating uniformity of conduct here, and permitting abortions avoids the coercion of those who think them morally permissible while not preventing those who think them morally wrong from following their consciences. (This is in essence the basis of the American Supreme Court decision that prevented the states from criminalizing abortion through ordinary legislative processes.)[c]

[c] I should perhaps mention here Ronald Dworkin's argument in favour of a constitutionally guaranteed right to an abortion in his book *Life's Dominion* (London: HarperCollins, 1993). Dworkin repudiates the preclusion principle as a general principle, but his argument in the specific case of abortion turns on a version of it. According to Dworkin, almost everybody agrees that human life is sacred (including foetal life), but there is disagreement about what follows from this about the moral permissibility of abortion. This promotes the issue to one of religious disagreement, and it is taken as axiomatic that religious disputes should not be settled by law: rather the law should allow people to act on their own convictions. There are two objections to this argument. The first is that the premise that Dworkin takes to be common ground is in fact the property of the anti-abortionists. Many people (including me) would say that there is no deep moral issue involved in abortion because if nobody comes into existence nobody is harmed. (Harming a foetus—e.g. by the mother's smoking and drinking during pregnancy—is wrong if the foetus is brought to term because then somebody *is* harmed.) If it is once conceded that all life (including foetal life) is within the realm of 'the sacred', it is hard to see how a mere preference on the part of the mother or the parents not to have a child could be sufficient to overcome the claims of the foetus. Even if this objection

It should be observed at once that this is not a case where Mill's harm principle can be invoked, because the issue at stake is precisely whether the foetus is to count as a human being (so that its protection triggers the positive harm principle) or not. Obviously, therefore, the harm principle cannot be used to settle the issue, which is one of the proper interpretation of that principle. The preclusion principle therefore has to stand on its own, and we have already seen how implausible it is as a theorem of justice as impartiality.[24] Thus, if we say that it is controversial whether or not a foetus is to count as a human being, and therefore the mother must be left to decide about aborting it, I cannot see how a similar move can be headed off in the case of female genital mutilation. This is also a controversial practice: some traditionalist Muslims regard it as religiously mandated and others would say that it forms part of a way of life that they value. So does it not follow that it would be unjust to have a law forbidding parents from subjecting daughters to genital mutilation? If justice entails a 'pro-choice' position for one, does it not entail a 'pro-choice' position for the other? Of course, it is perfectly possible to take a pro-choice position on one and not on the other. (This is as a matter of fact my own position.) But this can be done consistently only if it is acknowledged that the preclusion principle does not constitute a principle of justice.

I pointed out in my discussion of the harm principle that it would, in its negative form, rule out any laws aimed at preventing cruelty to animals, or more generally the infliction of suffering on them in the course of, for example, using them for medical research or raising them for food. Let me now draw attention to the way in which the 'pro-choice' argument for abortion from the principle of preclusion is used, apparently in all seriousness, by defenders of the continued legality of barbarous sports such as fox-hunting, stag-hunting, and hare-coursing—and could, presumably, be used with equal force for the restoration of legality to such things as cock-fighting, dog-fighting, and bear-baiting. Nobody, it was said in a recent parliamentary debate on the subject in Britain, has to engage in bloodsports unless he or she chooses to. And, since the morality of bloodsports is controversial, the decision should be left to the individual. Although this may seem like a mere parody of the 'pro-choice' argument in relation to abortion, the

could somehow be overcome by elevating the wish not to be encumbered by a child to the level of a competing 'sacred' interest, the argument would still run into the difficulty raised in the text: that the appeal to private judgement in matters of religion is strictly qualified. If abortion is the destruction of a human being, invocation of the realm of the sacred will hardly lead to the conclusion that abortion should be permitted by law. We would, after all, regard as absurd an argument that murder should not be prohibited on the ground that all human life is sacred.

point is that it is structurally identical, and I do not see how it is possible to reject it in the one case without rejecting it in the other.

The opponents of hunting will, of course, say that the result of leaving the decision to the individual is that a lot of animals will be torn to pieces by dogs. But equally, of course, the opponents of abortion will say the result of leaving that decision to the individual will be that a lot of foetuses get aborted. There is in the end no way round the point that there are different evaluations of the gravity of those states of affairs when put in the balance against the ability of women to control their own fertility and the enjoyment (sometimes claimed to be intense) that hunters derive from their pursuit.[d] And I do not believe that in either case it is plausible to suggest that there is a principle of justice demanding that the law must come down against the protection of foetuses or animals.

Finally, it is worth pointing out that, because the principle of preclusion is flawed, and can be seen to be flawed by anyone who is led to question it as a result of disliking the conclusions derived from it, the claim that it resolves conflicts by 'taking controversial issues out of politics' is actually the reverse of the truth. For the principle itself becomes the focus of even more violent controversy than the issue itself ever was. This is illustrated by the contrasting experience in relation to the abortion issue of the United States, where the Supreme Court committed it to the preclusion strategy, and Western Europe, where in each country some compromise between the extreme views was reached by ordinary legislative processes. The issue is in itself as controversial within Western Europe as in the United States. But the kind of violent opposition to the law found in America has been very largely absent in Western Europe.

Further support for the proposition that the cause of this difference is the way in which the abortion issue was 'taken out of politics' in the United States can be gained by looking at the situation in states that had already enacted liberal abortion laws before the Supreme Court preempted the issue. As Kristin Luker has shown, opponents of abortion in California (one of the states with a liberal law) had on the whole reconciled themselves to defeat in the ordinary legislative process. What mobilized them was the Supreme Court's insistence that the issue was

---

[d] It might be argued that there is a difference in the following sense. In the case of abortion there is a disagreement whether, if a foetus is not brought to term and does not suffer, aborting it is an evil at all. In contrast, if we leave aside obviously corrupt arguments on the lines of 'the fox enjoys being chased', we can say that nobody denies that the suffering of the quarry is *pro tanto* an evil. However, conceding the validity of the point, I do not think that it affects the parallelism in a significant way. For the question in the latter case is the relative importance to be given to animal welfare when compared to the interests of human beings, and the point is that there is apparently quite strong disagreement about this.

not one for political horse-trading in which each side took its chances but was one of constitutional principle.[25]

Imagine that the question of animal welfare were similarly 'taken out of politics' by a constitutional provision that prevented the legislature from abolishing hunting, controlling experimentation on animals more closely, abolishing battery farming, and so on. Would this pacify those who think that such measures are needed? Surely it would simply entail their disillusion with the constitution. And I do not see how they could be said to be misguided. In fact I would agree with them.

15. Social Justice in the Courts

I began this chapter by showing how substantive rules are assessed differently within utilitarianism and justice as impartiality. I have not, however, said anything yet about the way in which the latter theory approaches the design of constitutions. It would be convenient if I could say that, whereas the utilitarian approach is entirely bottom-up, the approach of justice as impartiality is entirely top-down. Unfortunately, things are not so simple.

I have shown how justice as impartiality can assess substantive rules directly, without referring to the outcomes produced by people acting within the environment created by those rules. We cannot say, however, that justice as impartiality is never concerned with outcomes, and I have in fact shown in the previous section the way in which the concept of harm functions to draw together kinds of outcome that it is the job of rules of justice to prevent. We also cannot say that constitutions could reasonably be drawn up in an entirely top-down manner. We cannot, in other words hope to be able to specify the characteristics of a just constitution in purely procedural terms. For we must be concerned with the substantive justice of the laws and governments policies that are produced within the framework for collective decision-making that it provides.

Some substantive rules of justice lend themselves to incorporation directly within a constitution. A good example is the one of freedom of religious worship discussed earlier in this chapter (Section 13). This can be guaranteed against attack by ordinary legislative majorities by writing it into the constitution. There are two features of religious freedom that are relevant here. One is that justice as impartiality reaches definite conclusions about it: that any departure from freedom of worship on equal terms for all is unjust. The other relevant feature is that this conclusion is capable of being embodied in a justiciable rule which sets limits on permissible legislation, setting bounds to the operation of the ordinary legislative process. Needless to say, any such rule would leave a good deal of scope for judicial interpretation. But experience attests that it is feasible to turn a principle such as that of freedom of religious worship into a rule that courts can get a grip on.

The implication is that a just constitution can build in freedom of religious worship as a substantive element. This will protect it against abridgement by the ordinary process of legislation, since amendment of the constitution will (I assume) require special procedures to be followed. That freedom of religious worship is an appropriate substantive element in a just constitution does not entail, however, that a constitution cannot be accounted just if it does not include it. For what ultimately matters is that freedom of religious worship should exist: the means by which this is achieved is of no significance in itself. There used to be a widely held view in Britain, for example, that an entrenched clause in a written constitution asserting the inviolability of religious liberty was unnecessary because there was no risk of its being violated by ordinary legislation. And if there was no need for it there was a certain advantage in not having it, since the spirit of religious freedom would be better protected by the whole mass of laws, without possibly perverse judicial intervention. The past fifteen years have damaged beyond repair the idea that governments in Britain can be trusted to operate within unwritten constraints. And since the argument has not appeared plausible anywhere else, it can now be pronounced dead. It is still, however, worth carrying from it the point that whether or not a potentially justiciable rule of justice should be incorporated in a constitution is a question of strategy and not one of deep principle. In practice, however, it seems hard to resist the conclusion that the drawbacks of the constitutional route are invariably outweighed by its advantages.

In addition to freedom of religious worship, I have argued, freedom to engage in consensual homosexual sex can also be derived from the theory of justice as impartiality. And this too is a limitation on the scope of the legislature that could feasibly be incorporated in the constitution. There are two other matters that constitutions invariably deal with: they set out some constraints on the operation of the legal system and they lay down the fundamentals of the political system. It is surely apparent that these are precisely matters where limits on the powers of the government and legislature are most needed, since office-holders are always open to the temptation of trying to take short-cuts to secure what they regard desirable results and are liable to rig the rules controlling electoral competition in their own favour. I shall say some more about the place of constitutional rules in politics later in this chapter

(Section 16). But I think there is little need for any argument in favour of the general point that *ex ante* nobody could reasonably reject the proposition that rules governing the legal system and the political system should be constitutionally entrenched.

I now want to ask what else courts might be able to do to further the cause of justice. I want to ask, specifically, what relevance if any courts have for the pursuit of social justice, understanding by that expression the justice of a society's basic social and economic institutions. Showing how this might affect constitutional design would best be done by taking as examples principles of social justice that I believe to be derivable from the theory of justice as impartiality. Unfortunately, however, I shall not be in a position to expound such principles until I get to the next volume in this *Treatise*, entitled *Principles of Justice*. As a surrogate, then, let me take as an example the 'difference principle' advanced by John Rawls. This is the general principle that social and economic inequalities should be accepted only if and to the extent that they benefit the least advantaged social group.[e]

Suppose we take the difference principle as our touchstone. What does it suggest in terms of constitutional arrangements? It has been suggested that the difference principle might actually be incorporated into a constitution as a substantive rule.[26] But it seems clear to me—and Rawls has expressed the same view on numerous occasions—that courts are wholly unsuited for the kinds of judgement that are needed. For what is at stake in any given society includes (to mention only some of the most obvious) the form of economic organization (private ownership, public ownership, workers' cooperatives, and so on), the system of taxes on income, inheritance and gifts, and the basis on which cash transfers are made. These are, if anything is, the stuff of politics. If the injunction to give priority to the socioeconomic interests of those who do least well is widely accepted as the right basis for public policy, it will provide a framework for debate on social and economic policy. But we must

---

[e] I have discussed Rawls's derivation of the difference principle in chapter 6 of *Theories of Justice*. I have been taken by a number of people to have intended to endorse this derivation, and I probably gave this impression by saying that Rawls's argument was valid (p. 214). I meant by this that the conclusion followed from the premises, but I did not offer a view of the correctness of the premises. The following is a valid syllogism: 'Socrates is a mouse; all mice have curly tails; therefore Socrates has a curly tail.' But in saying that this is a valid argument I do not commit myself to either the proposition that Socrates has a curly tail or the proposition that all mice have curly tails. Similarly, I do not in fact accept Rawls's premise that there is nothing for which people can claim credit because all differences in productive capacity arise from one kind of luck or another. However, the implications of the principles I shall advance in the next volume of this *Treatise* are close enough to those of the difference principle that the text would not have to be amended if they were substituted.

expect that there will be many views about what would be the precise institutional arrangements best calculated to benefit the worst off.

This is not enough, however, to show that social justice cannot be incorporated into a constitution in the form of substantive rules. Suppose, to take an analogy, that John Stuart Mill's 'harm principle' were a theorem of justice as impartiality (contrary to my arguments in the previous section). It would surely be leaving judges with too much discretion simply to state that principle in the constitution and let the courts decide on its application. Rather, the principle would form the basis for specific rules, prohibiting the state from interfering in religious worship, guaranteeing freedom of speech, and so on. Similarly, it might be argued, the courts should not be presented with the difference principle—or any other principle of justice for that matter. But, so long as there was sufficient agreement among the members of a society about the implications of social justice, these might be embodied in specific substantive rules and incorporated in the constitution.

All the new constitutions in the former Soviet states of central Europe incorporate a panoply of 'social' rights. 'The Albanian constitution is typical. It includes the right to work, the right to remuneration in cases of work stoppage, the right to a paid holiday, the right to recreation, the right to social security, guaranteed free medical service, and paid maternity leave. The Polish draft is quite similar.'[27] The Hungarian constitution 'protects not merely the right to equal pay for equal work, but also the right to an income conforming with the quantity and quality of work performed'. This would, if taken seriously, throw the entire system of wage-determination into the lap of the courts. Another provision of the Hungarian constitution with completely open-ended implications is that 'People living within the territory of the Republic of Hungary have the right to the highest possible level of physical health.'[28] There has also been a quite strong move in Canada to add to the constitution 'a social charter that would guarantee the right to health care, social assistance and education.'[29]

There are two difficulties inherent in the constitutionalizing of such objectives. The first is a practical one. 'Courts lack the tools of a bureaucracy. They cannot create government programs. They do not have a systematic overview of government policy.'[30] The other is a problem of principle: since almost all of these objectives costs money to implement, courts would be left controlling the lion's share of the budget, deciding the level of taxes, and making decisions about the levels of competing expenditures that lie squarely with the province of governments. Presented by the constitution with what is in effect a wish-list of desirable outcomes, judges would tend to duck controversy, deferring to the government's view of 'what [it] can or can't afford, given this or that level of deficit and taxation'.[31] As Cass Sunstein has said: 'If the Constitution tries to specify everything to which a decent society commits itself, it threatens to become a mere piece of paper, worth nothing in the real world.'[32]

The deeper point, which I shall not be able to support until much later in this *Treatise*, is that social justice does not determine the level or organizational form of health care, education, or social security. In a modern society, social justice certainly does require that all of these should be provided, but it leaves a good deal of scope for variation beyond that. If the French choose to fund children heavily and pensioners less generously while the Germans have very generous pensions but less generous child benefits, this is a legitimate reflection of (presumably) different collective preferences. Within any area covered by mobility of labour and capital and free flow of goods and services, there is a strong case for saying that the collective decision must be area-wide on standards of worker protection and environmental standards, and perhaps also on the overall 'social wage'. The implication is that what is needed is area-wide legislation, since this is the only way of creating sufficient uniformity. It still remains true that the concept of justice does not itself determine a unique right answer, and that throwing the question to a European court in order to provide a pan-European set of answers would be an inappropriate way of dealing with it.[f]

---

[f] It may be thought that what is said in the text is contradicted by the existence of the Social Charter of the European Economic Community. However, it actually supports my case. What is interesting is that the route taken to protect workers against exploitation is not that of justiciable rules to be interpreted by the European Court, as with the usual liberal rights. Rather, the Charter is a declaration of principles (corresponding roughly to the area of overlap between the basic ideas of Social Democratic and Christian Democratic political parties in Western Europe) which are then to be implemented by pieces of very specific Community legislation, such as a ban on anyone working more than forty-eight hours in a week, precisely stated minimum terms of maternity leave, and so on. This drive to create standards common to all the countries of the EEC stems from the fear of a competitive downward pressure on standards within the single market. Exactly the same fear animates some of the Canadian supporters of a social charter, who say that it 'would preserve and expand national standards in order to ensure that provinces are not forced into "downward harmonization" of social programs and regulatory measures by increased mobility of capital and citizenry. Provinces should not be competing with each other for capital investment in a manner which rewards the province with the lowest environmental or employment standards, for example.' (Kymlicka and Norman, (for citation see n. 29), p. 8, quoting Bruce Porter, 'Social and Economic Rights and Citizenship', prepared for the Institute for Research on Public Policy, November 1991.) I do not believe, however, that a justifiable social charter could achieve the goals set out by Porter. What the argument shows is that standards have to be set at the national level rather than being left to the provinces. But there is, I suggest, no alternative to legislation setting the precise levels to be maintained.

With public services, then, we can say that justice bears primarily on the way in which the money is raised and the way in which the services are distributed among claimants, but that the level of expenditure can (within certain limits) legitimately depend on what the citizens want to pay for. There is no similarly conventionalist element in justice as it concerns the distribution of income and wealth. (I shall argue for this conclusion in the next volume of this *Treatise.*) Nevertheless, if we cannot imagine a society turning over to the judiciary the authoritative interpretation of the difference principle (or any other principle of distributive justice such as the principle that desert should be rewarded), it is surely even harder to imagine that some specific formula for the progressivity of income tax and inheritance tax should be built into the constitution. For even if there were quite widespread agreement on, say, the difference principle, there would still inevitably be a lot of disagreement about its concrete implications. And there seems no good reason why the majority view current when the constitution is being drawn up should be given a special position *vis-à-vis* subsequent majority views.

Is the implication of all this that courts have virtually nothing to contribute to the pursuit of social justice? By no means so, but it is true that their efforts will for the most part play a subsidiary role to that of legislatures and governments. At the most modest—but still important—level, courts must oversee the application of the rules defining liability to taxes, eligibility for benefits, and so on. We can, however, envisage courts being given a considerably more ambitious role than this, which would still fall far short of the ability to set overall levels of expenditure or dictate forms of governmental reorganization. The key to this approach—which, as we shall see, has much wider applicability—is to draw a distinction between what gets done and how it gets done. Principles such as non-discrimination, equal educational opportunity and equal access to health care speak to the question of 'how' and are appropriate for judicial review; questions of 'what' (such as the overall level of expenditure and the general organization of the service) are more suited to the government and legislature, even when they too involve questions of justice.

Principles such as that demanding equality of access and of opportunity and that demanding non-discrimination are capable of generating widespread support, but they are by no means always instantiated in the actual policies that get enacted by governments, left to their own devices. This may arise deliberately as a result of prejudice or inadvertently through lack of attention to the impact of some policy on people in a particular situation. The judiciary can usefully operate interstitially to ensure that whatever general policies are pursued are carried through equitably.[33] As has been said of a proposal on these lines in the Canadian debate, this 'would assist those who might otherwise slip through the social safety net, but it would do little to determine the height of the net, so to speak'.[34]

We need not resort to speculation about the feasibility of this kind of judicial intervention. The Fourteenth Amendment of the United States constitution, which says that everyone should enjoy th 'equal protection of the laws', has been employed not only to outlaw racial segregation of public facilities but also to prevent inequities of funding. Thus, for example, schools have been required to reduce the gap between the amount per head spent on sports for boys (notably support for the football team) and sport for girls. In both cases, the overall level of financial support is not at issue. What is at issue is the equitable distribution of whatever funds are made available. American judicial activism is a familiar story, but what is worth observing is that examples of intervention by courts can be found even in Britain, perhaps the most unpromising source in any Western liberal democracy. It has been held that if a local education authority chooses to have a selective school system with single-sex schools, it cannot provide more places for boys than for girls. Similarly, the European Court of Justice has acted to eliminate inequities between the treatment of men and women within the system of cash benefits, such as different ages of compulsory retirement for men and women, and the extraordinary provision that married women could not claim a carer's benefit available for men and unmarried women.[35]

16. Procedures and Social Justice

Valuable as the interstitial activity of courts may be, it is clearly of limited significance. It cannot ensure the substantive justice of laws and policies. Thus, most of the burden of securing social justice has to rest on the procedures that result in laws and policies. In this section, I shall ask what procedures are best adapted to the task of fostering just laws and policies.

A good way of approaching this question is to reflect on the conditions required, according to the Scanlonian approach, for justice to prevail. We posit people who are well informed, concerned to further their own interests and conceptions of the good, but capable of recognizing reasonable objections on the part of others. The institutional setting is one that guarantees the parties an equal footing by giving them all a veto over proposals that they cannot reasonably accept. If these are the hypothetical conditions under which rules and principles of justice can be expected to emerge, an obvious implication is that just laws and policies are more likely to arise in actual societies the closer they come to instantiating these hypothetical conditions.[36]

In *Theories of Justice* (p. 347) I coined the expression 'the circumstances of impartiality' to refer to empirical conditions that approximate those of a Scanlonian original position. Employing the conception of rules of justice developed at the end of the previous chapter, we may define the circumstances of impartiality as the conditions under which the substantive rules of justice of a society will tend actually to be just. As we have seen already, the concept of rules of justice covers moral as well as legal rules. For the present, however, I shall confine my attention to substantive legal rules and authoritative policies, postponing until Chapter 8 the question of the circumstances of impartiality for a society's moral rules.

The most important and at the same time perhaps the most elusive of the circumstances of impartiality is a motivational one: the willingness to accept reasonable objections to a proposal regardless of the quarter from which they come. There is no way in which procedural rules can be expected to bring about just laws and policies in a country containing a stigmatized minority group (or several minority groups) whose concerns are given little or no consideration by the majority. One of the ground rules of public discourse must be that all claims are weighed in the same balance. Suppose I belong to the dominant group in my society, defined for example by race, language, religion, or ethnicity. And suppose further that I believe that the members of my group could validly object to some policy if it would have the effect of denying our children a decent education. Then I cannot say that a similar objection to a certain policy is to be discounted simply because it is made by or on behalf of the members of some minority such as gypsies or the residents of inner-city ghettos.

This is, it may be observed, a very weak requirement. But, weak as it is, it is unhappily quite enough to suggest that in many societies the conditions do not exist for ordinary political processes to bring about social justice. It is, indeed, possible to provide constitutionally for the representation of stigmatized minorities. In India this is done by reserving seats in the national legislature for members of the scheduled castes and tribes, and in the United States it has been held by the courts that the representation of blacks cannot be 'diluted' by denying them some seats in which they are a substantial majority. This will ensure that their voice is heard, but it cannot avert a situation in which a majority of politicians gets elected on a platform of neglecting or repressing the minority. (Indeed, it has the by-product of creating a majority of homogeneously white districts.)

There is, unhappily, no procedural alchemy whereby a majority bent on injustice can be made to pursue justice instead. This is a depressing conclusion, but who can look at constitutional regimes with stigmatized minorities and not be depressed? In spite of their limitations, substantive constitutional rules are the only hope for the protection of minorities in these conditions, examples being the Indian provision of guaranteed places in higher education and the public services for members of the scheduled castes and tribes, and (at least until recently) the vigorous prosecution of a certain ideal of racial equality in the schools by American courts. However, in the absence of the kind of support by popular majorities for such measures that would have made them unnecessary in the first place, they are inevitably vulnerable. For in the long run a large majority unwilling to accept the equal claims of the minority can, within a constitutional regime, change the constitution.g

We should observe, however, that, even where group members systematically discount others' claims, the circumstances of impartiality can arise if the leaders of the groups conclude (and can persuade their followers) that social peace demands that in politics claims should be counted as equal. Suppose that we have several groups, not necessarily equal in strength, but well balanced in the sense that none can hope single-handedly to hold down the rest indefinitely. These groups will typically be distinguished by religion, race, language, or ethnicity. Then justice as mutual advantage may actually lead to the outcomes that would be endorsed by justice as impartiality, provided the peaceful resolution of conflicts is seen as mutually advantageous.

It has to be said, however, that this is precarious. There is always present the alternative of a conflict in which two or more groups form a tactical alliance to crush those left out of their coalition. Thus, post-independence Nigeria quickly settled into a zero-sum game of two

---

g In India, the constitution itself requires that the provisions mandating quotas lapse unless they are periodically extended by a parliamentary majority. (This stems from their being envisaged as extraordinary measures responding to a situation of systematic disadvantage and prejudice which it was hoped by the founders would soon disappear.) In view of the sharp reaction to the most recent renewal and rise of political forces opposed to quotas, it must be doubted if the next renewal will go through when it comes up for a vote. In the United States, those who voted for Reagan and Bush were given to understand that they would put forward candidates for the Supreme Court (and the lower federal courts) who could be expected to dismantle much of the protection of minorities built up since the 1950s, and this was at any rate one promise that has been carried out. By such means the constitution is changed by interpretation to accord with majority preferences (or at any rate politically successful preferences) without the need for a constitutional amendment.

regions against one, and the elaborate arrangements for communal power-sharing in Lebanon collapsed into civil war, albeit under external pressure. In the long run, in fact, I am inclined to think that justice as impartiality founded on justice as mutual advantage is stable only if the practice of working together peacefully creates the conditions for justice as impartiality to stand independently of support from justice as mutual advantage. In other words, what one has to hope is that, after a long enough time spent practising a politics in which all claims are treated equally for the sake of social peace, the people in the society will begin genuinely to count all claims equally. The amount of time required for this to happen is, unfortunately, to be measured in decades or even centuries, if historical experience is to be our guide.

No constitution can prevent a majority coalition hell-bent on oppressing the other citizens from attempting to do so. What can be said, however, is that if politicians do want to operate a 'politics of accommodation' in a divided society, there are certain devices that they will typically use.[37] Narrow majorities will be eschewed and instead more inclusive support for the government and its measures will be sought. Political appointments will often be made according to some principle of proportionality, so that the major groups are represented according to their numbers in the population or their parliamentary strength. What has to be emphasized, is that these devices are the expressions of a commitment to the accommodation of the groups into which the society is divided, not the cause of that commitment.[h] That being said, however, it is surely clear that the operation of these devices will itself help to maintain the spirit of accommodation.

It is natural to ask if there are any lessons to be drawn from this for societies that are not deeply divided. Our present question is, let me recall, as follows: what are the conditions in which there is a widespread disposition to accept the force of reasonable objections to proposed laws and policies? So far I have argued that a necessary condition is a disposition to see fellow citizens as equals in a fundamental sense, so that the force of an objection is not discounted simply because it is

---

[h] If the effect is mistaken for the cause, it is natural to suppose that imposing consociational devices upon local politicians (as the United Kingdom government has attempted at various times to do in Cyprus and Northern Ireland) will create a practice of political accommodation. I argued in 1975 that this proposal rested on a mistaken analysis. I have since had the melancholy satisfaction of seeing its truth amply confirmed by experience. It is worth noting that the problems of group conflict in both Cyprus and Northern Ireland are especially intractable because both places are characterized by the existence of only two communities, one much larger than the other. See 'The Consociational Model and its Dangers', reprinted in my *Democracy and Power: Essays in Political Theory, Vol. I* (Oxford: Clarendon Press, 1991), 136–55.

made by or on behalf of some stigmatized group distinguished by race, religion, language or descent. But this is plainly not a sufficient condition. What is required is as far as possible a polity in which arguments are weighed and the best argument wins, rather than one in which all that can be said is that votes are counted and the side with the most votes wins. Of course, there must be some determinate decision rule specifying, say, a procedure for electing a parliament and a procedure for voting on legislation within parliament. But Michael Walzer could not be more wrong—in any sense except the banal one of endorsing democratic decision-rules of some kind—in saying that the authority of law 'is a function of popular will and not of reason'.[38]

The authority of a law does indeed depend on its having been made in accordance with constitutionally mandated procedures. But it also depends upon its having been adopted in a way that gave a full chance for objectors to be heard and upon its not being open to reasonable rejection—in other words on its not being unjust. Thus, the reform of local government taxation carried out by the Thatcher government in Britain, which replaced a tax based on house values ('rates') with a flat rate 'poll tax', was pushed through over the virtually unanimous advice of experts and was widely (and correctly) viewed as grossly unjust. The reaction was predictable, and was in fact predicted. Whereas non-payment of rates had been of negligible proportions, many people refused to pay the poll tax, clogging the courts and causing serious financial problems for local authorities. More seriously, unjust laws tend to undermine the authority of law in general: it has been surmised that it will take many years for the proportion of people paying local government taxes to return to its previous level, if it ever does, even though a new system (basically similar to the one before the poll tax) has been introduced.

To be worthy of respect, then, laws and government policies must arise from a process of 'open justifications openly arrived at'.[39] Legislation, for example, should be based upon consultation, in the course of which concerned individuals and organizations are given enough time to formulate comments on proposals; there should be hearings, where experts and others with something to contribute to a process of rational evaluation have a chance to state their case and answer questions; and the law that emerges should be both defensible and actually defended by engaging—not perfunctorily but seriously— with the arguments put forward by objectors. These are all procedural rather than substantive desiderata. I put it forward as an empirical claim that manifestly unjust legislation is less likely to come about under these conditions than in their absence.

If I am right, then, it is possible to set out procedures of a kind familiar within many liberal democratic political systems that will produce an empirical approximation of a Scanlonian original position by making it harder for rules that can reasonably be rejected to be adopted. Such procedures do not, however, lend themselves very well to embodiment in justiciable constitutional rules. That said, it should be allowed that even the relatively supine British judiciary held that some of Mrs Thatcher's ministers acted unreasonably in taking decisions (especially on town planning applications) without considering relevant evidence. But this did not, of course, prevent the decision from being reaffirmed after the evidence had supposedly been taken into account.

Respect for expert opinions, arguments, and evidence are in the end more a question of the spirit in which politics is carried on than something that lends itself to being captured in a set of rules.[i] In the end even the most elaborate rules can avail little in the face of a government with a parliamentary majority that is imbued with the Walzerian belief that 'the people are the successors of gods and absolutist kings'.[40] But we are, I suggest, focusing our attention on a point too close to that at which laws and policies are made if we are looking for rules that will enforce reasonableness. We should rather ask what can be said about the kinds of environment within which the weighing of reasons tends to displace the counting of noses, and then ask how constitutional rules can contribute towards the creation and fostering of these desirable kinds of environment.[41]

---

[i] This point is illustrated by the Thatcher episode in Britain. Without altering any of the procedural rules that would form part of a written constitution if the United Kingdom had one, she succeeded in expelling virtually all elements of civility in British political life. During her period in office (1979–91) there were no Royal Commissions, and the only committees that were set up were given in advance the conclusions they were to reach: their task was simply to work out ways and means of achieving a preset goal. The government was caught lying to parliament often enough to suggest that this practice was endemic, and the quality of public debate was further debased by the prostitution of the government information services, the suppression of inconvenient statistics (e.g. on income distribution) and the ruthless manipulation of others (e.g. unemployment figures). A climate was created in which the key to influence was the zealous and uncritical espousal of the leader's ideas while expert advice of all kinds was denigrated as the mere expression of professional self-interest. In addition to all this, the playwright Alan Bennett was perhaps right to say that 'Mrs Thatcher's worst legacy was to have deliberately destroyed that tradition of tolerant non-party cooperation on public bodies and community enterprises that had been one of the most valuable features of public life in this country,' Bennett, 'Peeved at Peregrine', *The Guardian*, 25 May 1992, p. 21. The last of these is particularly difficult to recreate once it has been destroyed, especially when a whole generation of politicians has now come into parliament that has never known anything else. A form of important social capital has been depleted. Getting back to conditions that were taken for granted before 1979 will now require more than a change of government; it will call for the kinds of constitutional arrangements mooted below.

Thus, public commissions and committees of inquiry are settings in which alternative laws and policies can be subjected to public scrutiny. Since the job of such bodies is defined as that of arriving at reasoned conclusions, they form a salutary part in the public life of a country over and above any influence they may exert within the specific area of their reports. Again, it has often been remarked upon that a parliamentary or congressional committee provides a forum in which witnesses can be called and evidence sifted. Surprisingly often, the dynamics of this process lead to a cross-party consensus (or something approaching a consensus) on some conclusion which may well not be to the taste of the government or the party leaders. In recent years there have been a number of occasions when a committee of the House of Commons has reached an agreed conclusion that some policy of the government was thoroughly ill-conceived. Unfortunately, however, this has had no practical effect because the government has been able to count on the support of its MPs in a vote of the House of Commons.

If we now ask what are the political conditions under which investigative and advisory committees (either of legislators or appointees) play an important role, we may say that their influence tends to be at a maximum when either parties lack cohesion (as in the United States) or where there is a multiparty system with no party making up a majority (as in most of continental Western Europe). Conversely, in the United Kingdom and those members of the British Commonwealth that have democratic political systems, where one cohesive party commonly has a majority, the influence of parliamentary and extra-parliamentary committees depends upon the disposition of the government and is thus extremely fragile.[42]

The final stage in the analysis consists of asking how far procedural constitutional rules can contribute to the creation of either weakly disciplined parties or a multiparty system. Parties whose members cross party lines in voting are possible only in systems such as that of the United States where the executive is independently elected and thus not dependent for its tenure in office on maintaining a majority in the legislature. It may well also be that weak parties are also necessary for the stability of the system, since it is otherwise perpetually at risk of deadlock. But there is nothing in the system that ensures the existence of weak parties and this may be the key to the almost total failure of the American model to export successfully: it has been the universal model for democratic regimes in Latin America, and deadlocks have invariably been resolved either by the president taking power at the expense of the legislature or by both being displaced by a military coup.

It is unfortunate that the only constitutional model more copied than the American is the British. This came about in the first instance because the constitutions of the many newly institutional countries that had been British colonies were drawn up by British constitutional experts, and this has proved a departing gift of dubious value. (A few years ago a senior Indian political scientist remarked to a conference in New Delhi that the 'Westminster model' had not served India well; I could not forbear to comment that it had not done too well at Westminister either.) The system of election by plurality voting in single-member constitutions tends to manufacture a one-party majority almost regardless of the distribution of party support within the electorate, and the power of the government is then compounded by its being able to call elections at a time of its choosing (without even requiring parliamentary approval) and by procedural rules within the House of Commons that give the government (backed by its party majority) complete control over the timetable.

The conditions under which political decision-making is guided by a norm of reasonableness are, I believe, closest to being achieved in some of the smaller Western European countries such as the Netherlands and Scandinavia. These countries have in common elections to the parliament in multi-member constituencies with a low threshold of representation and a less one-sided relation between government and parliament than is typical in the British system and those based on it. Perhaps smallness—a population of less than fifteen million, say—is itself a factor in the maintenance of political civility. If so, the implication is that inhabitants of larger countries should consider seriously the possibility of breaking them up into several independent countries or at least creating strongly autonomous regional governments.[j]

It might at first sight be thought that, since the Scanlonian original position gives everybody a veto, the best empirical approximation to it would make it a constitutionally laid down requirement that governments should be supported by a large majority (say two-thirds or three-quarters) of the members of the lower chamber, or that legislation should be deemed to be passed only if supported by a similar kind of qualified majority, or both. The same thought is liable to be reinforced

---

[j] It used to be argued that there were two important advantages to large countries. One was economic: only a large country could create a single internal market and thus reap the benefits of the division of labour. The other was military: a large country would be able to defend its borders against an aggressor more effectively than a small one. Trade liberalization and the current international regime (which has succeeded even in maintaining state boundaries whose only conceivable merit is that they exist) have greatly weakened the force of these arguments everywhere in the world. Within Western Europe, the EEC and the joint security system have reduced them to negligible proportions.

by the observation that, where practices of political accommodation exist, they quite often (though very far from always) go along with a practice of broad-based government coalitions and of key measures carried by very large majorities.[43] (I mentioned this earlier in the present section.) However, such super-majoritarian practices are not constitutionally mandated, and it is an example of the kind of magical thinking—the reversal of cause and effect—to suppose that mandating them would create a spirit of accommodation where none existed. The point is rather that, to the extent that a spirit of accommodation exists, it may (especially in times of emergency) express itself in an attempt to incorporate a wide range of political parties in government and to hammer out a working consensus on contentious legislation.

So far from ensuring that all interests are given equitable treatment, a constitutional requirement of extraordinary majorities would be liable in the absence of a spirit of accommodation to exacerbate conflict. There would be a danger that no government could be formed or that essential legislation such as the budget could not be passed. Alternatively, we might well find a minority exploiting the rest as the price of cooperation.[44] To put it formally: it is not true that the closest empirical approximation to a hypothetical situation in which anybody can reasonably reject a proposal is one in which a minority can reject any proposal whether reasonably or not. One especially significant application of this to social justice is that giving a minority the power to block change in effect entrenches existing injustices. Suppose that an existing society is marked by a concentration of wealth and income in a minority that is incompatible with social justice. (I shall in due course argue that this is in fact true of all the current liberal democracies.) Then requiring an extraordinary majority for change means that the beneficiaries have a veto on the creation of the basic conditions of social justice.

The remaining stipulation in the specification of a Scanlonian original position is that the people in it are well informed. I take this to mean not only that they know the bare facts about their society but also that they know that other societies do things differently and that their own could feasibly be different in various ways. (For example, an Indian untouchable in a remote village might, in earlier times, have been well enough informed about the realities of the caste system locally but unaware of its peculiarity within the social systems of the world.) The Scanlonian original position is envisaged as one of face-to-face discussion and argument, and requires people to be able to understand how alternative proposals will affect them and also to assess the claims of others about the way in which they would be affected. The equivalent requirement within a liberal democracy is that citizens should be able to comprehend the policies put forward by different political parties and be able to work out how they and others would be affected if these policies were put into effect. This is necessary if people are, as the Scanlonian construction requires, to press for the advancement of their conception of the good within reasonable limits.[45]

It is apparent that no country comes very close to approximating this complex information condition, but that some get a lot closer than others. I shall be brief here not because I underestimate the importance of the topic but because it would take me too far afield to enter into it fully. Constitutional provisions have a part to play here by guaranteeing freedom of speech and requiring the government to provide adequate information about its activities to enable citizens to form an intelligent view of them. All of this is, however, compatible with a grossly biased system of opinion-formation in which the wealthy and privileged are able, both in their individual capacities and even more by using their positions as owners and directors of companies, to set the political agenda by financing 'think tanks', political parties and political advertising, and by controlling the editorial policies of newspapers and magazines. Under these conditions, the circumstances of impartiality are very seriously violated, since views that represent the interests of the wealthiest and most powerful members of the society are given a massively disproportionate amount of influence. What is called for is the public funding of political parties, and stringent limits on the amounts spent (by both private individuals and firms) on contributions to political parties and on political advertising.[46] Subsidies to maintain political diversity in the press (as in Scandinavia) would go some way towards the remaining problem. However, in countries where systematic bias has gone furthest (as in Britain) I believe that nothing short of making newspapers licensed public corporations (on the model of British television) can meet the case.[47]

So far I have been asking what constitutional rules would be best adapted to bring it about that a society's laws and policies are just. I have argued that there is only quite limited scope for incorporating substantive rules of justice directly into the constitution, though it should be also said that the matters which can be dealt with in this way are very important. Courts can also operate to ensure that legislation and public policy observe certain requirements of due process and non-discriminatory treatment. But most of the burden of securing social justice still devolves on to the circumstances of impartiality: the most we can hope for is that the procedures by which decisions are made (and more generally the social context within which they are made) will be conducive to the justice of those decisions.

All this presupposes that we are dealing with issues where there is (at any rate in principle) an answer to the question: what, in the way of substantive legislation or policy, does justice demand? Such issues are worth a lot of attention because getting them right largely determines how just a society is. But it must be acknowledged at the same time that only a very small fraction of the work of a contemporary legislature and government deals with matters where justice is of the essence. As I pointed out in Section 15, any policy can be carried out unjustly, but justice is often unable to say whether or not the policy should be adopted in the first place. Suppose, for example, that the question concerns some public good: should there be a new road, swimming pool, fire station, and so on? Many things will, no doubt, be able to be said on both sides of each question; but, normally at any rate, neither party will be able to say that justice is on their side. Justice would, however, became relevant if the swimming pool were open only to the members of one racial group or if the money to finance it were raised by a tax unrelated to ability to pay.

The significance of these constraints on the way in which policies are carried out must not be underestimated. But they leave us with the question to which the rest of this section is devoted. This may be put as follows. Would the people in an appropriately constituted original position be indifferent to the question of what decision was taken in cases where justice is not determinative, so long as it was implemented in a way that did not conflict with the demands of justice? We must recall that they have, *ex hypothesi*, conflicting conceptions of the good. The people in the original position cannot therefore give what would otherwise be the natural response and say that the criterion by which decisions can be evaluated is their conduciveness to the good. Each person will, of course, evaluate decisions by this method. But different people will be coming at their evaluations from different premises. It must be expected therefore that any given decision will be evaluated in different ways by different people according to their conceptions of the good.

The upshot of this is that, where substantive justice is unavailable to provide a basis of agreement, we cannot hope to find consensus on the basis of any other substantive criterion. But that, fortunately, is not the end of the matter. For it is surely plausible to suppose that people in an appropriately constituted original position would not be indifferent to the procedures by which decisions were reached. I have argued that nobody could reasonably be asked (in the absence, anyway of some life-and-death emergency) to agree to less than equal civil rights. But by the same token it is hard to see why anybody of sound mind should be asked to accept less than equal political rights. Generalizing the point, we may say that, where substantive justice falls short, the search for agreement has to be pushed up to the procedural level.

Thus, while the theory of justice as impartiality is not (as I observed back in Section 15) a purely top-down theory, it does have a strong top-down element. Let us suppose, for example, that two alternative policies would both be compatible with the demands of justice. Then we might say that both are potentially just policies for the society in question. But which one actually *is* just for that society depends on the result of a fair decision procedure. Thus, if a referendum (held against a number of background conditions defining a fair campaign etc.) is a fair way of deciding the issue, the alternative that gets a majority in the referendum is the just one for that society.

In looking for intrinsically fair conditions for decision-making in cases where justice does not prescribe any particular decision, we can take advantage of the earlier discussion and say that what defined fairness there will likewise define fairness here. Thus, a decision-making process is fair to the extent that all those concerned are well informed and have their interests and perspectives expressed with equal force and effectiveness. It is fair to the extent that what counts as a good argument does not depend on the social identity of the person making it. And it is fair to the extent that it aims at consensus where possible, and where consensus is not possible it treats everybody equally (e.g. by giving everybody one vote).

From a properly constituted original position, nobody could reasonably object to this proposition: that, in cases where justice is not determinative, the constitutional rules, plus the relevant educational institutions, the organization of the mass media of communication, and so on, should provide for the decision to be made in conditions that instantiate the circumstances of impartiality. But I have already argued earlier in this section that the same proposition would be endorsed for cases where justice is determinative. Thus, the overall conclusion to be reached by putting these two results together is that a just constitution must be set up in such a way that all decisions are taken in ways that instantiate the circumstances of impartiality.

Does this mean that the whole discussion earlier in this section was a waste of time? Not at all. For it remains enormously important that a constitution should have a tendency to produce substantively just laws and policies. That the conditions conducive to that also define a fair decision-making process for cases where justice is not at stake is a piece of serendipity. It remains true that there are two independent (though, as I have said, related) arguments for the circumstances of impartiality: one is conduciveness to justice and the other is intrinsic fairness.

Where justice is relevant, we can go further and say that the fairness of the procedure has a value in addition to the justice of the decision. Justice, as the old saw has it, must not only be done but must be seen to be done. And that means that the decision must be arrived at fairly. Even if the decision is itself perfectly just, it is still tainted if the method by which it was arrived at was unfair. Conversely, there is a great deal of evidence to show that, even if people are unhappy with a decision, they are much more likely to accept it if they perceive it as having been taken in a fair way.[48] From an appropriately constituted original position, then, fair procedures would be endorsed not only because of their tendency to bring about just decisions but also because, where the justice of the decision is disputable (as may well quite often be the case) the fairness of the process leading to the decision will make it more acceptable.

17. Conclusion

I now draw to a close this first part of the book. In the next part (Chapters 5–7) I shall defend justice as impartiality against the charge that, contrary to the claims made for it, the theory rests covertly upon a conception of the good of its own. My response will entail that I develop my own justification for justice as impartiality, and I shall do that in Chapter 7. My objective so far has been more modest. I have endeavoured to explain how the idea of justice as impartiality emerges as a solution to an otherwise intractable problem—the problem, both practical and theoretical, created by unresolvable conflicts about the good. In particular, I have tried to make the case that the form of justice as impartiality proposed by T. M. Scanlon provides a superior solution to that put forward by John Rawls in *A Theory of Justice*.

Let me briefly retrace the path by which I arrived at this point. It is easy enough to see how conceptions of the good that are agent-relative are bound to lead to conflict. Even if you and I both agree about precisely what constitutes the good for a person, we shall reach different conclusions about the value of alternative states of affairs if I give a greater weight to my own good or the good of those close to me than to that of others, while you do likewise for your own good or the good of those close to you. The case argued in Chapter 1 is more interesting and more challenging than that, however. I pointed to the large variety of conceptions of the good that all meet the test of impartiality. And I suggested that, although these can be argued about, it is hard to believe that there is any rationally compelling case for any of them. At the

beginning of Chapter 2, I extended this contention from pure teleological theories to religious conceptions of the meaning of life, on the basis
of their being similarly open to interminable dispute. (I shall seek to
back up the claim made there in the course of my argument in Chapter
7.)

It is a fundamental assumption in this book that we do not need to
explain why people pursue their conception of the good. Whether
somebody's conception of the good be partial or impartial, I take it to
be unproblematic that it has motivational force. The problem is, rather,
to explain why people might do anything else. Why should somebody
deliberately draw back from the pursuit of the good? The three theories
of justice analysed in this book—justice as mutual advantage, justice as
reciprocity, and justice as impartiality—all offer answers to that
question.

Justice as mutual advantage does not call upon any fresh motive. That
is its great strength. The underlying idea is simply that the unconstrained pursuit of your conception of the good is not likely to be very
successful if everybody else is likewise pursuing their conceptions of the
good. Everyone therefore has an interest in agreeing on terms that avoid
mutual frustration and secure for each person a better chance of achieving his or her good than is offered by a free-for-all. In Section 6 I
pointed out the internal weaknesses of justice as mutual advantage.
Then, in Section 7, I argued that it is also open to external criticism:
unless the opposing forces happen to be in balance, the outcome is
liable to be monstrously unfair.

With justice as reciprocity we introduce a new motivation: we assume
that people can be restrained from pursuing their conception of the
good by the thought that it would be unfair to do so. However, I
argued in Section 8 that the theory of justice as reciprocity is internally
incoherent because a sentiment of fairness will not underwrite deals
arrived at according to the formula of mutual advantage. We are therefore left with the theory of justice as impartiality, which starts from the
motivation of fairness and then seeks to bring the criteria of justice into
line with that. The essential idea is that fair terms of agreement are those
that can reasonably be accepted by people who are free and equal. The
problem is how to capture that idea and give it some structure.

In Section 9, I argued that the first stage of Rawls's theory, in which
principles are chosen in an original position, does not succeed. I then
examined (in Section 10) his second stage, where we check to see that
excessive 'strains of commitment' would not be produced by the principles chosen in the first stage. This second stage, I suggested, constitutes
an independent version of justice as impartiality, and one that would if

systematized lead us to the theory proposed by T. M. Scanlon. This was presented in Section 11.

All the rest of Part I has been devoted to giving some content to the idea of justice as impartiality. What I have especially tried to emphasize is that the theory has strictly limited ambitions. In the last section of Chapter 3, I particularly made the point that justice as impartiality is designed to provide a framework within which people can live, but does not purport to tell them how to live. In this chapter, I have drawn special attention to the point that justice as impartiality does not have a substantive answer to every question. Rather, in very many cases it can set limits to what is just but has to leave the choice of an outcome within that range to a fair procedure.

I should make it clear that Scanlon is not to be held responsible for the use that I make of his ideas in this book. Although he has on occasion (in both published and unpublished work) deployed his construction in order to generate some practical conclusions about what rules could not reasonably be rejected, he sees it mainly as a device for explaining the nature of morality.[49] It might be said that, in the way in which I use it, the Scanlonian construction is little more than a device for talking about what is fair, on a certain fundamentally egalitarian conception of fairness. I would not regard that as a devastating criticism. I make no pretence of getting something for nothing: what you get out is what you put in. There are, however, two reasons for making use of the Scanlonian construction that seem to me to have much force.

The first reason for doing so is simply that the question 'Is it fair?' is illuminated by phrasing it as 'Could it reasonably be rejected?' The second is that the Scanlonian approach opens up the idea that I have introduced in this chapter of the circumstances of impartiality. I believe that this is an important extension of the theory of justice as impartiality because it generates the theorem that, as empirical conditions approach those of an ideal Scanlonian original position, the observed outcomes will tend to be those that could not reasonably be rejected in such an original position. I shall discuss the methodological implications of this idea at some length in Chapter 8 (see especially Section 32).

The notion of the circumstances of impartiality can be pushed one stage further. Justice as impartiality turns on what could reasonably be rejected, but are there empirical conditions for people recognizing what is reasonable? I conjecture that, if the circumstances of impartiality are violated beyond a certain point, those who gain from injustice may be unable to recognize the untenability of their position. G. A. Cohen has expressed a similar thought by saying that 'a slave need not be impressed when a master says: "Had you been born into the slaveholder

class, you too would have lived well and treated your slaves like slaves."
Such counterfactual predictions do not show that what people at a certain social level typically choose to do is justifiable.' We often find an
elaborate rationalization of the indefensible. Slavery, for example, may
be justified by maintaining that it is part of the natural order or by
claiming that the people who are enslaved are subhuman and hence outside the protection due to human beings.[50] Since justice as impartiality
requires the parties not to have false beliefs, it is hardly surprising that
there should be people to whom it is not accessible, given their existing
beliefs.

Some writers appear to believe that a theory of justice must somehow
pick people up by the scruff of the neck and force them to behave justly,
regardless of their beliefs or inclinations. This is an absurd demand, as a
moment's thought should be enough to show. What, then, can be said?
If a sense of justice were totally ineffective, the subject of this book
would be purely theoretical. Fortunately, though, a sense of justice can
be effective among third parties, as the movement against slavery in the
nineteenth century and the international anti-Apartheid movement
both attest. It can also invigorate those who would gain from an end to
injustice: there is all the difference in the world between *wanting* more
and being convinced that it would be *just* to have more. Even among the
beneficiaries of injustice, it would be wrong to assume that justificatory
beliefs will necessarily hold sway indefinitely. To a remarkable degree,
for example, the Soviet system fell apart because the people running it
had ceased to believe in it themselves.

If we insist on a theory of justice that simply takes existing beliefs
and desires as given, the only general theory available is justice as
mutual advantage. But that is, as I have already argued, sorry comfort
for anyone who thinks that the right answer is given by justice as
impartiality. Thus, if there is one thing that is straightforwardly contradicted by justice as impartiality, it is the creation of first- and second-
class citizens according to ethnic identity. For it is manifestly
unreasonable to expect those who are systematically disadvantaged in
this way to accept their inferior status. Yet exactly this has occurred in
most of the states that have succeeded to the territories of the Soviet
Union, the countries it controlled in Eastern Europe, and the former
Yugoslavia. Justice as mutual advantage can offer a case for conciliating
ethnic minorities by treating them as civic equals. But, from the point of
view of the ethnic majority, it is a purely pragmatic question whether
this is the most advantageous course or whether it would be better to
kill, expel or oppress even more thoroughly the minority or minorities.
In this context Claus Offe has spoken of 'the logic that Bulgarians apply

against their Turkish minority, and which Hitler proclaimed the day before the German invasion of the Soviet Union in 1941: "After what we have done to them, we will be devastatingly punished unless we continue doing it." '[51]

My object in this *Treatise* is to present the results of some twenty years of thought about what justice is and what it entails. My concern is with truth, not with popularity. If I am right, justice calls for radical changes. In many ways, these run against contemporary tendencies. I have mentioned the politics of ethnic inequality. In Part II, I shall focus especially on the inadmissibility of basing a polity upon a religious dogma. In later volumes, I shall argue in addition that justice entails large-scale international redistribution and also much more equality within countries. This again runs strongly counter to trends in the past decade. I shall argue in Volume III of this *Treatise* that some well-known arguments about the psychological impossibility of impartial justice are misguided. But how strong the desire to behave justly actually is, when it comes into competition with other desires, I leave open. I claim only to tell you what justice is; what you do about it, if you believe me, is up to you.

PART II

JUSTICE AND THE GOOD

CHAPTER 5

━━━

Is impartial justice a fraud?

18. Introduction

So far I have argued that justice as impartiality offers a fair basis of agreement for people with divergent conceptions of the good. In this chapter, I shall take up a line of criticism of justice as impartiality according to which these pretensions are fraudulent. Although criticism of this kind is quite common, I believe that the most forceful and persuasive statement of the case is the one to be found in Alasdair MacIntyre's book, *Whose Justice? Which Rationality?* In order to advance my own exposition, I shall at several points take up issues that are not raised by MacIntyre himself but have been put forward by others—both friends and foes of justice as impartiality. Nevertheless, the framework of the chapter will be provided by MacIntyre's allegation that justice as impartiality is in fact a 'partisan' account that embodies the distinctive assumption of 'liberal individualism'.

The theory of justice that MacIntyre intends to attack is set out by him as follows.

Rationality requires . . . that we first divest ourselves of allegiance to any one of the contending theories and also abstract ourselves from all those particularities of social relationship in terms of which we have been accustomed to understand our responsibilities and our interests. Only by so doing . . . shall we arrive at a genuinely neutral, impartial, and, in this way, universal point of view, freed from the partisanship and the partiality and onesidedness that otherwise affect us.[1]

To the extent that MacIntyre can be said to have depicted any actual theory of justice here, it is surely justice as impartiality. MacIntyre does at any rate record the aspiration to achieve an impartial point of view, and the notions of divesting and abstracting that MacIntyre introduces bear some relation to what happens in the Rawlsian and Scanlonian original positions. Thus, in Rawls's construction the people choosing principles know that they have conceptions of the good that they want to advance. (It is fairly clear from the context that these are what MacIntyre means by 'contending theories'.) But, since they do not know what their own conception of the good is, they cannot aim to promote it by opting for principles that will give their own conception a special advantage over others. Within the Scanlonian construction, people know what their conception of the good is, but they are constrained in proposing principles for general adoption by the need to reach agreement on reasonable terms. This, it is assumed, will rule out any attempt to privilege one conception of the good at the ground-floor level. For it would seem that anybody could reasonably reject a proposal that put his own conception of the good in a systematically disadvantageous position in relation to others. In these ways (but only in these) we may accept MacIntyre's statement that 'we first divest ourselves of allegiance to any one of the contending theories'.

It is necessary to handle with even more care the assertion that we have to 'abstract ourselves from all those particularities of social relationship in terms of which we have been accustomed to understand our responsibilities and interests'. This could easily be taken to mean that if we endorse the idea of impartiality this entails that we think people should go around behaving impartially all the time—not, for example, doing anything for their own families that they would not be prepared to do for anybody else with similar needs and deserts. (See Section 4 for an account of this Godwinian notion of impartiality.) A lot of criticism of impartiality stems from precisely this notion, and I shall devote the bulk of Part III of this book to showing that it is misdirected, if it is taken to be an objection to justice as impartiality.

In what sense, then, is MacIntyre's claim about 'abstraction' correct? Let us again take up the Rawlsian construction first. The people in Rawls's original position know that they have particular social relationships whose preservation and strengthening is of central importance to their lives. But, because they do not know their own identities, they are unable to press for principles that would provide them with special opportunities denied to others to further their own ends. They can therefore do no better than support principles that will have the general effect of giving everybody a chance to preserve and strengthen their own personal relationships.

Within the Scanlonian construction, the people who are choosing principles will, naturally, be concerned to ensure that those principles will be consistent with the preservation and strengthening of their personal relationships. But the requirement of reaching agreement on reasonable terms has much the same effect as the Rawlsian 'veil of ignorance' in inhibiting attempts by the parties to enhance their own position at the expense of that of others. Any proposal which can be supported only by saying 'This would advance my ends, and to hell with what it does for anybody else's' is manifestly a candidate for reasonable rejection. We may therefore suppose that whatever emerged from a Scanlonian original position would be favourable across the board to the sustenance of personal relationships. If this kind of thing is what is meant by MacIntyre's talk of 'abstraction', then what he says may be accepted. And I would, indeed, wish to defend abstraction understood in this way (but only in this way) as an essential part of any procedure for determining what justice calls for.

So far I have been concerned to ensure that MacIntyre's claims about the features of justice as impartiality are given an interpretation that saves the theory from being misrepresented. There is, however, one crucial aspect of his account that I want to reject outright. This is contained in his opening words, which suggest that the whole of justice as impartiality can be derived from the requirements of 'rationality'. This claim plays an important part in MacIntyre's general view of liberalism as the heir of what he calls the 'Enlightenment project'. For the Enlightenment project was, according to MacIntyre, precisely one of deducing moral and political principles from the bare concept of rationality. Since my object here is not to discuss MacIntyre's ideas in general but to focus on his claim that justice as impartiality is a fraud, I shall not take up this wider claim.[2] I wish merely to observe that the concept of rationality has played only a quite limited role in my exposition of the case for justice as impartiality.

Within the Rawlsian construction, rationality is significant in one context only. The people in the original position are said by Rawls to be rationally pursuing their ends, in as far as they can from behind the 'veil of ignorance'. It is important to recognize, however, that this construction is embedded within a wider theory, which explains (among other things) why we should suppose that the rational pursuit of ends under these conditions will lead to the principles that emerge being principles of justice. And this argument does not itself rest on the claim that everything can be derived from the concept of rationality. (See above, Section 9.) As far as the Scanlonian construction is concerned, the concept of rationality is even further in the background. For the crucial way in which the Scanlonian approach differs from the Rawlsian is in rejecting the notion that anything can be learned from the rational pursuit of ends behind a veil of ignorance. Instead it suggests that we should ask what happens when ends are pursued in a context that constrains demands by a requirement of reasonableness.

It is therefore plain that neither version of justice as impartiality rests on the kind of hubristic claim to get the whole thing from the concept of rationality that MacIntyre builds into his account. I believe, however, that it is possible to detach his charge that justice as impartiality is a fraud from this claim about the role of rationality. Let us start from MacIntyre's objection that the account of rationality he has attributed to justice as impartiality is 'contentious' because 'its requirement of disinterestedness in fact covertly presupposes one particular partisan type of account of justice, that of liberal individualism, which it is later to be used to justify, so that its apparent neutrality is no more than an appearance'.[3] If we drop the reference to rationality, we are left with the claims that the theory of justice as impartiality is contentious and that it presupposes liberal individualism. What can be said of these charges?

Let me begin with the objection that the theory is contentious. I can see no way of denying this, nor any reason for wishing to do so. Every theory of justice is bound to be contentious, if all that means is that some people will not like it. To look no further than the example provided by MacIntyre himself, it is surely clear that no unreconstructed Thomist can be reconciled to justice as impartiality in any of its forms. Invited to step behind the Rawlsian veil of ignorance, he will insist on taking with him his knowledge of natural law and divine revelation, thus subverting the whole exercise. Similarly, he is bound to upset the Scanlonian apple cart by rejecting (for example) the usual view that the appropriate level of interest rates is a matter of prudent economic management. Rather, he will insist, it must be seen as a question of justice in that only an interest rate of zero is consistent with the Thomist prohibition of usury. (More politically significant today are those who maintain that an 'Islamic state' must adhere to the Koranic prohition of usury.) A Thomist (at any rate one who follows MacIntyre's hard-line interpretation related above in Section 12) will argue that this is a conclusion that nobody can reasonably reject since only a zero interest rate will bring human institutions in line with natural law. Non-Thomists, however, will refuse to accept the validity of the system from which the conclusion is derived, and will therefore deny that they must accept it.[a] The result can only be stalemate.

---

[a] Can those who do not hold a religiously based view about the wrongness of usury say that it would be unjust to institute a prohibition on it? A familiar American line of argument would support this, claiming that the 'separation of church and state' calls for arguments on matters of public policy to cite only non-religious premises. (See for example Robert Audi, 'The Separation of Church and State and the Obligations of Citizenship', *Philosophy & Public Affairs*, 18 (1989), 259–96.) I do not accept this, since many issues unavoidably turn on conceptions of the good, and there is no reason for insisting that only secular conceptions be included. (See below, Ch. 6, and esp. Sect. 23.)

There is no prospect of finding an uncontentious theory of justice if that means finding a theory capable of leaving unchallenged views of the world such as that embodied in Thomism. If that is enough by itself to make justice as impartiality a 'partisan' theory, there is no more to be said. I concede the case but deny that this is any real objection. I do not believe, in fact, that any proponent of justice as impartiality (or any other generally liberal ideas) has been so naïve as to maintain that unreconstructed Thomists could be brought on board. Before a Thomist could assent to the claims of impartial justice, he would have to abandon the demand that all other conceptions of the good must give way before the Thomistic one. And this would represent a pretty profound reconstruction of Thomism as MacIntyre presents it.

Similarly, if we imagine that a neutral theory must be one that leaves everybody equally pleased with the outcome, regardless of their starting-point, it is obvious that there can be no such thing as a neutral theory. For, once we have more than two starting-points, there will in general be no way of finding a single point equidistant from all of them. (It would have to be possible to array all the starting-points on the perimeter of a circle in two dimensions, on the surface of a sphere in three dimensions, and so on for higher dimensions.) Again, however, this would be an objection to justice as impartiality only if its advocates had been so unwise to claim that their theory was neutral in this sense. But as far as I am aware none of them ever has, and I certainly would not wish to do so myself. There are, it is true, two senses in which justice as impartiality claims to be neutral: it does not rest on any particular conception of the good, and it proposes that all conceptions of the good should (in a way defined by the theory itself) be treated equally. Whether neutrality in either of these senses is either possible or desirable is, of course, a legitimate topic for debate. But it is no argument against them to say that they fail to accord with some different (and absurd) conception of neutrality.

The claim that is worth serious attention is that the impartialist account of justice is a version of 'liberal individualism'. Whether or not this conclusion is to be resisted depends entirely on the meaning to be ascribed to the expression 'liberal individualism'. The words have been used in recent years to refer to so many ideas that they no longer convey any distinct meaning, if they ever did. Resisting the temptation to discourse at large on this theme, I shall focus in this chapter on three possible definitions. The first equates liberal individualism with an

In Scanlonian terms, we may say: nobody could reasonably reject the proposition that, if a prohibition of usury is capable of gaining enactment through fair political procedures (see Sect. 16), its enactment should not be struck down by some constitutional provision.

atomistic sociology and an associated theory of natural, presocial rights. The second ties liberal individualism to the idea that a theory of justice should be neutral between different conceptions of the good. The third, to which I shall devote the most attention, equates liberal individualism with a certain distinctive conception of the good.

19. Three Varieties of Liberal Individualism

In accordance with the programme just set out, I shall begin by taking up the equation of liberal individualism with an atomistic sociology and an associated theory of natural, presocial rights.[4] I should make it clear that MacIntyre does not make any attempt to smear liberalism by suggesting that it must necessarily rest on such preposterous premises. But the charge is so commonly repeated by other less scrupulous critics that it is worth getting it out of the way at the beginning.

The refutation of this *canard* is best undertaken by considering it in two parts. First, does justice as impartiality (which I shall take to be the standard contemporary liberal theory) depend on 'atomistic' sociological premises? That is to say, does it presuppose that human beings can develop outside any social and cultural matrix, which makes their characters and abilities what they are? The answer is not merely that such ideas are inessential to the case for justice as impartiality, but that they are actually incompatible with it. The reason for this is that any such conception of the human condition conflicts fundamentally with many well-known facts about human development and the necessary interdependence of the members of any society and thus falls foul of the information condition built into the specification of the situation in which rules and principles of justice are to be chosen.

Consider the parties in a Rawlsian original position. They, according to Rawls, are to be taken to 'understand political affairs and the principles of economic theory; they know the basis of social organization and the laws of human psychology. Indeed, the parties are presumed to know whatever general facts affect the choice of the principles of justice.'[5] The parties therefore cannot base their deliberations upon a manifestly inadequate conception of the way in which human society works. As far as the Scanlonian construction is concerned, I pointed out in Section 11 that Scanlon himself stipulates a very strong information condition. But even on the more relaxed requirement that the parties in the original position should believe what it is reasonable (or at any rate not unreasonable) for them to believe, we can surely eliminate an account of human society that is contradicted by all our experience.

In the conception of liberal individualism currently under discussion, the other element is a doctrine such as that postulated (though never defended) by Robert Nozick in *Anarchy, State, and Utopia* according to which 'individuals have rights' that somehow exist before or outside society.[6] Now, Rawls and Scanlon are both clear that it is the job of the original position to generate a system of rights. The parties are supposed to take rights away from their deliberations; they are not supposed to bring them to those deliberations. Anyone seeking to insist that the results of the choice made in the original position must conform to some pre-existing structure of rights would have to be ruled out of order. Whether it is derived from theological premises (as with Locke) or left dangling in the void (as with Nozick), the doctrine of natural rights produces implications that can reasonably be rejected in a suitably constituted original position. Thus, the Nozickean system of natural rights would commit everybody in advance in accepting that, however wealthy their society might be, they should starve to death if their market-derived entitlements plus gifts from others did not add up to enough to keep body and soul together. It would surely be preposterous to imagine that people with the most elementary regard for their own interest would accept such a prospect. The myth of what Bentham called 'pre-Adamical' rights would therefore play no part in the reasoning among the parties in the original position.

Having dismissed a notion of liberal individualism that MacIntyre does not himself invoke, I want now to discuss two notions that are put forward by MacIntyre himself. One of these identifies liberal individualism with neutrality between competing conceptions of the good. The other notion of liberal individualism is that of a distinctively liberal individualist conception of the good. These two notions are closely interwoven in MacIntyre's argument, because the essence of his charge of fraud is that justice as impartiality purports to subscribe to the first of these notions but in fact embodies the second.[7] I shall, however, introduce them one at a time.

MacIntyre speaks of 'the project of modern liberal, individualist society' as being 'to provide a political, legal, and economic framework in which assent to one and the same set of rationally justifiable principles would enable those who espouse widely different and incompatible conceptions of the good life for human beings to live together peaceably within the same society, enjoying the same political status and engaging in the same economic relationships'.[8] He then proceeds to draw out what he takes to be the implications in the following terms:

Every individual is to be equally free to propose and to live by whatever conception of the good he or she pleases ... unless that conception of the good involves reshaping the life of the rest of the community in accordance with it. Any conception of the human good according to which, for example, it is the duty of government to educate the members of the community morally, so that they come to live out that conception of the good, may up to a point be held as a private theory by individuals or groups, but any serious attempt to embody it in public life will be proscribed.[9]

This is a quite accurate account of both the objective of justice as impartiality and at any rate a central feature in its view of the way in which its objective might be achieved. If MacIntyre wishes to attach the label 'liberal individualist' to that objective and that conclusion about the way to achieve the objective, there can be no gainsaying it: justice as impartiality is a liberal individualist theory. It has to be said, though, that it is a rather curious approach to the liberal tradition to define liberalism so that it is equivalent to neutrality. For it is fairly clear that, if we draw up a roster of famous liberals, we shall find that they neither started from what MacIntyre calls the liberal individualist objective of attaining agreement among people with diverse conceptions of the good nor advocated the kind of neutrality in public policy between different conceptions of the good that MacIntyre takes to be the hallmark of liberal individualist practice.

I believe that Thomas Jefferson, John Stuart Mill, T. H. Green, and L. T. Hobhouse (to take a few obvious names) would all have said (if the terminology had been explained to them) that they had a conception of the good—a liberal one, of course—and would wish public policy to be based on that. As far as agreement is concerned, they would presumably have hoped that the inherent attractiveness of their conception of the good would tend to produce over time a convergence towards it, just as MacIntyre presumably hopes that Thomism could become a consensual basis for public policy as a result of its intellectual superiority becoming generally recognized. But they would not have said, any more than does MacIntyre wish to say, that their objective was to find a way in which people who continued to adhere to different conceptions of the good could be brought to reach an agreement.

As it happens, none of this matters in the present context, since what I am defending is justice as impartiality and that is precisely what MacIntyre is attacking. If he chooses to dignify it, in a grossly unhistorical way, with the label 'liberal individualism', that is really neither here nor there. A label does not constitute an argument. Even if 'liberal individualist' is a term of abuse in some quarters, the adherent of justice as impartiality has only to respond that 'names can never hurt me'.

Since there is no point in arguing about definitions, and the labels are in any case quite useful for my own purposes, I shall take over

MacIntyre's proposed usage of 'liberal individualist'. I shall therefore talk about the liberal individualist objective as that of finding a basis of agreement capable of being accepted by people with very different conceptions of the good. And I shall say that the liberal individualist solution to the problem that it sets itself is that the correctness of some conception of the good cannot in itself form a legitimate basis for a society's basic institutions. It will not escape notice that we could equally well say that these are the objective and solution of justice as impartiality.

If we ask why MacIntyre should think that what I have quoted him so far as saying constitutes an *attack* on justice as impartiality, we arrive at the third notion of liberal individualism to be canvassed in this section. For MacIntyre wishes to maintain that the liberal individualist objective of adjudicating between different conceptions of the good is a smokescreen behind which liberals engage in pursuing their own, distinctively liberal, conception of the good. 'Liberal individualism,' he tells us, has 'its own broad conception of the good, which it is engaged in imposing politically, legally, socially, and culturally wherever it has the power to do so.'[10] Hence, 'the starting points of liberal theorizing are never neutral as between conceptions of the human good; they are always liberal starting points.'[11]

We have to be careful here (more careful than MacIntyre himself is) to get clear exactly what the charge is. MacIntyre still, as I understand it, holds to his description of the liberal individualist conclusion—the idea that no conception of the good can claim a privileged position in politics. What he is saying is that the liberal individualist premise from which this conclusion is derived, which has pretensions to being neutral between conceptions of the good, is not in fact neutral at all because it embodies a distinctively liberal individualist conception of the good. But how is the liberal individualist premise related to the liberal individualist conclusion? There are two possible answers. MacIntyre could be saying that there is at least one conception of the good which will underwrite neutrality. Alternatively, he could be taken as denying that there is any way of reaching neutrality except by making use of premises that include a distinctively liberal individualist conception of the good.

The two propositions are logically independent to this extent: that, although the second entails the first, the first does not entail the second. Suppose that the first one is true and the second one false. The implication of this will be that there are at least two different routes to neutrality, including one that runs via a liberal individualist conception of the good and one that does not. I believe that that is in fact how things stand. But if I am right about this, MacIntyre's charge of fraud against justice as impartiality cannot be sustained. For it is no objection to the claim that the starting point is (in a certain sense) neutral to say that there is also available a different starting point that makes use of a certain conception of the good. Only if the second proposition is true can MacIntyre be said to have exposed the hollowness of the pretensions of justice as impartiality to stand above the battle between rival conceptions of the good. It seems clear that this is what MacIntyre believes he can establish. For he says that 'liberalism, while initially rejecting the claims of any overriding theory of the good, does in fact come to embody just such a theory'.[12]

In the next two sections I shall take up two conceptions of the good that can with some plausibility be regarded as liberal individualist. In Section 20 I shall consider a conception of the good that equates it with autonomy and then in Section 21 I shall turn to a conception of the good that equates it with want-satisfaction. MacIntyre's argument is that the second of these conceptions of the good is the one that generates neutrality as a conclusion. I believe that he is right about this, in a certain sense that I shall specify. But, as I shall seek to show in the next chapter, justice as impartiality remains an alternative approach, and generates a different (and more acceptable) form of neutrality. The third and last chapter in Part II will be devoted to the crucial question that is raised by the neutrality of justice as impartiality. This is: what reasons can be given to someone with a strongly held conception of the good for moderating his pursuit of it so that he remains within the bounds set by impartial justice?

20. *Liberal Conceptions of the Good (1): Autonomy*

At the beginning of the present chapter, I said that I would organize it around MacIntyre's charge of fraudulence against justice as impartiality. But I have already illustrated, by taking up a notion of liberal individualism (as compounded of atomism and natural rights) not put forward by MacIntyre, that I do not regard myself as being bound to restrict my discussion to points made by MacIntyre himself. In this section, therefore, I shall look at the most popular conception of the good invoked by liberals, that of the good as self-determination or autonomy. Both terms, of course, can be used to refer to collectivities, and the original meaning of 'autonomy' was political: an autonomous polity was one that had self-rule, that is to say political independence. But in the usage I am concerned with here, self-determination or autonomy (which I shall use interchangeably) are predicated of individual human beings.

There can be no question but that a conception of the good as autonomy comes with impeccable liberal credentials, since it is one strand (though only one) in John Stuart Mill's *On Liberty*.[13] Moreover, among contemporary political philosophers of a liberal persuasion, those who do not appeal to justice as impartiality almost all invoke the value of autonomy. But does a conception of the good as autonomy lead to what MacIntyre calls liberal individualist conclusions, that is to say neutrality between divergent conceptions of the good? It has been argued that it does. I do not believe that the case can be sustained.

What plausibility the case can attain arises from a peculiarity that a conception of the good as autonomy shares with a conception of the good as want-satisfaction: both are second-order conceptions. Let us examine the conception of the good as autonomy a little more closely. According to this conception, then, what is of central importance in human life is that people should make up their own minds about how to live and what to think and that they should be able to express their beliefs freely and act on their conclusions about the best way to live, subject to rules assigning rights to speak and act that are designed to protect the ability of others to do likewise. This is a second-order conception of the good in that it does not specify what the good actually consists in. Anything could be regarded as good (in a second-order way) so long as the person who conceived it as good (in a first-order way) had arrived at this conception in a way that satisfied the requirements of autonomy. We may thus contrast autonomy as a conception of the good with a substantive conception, for example a religiously based conception, of the good.

Now it is, I think, quite easy to see how the kinds of civil rights normally associated with liberalism can be justified on the basis of a conception of the good as autonomy. Thus, if we say that it is important for people to be able to question, revise, and form their own substantive conception of the good, we shall naturally be led to endorse the 'traditional liberal concern for education, freedom of expression, freedom of the press, artistic freedom, etc.'. If we add that, having formed their substantive conception of the good, 'individuals must . . . have the resources and liberties needed to live their lives in accordance with their beliefs about value, without being imprisoned or penalized for unorthodox religious or sexual practices etc.', we can motivate 'the traditional liberal concern for civil and personal liberties'.[14]

We must, however, be careful to distinguish between characteristic liberal positions such as these and the idea of neutrality between substantive conceptions of the good. MacIntyre's tendentious equation of neutrality with liberal individualist conclusions would naturally lead us to think that, if a second-order conception of the good such as autonomy underwrites liberal conclusions of the traditional kind just listed, it must also underwrite neutrality. But we should avoid falling victim to such sleight of hand. In fact, as I shall argue, it is not simply that neutrality is not entailed by a conception of the good as autonomy. The two are actually incompatible.[15]

I should reiterate here that, although MacIntyre equates liberalism with neutrality as far as conclusions are concerned, and also says that liberal conclusions depend upon a distinctively liberal conception of the good, he does not himself suggest that the relevant conception of the good is one that makes it autonomy. There have not been lacking liberals, however, who have maintained that autonomy entails neutrality. Thus, Will Kymlicka, from whom I was quoting above, moves straight from the claim that autonomy supports traditional liberal policy prescriptions to the further claim that 'liberals say that state neutrality is required to respect people's self-determination'.[16] Another liberal who makes a similar claim is Bruce Ackerman. In his book *Social Justice and the Liberal State*, Ackerman works out the implications of what he calls a 'principle of Neutrality' which is precisely the principle that nobody should be able to press for public policies on the basis of the superiority of his conception of the good to those of other people. He suggests that support for Neutrality might be garnered in a number of different ways. Thus 'you might think that you can only learn anything true about the good when you are free to experiment in life without some authoritative teacher intervening whenever he thinks you're going wrong. And if you think this, Neutrality seems made to order.' I would regard this as a conception of the good as autonomy in that it suggests that ways of life have value only if they are freely chosen. Ackerman adds, however, as another route to Neutrality, that 'you may adopt a conception of the good that gives a central place to autonomous deliberation and deny that it is possible to *force* a person to be good'.[17]

A partisan of autonomy as a second-order conception of the good would, however, be wise to pause before accepting Ackerman's confident assertion that his view entails neutrality. The state is not, after all, the only possible source of authority figures who tell people to shut up and conform. A state dedicated to the furtherance of autonomy might plausibly adopt policies designed to undermine would-be authorities of this repressive kind. As Kymlicka says, it follows from a conception of the good as self-determination that 'people are . . . made worse off by being denied the social conditions necessary to freely and rationally question their commitments'.[18] These conditions are, for example, denied to children by schools that are dedicated to inculcating some religious belief which is also that of the parents (as is normally the case), so that the two forms of authoritarian socialization reinforce one another. A hard-line partisan of autonomy might well conclude that such schools should be prohibited. And it would be hard to be taken seriously as a partisan of autonomy at all unless one at least held that schools devoted to the suppression of autonomy should not be eligible for public funding. This would itself be enough to constitute a departure from neutrality.

Kymlicka also supports Ackerman's assertion that people cannot be coerced into being good.[19] The truth of this depends upon one's conception of the good. People can at any rate be coerced (to some degree) into behaving well, and that is for many purposes the most important thing. What Ackerman and Kymlicka are implicitly appealing to is a Protestant or Kantian account of virtue , which makes it a matter of the will.[b] An Aristotelian would counter that virtue is a habit—and habits can, we know, be acquired in the first place under coercion. Suppose, however, we concede that within the concept of justice as autonomy there is no room for coerced virtue. That proposition implies a neutral state only if we accept the question-begging assumption that the only *modus operandi* of the state is the criminal law. I have already suggested that states can foster autonomy through their educational policies, and the same selective use of subsidies could be carried through in relation to the arts, broadcasting, the print media, and so on. We should recall that T. H. Green's slogan that the duty of the state is to remove the hindrances to freedom did not lead him, or the 'new liberals' who followed his lead, to the endorsement of state neutrality.[20]

The error made by Ackerman and Kymlicka can be stated succinctly as follows: a conception of the good as autonomy does not imply that the pursuit of all substantive conceptions of the good is equally valuable. Only those conceptions that have the right origins—those that have come about in ways that meet the criteria for self-determined

[b] In the notes to his discussion of the basis of neutrality in *Liberalism, Community and Culture* (19 n. 1), Kymlicka acknowledges a diffuse debt to Ronald Dworkin's ideas, and it may be noted that Dworkin makes exactly the same argument as Kymlicka in some lectures originally delivered in 1988. Thus, he says that those who accept what he calls a 'challenge' model of value (which may for the present purpose be taken as equivalent to a conception of the good as autonomy) 'cannot make other people's lives better by the coercive means liberal tolerance forbids, because on the challenge model . . . someone's life cannot be improved against his steady conviction that it has not been', Dworkin, 'Foundations of Liberal Equality', in *The Tanner Lectures on Human Values,* XI, ed. Grethe B. Peterson (Salt Lake City: University of Utah Press, 1990), 3–119, quotation from p. 116. Dworkin, like Kymlicka, assumes that he can move from this to the claim that his preferred conception of what makes a life go well leads to neutrality. The objections to this move by Kymlicka are also therefore valid against Dworkin.

belief—can form a basis for activity that has value. It is therefore
unlikely that the good as autonomy will be advanced by distributing
resources in a way that takes no account of the autonomous or non-
autonomous origins of people's substantive conceptions of the good.

I anticipate here the protest that there must be something wrong with
this analysis because believers in autonomy do not normally conclude
that the state should discriminate against people who wish to pursue
non-autonomous ends. Liberals of this kind may wish to depart from
neutrality in order to foster autonomous preference-formation, but
they are liable to shy away from the suggestion that those who do not
respond to these efforts should be deliberately denied an equal chance
to pursue their ends. I accept the point, but for three reasons I do not
think it constitutes a decisive objection to what I am saying. The first is
that it would not be easy to devise a practical policy that would discriminate against the pursuit of conceptions of the good that had not
been autonomously arrived at. The second is that, even if one could
conceive of such a policy being carried out accurately by an ideally conscientious dictator, it would be impossible to frame an institution for
implementing a policy that would not be open to abuse, since it would
entail handing wide discretion to some body to act on ill-defined criteria. And the third reason, which works so as to reinforce the others, is
that few people are such fanatics for autonomy as to believe that it
should be maximized at the expense of all other considerations.

Another possible objection which is worth examining runs along
these lines. It will be recalled that I said myself in Chapter 4 that, within
the constraints imposed by a just constitution and by the requirements
of distributive justice (as determined by justice as impartiality), it is
open to people to pursue their conceptions of the good. If the partisans
of the good as autonomy had control of the political decision-making
apparatus, then, they would be able to foster educational and cultural
institutions conducive to the autonomous formation of beliefs and plans
of life. Does not this show that, when it comes down to it, there is no
difference between justice as impartiality and a conception of the good
as autonomy?

The answer is that, although justice as impartiality is compatible with
the existence of public subsidies for autonomy-inducing institutions, it
is equally compatible with their non-existence. All that the theory of
justice as impartiality insists on is that the decision should be the outcome of a fair political process. There is thus nothing built into justice
as impartiality that leads to its endorsing policy prescriptions derived
from a conception of the good as autonomy. It is procedurally neutral.
This is what, according to my argument, makes it appropriate as a fair

proposal for enabling partisans of different conceptions of the good to share common social and political institutions.

21. *Liberal Conceptions of the Good (2) : Want-Satisfaction*

There is something on the face of it paradoxical in MacIntyre's combining the claim that there is a distinctively liberal conception of the good with the claim that the conclusion derived from this conception of the good is that public policy should be in some sense neutral between different conceptions of the good. The discussion of autonomy in the previous section should help to suggest how the paradoxical air attaching to these two claims can be dissolved. For we saw that Bruce Ackerman displayed no intellectual discomfort in saying that one of the ways in which somebody might arrive at neutrality was to start from a conception of the good as autonomy. Fairly clearly, the solution is to restate MacIntyre's case so as distinguish between second-order and substantive conceptions of the good. Then we can put the point by saying that there is a distinctively liberal individualist second-order conception of the good from which can be derived the idea of neutrality between substantive conceptions of the good. MacIntyre himself never explains how he thinks it is consistent to say that there is a distinctively liberal conception of the good and at the same time that 'the liberal is committed to there being no one overriding good'.[21] But if by 'overriding' we understand 'substantive', we can make sense of what he says.

Autonomy is a genuinely second-order conception of the good because it does not specify the content of the good: there is no substantive conception that it rules out, just so long as that conception has been arrived at autonomously. But it does not lead to neutrality between conceptions of the good, precisely because value is attributed only to those conceptions with the right pedigree. It is thus quite natural to conclude that, if we are looking for a second-order conception of the good that will generate neutrality between substantive conceptions, what we should do is simply drop the requirement that substantive conceptions of the good must have the right pedigree in order to have value. Doing this will give a conception of the good as want-satisfaction. According to this conception, what has value is the satisfaction of whatever wants people happen to have, regardless of the way in which they came by those wants.[c]

---

[c] Thus, substantive conceptions of the good are treated as giving rise to wants, which are factored into the utilitarian calculus. The (second-order) conception of the good as autonomy can be accommodated on the same basis as substantive conceptions of the

MacIntyre himself equates the liberal individualist conception of the good with want-satisfaction. Thus, having said that liberal individualism has its own conception of the good and that its toleration of rival conceptions in the public arena is severely limited, he goes on to explain how these rival conceptions of the good are accommodated, as follows: 'What is permitted in [the public] arena is the expression of preferences. . . . It may well be that in some cases it is some nonliberal theory or conception of the human good which leads individuals to express the preferences that they do. But only in the guise of such expressions of preference are such theories and conceptions allowed to receive expression.'[22] Hence, 'the defense of rival moral and political standpoints is interpreted . . . as the expression of preferences by those individuals who engage in such defenses.'[23] The result of conceiving moral and political views within 'the culture of liberalism' as preferences is that 'debate at the first level [i.e. substantive debate on the issues themselves] has no outcome.'[24] However, issues are resolved at a second level where the raw material fed in consists of preferences. At this level, 'the participants in debate find that . . . their points of view are included in that tallying and weighing of expressions of preference which the institutionalizations of liberalism always involve: counting votes, responding to consumer choice, surveying public opinion.'[25]

In as far as it is consumer preferences that are to be aggregated, the market—'the dominant institution in a liberal economy'—functions so that 'through the expression of individual preferences . . . a heterogeneous variety of needs, desires, and goods conceived in one way or another are given a voice.'[26] And in as far as preferences are to be aggregated politically, this will be done through the voting mechanism or by decisions taken on the basis of consulting public opinion. Either way, technical problems will arise about carrying out an aggregation of diverse preferences. This explains why 'Arrow's theorem and its heirs [are] so relevant in modern social theory.'[27] But, however the aggregation is actually to be done, it is the liberal identification of practical rationality with the maximization of preference-satisfaction that 'makes both the preoccupations of utilitarianism and its distinctive idiom so ineliminable from modern public discourse as well as from modern moral and political philosophy.'[28]

The simplest and most familiar theory that makes want-satisfaction the good is the variant of utilitarianism in which the maximand is taken to be want-satisfaction rather than, say, pleasure or happiness. The

good. Anything that a proponent of autonomy thinks ought to be done to promote it can be treated as a want for that to happen, and aggregated with other people's wants for different outcomes.

rationale for maximizing aggregate want-satisfaction is that, if want-satisfaction is taken to be good, that must mean more of it is better than less, and it does not make any difference who the bearers of want-satisfaction are. (This is the significance of the slogan that 'Everybody is to count for one, and nobody for more than one.') Now, utilitarianism is manifestly a child of the Enlightenment, but it does not automatically lead to the endorsement of liberal institutions. The argument can be made, but it is undeniably less direct and straightforward than the case that can be made starting from a conception of the good as autonomy. The obvious difficulty is that it is possible to imagine illiberal preferences (e.g. for the suppression of beliefs or actions that are found offensive by a large majority of the population) giving rise to a state of affairs in which it might be that aggregate preference-satisfaction could be secured by illiberal public policies.[d]

However, two resources are available to help steer the conception of the good as want-satisfaction towards liberal conclusions. One is to posit what have been called 'stylized facts', in this case about the structure of preferences. Suppose that people in general care more about being able to do what they want than they care about stopping other people from doing what they want.[29] This implies that freedom will tend to generate more utility than repression. But it still leaves open the possibility that a mild preference on the part of a large majority of the population for preventing a minority from doing something (e.g. engaging in homosexual acts or Protestant forms of worship) might outweigh in the calculus of aggregate want-satisfaction a more intense preference on the part of the minority for doing it. Such an uninviting prospect can be cut off by a second move: the abandonment of simple aggregation.

Many philosophers who have been attracted to the equation of the

---

[d] It may be worth pointing out that the so-called liberal paradox invented by Amartya Sen does no more than demonstrate the same point: that illiberal preferences plugged into any calculus that assigns value to preference-satisfaction must inevitably produce illiberal implications (though not, as it happens, the ones that Sen claims in the case of his alleged paradox). In the canonical story about the reading or not reading of *Lady Chatterley's Lover*, each of the parties has a stronger preference for what the other person does than he has for what he does himself. It is therefore hardly surprising that the Pareto-optimal outcome is for each to do what the other wants him to do. This is an illiberal conclusion only in the sense that it says a situation is better when each conforms to the wishes of the other than when he does what he wants, considering only himself. But it would lead to illiberal institutional implications if we were to add that institutions should be designed to ensure Pareto optimality. Since the Pareto principle is entailed by utilitarianism (it is the ordinal form of cardinal utility maximization), the same holds for the application of the utilitarian principle. See for a discussion of the 'liberal paradox' my 'Lady Chatterley's Lover and Doctor Fischer's Bomb Party: Liberalism, Pareto Optimality, and the Problem of Objectionable Preferences', repr. in *Liberty and Justice: Essays in Political Theory*, vol. II (Oxford: Clarendon Press, 1991), 78–109.

good with want-satisfaction have been disturbed by the utilitarian corollary that more want-satisfaction is better than less, regardless of the way in which it is distributed. They have therefore proposed building in distributive considerations, so that the value to be attributed to a given situation depends both on the total amount of want-satisfaction and the way in which is distributed. (See *Theories of Justice*, 79–82.) One candidate is the proposition that, given a certain average level of utility, a more equal distribution is more valuable than a less equal one. Another is the proposition that a given average level of utility has more value the higher the level of those with the least. (If exclusive weight is attached to the level of the worst off, the criterion becomes one of maximin utility.)

If we retain the 'stylized fact' about the relative utility to be derived from doing something and preventing others from doing something, we can derive liberal conclusions with more confidence from these normative premises. For numbers now no longer count for so much. If it is worse to be repressed than to have one's desire to repress others frustrated, the position of the worst off will be better with freedom all round than with repression of some. On the same assumption, the distribution of utility will be more equal if all can do what they want and desires to prevent others from doing what they want are frustrated than if some people can get utility from doing what they want and also from preventing others from doing what they want while other people are denied utility from either source.

The conclusion I draw is that it is only with quite a struggle that a conception of the good as want-satisfaction can be induced to lead to the endorsement of liberal institutions. This should call into doubt MacIntyre's equation of want-satisfaction as the good with the so-called liberal individualist premise. In spite of this, however, MacIntyre might still be correct in saying that justice as impartiality is fraudulent in claiming to arrive at neutrality without invoking any conception of the good. For it could still be true that the only intelligible form of neutrality is that which can be derived from a conception of the good as want-satisfaction.

A utilitarian might say that the conception of the good as want-satisfaction is (*pace* MacIntyre) a genuinely neutral starting point, and therefore unobjectionable. Thus, Paul Kelly, in his recent study of Bentham, concedes that 'utilitarianism is not usually considered a neutralist theory because it is argued that the good is pleasure or welfare.' But he argues that this utilitarian criterion 'still provides a principle of right which is neutral between individuals' conceptions of happiness, pleasure, or welfare'.[30] This is correct in as far as want-satisfaction, as a conception of the good, allows each person to choose the content that he puts into it. But that does not, it seems to me, make it any less a distinctive conception of the good. MacIntyre is surely right in insisting that, when substantive conceptions of the good are conceived as preferences and given value only in that form, their status is transformed. Normally, people believe that they have a claim to something because it is good. They want it for the same reason, but that is not the basis of the claim to have it. When value is attributed to want-satisfaction, however, these relationships are turned around. The claim to have something is based on the fact of wanting it, and the goodness of what is wanted plays no part in the claim.

The difference becomes even clearer when we ask how, if I have a certain substantive conception of the good, I am supposed to think about the claims of others with different conceptions of the good. On the normal view, I use my conception of the good to judge claims by myself and others. A claim by somebody else for something that is valuable according to my conception of the good will carry weight with me. But a claim for something that has zero or negative value, according to my conception of the good, will carry no weight with me. That somebody wants it will not be relevant to my judgement, since (we are assuming) my substantive conception of the good does not attribute any value to want-satisfaction as such—only to the satisfaction of wants for what is good. But now suppose that I take want-satisfaction as my (second-order) conception of the good. Then the very fact of something's being wanted forms the basis in itself of a claim whose validity I must recognize. This is enough to show the want-satisfaction is a quite distinctive conception of the good, and perhaps a somewhat peculiar one. It is neutral in the sense that it can accommodate all substantive conceptions of the good, but only by transforming them into preferences. This was, of course, precisely MacIntyre's complaint, and what I have just said suggests that it is well founded.

This being so, it is important for my overall argument to be able to show that MacIntyre is wrong in maintaining that justice as impartiality reduces to a conception of the good as want-satisfaction. MacIntyre does not, as far as I can see, ever put forward an explicit case for thinking that there cannot be a conception of justice as impartiality which does not in the end rest on a conception of the good as want-satisfaction. He may, I suspect, have fallen into a fallacious line of thought along the following lines: 'Justice as impartiality claims to entail neutrality; want-satisfaction is a conception of the good that entails neutrality; therefore justice as impartiality must reduce to a conception of the good as want-satisfaction.' It is plain, however, that there could be different premises leading to the same conclusion, and I shall indeed argue that justice as impartiality constitutes a genuinely different premise from that constituted by a conception of the good as want-satisfaction. I shall also, however, dispute the notion that the two premises arrive at the same conclusion. It is true that both premises lead to the endorsement of a certain kind of neutrality between different substantive conceptions of the good. But the kind of neutrality generated by one premise is not the same as the kind of neutrality generated by the other.

CHAPTER 6

The idea of neutrality

22. *Two Kinds of Neutrality*

I have said that MacIntyre is right to claim that a certain kind of neutrality between conceptions of the good can be achieved on the basis of a conception of the good as want-satisfaction. Want-satisfaction is, I have suggested, a second-order conception of the good that can incorporate all other conceptions of the good in the guise of wants. At the same time, however, I wish to insist that there is another kind of neutrality, which is generated by justice as impartiality. In this chapter I shall argue that MacIntyre's attempt to conflate justice as impartiality with a conception of the good as want-satisfaction can properly be resisted. But I shall also show how MacIntyre could have been misled into making this conflation. For there is an undeniable parallelism between the two which is worth bringing out.

Let me begin, then, by asking what justice as impartiality does have in common with utilitarianism understood as the impartialist moral theory generated by a conception of the good as want-satisfaction. The fundamental point of commonality, from which other similarities flow, is that both theories are addressed to the same problem. They start from the recognition of the irreducible plurality of substantive conceptions of the good. They therefore share the project of finding a basis for a society's institutions and public policies that is in principle capable of appealing to every member of that society, whatever his or her substantive conception of the good may be.

This is, I take it, clear enough in the case of justice as impartiality, which presents itself quite explicitly as a solution to the problem posed by conflicting conceptions of the good. To show the same for utilitarianism, we have to dig a little below the surface. Consider, then, Bentham's argument against alternatives to the principle of utility in the *Introduction to the Principles of Morals and Legislation*.[1] What this argument comes to is that all the alternatives are too idiosyncratic to provide a consensual basis for public policy. They 'fail to provide a rational objective structure for moral judgement and thus undermine the conditions of social interaction. For without public and objective criteria of moral judgement, and a public framework for the resolution of disputes, the enterprise of society cannot continue, and the result is anarchy.'[2] The same point has recently been put by Richard Arneson.

If one gives up the thought that individuals would reasonably all agree on any one particular conception of the good, there is still the possibility that rational preference satisfaction could be agreed to as a formal goal, with substantive content being filled in for each person by that very person's tastes and values, insofar as they would withstand rational scrutiny. The proposal to use welfare as a measure in a theory of justice is not a denial of the fact of pluralism; rather, it is a device for coping with it.[3]

Arneson speaks here of rational preferences—that is, preferences that are based on good information and reflection—but for the present purpose nothing turns on the precise specification of the preferences. The essential point is that conceptions of the good are to be turned into preferences and brought into relation with one another *qua* preferences.

It is undeniable that this is a kind of neutrality in relation to specific conceptions of the good. Arneson, indeed, describes it as 'subjectivist neutrality'.[4] The rationale for this description is, he says, is that 'preference satisfaction is a proposed metric for amalgamating diverse conceptions of what is worth seeking in life on a common scale. . . . Whether acceptable or unacceptable, subjectivism is not another sectarian doctrine lacking the support of impartial reasons'.[5] Conceding this, the question is: does justice as impartiality constitute a genuine alternative to the form constituted by a comparison of utilities? Both MacIntyre (as an opponent of utilitarianism) and Arneson (as a supporter) suggest that, if it is made coherent, justice as impartiality will turn out to require utility as its metric.[a]

I want to deny that justice as impartiality collapses into utilitarianism whenever it is called upon to do any real work. The only way of making that denial plausible is to show in some detail how the two really do differ in their approach to a common subject-matter. The following two

---

[a] I use 'utilitarian' here to include any view according to which we can evaluate states of affairs using only utility information. I reject the term 'welfarism' for this because it incorporates the economists' typical equation of welfare with utility. In ordinary usage, which I think it is important to preserve because it incorporates an important distinction, welfare is an objective rather than a subjective concept. Welfare corresponds roughly to the absence of harm (i.e. the presence of adequate food, clothing and shelter, freedom from pain and suffering, and so on).

sections (which make up the rest of the chapter) will be devoted to that
project. In the next section, I shall show that utilitarianism and justice as
impartiality lead to quite different ways of understanding the significance of votes on policies. Then, in the following section, I shall take up
a slightly arcane aspect of cost-benefit analysis, the so-called Contingent Valuation Method (CVM). This is, I shall argue, squarely
founded in utilitarianism but is precisely for that reason controversial. I
shall try to show that the notorious difficulties that practitioners of
CVM have run into when attempting to apply it reflect resistance to the
assumptions about the appropriate way of taking decisions on which it
is based.

Before that, I shall complete the present section by returning to the
theme with which I began it: that the similarities between utilitarianism
and impartial justice should not be taken as evidence for their identity. I
have spoken so far of their having a common objective in offering a
response to the variety of substantive conceptions of the good. My
argument has been that this common aim is nevertheless pursued in different ways by the two theories. What I shall now suggest is that there
are also some similarities between the practical conclusions to be drawn
from utilitarianism and those to be drawn from justice as impartiality.
But I shall, again, argue that this does not make the two theories the
same. For they arrive at their conclusions by different routes.

The first case I shall take up is that of harm. Harm plays a part in
both theories, but it does so in quite different ways. Thus, within utilitarianism, harm is simply an important form of negative utility, to be
factored in with all other utilities. It has no significance apart from this.
For justice as impartiality, however, the significance of harm lies in its
being recognized as bad within a wide variety of conceptions of the
good, of which the utilitarian conception is only one. (See above,
Section 14.) It is quite often claimed in criticism of this move that the
concept of harm cannot function in this way because the content of
'harm' reflects the particular conception of the good of the person
employing the term. I have never, however, seen this assertion backed
up by convincing evidence, and I do not believe it could be. It is worth
noticing, for example, that every society falls back on a quite limited
range of punishments such as deprivation of money or property, physical confinement, loss of bodily parts, pain, and death. Unless these were
regarded by people with a wide variety of conceptions of the good as
evils, they would not function reliably as punishments. It is also relevant that, even in societies with ideas about the causation of harm that
we do not share, the conception of the kinds of thing that constitute
harm is familiar. Thus, in societies (either recently in Africa or several

centuries ago in Europe and America) where it was widely believed that people could be harmed by witchcraft, the things complained of were diseases and injuries, destruction or damage of property (including diseases and injuries of livestock) and similar misfortunes of a kind that we have no difficulty in recognizing as harms.

I also argued in Chapter 4 (see especially Section 13) that justice as impartiality will underwrite constitutional provisions mandating freedom of religious worship and freedom of sexual expression. Utilitarianism can, as we saw at the end of the previous chapter, arrive at the same conclusions, by helping itself to some 'stylized facts' about the relative intensity of active and repressive desires. (These 'stylized facts' were not, however, pulled out of thin air. The strength of both religious convictions and sexual desires is suggested by the willingness of people at a whole variety of times and places to risk enormous penalties, including torture and death, to uphold forbidden religious beliefs and engage in forbidden sexual practices.) The point I want to make here, however, is that the argument set out in Section 13 was not utilitarian in form. In essence it went as follows. Suppose you were to say: 'The reason why I should be able to practise my religion but you should not be able to practise yours is that mine is right and yours is wrong.' You would, obviously, reject a claim made in similar terms by somebody else with opposing ideas about what was right and what was wrong. In rejecting that claim you would be acting reasonably. But then it follows that you cannot reasonably object when others reject your claim.

The argument here appeals to a certain notion of consistency. It makes no reference to the strength of the opposing desires at work. You could conclude that the desire of somebody else to suppress your religion is more powerful than your own desire to practise it. That does not change the fact that you could reasonably reject his claim to prevent you practising your own religion. For the ground on which you can reasonably reject his claim is quite independent of such considerations. You can reasonably say that his presumption of rightness is inadequate as a basis for his demand to be able to practise his religion and prevent you from practising yours. The price of taking this line is, however, to recognize that your own demand for a special status for your own beliefs is symmetrical with the one you have just rejected.

These examples are enough to suggest that the neutrality of justice as impartiality is quite a complicated matter. The basic idea is simple enough: that nobody should be able to claim a privileged position for any conception of the good on the basis of its correctness or its superiority to others. But following that basic idea through will entail several different kinds of move. Thus, we say that the prevention of harm is required by justice as impartiality because what is harmful is deleterious to the furtherance of virtually any conception of the good. We do not therefore have to invoke any particular conception of the good to arrive at the conclusion that rules of justice must prohibit the doing of harm. We cannot, obviously, appeal to any similar consensus on the value of religious and sexual freedom. Here we have to move to a higher level of generality and argue that people who accept the good of religious worship and sexual expression for themselves cannot consistently deny it to others. Neutrality comes in here to block the only move that could prevent the issue from being raised to a higher level: the claim that the difference between my religion (or sexual preference) and yours, which justifies a difference in treatment, is that mine is true (or 'natural') whereas yours is heretical (or 'deviant').

These are cases where the theory of justice as impartiality reaches definite conclusions about what justice requires. But as far as the great bulk of contemporary legislation and policy-making is concerned, justice as impartiality will have things to say about *how* the legislation or policy can be framed consistently with the demands of justice, but it is silent on the question of *what* the content of the legislation or policy should be. In all these matters, the neutrality inherent in justice as impartiality leads to an insistence on the point that the decision-making rules should not give any special advantages to certain conceptions of the good over others. Subject to that, however, the process must be one in which the partisans of different positions defend them on the basis of their conception of the good and seek to win converts to it or to persuade holders of other conceptions of the good that their own conception, rightly understood, supports the same position.

This is worth emphasizing because it seems to be widely believed that neutrality, in the sense relevant to justice as impartiality, entails that every law and policy has to be argued about in ways that avoid invoking any conception of the good. This conception of the scope of neutrality has been advocated especially strongly by Ronald Dworkin[6] and has been picked up by critics[7] and commentators.[8] However, Dworkin has never made any serious effort to show how public policy could be made in a way that is neutral between different conceptions of the good. It is significant that all his arguments for the superiority of allocations based on resources (rights, money, etc.) over allocations based on utility are concerned with the distribution of private goods.[9] As far as I am aware, his only contribution to the assessment of public policies (say, protection of the environment) where individual rights are not at issue remains the proposal that the criterion should be a utilitarian one, with preferences 'laundered' to eliminate from the calculus so-called 'external' or 'moralistic' preferences.[10] And if we are looking for neutrality at the level of policies rather than procedures, the sort offered by utilitarianism is, indeed, the only sort available. But it is, I am arguing, a kind of neutrality foreign to the logic of justice as impartiality.

Utilitarianism has a criterion that is (in principle, anyway) able to give an answer to every question about what is the right public policy. Justice as impartiality can in many cases do no more than set the outer limits to what is acceptable, and in other cases all it can do is specify that the decision must be made by a fair procedure. (See above Chapter 4, especially Section 16.) It is interesting in this context to observe that Rawls has recently endorsed the same conclusion. 'Public reason' is a standard of impartial justification whose limits on decision-making 'do not apply to all political questions but only to those involving what we may call "constitutional essentials"'.[11] Examples of issues that fall outside are 'much tax legislation and many laws regulating property; statutes protecting the environment and controlling pollution; establishing national parks and preserving wilderness areas and animal and plant species; and laying aside funds for museums and the arts'.[12]

This list contains, I suggest, two distinct kinds of item. One set of items (tax and property laws) contains matters that are in principle within the realm of 'justice as fairness' but are subject to reasonable disagreement about the implications of the principles of justice.[b] (This is

---

[b] In *A Theory of Justice*, this appears to be the only source of indeterminacy allowed for. Thus, Rawls says that 'the question whether legislation is just or unjust, especially in connection with economic and social policies, is commonly subject to reasonable differences of opinion. . . . Often the best that we can say of a law or policy is that it is at least not clearly unjust. The application of the difference principle in a precise way normally requires more information than we can expect to have. . . .', (John Rawls, *A Theory of Justice* (Cambridge, Mass.: Harvard University Press, 1971), 198–9). There is nothing inconsistent here with the admission that the principles of justice might leave the just outcome open in a more radical way. It is simply that the only difficulty canvassed is that of applying the difference principle—that is to say, deciding what laws and policies would in fact be most advantageous (in terms of primary goods) to the worst-off social group. It is, incidentally, an error to suppose that Rawls is somehow precluded from permitting legislative decisions to be made on the basis of conceptions of the good by his being an 'anti-perfectionist'. Thus, for example, Joseph Raz (see reference note 18 for citation) depicts Rawls as one of the 'antiperfectionist writers . . . who deny that political decisions may be based on conceptions of the good life' (772 n. 16). But for Rawls 'perfectionism' is understood as one of the three candidates between which the choice is to be made in the original position (the others being Rawls's own principles and utilitarianism). Thus, it is as a potential criterion of social justice that perfectionism is rejected. As Rawls says, 'the argument is . . . that in view of their disparate aims the parties have no reason to adopt the principle of perfection given the conditions of the original position' (p. 328). And 'even in its intuitionistic [i.e. pluralistic] form, perfectionism would be rejected as not defining a feasible basis of social justice' (p. 331). Thus, 'anti-perfectionism' means that the basic social and political institutions of a society cannot be moulded to advance any one idea. On this understanding of it, Rawls remains an

something that could equally well happen with the utilitarian criterion.) The other set, comprising the rest of the list, contains issues that in the nature of the case cannot be resolved without giving priority to one conception of the good over others. Here the requirement of impartial justifiability can extend only to insisting that the procedure by which the decision is taken should be fair and that the policy should be implemented fairly, e.g. that the taxes to support public expenditure should be raised in an equitable way. In this context, however, there is no room for a complaint of discrimination simply on the ground that the policy by its nature suits those with one conception of the good more than it suits those with some different one. This is unavoidable.

Associated with the incompleteness of impartial justice as a decision rule is another contrast with utilitarianism. This is that there is nothing in justice as impartiality corresponding to the single kind of stuff, utility, with which utilitarianism works. A number of attempts have been made to determine 'the currency of egalitarian justice'.[13] Each of these is successful in pointing to examples that support the particular currency proposed and do not fit some rival currency. The common error lies in supposing that there is one answer waiting to be found. The currency of justice as impartiality is irreducibly heterogeneous: justice is not to be defined in terms of the distribution of one fungible quantity. Rather, the theory of justice as impartiality issues in a set of discrete conclusions, each with its own distinct subject-matter. A corollary is that a just society is one that gets millions of decisions right. It is not one that approximates an ideal distribution of some single kind of stuff—for example an equal distribution of utility or generic 'resources'.[14]

23. Rival Conceptions of Voting

The comparison between utilitarianism and justice as impartiality can be carried forward usefully by imagining that a decision-making system is in place and that some issue falls to be decided by a certain procedure—say a referendum. How will the two approaches deal with this? Let us, to give our discussion some content, suppose that the issue before the polity is whether or not to build a dam that would, if built, destroy the habitat of an endangered species of fish—for convenient reference, call it the snail-darter.

anti-perfectionist even while accepting that legislation within a just constitutional framework can reflect specific conceptions of the good. As is always the case with Rawls, much more might be said, but this much is perhaps worth saying.

As we saw in the previous chapter, MacIntyre assumes that the rationale of voting in a liberal society must rest upon want-satisfaction. Although I wish to deny, of course, that this is the only possibility, it is quite true that such a rationale does exist. Let us begin, then, by exploring it. The most sophisticated treatment of the idea that a voting procedure should aggregate wants for outcomes is to be found in social choice theory. This is an ordinalist development of utilitarianism. That is to say, it does not make any explicit use of the notion that preferences have different intensities. The problem that it sets itself is that of starting from individual preference-orderings and then aggregating them to form a single so-called 'social preference ordering'. A voting procedure is thus seen as a way of eliciting and aggregating preferences. However, eliciting preferences is a less simple matter than might appear, because all voting procedures (except where the choice is limited to two alternatives) provide incentives for people to misrepresent their preferences— that is to say to vote in a way that does not correspond to their actual ordering of the alternatives.[15] But some procedures are more prone to strategic manipulation than others, and this is one consideration that is relevant in recommending a voting procedure. There is no need here to enter into the travails of social choice theory in trying to find a way of aggregating preferences so as to satisfy what are supposed to be intuitively appealing axioms.[16] What we can say, which suffices for the present purpose, is that every voting procedure can be construed within this framework as a device for aggregating preferences, each with its own advantages and disadvantages.

The construction of social choice theory in ordinal terms arose out of the denial of the meaningfulness of the notion of intensities of preference.[17] If we assume that there are only two alternatives in the dam-building case, an epistemological ordinalist of this kind would find the problem easy. He would say that the social choice should correspond to the side that gets the most votes. For with only two alternatives no difficulties arise about preference-revelation, and if it makes no sense to talk about intensities of preference then a majority of preferences must beat a minority.

It is possible, however, to accept that as a practical matter votes must be expressed in terms of orderings of alternatives while still retaining a rationale for voting systems that rests of utilitarian foundations. An example of this approach is provided by Michael Dummett's book *Voting Procedures*.[18] Dummett assumes that the choice between a voting system that sums rankings (such as the Borda count) and some form of majoritarian system 'turns on whether it be thought more important to please as many people as possible or to please everyone collectively as much as possible'.[19] Once the question is set up in this way, the second answer seems persuasive, with the implication that (subject to the difficulty of its vulnerability to manipulation) a Borda type of system should be preferred. Ideally, it seems clear, Dummett would like to take account of *strengths* of preference for alternative options. The Borda system, which counts only rankings, is thus a second best for him, and it is significant that he suggests its accuracy might be improved by introducing dummy alternatives so as to get a better measure of the distance between the actually available alternatives. In effect, this analysis involves us in treating each step down a ranking as a loss of a standard amount of want-satisfaction. On this view of the matter, 'the rule to do as the majority wishes does not appear to have any better justification than as a rough-and-ready test for what will secure the maximum total satisfaction'.[20] Thus, in the dam case, Dummett might wish to have the field of choice widened (if necessary by adding infeasible alternatives) and then using preference-rankings as surrogate measures for strengths of preference between the real alternatives.

As David Miller has pointed out, however, Dummett's rationale of voting fits only a limited range of decisions where gratifying the voters is the object—for example, choosing the fixed menu for a meal to be consumed in common.[21] Here, aiming to please the majority rather than trying to please everyone to the greatest extent possible would indeed seem out of place. An aggregation mechanism such as a Borda count, summing the scores of alternative menus, would here seem appropriate. For we might reasonably regard this as a practical procedure for approximating the utility-maximizing outcome—so long as everybody listed the alternatives in accordance with their true preferences.[c] But the objective of maximizing the utility of the voters in this way is, Miller suggests, irrelevant and indeed offensive where the decision is 'better represented' as being about 'what is the right thing to do'.[22] (Miller's own example is that of imposing the death penalty for a crime of a

[c] Even in the choice of a menu, it is actually an oversimplification to say that the only thing to enter in are likes and dislikes based on taste. For any satisfactory formula would have to let people exercise a veto over menus that offended against their religions or zoo-centric convictions or included items ruled out on medical grounds. In terms of the machinery of a Scanlonian original position: anyone could reasonably reject the proposition that dietary restrictions based upon a conception of the good could be overridden by an accumulation of personal preferences based on likes and dislikes. (As far as restrictions based on medical criteria are concerned, nobody could reasonably reject giving health a certain priority because the value of health is integral to so many different conceptions of the good.) It may be observed, incidentally, that the constraints imposed on the menu by vetoes might well be so severe as to leave little scope for personal likes and dislikes to come into play. For this reason a prior decision is very commonly made to provide separate vegetarian and non-vegetarian menus.

certain kind.) Here, as Miller says, it does seem 'that the natural procedure would be to use one of the majoritarian methods, since what seems
important is that whatever is done is done by the will of the majority—
if possible what the majority wills in preference to all other options'.[23]

It is important to recognize that Miller's criticism of Dummett's utilitarian approach to voting carries over to the ordinalist theory of social
choice that I discussed earlier. It is true that this leads (as I pointed out)
to the conclusion that the decision should go with the majority where
the choice is between only two alternatives. But the rationale is, as we
have seen, still in terms of preference-aggregation. That is to say, the
argument for saying that the outcome should be what the majority
voted for is that this will be the outcome that satisfies more wants than
the alternative.

Suppose we reject this whole approach and say that the issue involving the dam is one where there are competing views about the right
answer rather than conflicting wants. There are then two ways of getting to the conclusion that the outcome should be the one supported by
a majority. We must be careful how we proceed here, because only one
of them is compatible with justice as impartiality. The one which is not
was classically stated by Rousseau and formalized by Condorcet. It says
that, if everyone sincerely expresses his opinion as to what is the right
answer, what a majority believes to be right will very probably be right
provided that each voter has a better than fifty-fifty chance of being
right.

To consider the application of this, imagine a society in which everybody has the same conception of the good. If all the voters ask themselves what decision their shared conception of the good calls for, what
the theorem tells us is that their collective wisdom is very likely to
arrive at a decision in favour of the alternative that this conception does
call for.[d] But where there is no shared conception of the good, this

---

[d] It is in this spirit that I interpret Rousseau's doctrine of the General Will. The
General Will is a will for the common advantage, which Rousseau (as I understand him)
takes to be objective—a question to which there is, in principle, always a right answer. In
a well-ordered society, then, 'the general will is in the majority'. I interpret this as meaning that, if everyone is seeking the right answer, the majority has a good chance of reaching the right answer—the bigger the majority the better the chance. Condorcet explicitly
calculates in terms of *verité* and *erreur* in his proof that, if a large number of people each
have a probability of getting the right answer that is better than 0.5, the probability that a
majority will reach the right answer is much higher. (See Jean-Jacques Rousseau, *The
Social Contract* trans. Maurice Cranston (Harmondsworth, Mddx: Penguin, 1968), bk. 2
ch. 3; and Keith Baker *Condorcet: From Natural Philosophy to Social Mathematics*
(Chicago: University of Chicago Press, 1975), 228.) I made use of Condorcet's work in
an exposition of Rousseau, without being aware at that time that Condorcet had himself
drawn his inspiration from Rousseau: see 'The Public Interest', in *Proceedings of the
Aristotelian Society*, Supplementary Volume 38 (1964), 1–18.

rationale has no application. If the holders of each different conception of the good were to caucus separately, we might use the same argument in favour of majority voting within each of these groups to determine a common line. But there is no basis for talking of a superordinate 'right answer' which the votes of those who subscribe to different conceptions of the good might be thought of as contributing to by their votes.

The alternative way of looking at voting on an issue, which fits in with justice as impartiality, is as follows. Let us suppose that at the constitutional stage it has been determined that building or not building the dam is the kind of issue that is not settled by the criteria of justice as impartiality. Instead, some procedure is laid down by which a definite decision may be reached about controversial issues such as this. We are supposing that in the case at hand the procedure is a referendum. Then casting a vote is simply taking part in that procedure, and the result of counting up all the votes has no significance except that it is the outcome of a fairly-conducted procedure applied in the appropriate conditions. There is no call for attributing any particular value to the outcome.

Suppose that you have an ecocentric conception of the good, and that on the basis of this you vote against the construction of the dam. Now let us assume that when the votes are tallied it turns out that there is a majority in favour of building the dam. How should you react to this? If your rationale for accepting the decision procedure was that it would tend to produce want-satisfying outcomes, you will have to say that building the dam will more likely than not on balance be valuable: in accordance with your (second-order) conception of the good, building the dam may be expected to advance the good more than not building it. You could have some qualms about that conclusion if there were reason to believe that those in the minority had on the average more intense preferences than those in the majority, but it would be only on lines such as those that you could question the superior value of the dam-building option.

We have not, however, said anything about your having in addition to your ecocentric conception of the good a second-order conception of the good as want-satisfaction. Let us posit explicitly that you do not have any such conception. On the contrary, let us say that satisfying human wants inimical to the integrity of the ecosystem is, as far as you are concerned, bad. Suppose that you nevertheless endorse the theory of justice as impartiality, and on the basis of that accept that the right thing is for the dam to be built. Must you, on pain of self-contradiction, revise your initial view that building the dam is a bad thing? I do not see that you do. You believed before the referendum that building the dam would reduce the amount of value in the universe (to put it in a rather highfalutin way), and there is nothing in the mere result of the referendum to make you change your mind about that. You now know that building the dam will probably increase the amount of human want-satisfaction, but since you do not hold a want-satisfying conception of the good that does not concern you.

What status, then, does the result of the referendum have for you? You will accept that it should be implemented because it was the outcome of a fair procedure, fairly conducted. That is all. You need not adopt an alien conception of the good so as to make the outcome turn to be a value-maximizing one. Unless you change your mind about the ecological ethic or its implications for the case in hand, you must continue to regret that the wrong decision was made. But you can still say, if you adhere to justice as impartiality, that majority voting was a fair way of resolving the issue and that you must, therefore, accept that what the majority supports should become public policy. The outcome is, as far as you are concerned, legitimate but bad—bad in the precise sense that it offends against your conception of the good.[e]

We can reinforce the conclusion if we go back to the period of the campaign preceding the vote on the building of the dam. If we assume

[e] It is, of course, always possible to maintain that, if you accept the outcome, this *must* mean that you impute greater value to it than to the alternatives. An illustration is provided by Robert Goodin's defence of what he calls the 'green theory of value'. (I mentioned it earlier in Section 3.) According to this, two physically identical states of affairs can have different value if they came about in different ways, one having occurred naturally and the other as a result of human artifice. In seeking to render this plausible, Goodin argues that there is nothing strange in the idea that things can acquire value as a result of their having the right history. An example is, he claims, 'the rule [*sic* -read 'role'] of process based considerations in imparting legitimacy to the outcomes of political deliberations'. Goodin considers the objection that 'conferring legitimacy' is not the same thing as 'imparting value'. He imagines an objector saying (as I would indeed wish to do) that 'far from valuing those outcomes more highly on account of their histories, what we are actually doing when accepting those outcomes as "legitimate" might be no more than merely saying that we are prepared to accept even less valuable outcomes, just so long as they have the right histories'. Goodin's reply to this challenge simply begs the question. Why, he asks, should we be willing to accept less valuable outcomes with the right histories? 'Only, presumably, because we attach some independent *value* to the process of the creation of those outcomes. If so, then what is really going on is just this: outcomes which are less valuable to us, in purely substantive terms, nonetheless turn out to be more valuable to us overall once the extra value derived from the process of their creation has been added in', Robert Goodin, *Green Political Theory* (Cambridge: Polity Press, 1992), 28, italics in original. All the work is being done here by the word 'presumably'. Why should we make the presumption we are invited to make unless we are wedded to the dogma that nobody ever has any (ethically sound) reason for accepting any outcome other than that it advances his conception of the good? If we do take that step then of course we have to add a 'fudge factor' on the lines proposed by Goodin in order to make the answer come out in the right place. But he does not tell us why we should, and I do not believe that he (or anybody else) could do so.

that the only possible rationale for having a referendum is the want-satisfying one, there will be only one possible line along which you can campaign. You will have to say that the case against building the dam is that a lot of people (including yourself) want to save the snail-darter, and that, if enough people want to save it, want-satisfaction will be increased by not building the dam. You can of course, try to get more people to want to save the snail-darter, perhaps by appealing to your ecocentric first-order conception of the good. But the argument against the dam will still have to be pitched ultimately in terms of its effects on aggregate want-satisfaction.

This is enough to show how absurd is the assumption that the rationale of the referendum must be a want-satisfying one. For the basis of your opposition to the dam is that, from the point of view of an ecocentric conception of the good, it would be wrong to extinguish a species in pursuit of human interests of less than critical importance. In campaigning for a 'No' vote on the proposition to build the dam, you will not say 'Building the dam would be a bad thing because it will diminish aggregate human want-satisfaction (provided enough people share my wants in the matter).' Rather, you will say that building the dam will be bad because it will destroy the snail-darter. In other words, you will appeal to your own conception of the good and try to convince others of your case on the basis of that. If the referendum goes against you, that gives you no reason for thinking that there was anything wrong with the case. You can continue to affirm your ecocentric conception of the good and to conclude that, in terms of it, the outcome was regrettable. This is perfectly consistent with accepting that justice as impartiality underwrites the implementation of the decision supported by the majority.[24]

Suppose, conversely, that the decision is against building the dam. In practice, there will normally be many different reasons for people voting on one side or other of an issue. (For example, if one side is backed by the government, a vote against that side may be primarily an expression of general discontent with the government.) Let us simplify matters, however, by stipulating that the reason underlying every vote against building the dam is that not building it will save the snail-darter. Thus, the justification for the decision appeals to an ecocentric conception of the good. But the justification for *that being* the decision is that there was a majority in a referendum against building the dam. Assuming that justice as impartiality endorses that procedure, then it also indirectly endorses the outcome as just. If the referendum had gone the other way, however, then it would have concluded that the opposite outcome was just. (For a discussion of Rawls's related ideas about 'procedural justice' see Section 35.)

24. A Test Case: The Contingent Valuation Method

Decisions about building dams are not normally taken by means of a referendum. In a parliamentary system the decision will normally be taken by the government, and if legislative approval is required this can be counted on to be forthcoming so long as the government party or parties have a parliamentary majority. Within the system of the United States, the Congress can be expected to play an independent role in the decision, though the administration will obviously also be involved. Either way, a decision has somehow to be made. Justice as impartiality does not have much to contribute—a point which demonstrates that it has no pretensions to being a complete political ethic, let alone a complete personal ethic.

It would, of course, be possible to simulate a referendum by taking the decision on the basis of public opinion surveys; and, even where governments do not themselves undertake surveys, lobbying organizations often commission them in the hope that the results will strengthen their hand. Opinions expressed in surveys have exactly the same status as votes in this sense: both can be regarded as expressions (veridical or not) of preference. An opinion or a vote can then be aggregated with others, and the policy with the most support can be said to be the best (at least presumptively) on a utilitarian conception of the good. Alternatively, however, a survey and a referendum can be thought of as different ways of eliciting information about what people think is the right policy to adopt. It can then be said that it would be fair (procedurally) to adopt the policy with the most support.

Simulating a referendum by following the course of action supported by a majority is a way of taking a decision mechanically, without any interposition of independent judgement by elected politicians. This is quite compatible with justice as impartiality but it is certainly not required by it. Provided legislators or ministers have reached their positions as a result of the operation of procedures that could be endorsed in a suitably constituted original position (see above Section 16), there is no reason why they should not exercise their own judgement about the right thing to do. This is what would be endorsed in the original position, especially for issues about what the average citizen's views are unlikely to be well informed or well considered. It is what the neutrality of justice as impartiality entails in such cases.

In contrast with this, utilitarianism, as we have seen, converts into a common currency of wants for outcomes all views about what ought to be done. And, once everybody's input has been expressed in this common currency, there is (in principle) only one outcome that can be endorsed by the utilitarian criterion. There remains, however, the problem of finding some procedure for identifying this outcome. And, since the objective of utilitarianism is to create a basis of agreement, the procedure must be publicly defensible. There might, for example, be a small group of utilitarian adepts whose calculations were almost always correct. But, unless these wizards of the utilitarian calculus were able to explain to the satisfaction of most of the population the method by which they arrived at their results, any proposal to turn over all decisions to them would fail to elicit agreement, even in a society where everyone accepted that public policy should be based on utilitarian criteria.

How might a society of utilitarians escape from this impasse? Let us suppose that the decision about the dam is to be made by the government. (For simplicity let us leave the legislature out of it.) How could members of the government defend themselves against the charge that they had acted arbitrarily or capriciously, or had used the utilitarian criterion as a smokescreen behind which they had pursued their own substantive conceptions of the good? As I have suggested, they might simulate a referendum by carrying out a public opinion survey. But if we ask why the government should do what a majority wants, the only answer available in a utilitarian society is going to be fairly feeble: that, in the long run, more want-satisfaction is likely to be generated by following a fixed policy of going with the majority than by following any other fixed policy. The basis for this claim is as follows: it must be assumed a priori that on any issue the intensity of want registered by a 'yes' answer will be on the average the same as the intensity of want registered by a 'no' answer.[25]

This is clearly an unrealistic assumption. We might suppose, therefore, that there has to be a good deal of room for improved methods of applying the utilitarian criterion, to take account of intensities. We should bear in mind, however, that any such method must be capable of being defended publicly as being in a certain (and probably misleading) sense 'objective'. Simulating a mechanical political device, a referendum, can be presented as having that virtue—provided, of course, that we overlook all the usual problems about the wording of the questions and the interpretation of the results inherent in survey methodology. The proposal that I now want to consider is for another technique that supposedly eliminates the need for judgement. This is cost–benefit analysis. Let me illustrate it by taking the example of the dam again. We estimate the total costs of building it—from sacks of cement to the destruction of the snail-darter's habitat. Then we estimate the total benefits—extending from flood control and electricity generation to sailing and fishing. The government should take its decision according to the way in which these estimates come out. If benefits exceed costs the dam should be built and if not then it should not be built.

It may be recalled that MacIntyre's depiction of the 'culture of liberalism' made it one in which 'the defense of rival moral and political standpoints is interpreted . . . as the expression of preferences by those individuals who engage in such defenses'. And, when their views have been treated in this way, 'the participants in debate find that . . . their points of view are included in that tallying and weighing of expressions of preference which the institutionalizations of liberalism always involve: counting votes, responding to consumer choice, surveying public opinion'.[26] I have so far talked about the ways in which votes and answers to surveys might be construed in this spirit as expressions of preference to be amalgamated with others by some counting procedure. With cost–benefit analysis, we get to the remaining member of MacIntyre's triad of liberal devices, 'responding to consumer choice'.[27] For the essence of cost–benefit analysis is to refigure citizens as consumers, whose views about the importance of saving the snail-darter are turned into costs with a notional cash value and factored in with other costs of the dam such as sacks of cement.

The method used by cost–benefit analysts to establish these notional costs is called the Contingent Valuation Method (CVM). Suppose the question is what monetary value should be attached to the survival of the snail-darter—or, to put it the other way round, what loss of monetary value should be attached to its extinction. Then a sample of the public will be asked either of two questions. One kind of question is designed to tap willingness to pay (WTP) for the preservation of the snail-darter: each respondent is asked how much money he personally would be willing to pay to see the snail-darter saved. The other kind of question is designed to tap willingness to accept (WTA): here each respondent is asked how much money he personally would need to be paid in order to compensate him for the extinction of the snail-darter. Orthodox economic analysis tells us that—leaving aside income effects, which are unlikely to be significant in such a case—WTP and WTA should be very similar for any given person. The idea is, then, that the answers to questions about WTP and WTA should be used to establish an 'existence value' for the snail-darter, which can then be factored into the overall cost–benefit calculation.

The technique of contingent valuation provides us with a perfect test for MacIntyre's thesis that the culture of the liberal democracies is saturated with utilitarianism. For we should expect to find, if this were so, that attempts to assign monetary value in this way would be easy to carry out and uncontroversial. Conversely, if (something like) justice as impartiality is firmly established as an alternative view of the way in which political decisions should be made, we may expect CVM to run into difficulties. Aaron Wildavsky suggested that 'disagreements over degrees of environmental protection are not about relative costs and benefits but about the validity of economics itself as a form of interaction—its basis in exchange, costs, and cash—as a measure of the way we ought to relate to one another'.[28] To the extent that this turns out to be so, we can conclude that MacIntyre is wrong and that utilitarianism is not the unquestioned political philosophy of liberal democracy.

There is massive evidence supporting the hypothesis that very many people are not willing to play the game that they are asked to play by the practitioners of CVM. In order to evaluate this evidence we have to be clear precisely what is the nature of this game. For the questions about WTP and WTA have to be construed in a rather peculiar way if the answers are to play the part assigned to them by CVM. Consider first WTP. Somebody who thinks he is being asked questions in his capacity as a citizen rather than as a pseudo-consumer might imagine that he is being asked what he, as a taxpayer, would be prepared to contribute to some public good such as cleaning up beaches—what he would regard as his fair share of the total cost. CVM requires something quite different from this. It needs from each respondent a report on the monetary equivalent of the utility he would gain if the beaches were cleaned up. (If he has no expectation of visiting the beach, the value he assigns will be a pure 'existence value'. Otherwise it will incorporate a 'use value' element.)

Asked how much he would be willing to pay for a certain kind of chocolate bar, it is natural enough for a respondent to construe this as a question about the monetary value of the utility he would derive from (literally) consuming the chocolate bar. It makes sense for him to ask himself questions such as the following. Is it worth anything to me? If so, is it worth less to me than the actual price, just worth the actual price, or is it worth more than the price? Questions about, say, cleaning up oil slicks have to be understood in the same kind of way. The question is not really about willingness to pay (which could be a response to many factors that one might take into account as a citizen) but about the size of the monetary loss that one could incur without a loss of utility, provided that in return the oil slicks were to disappear.

If we think again of the chocolate bar, we can see why theoretically WTA should be close to WTP. If I would be willing to pay a maximum of forty-five pence to own a chocolate bar of some particular description, it would seem rational for me to be prepared to give up an identical chocolate bar that is in my possession so long as I receive a minimum of forty-six pence. For my utility would presumably be slightly enhanced if I obtain in return an amount of money slightly greater than the amount the chocolate bar is worth to me. The parallel question within the framework of CVM is to be understood as follows: How much money would it take to make you feel indifferent to the news that some pristine coastline had been fouled by oil, that a stand of redwoods had been destroyed, that whale hunting had been resumed, and so on?

The big practical difference between WTP and WTA is that it is less easy to misunderstand the intended import of a question about WTA. Questions about WTP can, as we have seen, be taken as questions about public action. But questions about WTA are hard to see as anything except questions about the monetary equivalent of utility loss: how many bottles of Scotch would you need to stop feeling bad about the whales?

If most people were utilitarians at heart, this difference between WTP and WTA would imply that WTA ought to be a more reliable indicator of what CVM is supposed to measure. The best evidence that most people are not utilitarians is that practitioners have been forced to abandon WTA because of the problems that have been encountered in trying to estimate it. These problems take two forms. First, many respondents—up to a half in some surveys—become very angry when asked how much they would take in return for some degradation of the environment, saying that they are not in the business of accepting bribes. Quite a few are so indignant that they throw the interviewer out as soon as the question is asked. Moreover, even when respondents are prepared to answer a question about willingness to accept, they will commonly name a sum for WTA that is a large multiple of the amount that they stated in answer to a question about WTP. Some say that it would require an infinite amount of money, or some finite but immense amount, to compensate them for losses to the environment.[29]

What is going on here? Plausibly, the answer is that the respondents are refusing to accept that their views on environmental policy are being appropriately elicited by asking them what they would need to compensate them personally for the loss of utility that they would feel from either experiencing or simply knowing about some degradation of the environment. What they want to be asked is for their views as citizens about the right environmental policy. In refusing to answer questions about WTA or naming enormous sums, they are expressing their rejection of the whole approach. They do not want to be turned into pseudo-consumers, providing information about their own utility functions to go into a cost–benefit analysis. Rather, they want to state their convictions about the right thing to do.

Because of the very large discrepancy between average WTA and average WTP, adepts of CVM have tended to propose that WTP should be used in lieu of WTA, even where WTA is the theoretically appropriate measure. This is, of course, good news for those who have an interest in lowering the quality of the environment, since average WTA can be more than ten times the size of average WTP.[30] But it is in any case extremely questionable that WTP measures what it would have to for CVM to work as advertised, at any rate in most of its uses.

The qualification introduced above is designed to accommodate uses of WTP that ask about willingness to pay for some good or service that can be sold to individuals. Thus, for example, WTP has been employed to find out how much people would pay as an entry fee to a public park. This is in principle no different from the market research that a firm might carry out before introducing a new variety of chocolate bar. Even here, it is true, there may be some difficulty in getting people to focus on the questions being asked, which is the maximum they would pay rather than give up a visit to the park. They may instead, it has been suggested, ask themselves what would be a fair price, based on charges for comparable amenities elsewhere. 'Thus, while they may in fact have a true WTP of $13 for a particular amenity, they may bid less than this amount if their view of a maximum fair entrance fee is $10 or $7 or $5 etc.'[31] Thus, even here people are liable to 'contaminate' the results by responding as citizens rather than simply reporting the monetary equivalents of their utilities. However, the question is at least intelligible, since people are familiar with paying money for a good or service.

The standard use of WTP is not like this. Rather, people are asked what they would be willing to pay for some public good (in the broadest sense). The questions they should really be asking themselves in order to produce the kind of answer needed by a cost–benefit analysis would run along these lines: 'Suppose that the coast of Alaska could be cleaned up for $10 would I be willing to pay it? What about $20?' And so on. This is, obviously, an extremely artificial—and wildly counterfactual—question. People realize perfectly well that cleaning up the Alaskan beaches would cost millions of dollars. They therefore turn the question into the more natural one: 'What would you be willing to contribute to the total cost?'

To provide a sensible answer to that question, it would be necessary to have an estimate of the total cost and to decide what group of people should pay (Alaskans? Americans? Americans and Canadians? Everybody in the world?) Then, it would be necessary to invent a fair tax system for raising the money from among the group, and work out one's contribution under it. The question could then be restated as:

would I be willing to pay that amount, on the assumption that all those in the appropriate group were also paying their fair share?

Since this is not the question that the practitioners of CVM want people to ask, respondents are provided with none of the information relevant to answering it. This means that none of them has any idea of the answer. It is not therefore surprising that they tend to seize the only clue available: the first figure mentioned (e.g. $10) or the range of amounts offered to choose from on a 'bidding card' (e.g. $10 to $50). When respondents orient themselves to the starting point this is called 'starting point bias', and when they orient themselves to the midpoint of the range they are offered this is referred to as 'anchoring'. These phenomena are commonly regarded as presenting technical problems, to be solved by some ingenious 'fix'. But the problems are far deeper.

Daniel Kahneman has proposed 'a hypothetical reconstruction of the thinking that a respondent may do in answering a valuation question. They ask whether I would be willing to pay $25 to clean up the lake. I have no idea, really, but $25 is probably a number that divides the population about equally. What I do know about myself is that I seem to feel (more/less) strongly than many other people on environmental issues . . . I feel the government isn't doing enough . . . or there are too many environmentalist crazies blocking economic progress for the sake of fish and ducks. The initial Yes or No could well be determined in this manner and the magnitude of the anchoring bias suggests that it often is.'[32]

Strong evidence for the essentially symbolic nature of the responses to questions about WTP is provided by research carried out by Kahneman with a colleague. This shows that responses are subject to what he calls 'embedding'. Thus, for example, he found that respondents in a survey were willing to pay little more for a cleanup of all the lakes in Ontario than for a cleanup of lakes in just one part of Ontario.[33] Kahneman suggests that 'people seem to answer such questions as if they had been asked "What do you want to do about keeping fish in our lakes?" and "How important is the issue to you?" The dollar number merely expresses the strength of the feeling that is aroused by these questions. Because the questions all elicit symbolic expressions of the same attitude, there is not much difference between the numbers that are attached to a single region and to all of Ontario.'[34]

For anyone who does not endorse a conception of the good as want-satisfaction, attempting to settle the fate of the snail darter by assigning it an existence value is, as Mark Sagoff has said, failing to distinguish between 'the competition of preferences and the contradiction of ideas'.[35] But this, it may be observed, is exactly the same objection as was made in the previous section to treating votes as expressions of preference. As I argued there, non-utilitarians who voted against the dam because they thought the snail-darter should be saved would deny that their object was to express the amount of gratification they would personally lose if the snail-darter were exterminated. Rather, they would say that they were recording their view about the right public policy. Similarly, those who rejected the cost–benefit framework would deny that their case against the dam was that they would lose private gratification from the extinction of the snail-darter. And this would explain their refusal to cooperate with attempts to measure that loss of gratification by asking a WTA question, or their converting a WTP question into one about their views on the right public policy to be pursued.

In the case of voting, my argument had to be purely conceptual. I could establish that there was an independent rationale of voting based on justice as impartiality. But, since this led to the same institutions as a conception of the good as want-satisfaction, there was no way of demonstrating that this alternative had widespread support. In contrast, the attempt to measure existence values is unequivocally utilitarian in inspiration. We can therefore deduce from the widespread rejection of this attempt the widespread rejection of a conception of the good as want-satisfaction.

CHAPTER 7

Justifying impartial justice

25. Introduction

I can best introduce the topic of this chapter by presenting in summary form the relevant points that have emerged from the preceding two. If we start, then, from the problem posed by the irreducible plurality of conceptions of the good, we can say that utilitarianism and justice as impartiality offer alternative solutions. Both purport to provide a generally acceptable basis for bringing diverse conceptions of the good into relation with one another by putting them on an equal footing. Utilitarianism reduces them to a lowest common denominator by treating them all as giving rise to wants, which are then given equal value *qua* wants regardless of their origins in different conceptions of the good. A utilitarian doctrine based on want-satisfaction as a conception of the good assesses outcomes according to their prospects of maximizing aggregate want-satisfaction. Rules of justice and constitutional arrangements are then to be assessed by asking how well their expected outcomes fare on the utilitarian criterion. Principles have a purely derivative status and are to be judged in the same way.

Justice as impartiality does not have any system for turning conceptions of the good into something else in order to bring them into relation with one another. Nor does it have a calculus for estimating the value of all outcomes according to a common measure. How, then, does it put different conceptions of the good on an equal footing while leaving their status as conceptions of the good intact? It does so by insisting that, at the point where the basic principles and rules are being drawn up, no conception of the good should be given a privileged position. Putting the same idea less abstractly, we may say that nobody is to be allowed to assert the superiority of his own conception of the good over those of other people as a reason for building into the framework for social cooperation special advantages for it. This will not prevent people from pursuing their own conception of the good, in public life as well as in private, but it will mean that they can do so only by means—casting votes, spending money, and exercising rights, for example—that are available to others on the same terms within a neutral constitutional framework.

Thus, public policy will in many matters reflect some conception of the good by, for example, preserving ancient monuments and historical buildings, protecting areas of natural beauty from development, subsidizing the arts, and so on. Similarly, decisions about what the publicly run schools are going to teach must obviously involve a view about the value of learning some things rather than others. (So must the imposition of minimum scholastic standards on private education.) It would be absurd to suggest that there is some way of determining a curriculum that is neutral between all conceptions of the good, and it is significant that those who support the idea of legislative (as against constitutional) neutrality have never attempted to lay out a neutral curriculum.[a] The requirements of neutrality here are procedural: that decisions should be open to public debate, capable of being defended by rational arguments, and so on.

Utilitarianism and justice as impartiality both therefore have an answer to MacIntyre's charge of resting upon a partisan conception of the good. Justice as impartiality does not rest on any conception of the good at all, so the issue simply does not arise for it. But a utilitarian can also reject MacIntyre's charge. For he could accept that he does indeed have a distinctive conception of the good but deny that it is partisan, precisely because it has a way of reducing all substantive conceptions of the good to a single currency of want-satisfaction. I do not believe that MacIntyre ever explains exactly what would be wrong with a defence along these lines: he seems to regard its inadequacy as self-evident. Nevertheless, it is possible to show why it won't do. The key point is that utilitarianism requires people to accept a way of regarding their own conceptions of the good that they could quite reasonably find repugnant.

---

[a] Absurd or not, the notion of neutrality has been invoked by the partisans of so-called 'creationist science' in the United States to argue that the Darwinian theory of evolution should be taught as a mere hypothesis and forced to share equal time with the theory that the species were created in succession by God. On the same basis it might as well be urged that the National Science Foundation's budget for astronomy should be split into two, with half going to astrology. For the purposes of both teaching and research, the consensus of the scientific community is precisely what government within a neutral constitutional system should defer to. See Stephen Holmes, 'Gag Rules or the Politics of Omission', pp. 19–58 of Jon Elster and Rune Slagstad, eds., *Constitutionalism and Democracy* (Cambridge: Cambridge University Press, 1988), esp. p. 55.

Let me illustrate this by going back to the example introduced in the previous chapter. Suppose that someone has an ecocentric conception of the good but also accepts that public policy disagreements should be settled according to the utilitarian criterion. Then he is committed to saying that it is right to build the dam which will be the nemesis of the snail darter if it is determined that aggregate want-satisfaction will thereby be increased, according to some measuring device such as voting or cost–benefit analysis. Assuming that his ecocentric conception of the good leads him to the conclusion that building the dam is the wrong thing to do, his endorsing the utilitarian conclusion is surely tantamount to giving it up. For he is saying, in effect, that when it comes down to it what really matters is not the integrity of the ecosphere but the satisfaction of human wants. To say that he can keep his conception of the good, but only on condition that the conclusions he reaches on the basis of it are to be treated as wants and aggregated with other people's wants, is really saying that he cannot keep it.[b]

Let us concede that the kind of neutrality generated by utilitarianism cannot save it from the charge of being partisan. Can the kind of neutrality inherent in justice as impartiality avoid that charge? That is the question I shall address in this chapter. I hope that I have already refuted MacIntyre's claim that the reason for its being a fraud is that it has a partisan conception of the good. But I am not interested in scoring debating points. Even if MacIntyre's charge falls as stated, he might still be on to something in complaining that justice as impartiality is partisan. It could then be concluded that it is indeed a fraud, even if not the kind of fraud alleged by MacIntyre.

To probe this question further, let me go back to the beginning of Chapter 5, where I introduced MacIntyre's attack on justice as impartiality (Section 18). I conceded there that it was a controversial doctrine and I cited as an example of this that it was incompatible with unreconstructed Thomism. For an unreconstructed Thomist would not be prepared to have Thomism treated as one conception of the good among many. Rather, he would insist that the truth of Thomism should be

---

[b] The advantage claimed by Arneson (Section 22) for utilitarianism in the form that takes want-satisfaction as the good turns out to be double-edged. Arneson says that it enables each person to insert into the utility calculus his own preferences, whatever they may be. But in fact a utilitarian society would be generally acceptable only if there were a great deal of uniformity in the kinds of thing that its members wanted. Thus, it could work if each person thought that all that mattered to him were his own pains and pleasures. It would not then be unreasonable to accept that, for public purposes, what should count was everybody's pains and pleasures. Bentham's strong hostility to Christianity (the only politically significant form of religion in Britain at the time) was not a detachable feature of his utilitarianism: unlike some of his modern followers, he realized that the whole scheme would be subverted by the inclusion of otherworldly interests.

taken as the starting place, and that the proper basis for a constitution and rules of justice should be the tenets of Thomist doctrine. Before he could be accommodated within the framework of justice as impartiality, he would have to be prepared to drop the demand that Thomism should be given a privileged position on the basis of its truth. But why should he agree to be reconstructed in such a way?

One possible answer is that he need not be reconstructed at all. He can continue to believe that Thomism contains the truth, and that it would be legitimate to impose it. But prudential arguments can be offered for his nevertheless embracing justice as impartiality. One such argument is that imposing Thomism, if it could be done at all, could be achieved only at a high cost of turmoil and bloody resistance. Another argument is that, if the rules of the game permit any group to impose its conception of the good on the whole society so long as it has enough power to do so, Thomism may well turn out to be on the losing end. Rather than take this risk, it may be urged, the path of prudence lies in endorsing justice as impartiality on condition that other groups with significant power do likewise.

Arguments of this nature were of great importance in establishing a practice of (at any rate partial) religious toleration in Europe from the sixteenth century on. They are perfectly good arguments as far as they go. But their scope is manifestly limited. Ultimately, they rest on an appeal to justice as mutual advantage. I pointed out in Section 7 that, under conditions of approximately equal power, justice as impartiality could be seen with some plausibility as offering terms on which agreement might be reached by people committed to pursuing their own conceptions of the good. The reason I put forward was that it might be seen as giving each of the parties more than they could hope to achieve by fighting it out, once the costs of fighting were counted in. The first argument for toleration, which urges the advantage of peace over war or repression, is simply an application of this. The second argument, which is designed to appeal to those who give little weight to the costs of conflict, still proposes religious toleration as a mutually advantageous deal. Here, the reason offered is that the gains to be hoped for in going for a favourable outcome are outweighed by the risks of getting a less favourable one. Toleration thus emerges as a maximin strategy.

An appeal to mutual advantage might suffice to resolve a stand-off between two well-entrenched religious groups. But it is apparent that justice as impartiality goes far beyond anything that could be underwritten by such considerations of mutual advantage. Protestants and Catholics might agree to set their differences aside and allow freedom of worship, and then combine to condemn homosexuals to death amid appalling torments—as they did in parts of Western Europe in the seventeenth and eighteenth centuries. The point of justice as impartiality is that powerless minorities should be protected as well as groups that are able to look after themselves. Pragmatic arguments cannot succeed in making the case for justice as impartiality as a general approach, though they may under favourable conditions lead to certain specific conclusions that would also be endorsed by justice as impartiality.

26. The Agreement Motive

In this section I shall offer a general argument designed to give a reason for voluntarily constraining the pursuit of the good within the limits set by justice as impartiality. If my claims are justifiable, this reason will be equally compelling regardless of the nature of the conception of the good held. In another way, however, my pretensions fall short of universality. This arises because my argument presupposes the existence of certain desire: the desire to live in a society whose members all freely accept its rules of justice and its major institutions. Given the existence of that desire, the reason for observing the constraints of impartial justice is that it sets out the only terms upon which there is any hope of reaching agreement. To the extent that the major institutions conform to the demands of justice as impartiality they are legitimate. This means that the members of the society can justifiably demand the cooperation of others in maintaining those institutions.

Now consider a society whose institutions are more favourable to some conception (or conceptions) of the good and less favourable to others than justice requires. The greater the degree that this is so, the less can those who stand to benefit from such arrangements reasonably expect the others to acquiesce freely in them, and the more the stability of the society will have to depend on the repression of a disaffected minority. Thus, justice as impartiality requires that all religious organizations should face a set of uniform laws. This means for example that they should be treated in the same way for tax purposes and that their applications for building permits should be assessed by the same criteria. Then it must be the case that, if some religious group is treated more favourably than this (by being given special tax breaks or exemption from the usual planning requirements), the rest are being treated less than equally, even if they are treated the same as non-religious organizations. Of course, if some religious groups are treated more favourably than non-religious groups and others less favourably (perhaps by actually being refused permission to build places of worship at all), the argument is completely straightforward. My point is that, even in less blatant cases than these, we can still show relative disadvantage, taking the requirements of impartial justice as a baseline.ᶜ

What I have called 'the agreement motive' plays a central role in contemporary arguments for justice as impartiality in all its forms. Consider, first, the Scanlonian variant. The people in a Scanlonian original position are assumed to be motivated by the desire to find terms for living together that could not reasonably be rejected by other people who were similarly motivated (see Section 11). But why should we— flesh and blood people—take any interest in the terms on which the people in such a hypothetical situation would reach agreement? Scanlon's answer runs as follows. 'According to contractualism, the source of motivation that is directly triggered by the belief that an action is wrong is the desire to be able to justify one's actions to others on grounds they could not reasonably reject.'¹ Scanlon adds a little later that 'the desire to be able to justify one's actions (and institutions) on grounds one takes to be acceptable is quite strong in most people. People are willing to go to considerable lengths, involving quite heavy sacrifices, in order to avoid admitting the unjustifiability of their actions and institutions.'²

Thus, a Scanlonian society would be one in which the institutions could be justified to everybody and would therefore be freely acceptable to everybody. And the criterion for a justifiable institution is nonrejectability in a Scanlonian original position—that is to say, one with the motivations, information conditions and decision rules stipulated by Scanlon. We can therefore see how there is a direct connection between on one side the test for a rule or institution's meeting the demands of justice as impartiality and on the other side the motivation that, on Scanlon's account, people in real life have for observing the constraints imposed by impartial justice.

What about Rawls, whom I am taking as the other exemplar of justice as impartiality? There is no question that Rawls has always attached great significance to agreement. The fundamental argument for the

ᶜ We must, of course, keep a sense of proportion. The advantages of establishment enjoyed by the Church of England or by the Lutheran Church in Sweden are scarcely on a scale as to lead anyone to feel seriously discriminated against. In contrast, denying the vote to Roman Catholics or requiring subscription to the Church of England as a condition of entry to Oxford or Cambridge did constitute a serious source of grievance. Strict adherence to justice as impartiality would, no doubt, be incompatible with the existence of an established church at all. But departures from it are venial so long as nobody is put at a significant disadvantage, either by having barriers put in the way of worshipping according to the tenets of his faith or by having his rights and opportunities in other matters (politics, education, occupation, for example) materially limited on the basis of his religious beliefs.

principles of justice—from *A Theory of Justice* until the present—has always been that they form a basis (and perhaps the only one) of agreement among people with divergent conceptions of the good. Thus, he says in *A Theory of Justice* that 'it is partly' in order to reach 'the greatest convergence of opinion' that 'we accept the constraints of a common standpoint, since we cannot reasonably expect our views to fall into line when they are affected by the contingencies of our different circumstances'.[3] He goes on to emphasize that 'the numerous simplifications of justice as fairness'[4] are justified by their role in making agreement more feasible. The hope of the parties in the original position is that, by settling for two relatively simple principles lexicographically ordered, they will succeed in 'simplify[ing] political and social questions so that the resulting balance of justice, made possible by the greater consensus, outweighs what may have been lost by ignoring certain potentially relevant aspects of moral situations.'[5] Thus, the requirement that the principles of justice should form the publicly acknowledged charter of a society sets limits on how complex they can be.

Before moving on, I want to discuss one more theorist who places this motive in a central position in his work. This is Charles Larmore, whose book, *Patterns of Moral Complexity*, contains a much-cited argument for neutrality between conceptions of the good.[6] I shall be assessing his argument later in this chapter (Section 28). For the present purpose, I shall focus on just one aspect: the way in which it relies on an overt appeal to the agreement motive. Larmore starts from a proposal about the way in which a conversation can be kept going in the face of disagreement between the parties. 'When two parties disagree,' he says, 'they can adopt a neutral stance by setting aside, for the time being, the opinions in dispute and continuing to converse on the basis of the rest of their beliefs. The sensible strategy for achieving neutrality is not to assume that the conflicting views will themselves share some common denominator. . . . Instead, the strategy is to *abstract from* what is in dispute.'[7] This manifestly presupposes that the parties do want to reach agreement, by some means or other. (These means, it is clear, are not to include coercion: what Larmore assumes is a search for free, unforced agreement.)

Larmore concedes that the 'retreat to neutral ground' may need to be only temporary. Although, as he says, the existence of common ground cannot be assumed, we are not entitled to assume that it cannot exist. The parties may, he suggests, be able to find shared premises from which they can resolve their disagreement and arrive at the same substantive conclusions.[8] Larmore does not offer any examples of the way in which this process might work, but it is not hard to think of some.

Suppose, for example, that we have common standards of biblical inter-pretation and start from an acceptance of Christianity in broad outline. Then we may be able to resolve some specific doctrinal dispute by his-torical or textual arguments from shared premises. Another example might be drawn from moral argumentation. I may be able to convince you that some particular conclusion to which you are strongly attached is incompatible with the conception of the good that you claim to hold. If this conclusion can be derived from my conception of the good, I may be able to convince you that you should abandon yours and adopt mine.

It is true and important that conceptions of the good are open to argument along lines such as these. Conceptions of the good are com-plex systems of belief and open to rational argument. We must resist any temptation (always liable to be pressed on us by economists and utilitarians) to treat them as 'preferences', of the same underlying nature as a taste for strawberry ice cream. Nevertheless, it is hard to challenge Larmore's conclusion that 'to a large extent these conflicts about the nature of the good life will remain unresolved'. (I shall offer support for this view in the next section.) To the extent that this is so, Larmore argues, the retreat to neutral ground will require that the parties 'elabo-rate principles of state action upon this neutral basis itself, without resolving that dispute [about the nature of the good life]'.[9] Thus, 'the norm of rational conversation would serve to shape a political culture in which the public could continue to discuss disputed views about the good life with the hope of expanding the scope of agreement, but in which it would also agree that the state's decisions cannot be justified by an appeal to the intrinsic superiority of any such view that remains disputed'.[10]

Larmore makes no attempt to suggest what principles might emerge from the retreat to 'neutral ground'. And he accepts that neutrality may offer 'too weak a basis for deriving any political principles that assign basic liberties and distribute wealth'.[11] He suggests that there is a satis-factory answer to be had along the lines that 'neutrality should be made more restrictive until a decision does become possible'.[12] The 'least restriction' might, he says, be sought by 'admit[ting] beliefs that are the least central to anyone's idea of the good life, or . . . admit[ting] beliefs that the least number of people do not hold.'[13] I agree that restrictions are needed, but I believe that they are to be looked for in the specifica-tion of the Scanlonian original position. What cannot be accepted is that agreement should be stymied by objections based on misinformation or objections that are unreasonable because, for example, they are based upon nothing but the self-interest of the speaker.

Larmore cites with approval the Habermasian notion that 'to put forward our claim to others in the actual conversation as a claim backed up by good reasons is to assert, in effect, that these good reasons should command the assent of others.'[14] This idea is also at the core of Scanlon's theory: 'If I believe that a certain principle, *P*, could not reasonably be rejected as a basis for informed, unforced general agreement, then I must believe not only that it is something which it would be reasonable for me to accept but something which it would be reasonable for others to accept as well, insofar as we are all seeking a ground for general agreement.'[15] But Larmore does nothing with the notion, which accounts for his pessimism about the possibility of arriving at definite conclusions about basic liberties and the distribution of wealth. I contend that, if the idea of good reasons is fleshed out on Scanlonian lines, the problem of indeterminacy can be solved—to the degree that it is sensible to expect it to be solved (see Section 16).

27. The Need for Scepticism

The argument developed so far has three elements. It presupposes the existence of a desire to reach agreement with others on terms that nobody could reasonably reject. The argument then proceeds by suggesting that no conception of the good provides a basis for agreement on terms that nobody could reasonably reject. Neutrality of the kind defended in the previous chapter therefore appears as the solution to the agreement problem. In the rest of this chapter I want to see what can be said to strengthen the case.

I do not think that the agreement motive presents a serious problem. The desire to be able to justify actions and institutions in terms that are in principle acceptable to others is, fortunately, widespread. I should, at any rate, be more than happy if I could persuade everybody who possesses this motive that acting on it has the practical implications that I claim it has. To do that, however, I have to be able to make the case that only conclusions of the kind I advance are (reasonably) acceptable. That is, quite plainly, a formidable task.

The essence of the problem is this. Suppose that somebody accepts the burden of public justification but says that his own conception of the good provides a basis for a society's major institutions that every reasonable person should be prepared to accept. This, and not the blank denial of any concern for the reasonableness of one's claims, is the threat to justice as impartiality that must be taken seriously. I do not intend to deny, of course, that people who hold the idea of reasonableness in contempt have to be taken seriously. But the only response worth making is to try to defeat them politically and, if necessary, seek to repress them by force.

The position on which I propose to focus is by no means hypothetical. As we have seen, a persistent strand in utilitarianism is the claim that it provides a basis on which reasonable people should be able to agree. And the tradition of natural law thinking has at its core the idea that the contents of the natural law are in principle accessible to human reason. (It is held to be simply an odd coincidence that the only people who find this plausible happen to be Roman Catholics.) What response can be made? The only one that seems to me adequate is to deny that there is any conception of the good that nobody could reasonably reject. If this can be made out, it follows that reasonable terms must be terms that do not presuppose the correctness of any conception of the good.

How, then, are we to establish that there is no conception of the good that nobody could reasonably reject? The answer that I wish to defend is that no conception of the good can justifiably be held with a degree of certainty that warrants its imposition on those who reject it. I shall dub this the argument from scepticism. I confess that, to anyone steeped in ancient philosophy, 'scepticism' may well have more negative connotations than I intend, suggesting that belief is ill-founded rather than (as I wish to maintain) that certainty is ill-founded. However, I should like to claim that my use of 'scepticism' corresponds to that in everyday speech, where the central idea is that of doubt rather than denial.[d]

How can the case for scepticism be made out? I am inclined to think that there is a strong a priori argument for the inherent uncertainty of all conceptions of the good. Any chain of reasoning of this sort is, however, open to the objection by a dogmatist that it is too speculative to overcome his powerful sense of being privy to the truth. I therefore prefer to appeal to experience. In doing so I am simply recapitulating the basic argument for scepticism as it was developed in the sixteenth and seventeenth centuries.

The idea that public authority should not be thrown behind any conception of the good took its rise from the narrower claim that attempts to enforce religious orthodoxy should be abandoned. The case for

[d] Perhaps the most historically accurate term would be 'latitudinarianism'. According to Barbara J. Shapiro in her *Probability and Certainty in Seventeenth-Century England* (Princeton, NJ: Princeton University Press, 1983), 'the latitudinarians attempted to take a position somewhere between skepticism and dogmatism. They rejected the skeptical position which denied the possibility of any knowledge. They also rejected a zealous dogmatism which was overly confident in opinions that lacked adequate certainty and which, given the opportunity, would impose its opinions on others' (p. 110).

religious toleration arose out of the intractability of the conflicts between Catholics and Protestants in post-Reformation Europe. It became evident that there was no prospect whatever of one side or the other simply converting the members of the other by a process of rational argument, thus establishing religious harmony. Even legally prescribed penalties—civil, political, financial, and in extreme cases physical—proved remarkably ineffective in producing a genuine and lasting change in beliefs. Nothing much short of mass expulsion or genocide could be counted on with any reliability to restore orthodoxy to a society in which religious divisions had become well-established. Freedom of religion (to begin with extended perhaps only to Christians or to believers in a god of some description) appealed as a humane practical response to the situation.[e]

We should not, of course, assume that the experience of Europe in the sixteenth and seventeenth centuries is typical. The issues at stake in the conflict surrounding the Reformation and Counter-reformation were, after all, to a large extent ones involving organizational forms and in particular the location of religious authority. That these issues proved recalcitrant to rational persuasion need not show that broader questions of religious belief could not be resolved. If we extend the scope of our inquiry we shall, indeed, find a good deal of voluntary religious conversion in history. But it would be hard to establish any pattern suggesting a direction towards which conversions tend.

In as far as there is a pattern to be discerned, it appears to me to be one in which people change religions for two kinds of reason external to the intrinsic truth or falsity of either the religion they leave or the religion they join. One is the desire for individual social advancement, economic advantage, or political emancipation. One example is the conversion of many Jews in Germany and Austria in the eighteenth and nineteenth centuries to Christianity. Another more trivial example is the American phenomenon of 'trading up' denominations (e.g. from Baptist to Presbyterian or Episcopalian) in keeping with rising status aspirations. The other reason for converting, which is basically similar but can

---

[e] For someone who is otherwise sensitive to the historical development of traditions, it has to be said that MacIntyre is strangely myopic in his treatment of liberalism. Anyone who knew nothing about the matter except what MacIntyre has to say about it would come away with the impression that liberalism was simply willed into existence quite gratuitously by something called 'the Enlightenment'. In as far as it could be said to have any driving force behind it, this was what MacIntyre calls 'the Enlightenment project': the desire to deduce all morality from the bare notion of rationality as such, rather than this or that historically conditioned conception of rationality. (See Alasdair MacIntyre, *Whose Justice? Which Rationality?* (Notre Dame, Ind.: University of Notre Dame Press, 1988), 334–5.) This account simply ignores the role played by the religious conflicts that accompanied and followed the Reformation.

work on a mass scale, is the desire to associate oneself with a more sophisticated or at any rate more powerful culture. Taking the religion of a certain culture is a relatively easy way of asserting an identification with it—much easier than acquiring a mastery of its literature or its science, for example. Islam in earlier times (and still in parts of west Africa) and Christianity in more recent times have both been beneficiaries of this tendency.

All this is, I need hardly say, very superficial. Nevertheless, the sheer weight of the evidence in favour of scepticism seems overwhelming. It is hard not to be impressed by the fact that so many people have devoted so much effort over so many centuries to a matter of the greatest moment with so little success in the way of securing rational conviction among those not initially predisposed in favor of their conclusions. MacIntyre may, of course, think that this was true before he came along but that now things are different. I have to say, however, that I shall be surprised if *Whose Justice? Which Rationality?* makes as many converts to Thomism as Peter Singer's *Animal Liberation* has to vegetarianism.[16]

I assume that, if the case for scepticism can be made out for religiously based conceptions of the good, it will *a fortiori* hold for other conceptions. Thus, to give a personal example, I am myself quite strongly attracted to an ecocentric ethic and would favour sacrificing a good deal of human want-satisfaction (especially if the sacrifice were equitably distributed) in the pursuit of the ecological conception of the good. I think that arguments can be made for it by showing as vividly as possible the implications of following it or not and by appealing to a kind of sentiment that is ultimately, I believe, of the same nature as that which supports many religions. But I do not see how its claims can be presented in such a way as to show that it would be unreasonable to adopt a different view, and I take it that any other conception of the good is subject to the same liability.

A pat response to this argument for scepticism is that, in the last analysis, scepticism is on all fours with dogmatism. If you are imbued with faith, you will reject scepticism; if you have a sceptical turn of mind you will reject certainties: that is all there is to be said for it. Now, I am not engaged in prophecy, so I do not wish to claim that dogmatists *will* be persuaded of the case for scepticism. I am even prepared to concede that there has recently been something of a turn to the comforts of dogmatism in a number of parts of the world. But I do wish to assert that, whether or not dogmatists are actually convinced by the case for scepticism, they ought to be. For the impression that there are two positions—scepticism on one side and dogmatism on the other—is misleading.

What we really have is scepticism on one side and a host of conflicting dogmatisms on the other. These dogmatisms cancel one another out, in a manner of speaking. Each dogmatist can be confronted with other people who are equally dogmatic but hold something quite different from him. He has to explain why they are all wrong to be certain about what they believe in while he is right to be certain about what he believes in. And the others all have to do the same. The sceptic is in the happy position of agreeing with each about 99 per cent of what he maintains, that is to say the inherent lack of certitude in everybody else's beliefs. He disagrees with each only at the point where he maintains that his own beliefs provide the unique exception to what he claims to be the case for everybody else's.

It has often been pointed out, quite correctly, that from scepticism alone nothing follows in the way of political principles, including the principle of neutrality. Scepticism of the strong kind that reduces all normative statements to expressions of personal preference obviously undermines the possibility of putting forward any political principles with claims to general allegiance.[f] But it is equally true that nothing follows immediately from the kind of moderate scepticism I am espousing here. There is nothing to prevent anybody from accepting that his conception of the good could reasonably be rejected by others and saying 'All the same, I'll pursue it as hard as I can'. More seriously, there is nothing to prevent a majority in a society who share a certain conception of the good from taking the same line and making it the basis of the society's institutions. It is only when moderate scepticism is combined with a commitment to finding reasonable terms of agreement that it generates neutrality.

I have been arguing that scepticism supplies the premise that is needed to get from the desire for agreement on reasonable terms to the conclusion that no conception of the good should be built into the constitution or the principles of justice. But the claim that I wish to make is not simply that this premise can do the job: I also maintain that it is the only one that can. I do not see any way of establishing the correctness of this claim by a general argument. What I shall therefore do in the rest

---

[f] This rather tired argument is revived, for example, by Susan Mendus in her *Toleration and the Limits of Liberalism* (see n. 51), who says (p. 78) that liberal conclusions can be defended morally only on the basis of some 'values'. It is a tautology that complete scepticism undermines the attempt to defend anything. It is in fact clear from her discussion that none of the people she mentions as sceptics (pp. 75–8) were sceptical about *all* values. The seventeenth-century sceptics she cites were (on her own account) attached to the value of civil order, while the argument from scepticism to neutrality that she quotes from Bruce Ackerman's *Social Justice in the Liberal State* (New Haven: Yale University Press, 1980) very clearly rests on an egalitarian ethical premise. (It is closely related to the 'conversational' line of argument developed by Larmore.)

of this chapter is support my claim by showing that alternative premises that have been put forward in recent years either presuppose scepticism or can be made coherent only if taken to entail scepticism. Needless to say, even if I am right about the failure of these attempts to come up with an alternative to scepticism, that does not prove the non-existence of an alternative. All I can say is that it carries the argument as far as it can at present be carried.

28. *Equal Respect*

In this section I shall take up Charles Larmore's suggestion that neutrality follows from a commitment to 'equal respect'. In the next section I shall examine an argument put forward by Thomas Nagel deriving neutrality from 'epistemological restraint'. Nagel has subsequently repudiated this argument—without replacing it by another. I shall seek to show that there is nothing wrong with it once it is made consistent. But making it consistent, I shall argue, brings it into line with my argument from scepticism. In the final section, I shall take up the case of Rawls, who has been claimed by Nagel (probably correctly) as an adherent of the view that he has now himself renounced.

I have already laid out the initial move in Larmore's theory in Section 26. What I want to concentrate on here is the way in which Larmore proposes to get from the idea of a withdrawal to common ground to the conclusion that agreement will be obtainable on a basis of neutrality between conceptions of the good. I shall argue that his case depends upon a covert reliance upon scepticism, in the sense of the word that I defined in the previous section.

Before coming to that, I shall look at Larmore's own discussion of scepticism. Apparently, Larmore's view is that scepticism can be deployed validly to underwrite neutrality.[17] However, scepticism as he understands it seems to me to lead not to the kind of neutrality that he wants to defend (which is the kind I am defending) but to the kind inherent in utilitarianism. Thus, he takes scepticism to entail that 'when ideals clash, . . . there is no reason to prefer any of them, and so no government should seek to institutionalize them'.[18] The natural development of this line of thought would be to conclude that it does not make any difference what conception of the good people pursue. But then it would seem that there is no particular reason for favouring neutrality between conceptions of the good. If there is nothing to choose between conceptions of the good, what objection could there be to the government's picking one (perhaps at random, even) and enforcing it?

Some additional premise is needed in order to get from scepticism as Larmore defines it to neutrality. But the premise that is most often supplied here leads not to the neutrality of justice as impartiality but rather to the kind of neutrality created by the utilitarian calculus. The crucial move is to say that conceptions of the good are purely 'subjective', and hence should be regarded as 'preferences'. If we then add that value should be attributed to the satisfaction of preferences, we have an argument from scepticism to utilitarianism. (See the discussion of Richard Arneson's argument along these lines in Section 22 above.) But it is apparent that the sceptical premise (in Larmore's sense of 'scepticism') cannot by itself establish the value of want-satisfaction: that is itself a (second-order) conception of the good—and scepticism about *it* would be self-defeating.

Larmore's own reason for rejecting scepticism is curious. The context is a discussion of three 'familiar arguments' that 'invoke some view of human flourishing that can best be promoted if government maintains a neutral posture toward the variety of human aspirations'.[19] These arguments 'appeal to the values of skepticism, experimentation, or individual autonomy, respectively'.[20] And the same objection is said to apply to all three: that they embody 'controversial ideals of the good life'.[21] Now, it seems fair to say that this is true of autonomy, and I myself argued as much in Section 20. As far as the value of experimentation is concerned, I do not believe that this is really an independent conception of the good life but rather a corollary of the value of autonomy.[g] In that sense, it may also be said to embody a (controversial) conception of the good life.[22] But scepticism (either in Larmore's sense of the word or in mine) is not a 'view of human flourishing'. It is an epistemological doctrine about the status of conceptions of what constitutes human flourishing. Scepticism is, of course, a controversial view in that some people would deny it. But there is no way of avoiding the affirmation of a position that is not universally accepted if one is to get anywhere at all. My claim is that the case for scepticism cannot reasonably be rejected. I also wish to maintain that Larmore himself is unable to do without scepticism in my sense of the word.

As we have already seen, Larmore's fundamental idea is that, if two people disagree on some point, they can continue the conversation only by withdrawing to neutral ground—that is to say taking up the discus-

---

[g] Larmore's own account of autonomy suggests that the possibility of experimenting with different ways of living is essential to its exercise. For he takes a partisan of autonomy to be somebody who 'hold[s] that people cannot properly understand what it is to have a flourishing life unless they have worked out their ideal for themselves, making their own mistakes and learning from them' (pp. 51–2).

sion at points that they do agree on. Where their disagreement turns on differing conceptions of the good, they may attempt to resolve their dispute by arguing from shared convictions. But, Larmore says, any such attempt is liable to fail. Then they should agree to disagree about what divides them and endeavour to reach a mutually agreeable settlement which does not involve coming down on one side or the other. This will entail neutrality between their conceptions of the good. And, if we expand the conversation to include the holders of a wide variety of conceptions of the good, it is plausible to suppose that the only mutually acceptable basis of agreement will be one neutral between all conceptions of the good.

But why should I, as a participant in such a conversation, choose to go on to the second stage? Imagine that my interlocutor refuses to agree that the earth goes round the sun. I might consent to retreat to neutral ground—say, observations about the movements of the planets across the sky—in order to attempt to persuade him. But if that attempt were to fail, I should not willingly engage in further discussion premised on the understanding that nothing is to be assumed either way about the heliocentric hypothesis. If I thought that the proof of a certain conception of the good had the same epistemological status as that enjoyed by the Copernican theory, I would not be any more willing to seek agreement on a basis that did not presuppose its correctness.

Larmore canvasses two answers to this question. One is that there is no problem 'when those with whom we are in disagreement have views for which we nonetheless feel some sympathy'.[23] Larmore assumes that these will be people who 'stand at least close to us in their views'.[24] But it is notorious that the most bitter enmity often obtains between those who are divided only by one point of doctrine. If we feel sympathy for some view this is normally because we think there may be something in it. We accommodate it then because we have a suspicion that it may be correct. This clearly entails a quite strong degree of scepticism about our own current view. However, as Larmore rightly says, sympathy grounded in this way does not extend to anywhere enough views to underwrite general neutrality with respect to conceptions of the good.

The other answer offered by Larmore is our old friend from the first section of this chapter, the 'desire for civil peace'.[25] This is of interest because it is a motive which can under certain conditions lead to neutrality without requiring any appeal to scepticism. If the flat-earthers and the round-earthers (say) are both well-entrenched in a society, the desire for civil peace will lead to an agreement to shelve the issue, even if those engaged on one side or on both sides are convinced that their view cannot reasonably be rejected. It has to be said, however, that

Larmore is far too sanguine about the range of conditions under which the desire for civil peace will point towards neutrality. He says that 'continuing the conversation with those . . . who are powerful will in the end commit us to finding political principles of already considerable neutrality'.[26] But the desire for civil peace can be gratified by a settlement on any terms that can be enforced. Neutrality has no privileged status. Thus, it could plausibly have been put to the Albigensians that, given the balance of forces, the best way of ensuring civil peace would have been to convert to Catholicism. Larmore takes it for granted that we should want to 'continue to talk' (by retreating to neutral ground) with those who 'have enough power to make us pay attention'.[27] But if they are sufficiently powerful, they will have no need to continue to talk to us. Only if the opposing forces are evenly balanced does the desire for civil peace lead to the solution espoused by Larmore.

In the end, however, nothing crucial turns on the specific scope of either sympathy or the desire for civil peace, since Larmore concedes in any case that they leave us with the question of 'whether there exist similarly neutral reasons for continuing to talk with those who lack the power to call on our desire for civil peace and whose ideals seem quite foreign to ours'.[28] The answer offered by Larmore is 'that the neutral reason for continuing the conversation with them must lie in the wish to show everyone *equal respect*'.[29] By 'a neutral reason', Larmore means one that does not rest on any particular conception of the good life. As we have seen, Larmore claims that scepticism rests on a conception of the good life. I have denied this. What I now want to argue is that Larmore's invocation of 'equal respect' can do the job he wants it to do only in conjunction with scepticism.

Larmore tells us that 'the sense of equal respect to which [he will] appeal . . . is roughly that however much we may disagree with others and repudiate what they stand for, we cannot treat them merely as objects of our will, but owe them an explanation for those actions of ours that affect them'.[30] This is undeniably a way of motivating the desire to act in ways that can be justified to others. It is, indeed, simply a reformulation of the agreement motive discussed in Section 26. But it runs into the problem that I raised in the previous section: it does not by itself lead to the conclusion that disagreements about the good life should be resolved by a retreat to neutral ground. It is perfectly consistent with everything that Larmore says about equal respect that we should believe that the explanation required is an explanation of the superiority of our conception of the good. If we are convinced that nobody could reasonably reject our explanation, we would seem to have done all that 'equal respect' can demand of us.

Suppose we accept Larmore's assertion that 'the obligation of equal respect consists in our being obligated to treat another as he is treating us—to use his having a perspective on the world as a reason for discussing the merits of our action rationally with him (in the light of how we understand a rational discussion)'.[31] This obligation could be discharged adequately, in the absence of an additional proviso, by our putting forward what we regard as a rationally compelling argument in favour of our own conception of the good. The missing proviso is, of course, the sceptical premise introduced in the previous section. If we acknowledge that we cannot produce any such rationally compelling argument, we have to acknowledge also that it would be unreasonable to create constitutional arrangements and rules of justice based on our own conception of the good.

Larmore's idea of 'equal respect' is, then, a backing for the agreement motive. But to get the agreement motive to lead to neutrality we need a dose of scepticism. Larmore himself concludes his discussion of the case for neutrality by saying that 'the fact that lies at the heart of liberalism is that reasonable people differ and disagree about the nature of the good life'.[32] I suggest that it is only with this move that Larmore gets beyond considerations backing the agreement motive and arrives at one that begins to lead from the agreement motive to neutrality. But if it is fully developed to form a coherent argument, it has to amount to scepticism of the kind I put forward in the previous section.

29. Epistemological Restraint

The term 'epistemological restraint' was introduced by Thomas Nagel in an article published in 1987.[33] The core idea is that it is perfectly consistent to be convinced of the truth of some religious or other doctrine while acknowledging as a matter of principle that it would be wrong to make it the basis of public policy in a society some of whose members reject it. As it happens, Larmore endorses this idea in passing: he says that 'abstracting from a controversial belief does not imply that one believes it any the less, that one has had reason to become skeptical toward it. One can remain as convinced of its truth as before, but for the purposes of the conversation one sets it aside.'[34]

The problem to which epistemological restraint is proposed as a solution by Nagel is precisely that which I raised in Section 27. Liberalism, he supposes, requires that the truth of some religious belief cannot be advanced as a reason for basing a society's institutions on that belief. Within Rawls's theory, for example, this axiom is instantiated in the

178 *Justifying Impartial Justice*

denial to the people in the original position of any information about
their own religious beliefs. But how do we persuade somebody who is
convinced he has true religious beliefs to leave them at the door when
entering the original position? 'It is not sufficient,' Nagel correctly
insists, 'to exclude knowledge of one's religious beliefs from the
Original Position on the ground that this is needed to make agreement
possible.'[35] Nagel does not, as far as I can see, ever say exactly what is
wrong with an attempt to get straight from the agreement motive to
neutrality, but he concludes that 'the demand for agreement, and its priority in these cases [e.g. religious beliefs] over a direct appeal to the
truth, must be grounded in something more basic.'[36]

What is this 'something'? Nagel, like Larmore, explicitly repudiates
scepticism as the answer. 'True liberalism,' he suggests, does 'not rely on
a skeptical premise about individual belief. Rather it must depend on a
distinction between what justifies individual belief and what justifies
appealing to that belief in support of the exercise of political power.'[37]
According to Nagel, 'the distinction between what is needed to justify
belief and what is needed to justify the employment of political power
depends on a higher standard of objectivity, which is ethically based.'[38]
This could be taken as resting on what I call scepticism, even if Nagel
does not wish to call it that. For the argument that I have put forward
makes a distinction that could be expressed in the terms used by Nagel.
That is to say, I want to make a distinction between what it is reasonable to believe oneself and what it is reasonable to impose on others. It
appears, however, that Nagel would not accept the way in which I propose to work the distinction.

The nub is this. Suppose I hold a certain set of religious beliefs. Then,
on the view set forward in the previous section, I should recognize the
inherent uncertainty of these beliefs. While having enough confidence in
them to live by them, therefore, I should at the same time recognize that
others can reasonably reject them, and can reasonably reject any political
claim based directly upon their truth. Where Nagel departs from this line
of argument is in denying that acceptance of the proposition that others
could reasonably reject my views entails that I must to be consistent admit
to myself their inherent uncertainty. It is this denial that makes it accurate
to describe Nagel's proposal as 'not skepticism but a kind of epistemological restraint'.[39] Nagel puts the point as follows: 'We accept a kind of epistemological division between the private and the public domains: in
certain contexts I am constrained to consider my beliefs merely as beliefs
rather than as truths, however convinced I may be that they are true, and
that I know it. This is not the same thing as skepticism.'[40] Indeed, it is not
scepticism, in my sense or any other. But is it a sound idea?

If Nagel's distinction between the public and private domains were valid, it would underwrite the same conclusion that I invoked scepticism to reach. I could happily drop any reference to scepticism, defined as the illegitimacy of certainty. I could simply say that, however legitimately certain somebody may be of his own conception of the good, he cannot justifiably seek to impose it on others who reject it. Unfortunately, however, I do not think that the doctrine of 'epistemological restraint' is internally coherent.

The essence of Nagel's position is a very sharp distinction between what can be said about beliefs when viewed from the inside and what can be said about them when viewed from the outside. 'The idea is,' he says, 'that when we look at certain of our convictions from outside, however justified they may be from within, the appeal to their truth must be seen merely as an appeal to our beliefs, and should be treated as such unless those beliefs can be shown to be justifiable from a more impersonal standpoint.'[41] I question, however, whether certainty from the inside about some view can coherently be combined with the line that it is reasonable for others to reject that same view. The most promising case would seem to be that of a private religious revelation. Suppose that God were (as it seemed to me) to grant me a vision in which certain truths were revealed. A partisan of epistemological restraint would suggest that I might be absolutely convinced of the veridical nature of this revelation while nevertheless admitting that others could reasonably reject my evidence. But is this really plausible? If I concede that I have no way of convincing others, should that not also lead to a dent in my own certainty?

Hobbes conceded that 'God Almighty can speak to a man, by Dreams, Visions, Voice, and Inspiration.' But he added (taking up what Nagel would call the perspective from the outside) that 'yet he obliges no man to beleeve he hath so done to him that pretends it; who (being a man) may err, and (which is more) may lie'.[42] There are thus two grounds for doubting the validity of somebody else's report of a divine revelation: he may be mistaken about its status or he may simply be an impostor. If I have experienced the revelation myself, I can rule out the latter source of doubt, and this is sufficient to explain why it might be reasonable for me to reach a different conclusion from others about the genuineness of my claim to have received a true revelation. But if I am prepared to concede that others could at the same time believe that I am not simply making it up and also still reasonably reject my alleged revelation, then I must in consistency allow that I may be mistaken about its validity myself.

Now it is easy to see why, even if someone is totally convinced of my sincerity, he might still reasonably reject the claim that my inspiration is veridical. There have, after all, been many people who have claimed direct divine inspiration for some belief. Very likely some were impostors who simply made up a story to impress others. But it seems immensely plausible to suppose that many were sincere—especially when we bear in mind that a number have been prepared to undergo excruciating torments rather than repudiate their belief. Yet these revelations have had incompatible content, so they cannot all be valid. What, then, are the odds that any given sincerely believed-in revelation is true and all those incompatible with it false? The point, now, is this: if considerations such as these should move those who hear a report of a revelation, then they should move just as strongly the person who claims to have had the revelation.

Nagel makes the distinction between the inside and the outside turn on a difference in the available evidence. According to Nagel, if you make a belief of yours a basis for public policy, 'it must be possible to present to others the basis of your own beliefs, so that once you have done so, *they have what you have,* and can arrive at a judgment on the same basis'.[43] It is this requirement that Nagel asserts is violated by convictions whose 'source . . . is personal faith or revelation'.[44] But if somebody believes my report of a certain experience, he has what I have, in the only sense that is relevant. Suppose I have a pain and describe it to you with some precision (intense, throbbing, and located six inches below and to the right of the navel, say). Obviously, I still have the pain and you don't acquire it. In that sense, then, you do not have what I have. But if the issue is what causes this pain, then you do have what I have. And if you are a doctor while I am not, your view about the cause will probably be better founded than mine.

I wish to argue that there is a precise analogy between what can be said about a pain and what can be said about a religious revelation. Suppose I hear a voice in my head which claims to be that of God, or some other religious personage. If I report its content faithfully to you, then you have what I have in the relevant sense. We can both form views about the probable validity of this experience as a genuine religious revelation. In principle, there is no reason why I should be more impressed by the experience than you by my report of it, so long as you do not believe that I am deliberately deceiving you. It is a piece of information whose significance we both have to evaluate, and we may legitimately arrive at different conclusions about it. The phenomenon is perfectly general: faced with the same form books or the same meteorological data, two people can reasonably make different predictions about which horse will win or what the weather will be. This is what we mean by calling something a matter of judgement. The one thing we should agree about is that nobody is entitled to claim certainty.

Now it is undeniably true that, as a matter of fact, people are more likely to be impressed by their own experience than by the testimony of others, even if we exclude doubts about the sincerity of the deponent. We all tend to operate on the maxim that says that 'seeing is believing'. Yet psychologists have demonstrated *ad nauseam* how unreliable people's beliefs about what they have witnessed often are—even when the witnesses are absolutely convinced that they have got it right.[h] Thus, although we no doubt do have a greater propensity to be impressed by our own experiences than by reports by others of theirs (even if we rule out deliberate deception on their part), I maintain that this propensity has no rational foundation.

The upshot of the discussion so far is that, if epistemological restraint was a coherent idea, it would be an alternative to scepticism as a foundation for neutrality. But if I am correct it is not a coherent idea. Coherence requires narrowing the gap between what can be claimed 'from the inside' about the status of your own conception of the good and what can be pressed on others about the status of their conceptions where these differ from yours. This can, obviously, be achieved in two alternative ways. One is proposed by Joseph Raz. He picks up on Nagel's claim that 'however justified [some of our convictions] may be from within, the appeal to their truth must be seen merely as an appeal to our beliefs'.[45] In response to this Raz writes: 'If it is an appeal to their truth, rather than merely to their existence, from the inside, it must be recognized as such from the outside as well.'[46] If Nagel were to attain coherence by following this suggestion, he would have to drop his neutralist conclusion. Raz would himself be happy with that outcome.[47] But I have been arguing that the conclusion is right. My own suggestion is therefore that Nagel should move in the opposite direction to that proposed by Raz. He should retain the conclusion and modify epistemological restraint so that it corresponds to what I am calling scepticism.

In the event, Nagel has taken neither of these courses. He has said in a book published subsequently to the article I have been discussing that he 'no longer think[s] that "epistemological" argument works' but that

---

[h] The phenomenon of 'false memory syndrome' provides another telling illustration. Sometimes under hypnosis, adult clients are induced by 'therapists' to 'remember' incidents of childhood sexual abuse that are in some instances demonstrably impossible. Yet these 'memories' are usually believed by the 'victim' to be unquestionably veridical. 'Parent and child could take a stringent lie detector test and both would pass', Simon Hoggart, 'Tricks of Memory', *The Observer Magazine* 27 March 1994, pp. 42–5 at p. 45.

he 'still believe[s] the conclusion'.[48] But on what does the conclusion now rest? As best I can tell, Nagel wishes to appeal to a notion of 'Kantian respect', which entails respect for the beliefs of others (e.g. about matters of religion) even when one is convinced that they are false. I take this to be conceived along the same lines as Larmore's argument from 'equal respect'. I explained in the previous section why I believe this to require the addition of scepticism in order to arrive at neutralist conclusions.

With commendable but disconcerting frankness, Nagel himself concedes that the argument from equal respect is inadequate, but he seems to me to misidentify its weak point. He takes the problem to be one of persuading somebody that 'the ideal of reasonable unanimity' should prevail over 'the desire to pursue the transcendent good as one sees it'. Suppose, he says, that 'someone is willing to commit his own life to a particular conception, and convinced that the alternative is catastrophic'. Then 'it may be difficult to subordinate a concern for [the] good [of others] as he sees it to a requirement of Kantian respect, if he is really convinced that Kantian respect will allow them to doom themselves'.[49] I conceded at the beginning of Section 27 that there is no argument capable of instilling in someone who lacks it the desire to act in ways that can be justified to others. To that extent I can only share with Nagel the 'hope' that 'the ideal of reasonable unanimity . . . will be able to contain most of the disagreement that divides democratic societies, and that the forms of fanaticism which it cannot accommodate will gradually die out'.[50]

There remains, however, the problem that I identified in the previous section. Nagel appears to assume (like Larmore) that, so long as somebody adheres to 'the ideal of reasonable unanimity', this is bound to lead to an endorsement of neutrality. But there is a missing step here, as I pointed out in the previous section. For it is quite possible to accept the claims of 'equal respect' and 'the ideal of reasonable unanimity' and yet still maintain that they are compatible with the imposition of your conception of the good. All you have to do in order to arrive at this conclusion is assert that your conception of the good is one that nobody can reasonably reject. This is the move that Nagel's now discarded argument from 'epistemological restraint' was designed to block. I have suggested here that Nagel was right to discard it but wrong to think that he could still get from reasonable agreement to neutrality without something like it. My proposal is to substitute scepticism, as I define it, for 'epistemological restraint'.

The official business of this section is now concluded. Before bringing it to an end, however, I should like to address an objection that may have occurred to more than one reader. It may be felt that the argument put forward by the name of 'epistemological restraint' is not the only one that might be so described, and that there is in fact a better one to be made. This runs as follows. I may have 'a firm belief that one way of life is best' but also hold 'the equally firm belief that that way of life is valuable only if chosen freely'. Thus, 'liberals may be committed to truth in moral matters [i.e. believe that there is a truth and that they know what it is], but nevertheless think that the value of truth is less than the value of allowing people to choose for themselves.'[51] I have suggested (in Section 20) that the argument from the value of autonomy does provide a basis for liberal institutions. But my object in Part II is to seek an answer to MacIntyre's charge that justice as impartiality is a fraud because it purports to rest on neutral foundations while in reality resting upon a distinctively liberal conception of the good. Since the argument from autonomy does rest on a distinctively liberal conception of the good, it does not represent a form of 'epistemological restraint' that is relevant in the present context.

30. The Case of Rawls

In Section 26, I showed that the agreement motive plays a central role in Rawls's argument for the principles of justice. But how does he negotiate the move from the premise that we must look for an acceptable basis for agreement to the conclusion that no conception of the good can function as the basis for agreement? In his article advocating 'epistemological restraint' as the foundation of neutrality, Thomas Nagel enlists Rawls as a fellow adherent.[52] However, the passage that he quotes from *A Theory of Justice* does not seem to me to advance his case. Nagel simply assumes that, since Rawls does invoke the agreement motive and does arrive at neutrality, he must be appealing to epistemological restraint.[53] But this cannot be assumed.

It is true that Rawls says in *A Theory of Justice* that the case for liberty of conscience does not 'imply skepticism in philosophy or indifference to religion'.[54] More recently he has expressed what I take to be the same idea by saying that 'skepticism *and* indifference to religious, philosophical, and moral values' is a less adequate basis for his principles of justice than the appeal that he now favours to 'overlapping consensus'.[55] (I shall discuss the argument for 'overlapping consensus' in the next volume of this *Treatise*.) What, we must ask, is being rejected here under the name of scepticism? It is, I suggest, the same conception of scepticism that I attributed to Larmore in Section 28. The coupling of scepticism with indifference is surely significant. Whereas the kind of scepticism that I take to underlie neutrality is simply a denial of the legitimacy of certainty, Rawls's conception of it seems to equate scepticism with the idea that 'religious, philosophical and moral values' are chimerical.

I do not therefore think that the issue is settled by Rawls's own pronouncements about scepticism. What we need to look at is the course taken by his arguments in favour of, for example, freedom of conscience. In *A Theory of Justice*, the most explicit appeal to the limits imposed by the agreement motive on the kinds of claim that can be made in politics occurs in a passage about the terms in which arguments for restricting liberty of conscience can legitimately be couched. Rawls insists that they 'must be based on evidence and ways of reasoning acceptable to all'.[56] The claim that something (e.g. preaching heresy) would be publicly harmful and can hence properly attract criminal sanctions must 'be supported by ordinary observation and modes of thought (including the methods of rational scientific inquiry where these are not controversial) which are generally recognized as correct'.[57] This requirement is confidently deployed to shoot down arguments for restricting liberty based on religious grounds. 'Thus, for example, Aquinas justified the death penalty for heretics on the ground that it is a far graver matter to corrupt the faith, which is the life of the soul, than to counterfeit money which sustains life. . . . But the premises on which Aquinas relies cannot be established by modes of reasoning commonly recognized. It is a matter of dogma that faith is the life of the soul and that the suppression of heresy, that is, departures from ecclesiastical authority, is necessary for the safety of souls.'[58]

The context of this passage is an examination of the principle that 'liberty of conscience is to be limited only when there is a reasonable expectation that not doing so will damage the public order which the government should maintain'.[59] Such a statement obviously invites the question: 'When is an expectation reasonable?' (Aquinas presumably thought there was a reasonable expectation that not suppressing heresy would result in more people than otherwise being rendered liable to eternal damnation.) Rawls replies that the 'expectation must be based on evidence and ways of reasoning acceptable to all'.[60] However, when we look at Rawls's rationale for this restriction, we find that all is not what it seems. For it turns out that the whole discussion up to this point presupposes that the first principle of justice, which establishes freedom of conscience, has already been derived from the original position. Thus, Rawls says that 'this reliance on what can be established and known by everyone is itself founded on the principles of justice. It implies no particular metaphysical doctrine or theory of knowledge. For this criterion appeals to what everyone can accept. It represents an agreement to limit liberty only by reference to a common knowledge and understanding of the world. Adopting this standard does not infringe upon anyone's equal freedom. On the other hand, a departure from generally recognized ways of reasoning would involve a privileged place for the views of some over others, and a principle which permitted this could not be agreed to in the original position.'[61]

Since it is a defining feature of Rawls's original position that nobody knows his or her views (e.g. religious beliefs), it follows trivially that agreement will be reached on terms for living in a society that do not privilege any particular view. For it would, from within the original position, be perfectly arbitrary to pick out one view—say Thomism—and agree that the society's institutions are to be based on the assumption that it is true. Even Aquinas would have to concede that, were he to be placed in a Rawlsian original position, he would not demand that heresy be suppressed, since he would have no motive for attaching himself to any particular orthodoxy. But, precisely for that reason, he would refuse to enter a Rawlsian original position. For he would deny that the deliberations of a collection of people who had been artificially denied the possibility of knowing the truth about God could have any bearing on the question of the right institutions for a society to have. The appeal to the original position thus presupposes precisely the point that needs to be established if the case for religious liberty is to be made.

When real people with real religious convictions ask why they should have to set them aside in arguments with the other members of their society about state policy towards religion, it is useless to answer that this is what they would have agreed to in a Rawlsian original position. What we need to be able to tell them is that agreement with their fellow citizens can be reached only if there is a prior understanding that no arguments resting on the assumed truth of a particular religious view will be admitted. And we do actually find Rawls making this case in the section of *A Theory of Justice* immediately preceding the one that I have been analysing so far. Although most of the discussion here is again carried on in terms of choice in the original position, Rawls also has a paragraph that is addressed to actual people. Thus, he considers the argument 'that religious sects, say, cannot acknowledge any principle at all for limiting their claims on one another. The duty to religious and divine law being absolute, no understanding among persons of different faiths is permissible from a religious point of view. Certainly men have often acted as if they held this doctrine.'[62] What is his response?

Curiously at first sight, Rawls begins his answer to this challenge to the principle of religious liberty by saying that 'it is unnecessary . . . to argue against it'.[63] Properly understood, however, this remark is highly significant. It is clear from what follows that Rawls is denying the necessity of engaging directly at the first-order level with such religiously based claims. We do not, in other words, have to refute them by launching an argument designed to show that they are wrong. Rather we simply say that, true or false, they cannot form the basis of general agreement. 'It suffices that if any principle can be agreed to, it must be that of equal liberty.'[64] That this agreement has to be among real people rather than people in the original position is shown by the continuation. For Rawls says that somebody might think that 'others ought to recognize the same beliefs and first principles that [*sic*] he does, and that by not doing so they are grievously in error and miss the way to their salvation'.[65] (These must be real people, because people in the original position would not know what they thought about such matters.) Rawls's response is that 'an understanding of religious obligation and of philosophical and moral first principles shows that we cannot expect others to acquiesce in an inferior liberty. Much less can we ask them to recognize us as the proper interpreter of their religious duties or moral obligations.'[66]

The import of the penultimate sentence in this passage is far from plain, and is not given any further explanation. Taken in isolation, it would bear being read to mean that the religious sectarians who think that 'the duty to religious and divine law [is] absolute' can be shown to be wrong by invoking a correct 'understanding of religious obligation'. But this would entail producing precisely the kind of argument that Rawls has just said is unnecessary. To be brief, then, I suggest that we should take the argument as a whole to run as follows: if we are seeking principles for living together capable of attracting the agreement of all, 'we cannot expect' others to accept that our religious views should be invested with public authority, leaving them at a disadvantage. Our belief that they 'are grievously in error and miss the way to their salvation' as a consequence of a regime of equal religious liberty does not provide them with an adequate reason for 'acquiesc[ing] in an inferior liberty'.

The upshot is, then, that Rawls's doctrine with regard to religious liberty in *A Theory of Justice* has two parts. The first—the one we have just been looking at—invokes the agreement motive and says that only equal religious liberty is capable of eliciting general agreement, since anyone disadvantaged by unequal religious liberty can legitimately object. The second part, which I began by discussing, says that the principles agreed to at the first stage will include in them an agreement limiting the kinds of reasoning that can properly be used in arguing about their implementation. In particular, the principle of religious liberty will incorporate a clause permitting its restriction on the basis of 'the common interest in public order and security'.[67] But this clause is to be read in conjunction with the stipulation that a threat to public order and security must be established only on the basis of 'evidence and ways of reasoning acceptable to all'.[68]

In his more recent work, Rawls has collapsed these two stages into one, as far as the appropriate modes of reasoning in them are concerned. Thus, in *Political Liberalism*, he says that arguments of the first-stage kind (about 'matters of constitutional essentials and basic justice')[69] are to be conducted by observing the limits previously imposed at the second stage. The wording is indeed in part identical with that quoted above from *A Theory of Justice* and wholly in the same spirit: 'we are to appeal only to presently accepted general beliefs and forms of reasoning found in common sense, and the methods and conclusions of science when these are not controversial. . . . As far as possible, the knowledge and ways of reasoning that ground our affirming the principles of justice and their application to constitutional essentials and basic justice are to rest on the plain truths now widely accepted, or available, to citizens generally.'[70] Rawls describes these limits as being imposed by the requirements of 'public reason'. Although the expression is new, I hope I have shown that there is underlying it a considerable continuity in Rawls's thought from *A Theory of Justice* to *Political Liberalism*.

It is time to return to the question that introduced this discussion. We want to know precisely how Rawls gets from the agreement motive to his conclusion, that 'in discussing constitutional essentials and matters of basic justice we are not to appeal to comprehensive religious and philosophical doctrines'.[71] I have canvassed three possible answers to the question in this chapter. All are, it seems to me, consistent with what Rawls has had to say about the matter, either in *A Theory of Justice* or more recently. Thus, Larmore's prescription that agreement should be sought be prescinding from controversial premises is, as we have seen, echoed by Rawls. Nagel's 'epistemological abstinence' is reflected especially in Rawls's insistence that 'we may with perfect consistency hold that it would be unreasonable to use political power to enforce our own comprehensive view, which we must, of course, affirm as either reasonable or true'.[72] But my conception of scepticism is also consistent with the same sentiments: it rules out only a claim of certainty.

The three lines of argument are very similar. All of them turn on the crucial move of distinguishing between what can reasonably be believed and what can reasonably be advanced as the foundation of a society's basic institutions; and all three appeal to the agreement motive, claiming that only by ruling out certain kinds of beliefs can agreement be hoped for. However, I think the evidence from *Political Liberalism* supports Nagel's claim that Rawls is an adherent of 'epistemological restraint'. For Rawls here explicitly says that 'political liberalism . . . does not argue that we should be hesitant and uncertain, much less skeptical, about our own beliefs'.[73] This would seem to rule out even what I am calling scepticism. Furthermore, Rawls acknowledges a debt to Nagel's article and book.[74] He mentions that *Partiality and Equality* contains 'some revision' of the earlier article, but does not make the point that the book effectively withdraws the argument from 'epistemological restraint'. If I am correct, however, Nagel's conclusions can be reached only by invoking scepticism in my sense of the word. And if this is so, Rawls's 'public reason' must likewise demand an acknowledgement of what I have here called scepticism.

PART III

SOME MISTAKES ABOUT IMPARTIALITY

CHAPTER 8

Impartial justice and individual discretion

31. *Partialists versus Impartialists: An Ill-Joined Battle*

It is a commonplace that anglophone moral and political philosophy has for the past decade been the scene of a running battle between defenders and critics of impartiality. In one camp are Kantians, utilitarians, and supporters of what I have called justice as impartiality. Ranged against them are a variety of anti-impartialist philosophers of whom Bernard Williams is probably the best known and certainly the funniest. These are joined by a school of feminist critics of impartiality from several disciplines, including notably social psychology as well as philosophy. The most distinctive theme of these feminist critics is that the typical impartialist concern with rights and duties is a distinctively male concern and that an 'ethic of caring' more characteristic of females is equally valid or, according to some, should drive impartialist ethics from the field altogether.

This picture of the current situation is given a certain undeniable plausibility by the fact that many participants in the debate define themselves as being for or against impartiality. Yet there is no set of doctrines supported by one side and opposed by the other. The battle is ill-joined in this sense: that what the opponents are attacking is not what the supporters are defending. I believe that the core contentions of the friends and foes of impartiality (as they conventionally represent themselves) are equally valid. If this is so, there can be no contradiction between them.

What unites the members of the impartialist camp is the quest for a set of rules for living together that are capable of attaining the free assent of all. This ambition is quite explicit in the notion of justice as impartiality. But I think it is also fair to attribute to Kant the same Enlightenment hope that social arrangements might be made transparent—that all rational agents should be able to appreciate their rationale and thus accept them of their own free will. Kant's formulation of the categorical imperative in terms of universal participation in the Kingdom of Ends—the version that has been put in the foreground by a number of Kantian scholars in recent years—is especially significant in this respect.[1]

Utilitarianism presents us with a less clear-cut case, but I should like to recall here the suggestion I made in Section 22 that utilitarianism might be seen as a forerunner of justice as impartiality. In the utilitarian calculus, everybody counts for one in that all want-satisfaction is given the same weight regardless of the identity of its bearer. Everybody is thus treated equally in a certain sense, and it is upon this that (in different terms) Bentham, Mill, and Sidgwick all rest their claim that utilitarianism constitutes a generally acceptable basis for the law and positive morality of any society. I have argued that this sort of equal treatment is not adequate to the task because there is no way of showing that everybody has reason to accept want-satisfaction as a (second-order) conception of the good. But I am concerned here with the rationale of utilitarianism, which bases its claim to universal acceptability on its impartiality.

I now want to extend to all forms of impartialist theory thus defined another point that I have already made for the particular case of justice as impartiality. It would, I suggested in Section 12 , be an error to ask of it that it should provide a complete guide to the art of living. Justice as impartiality provides a framework within which people can conduct their lives—a set of mutually consistent rights and duties that prohibit some kinds of act, demand some other kinds, and leave the rest open to individual discretion. Once again, the extension of my argument is easier for Kantianism than utilitarianism. For it seems clear that the legal and moral constraints flowing from the Kantian categorical imperative would leave open a wide sphere of discretion within which people would be free to pursue their own ends. As far as utilitarianism is concerned, I must hark back to the point made in Section 21 that the utilitarian conception of the good is a second-order conception. This means that if the members of a society take want-satisfaction as the good for purposes of public policy and positive morality, this still leaves it open to them to decide what it is that they actually do want. (See also Section 22.) The idea of want-satisfaction as a conception of the good is entirely silent on that point. Hence, once again, we can conclude that impartialist theories do not offer a guide to the art of living.[a]

---

[a] There is a school of thought according to which anyone who attributes value to want-satisfaction is obliged, on pain of self-contradiction, to accept the implication that people should always be prepared to change their preferences (in as far as they can) so as to have more easily satisfied preferences, thus improving their prospects of satisfying

I began this chapter by saying that the battle between impartialists and non-impartialists as currently conceived is bogus. That does not mean that there is not a real conflict about the validity of impartiality. We need look no further than justice as mutual advantage to find a theory that rejects the impartialist objective. It might, indeed, be said to share the premise that the goal is a basis for general agreement. But if it is said to you that you should accept the rules generated by justice as mutual advantage, this means only that you should recognize them as offering you the best outcome you can realistically hope to obtain. Your interests will be taken account of only to the extent that you have the power to disrupt arrangements that are less advantageous to you than those you might hope to achieve from a new deal. Justice as mutual advantage thus rejects the key feature of justice as impartiality: the idea that constraints should be accepted freely as reasonable.

The impartialist vision of a society in which the major institutions are freely accepted by all may, of course, be repudiated more brutally than this. The holder of an avowedly élitist theory of the good such as Nietzsche would not be interested in the reception of his ideas among those who are designated by it as inferior specimens of humanity. 'A great man . . . wants no "sympathetic" heart, but servants, tools; in his intercourse with men he is always intent on *making* something out of them. . . . There is a solitude within him that is inaccessible to praise or blame, his own justice that is beyond appeal.'[2] MacIntyre quotes that passage in his *After Virtue* (the predecessor to *Whose Justice? Which Rationality?*) in the context of an argument to the effect that the only way of rejecting Nietzsche is to embrace the Aristotelian tradition of the virtues. From the present standpoint there is a certain irony in this, since it is apparent that Aristotle's conception of the good is also highly élitist (only well-off male citizens need apply) and anticipates Nietzsche

their wants. (See especially John Rawls, 'Social Unity and Primary Goods', in Amartya Sen and Bernard Williams (eds.), *Utilitarianism and Beyond* (Cambridge: Cambridge University Press, 1982), 159–85.) Since it is a rather unappetizing idea that people should be prepared to abandon everything that gives them their existing character if doing so would enable them to gain more want-satisfaction, this is taken to be a strong anti-utilitarian argument. However, the argument is based on a false premise. What is entailed in attributing a value to want-satisfaction is that the satisfaction of the wants people actually have is valuable. This can be expressed by saying that want-satisfaction has value, but that statement must be construed simply as an alternative way of saying the same thing as the other one. It is a fallacy to suppose that it is somehow a more general statement from which can be derived the proposition that it is just as good for people to change their wants so as to have more easily satisfied ones as for them to have their existing wants more effectively satisfied. The notion that want-satisfaction is good should be taken as agnostic on the question of what are good wants to have. (I have made this argument more extensively in 'Utilitarianism and Preference Change', *Utilitas*, 1 (1989) 278–82.)

in writing off a part of the human race as 'living tools'. He would presumably have been no more discomfited by the unacceptability of his theory among those designated natural slaves than would a Nazi by the rejection of his ideas among Jews.

When it is supposed that there is currently a battle between impartialists and anti-impartialists, the anti-impartialist camp is not taken to consist of either Hobbesians or élitists. On the tender-minded/tough-minded continuum, the anti-impartialists would see themselves as further towards the tender-minded end than the impartialists, whereas Hobbesians and élitists are located at the opposite end. What, then, do contemporary self-styled anti-impartialists stand for? They are united on one central contention, which is that there would be something crazy about a world in which people acted on an injunction to treat everybody with complete impartiality. There must, they maintain, be something fundamentally at fault with any moral system which has the implication that, for example, children should not be regarded as having special claims against their parents, or that a fully conscientious man would toss a coin to determine whether he should rescue from a burning building his wife or a total stranger. Such a world, the anti-impartialists say, might be suitable enough for some other race of creatures. But it is not one in which human beings can find a place.

This central contention of the anti-impartialists is surely correct. But if, as I am claiming, the impartialists are also right, the supporters and critics of impartiality must be talking about different things. I do not think it is hard to show that this is indeed so. What the supporters of impartiality are defending is second-order impartiality. Impartiality is here seen as a test to be applied to the moral and legal rules of a society: one which asks about their acceptability among free and equal people. The critics are talking about first-order impartiality—impartiality as a maxim of behaviour in everyday life. In terms of the discussion in Chapter 1, they wish to insist on the common-sense view of the scope of impartiality (set out in Section 2) and resist the extension of the demands of impartiality to the whole of life that I attributed to Godwin and Kagan in Section 4.

If second-order impartiality entailed universal first-order impartiality, the idea of a battle between friends and enemies of impartiality would make sense. Otherwise, it will be possible to adhere to second-order impartiality while rejecting universal first-order impartiality. The question that has to be asked is, therefore: does second-order impartiality entail universal first-order impartiality? The whole of Part III—this chapter and the next two—is structured around this question. In the remainder of this chapter I shall show that neither of the forms of justice as impartiality introduced in Chapter 3 entails universal first-order impartiality. I shall devote most of my space to the Scanlonian version, taking the opportunity to develop further my exposition of it. I shall then in the final section turn my attention to the Rawlsian version of justice as impartiality, arguing that Rawls's emphasis on procedural justice rules out universal first-order impartiality.

The following two chapters apply the analysis to second-order impartialist theories other than those falling under the heading of justice as impartiality. I shall argue in the next chapter that neither utilitarian nor Kantian impartiality entails universal first-order impartiality. Chapter 10 extends that discussion by arguing that much of the feminist criticism of impartiality is addressed to universal first-order impartiality and leaves second-order impartiality, properly understood, unscathed. (I acknowledge that some feminist critics of impartiality are genuinely opposed to second-order impartiality, but I argue that partiality all the way down is either incoherent or has to lead to justice as mutual advantage.) This discussion of the feminist critique is preceded by a discussion of the work of Lawrence Kohlberg. On the basis of this I suggest that the conflation of first-order and second-order impartiality among feminist writers can be explained by their taking seriously Kohlberg's theory of the stages of moral development, which (among other deficiencies) fails to distinguish between levels of impartiality.

32. *The a priori Approach and the Empirical Approach*

The terms 'a priori approach' and 'empirical approach' were first employed in *Theories of Justice* (Section 42). Although they have not been used until now in this book, the ideas that they represent should already be recognizable. By 'the a priori approach' I mean no more than the direct appeal to a Scanlonian original position in order to argue that certain rules or principles would emerge from it. This approach has been exemplified in the derivation of rights from a Scanlonian original position in Sections 11 and 13, and more generally within Chapter 4.

The 'empirical approach' exploits an idea already introduced, that of the circumstances of impartiality. Let me recall a suggestion made in Section 16: that, the more the actual conditions in a society approximate those of the Scanlonian construction, the more reason we have to regard the rules that are established and maintained in it as prima facie just. The empirical approach to the study of justice as impartiality picks up on this idea and systematizes it. Suppose we observe that a rule of a certain kind is found only in societies that approximate the circumstances of justice. The more often it is found in those societies, the more confident we can be that it would emerge from a Scanlonian original position. Conversely, if an institution (e.g. chattel slavery) exists only in societies that depart very far from the circumstances of impartiality, this provides strong support for the surmise that such an institution could reasonably be rejected in a Scanlonian original position.[b]

Too much should not be read into the names that I have chosen for the two approaches. Thus, it should not be supposed that the distinction between them is that one is grounded in experience whereas the other echews any appeal to experience whatsoever. What we should say rather is that they call upon experience in different ways. To pursue the empirical approach we have to study two things: the rules of justice that a society has, and the extent to which the conditions of the society approximate those of a Scanlonian original position. The a priori approach does not pay any attention to either of those phenomena. It is concerned to ask what rules of justice would emerge from the hypothetical choice situation specified in the Scanlonian variant of justice as impartiality. For this purpose, it imputes to the parties in the original position accurate information of a general kind about the characteristics of human beings and human societies, as well as the kind of knowledge that people normally have about themselves. It is then the task of the theorist to ask what would be agreed upon by people endowed with this information and motivated by the desire to reach agreement upon terms that could not reasonably be rejected. It is thus clear that, via the information imputed to the parties in the original position, the a priori approach appeals to features of human beings and human societies that are pervasive and deep-seated but are ultimately contingent, in the sense that it is logically possible that the world might have been differently constituted.

The a priori method and the empirical method provide a check on one another. If the theory is on the right general lines, we should find

[b] As a number of reviewers of *Theories of Justice* remarked, what I am calling the empirical method bears some relationship to the notion of ideal discourse in the work of Jürgen Habermas. (See, for example, his *Moral Consciousness and Communicative Action*, trans. Christian Lenhardt and Shierry Weber Nicholson (Cambridge, Mass.: MIT Press, 1990).) However, Habermas holds that we have to wait patiently until an ideal speech situation exists rather than try to anticipate what might emerge from it if it did exist. One follower of Habermas comes closer to my own twin-track approach by speaking of 'the counterfactual ideal of an uncoerced moral–practical discourse as the final justification for . . . various forms of institutionalized debate' (Kenneth Baynes, 'The Liberal/Communitarian Controversy and Communicative Ethics', in David M. Rasmussen (ed.), *Universalism vs. Communitarianism* (Cambridge, Mass.: MIT Press, 1990), 61–81, quotation from p. 74). It is still not clear, however, that he is proposing the attempt to draw conclusions from what happens in real situations that to some degree approximate the idea.

inherently suspect because of the biased way in which ideas are propagated—in modern societies as in others. 'What people can be induced to swallow in the name of justice' is not the same thing as justice. When it is said that justice is an acceptable basis for reconciling conflicts between different interests and conceptions of the good, the word 'acceptable' has an ineliminable normative content. If we take that away, the statement loses its initial plausibility. The normative element is, I wish to maintain, supplied by second-order impartiality.

Although it is worth making the point that consensus would not be the end of the story even if it existed, it is of no practical significance because it remains true that there is no actual consensus. The superficial appearance of a consensus may occur in a society marked by an official ideology, which provides support for the socioeconomic *status quo* by suggesting that successful individuals got where they are by their merits in a fair competition and that large economic rewards reflect large contributions to the economy. This is obviously congenial to the beneficiaries, and offers a rose-tinted view of their own lives. Even if some of the more thoughtful or perceptive have some qualms, it does not jar with their experience in a sufficiently jolting way to cause them to question it seriously. Those who do poorly from the system, in contrast, find that this official ideology fails to square with what they see around them.[4] In the USA, where there is no social democratic party capable of articulating an alternative picture of society, they tend to finish up with the incoherent set of beliefs that researchers typically uncover. Western Europe is manifestly moving towards the condition of the United States as its Social Democratic parties increasingly fall prey to the official ideology, talking the language of self-help and rewards for enterprise.

It may be asked why the process of electoral competition does not lead to the articulation of a counter-ideology corresponding to the experience of those who do poorly out of the system. The answer is that trying to create an electoral base by changing beliefs is a long-term strategy which makes sense only if party leaders have a time horizon extending well beyond the next election. For party leaders interested only in short-term electoral success, it is more efficient to manoeuvre in a policy space that is taken as given.[5] Reluctance to concentrate on the propagation of an ideology to challenge the official one is strengthened by the increasing heterogeneity of the disadvantaged. For this makes the job of creating a view of the world that chimes in with the experience of over half the population much more difficult.[6]

33. *A priori* Approach

I said in the previous section that the reconciliation of the two approaches could take either of two forms, depending on whether a society's institutions could be endorsed by a priori reasoning or not. In those areas where the institutions can be endorsed by the a priori approach, the task is to show that (at any rate in the relevant respects) the society exhibits the circumstances of impartiality. In those areas where the institutions lie outside the range of acceptable variation, determined by a priori reasoning, the two approaches can be reconciled if it can be shown that there are other features of the society (notably the unequal distribution of power) that can explain the deviation as a result of the failure of the society to exhibit the circumstances of impartiality to a sufficient degree.

My subject in this chapter is first-order impartiality. I shall pursue the a priori approach in this section and then ask in the next section if the conclusions reached here are confirmed by the empirical method. I shall argue here that there are both gains and losses inherent in a norm of first-order impartiality. On the basis of this, I shall suggest that the people in a Scanlonian original position could not reasonably reject established norms governing first-order impartiality provided that they fell within a certain range. However, this range does not extend as far as a norm of universal first-order impartiality or anything like it. The people in a Scanlonian original position could reasonably reject a norm that did not leave sufficient scope for individual discretion. My arguments for this conclusion will be conducted under three heads. Taking up in turn issues of control, coordination, and compliance, I shall try to show that each sets limits to the reasonable extension of first-order impartiality.

Let me begin then with control. Regardless of our conception of the good, we all want some ability to control our own corner of the world, and in return for that we are prepared to relinquish the chance of exerting control over others in their corner of the world. To put it another way, we want some room for discretionary choices within the areas that are the most important to us, and in a Scanlonian original position we would have to recognize that we cannot have that for ourselves unless we concede it to everybody.

The only valid argument in favour of a system of private property in personal possessions (and money with which they can be purchased) is rooted in considerations of control. I dismissed Nozickean ideas about presocial rights in section 19, and I have no intention of letting them in through the back door here. Justice as impartiality, I wish to insist, has a lot to say about the legitimate bases of ownership and the legitimate degree of inequality of ownership. The point is, however, that rights are a conclusion, not a premise. From the perspective of impartial justice, the case for property rights is that they operate so as to establish an area within which people can act as they choose. Imagine as stringent a control over the distribution of personal property as you like—a strict system of rationing under conditions of general scarcity, for example. It will still be true that, once a person has been assigned something as his legitimate property, he is not normally to be held accountable under the rules of justice (whether legal or moral in form) for the use that he makes of it. It can be consumed by him, given to somebody else, exchanged for something else of value (informally if not in an official market) or destroyed.

What William Godwin called—pejoratively—'the magic of the pronoun "my"' can be explained in this context by saying that life goes better if what I do with my toothbrush is my business. (See Section 37 in the next chapter for a discussion of Godwin.) I should not be under any obligation to ask myself whether somebody else could make out a better case for using my toothbrush than I can, on the basis of impersonally applicable criteria such as need or want-satisfaction. This is not, of course, to say that an occasion might not arise where the right thing to do was to lend somebody my toothbrush. But that is very different from maintaining that, if I were ideally conscientious, I would be constantly on the look for alternative uses of my toothbrush before using it myself. The point of a system of private property in personal possessions is precisely to exclude that.

The magic of the pronoun 'my' is not, of course, limited to personal possessions. Rather, we might say that having an area of discretion in the disposition of personal possessions constitutes the material basis for something that is actually more important: having an area of discretion in personal relations. All of us have only a finite amount of time, attention, care, and affection to devote to other people (or to ourselves for that matter), and life would scarcely be worth living if we could not decide for ourselves—once we had met our general social obligations— on whom these should be bestowed.

I now want to reinforce the conclusion reached so far by adding to the problem of control the problem of coordination. To show how the problem of coordination arises, I shall pick up and then extend an idea that I discussed in Section 12. Every society is faced with the need for rules of justice (legal and moral) to regulate the conduct of its members so as to minimize mutual frustration and conflict and, more positively, so as to promote cooperation. Now, the subject-matter of justice as impartiality is the content of these rules of justice. Our question is: how closely should they regulate conduct? Should a society's rules impose a lot of coordination, a little coordination, or some intermediate amount?

At one extreme is a Nozickean minimal state, with a minimalist positive morality to go along with it. The rules here are restricted to prohibiting people from inflicting physical harm on others or violating their property rights. This immediately has two implications. The first is that no collective decision can legitimately provide for money to be transferred from those who do well to those who do badly as a result of the way in which the system of private property works out. The second is that cooperation on collective projects of mutual advantage to the participants cannot be mandated by either the positive morality or the laws. (The only exception is that people can legitimately be required to contribute to the cost of enforcing contracts and the criminal law.) This does not, of course, entail that cooperation will be unknown. Sometimes people will see an advantage to themselves in joining some cooperative venture on certain terms, and will be prepared to enter into a contract that binds them to perform in return for others binding themselves similarly. However, since people are free to bind themselves in this way or not, nobody can be criticized for refusing to join in a mutually advantageous undertaking.

We can add that the scope of first-order norms of impartiality in such a set-up is bound to be extremely narrow. Since people have a right to dispose of their property as they see fit, there can be no room for norms stipulating that they must not discriminate (e.g. on racial grounds) in offering employment or in deciding whom to serve in a restaurant or whom to accommodate in a hotel. Similarly, schools and universities will be private institutions, and will be able to pick their students on any basis they like. Strict impartiality will in such a society be an obligation almost entirely confined to people acting in judicial or bureaucratic capacities, whose functions will be very limited.

A set of Nozickean rules would minimize the burden of cooperation. People would be free to do anything they chose to do provided only that they did not overstep the boundaries set by the persons and property of others. However, against this advantage have to be offset the disadvantages of leaving people on such a loose rein, and these tell conclusively against it. I have already made the point in Section 19 that a Nozickean society could not emerge as the choice of the parties in a Scanlonian original position, but it will be helpful to restate the case in the light of what has just been said. Thus, all three of the distinctive features of a Nozickean society would, I maintain, cause it to be unattractive to people who could reasonably insist on its being rejected.

To begin with, almost everyone would have reason to fear the prospect of being reduced to destitution by the operation of an economic system in which the only sources of money were inheritance, gift, savings, selling one's labour power to an employer, and providing goods and services for the market. Nobody can be sure of continuing to be physically and mentally capable of working or of finding a line of work that pays enough to live on, and unemployment is by its nature not an insurable risk.[7] Moreover, even those with substantial unearned incomes based on inherited wealth or savings cannot be confident that they will not be wiped out by a stock market collapse or the failure of banks, insurance companies, and other financial institutions (all of which will, of course, be private). At the very least, the parties to the hypothetical contract would insist on a 'safety net' to avert destitution.

A Nozickean society would, I have noted, impose neither a legal nor a moral obligation to contribute to mutually beneficial projects. In some instances this would not be a serious drawback, since those who did not choose to contribute could be left out of the cooperative scheme, neither contributing to it nor benefiting from it. The only loss to those who joined in might be a failure to reap otherwise attainable returns to scale or suffering a certain degree of inefficiency from providing a service only to some of those living in an area. In many other cases, however, the inability to ensure general cooperation would jeopardize the very possibility of carrying on the collective enterprise at all.

Almost all of the public services provided by government agencies and paid for by taxation have the characteristic that it is impossible or at any rate very awkward or expensive to exclude anyone from their benefits. Those who chose not to contribute to the cost in a Nozickean society would thus be able to 'free ride' on the efforts of those who did contribute. This would obviously be highly inequitable if the cooperative scheme was brought into existence but the alternative, which is highly plausible, is that the scheme would not be brought into existence at all or (as with American 'public television') would be supported by a relative handful of altruists and would be a shadow of what it might be if all the beneficiaries contributed their fair share. The parties in a Scanlonian original position would be prepared to accept neither the prospect of being exploited by 'free riders' nor the prospect that many mutually advantageous public services would fail to be provided at all. They would insist on some version of what Rawls has dubbed 'the duty of fair play'—the principle that beneficiaries from a cooperative scheme should not have the option of refusing to contribute to it.

The third feature of a Nozickean society that could reasonably be rejected by the contracting parties is the extremely limited role given to the norm of first-order impartiality. A Nozickean society would give impartiality little scope in two ways. It would minimize the role of public institutions with their function of applying without fear of favour a uniform set of rules to everybody; and it would also have the characteristic that no firm, club, school, or other body that was privately owned could be held accountable for its decisions, however discriminatory their impact. Many people in a Scanlonian original position would find the idea of such a society distinctly unappetizing, and could reasonably reject any proposal for bringing it into existence. They would, quite properly, insist that the major institutions whose operations affect life chances in a significant way must either be run publicly (according to the requirements of Weberian bureaucratic rationality) or, if left in private hands, should be subject to whatever norms of impartiality appeared necessary to avert systematic and cumulative disadvantage to those with low social status, poor economic standing, and little power.

To sum up: the plus side of a Nozickean society would be the relatively small amount of coordination through institutions or norms that would be called for; its disadvantages would be those that I have just spelt out. Now consider the polar opposite to a Nozickean society: one in which there was a norm of universal first-order impartiality. This would have all the advantages lacking in a Nozickean society, but would carry with it crushing disadvantages. One, which I have already talked about, is the way in which people would feel that they did not have control over their personal possessions and their personal relationships—in a word, their lives. Another is that such a society would encounter an insurmountable burden of coordination.

A general expectation that people will in the first instance care for themselves and their dependants has the effect that a good deal of life can be carried on without much need for coordination. People get on with what is designated as their own business within the constraints set by the rules of justice. These rules, I must emphasize, could be a lot more restrictive than those to be found in a Nozickean society and still leave the burden of coordination at a tolerable level. A society with a norm of universal impartiality, however, would be one in which everybody was supposed to show equal concern for all. It would be regarded in such a society as wrong to show special concern for the welfare of oneself or those close to one. (We cannot say 'dependants' here, because the concept of a dependant would disappear: everyone would be equally a dependant of the society as a whole.) It is apparent that such a society would throw up horrendous problems of coordination, simply because everything would be everybody's business. Either coordination would have to be done by some public authority operating impartially according to general norms, or it would have to come about through private actions governed by a norm of universal first-order impartiality. Neither could be expected to deal effectively with the problems of coordination.

The inconveniences arising from the problems of coordination are further intensified by the problems of compliance, the last of my three headings. A Nozickean society would have relatively little difficulty in securing compliance with its norms. All that would be required would be the enforcement of contracts and the punishment of offences against property or person: theft, embezzlement, fraud, and suchlike or the infliction of physical harm. The main challenge to public order would come from the mass of homeless, starving people who would be thrown up by the economic system—the 'sturdy beggars' that the Elizabethan Poor Law was created to repress. Experience between then (or indeed before then) and now has shown that with enough brutality this repression can usually be accomplished. But the very existence of such a mass of people in desperate circumstances in a Nozickean society is one of the main reasons why the rules of justice constituting it could never emerge from a Scanlonian original position.

Once again, a society in which universal impartiality was the norm would fall at the opposite extreme. In an attempt to secure strict impartiality in all areas of life a huge number of decisions that are now left to private judgement would have to be turned over to public officials; and all decisions left in private hands would be open to scrutiny and censure on the basis of the hypertrophied positive morality of the society. A Nozickean society concentrates the burden of compliance heavily on those reduced to destitution by the workings of a market system unmodified by transfers or public services. In a society committed to universal first-order impartiality, however, compliance would be experienced as extremely burdensome by everybody. This is because its demands would constantly run counter to sentiments whose long-term survival value no doubt means that they have a basis in human biology—as they have in the biology of all other animals. There is a natural inclination to make special efforts on one's own behalf and on behalf of those whom one cares about. It is the role of rules of justice (including norms of strict impartiality) to set bounds to the working of this inclination, by ruling out actions that injure others and prohibiting such violations of impartiality as nepotism. But it is one thing to channel people's attempts to advance the welfare of themselves and those to whom they are closely attached and altogether another to seek to extirpate any tendency in this direction. The burden of compliance that this would give rise to would be insupportable.

The felt burden of compliance in a society wedded to universal first-order impartiality would provide a strong incentive for non-compliance, and the difficulty of enforcing the sheer mass of rules would mean that fear of sanctions would be a weak counteracting force. Moreover, the integrity of those charged with applying and enforcing the rules would be severely tested, since very often the loser from the application of a rule would be specific whereas the beneficiaries would be diffuse. The opportunities for corruption would therefore be enormous. Nor would the sphere of public morality be immune to its own form of corruption. There is ample record of what happens in societies where censoriousness about private conduct is rampant, and from this it is clear that the system of informal sanctions can very easily be hijacked by people who are pursuing grudges and vendettas of their own. (The Puritan colonies of New England and China under the 'cultural revolution' both exemplify this, despite their differences in almost all other respects.)

A final point to be made is that a society dedicated to universal impartiality would not only be liable to a great deal of non-compliance but it would also be vulnerable to even a small amount.[8] This point connects the problem of compliance back to the problem of coordination. In a loosely coordinated society, a certain amount of non-compliance can be tolerated without difficulty. It will for the most part create only a local disturbance in the system. But in a highly coordinated society, all cogs must mesh together smoothly or the result is liable to be chaos. To put it concretely, where strict impartiality is the universal norm, my wellbeing will depend very little on what I do and very much on a large number of others all performing their assigned roles. A failure by any of them may well have devastating consequences for me.

The moral of all this is the one to be found in the story of Goldilocks and the Three Bears, or, for those who prefer more august authority, in Aristotle's doctrine of the mean. (Indeed, my objections to a society of universal first-order impartiality have something in common with Aristotle's criticism of Plato in the *Politics*.)[9] What justice as impartiality calls for is, in other words, neither too much first-order impartiality nor too little first-order impartiality but just the right amount—or, more precisely, an amount within a range whose limits would be established by the parties to a Scanlonian original position. A Nozickean society would display too little impartiality; one with universal first-order impartiality would have too much. What is required is a set of rules of justice (including, it should be recalled, both legal and moral norms) that provide everybody with a fair opportunity of living a good life, whatever their conception of the good may be, while leaving room for the kind of discretion in shaping one's life that is an essential constituent in every conception of the good life. This is the conclusion that I undertook to establish: that the variant of second-order impartiality that I have been discussing is so far from entailing universal first-order impartiality that it actually rules it out.

34. *The Empirical Approach*

In this section, I shall endeavour to support the conclusions of the previous one. I begin by observing that the common-sense morality I analysed in Section 2 does not endorse universal first-order impartiality. We cannot conclude, of course, that this settles the matter as far as the empirical approach is concerned, because the positive morality of a society might embody systematically unequal relations of a kind that could reasonably be rejected by those who lose out from them.[10] The positive morality of most societies would fall foul of this proviso in its treatment of relations between the sexes; and in many societies the norms governing relations between different races or castes would similarly be liable to reasonable rejection.

I shall not repeat here my discussion of the circumstances of impartiality in Section 16. I do want, however, to add to it by pointing out that within a single society the circumstances of impartiality may obtain to a different degree in different areas. For example, it could well be that, in societies where labour organization is weak, the rules operating within the workplace are especially suspect because the circumstances of impartiality are very far from obtaining, even if they obtain rather better in the political arena. The more cheerful aspect of the same idea that I want to focus on here is that, while a society's laws may arise from conditions that violate the circumstances of impartiality pretty seriously, there may be reasons for thinking that its positive morality is less suspect from a Scanlonian point of view.

The cases I have in mind here include countries such as Britain and the United States. These do not score very well on the criteria I put forward in Section 16—though they would no doubt fall within the top quartile in any ranking of all the members of the United Nations. The implication is that we have to treat with great caution any claim that we can draw inferences from the laws and public policies prevailing in those countries to the content of an agreement in a Scanlonian original position. However, the positive morality of the same countries is less suspect because it depends on the internalization of the rules and their reinforcement by public opinion. Not every society's positive morality is entitled to the same kind of respect. Calvin's Geneva or John Knox's Scotland are examples (and there are of course many others) where the sanctions backing the society's positive morality were not diffused as they are typically in modern Western societies. Since they flowed from a (formal or *de facto*) political authority whose basis violated the circumstances of impartiality, we can speculate that any features of positive morality found only in such societies could probably be reasonably rejected in a Scanlonian original position. The basis for this conjecture is that these features do not arise in societies where the conditions instantiate the circumstances of impartiality more fully.

Even where a society's positive morality is maintained by the diffuse force of public opinion, this is not enough by itself to offer any assurance that its norms could not reasonably be rejected in a Scanlonian original position. For the conditions under which those norms are maintained may still violate the circumstances of impartiality. Thus, one of those circumstances is that the people concerned should not harbour false beliefs. Consent to some systematic inequality is suspect if the victims of it accept it on the basis of a pervasive set of beliefs that defines them as 'naturally' inferior. To explain what I mean, let me go back to the point made in Section 3 that even a self-proclaimed 'anti-speciesist' such as Peter Singer concedes that it is appropriate for adult human beings not suffering from specific moral or mental disabilities to share rights and privileges from which other animals are excluded *en bloc*. Obvious examples are the right to vote and the right of free speech. In fact, about the only right attributed to most non-human animals by anti-speciesists is a right to humane treatment by human beings.[11] The line that in contemporary liberal societies is drawn in this way between human beings and non-human animals has in most societies that have ever existed been drawn in a place that divides adult human beings into virtually separate species. Thus, there is commonly a division between free and slave, where slaves have at most a right (dubiously enforceable) to humane treatment. Again, in only a few societies have women had the same civil and political rights as men and their rights have been mainly defined in terms of financial support and freedom from illtreatment of certain kinds.

Such divisions within the human race have normally been justified by claims that there are such marked differences in capacity between men and women or between different races that it would make no more sense to give them equal rights than to give chimpanzees the vote. Where this is put forward as an empirical claim, it can be dismissed as straightforwardly false. From the point of view of the empirical approach, the acceptance of inferiority on the basis of false beliefs is worthless as evidence of what could not be reasonably rejected in a Scanlonian original position. A slightly different tack has to be taken when superiority and inferiority are ascribed to groups on the basis of their greater or lesser spiritual worth, as stipulated by some system of religious belief. The Hindu varna system is an obvious example. Another is the position of the Dutch Reformed Church in South Africa that the descendents of Ham are condemned to be servants because Ham saw Noah naked while in a drunken stupor, and that descendents of Ham can be recognized by having black skins. I am assuming that the claims advanced by religions cannot be shown to be straightforwardly false. But I have also argued that demands based upon them can reasonably be rejected in a Scanlonian original position. This means that it would be incompatible with justice as impartiality to base a system of social inequality on the Hindu varna system or the theology of the Dutch Reformed Church in South Africa.

There is another reason for caution about the quality of consent to a decentralized system of public morality. This is that biases may persist in such a system of public morality precisely because there is no way of making changes to its content through any collective decision-making mechanism. Let us suppose that a certain positive morality is in place in a society and that, because of its unequal impact on different sections of the community (men and women, blacks and whites, for example), it could reasonably be rejected in a Scanlonian original position. If all the members of the society were debating what content their positive morality should have, this one would not emerge as an agreed outcome. But since the occasion for such a debate never arises in real life, a positive morality that would not survive a process of Scanlonian collective decision-making may nevertheless prove very resistant to modification. And this, I should emphasize, may be so even if those who are put at an unfair disadvantage recognize this fact about their situation.[d]

[d] This point may throw some light on the practice of female genital mutilation, mentioned earlier in Section 14 in the context of the positive harm principle. This is painful, introduces a quite serious risk of infection, and makes for complications in childbirth. Contrary to what is sometimes supposed, it is not required by any religion. It therefore seems straightforward that this practice could reasonably be rejected, by those liable to be subjected to it, in a Scanlonian original position. Why then are mothers so keen in places where the practice exists to have the operation performed on their young daughters, even where this entails breaking the law? The answer is that, under the prevailing norms, girls are considered not marriageable (or at any rate not as advantageously marriageable) otherwise. There is a precise analogy with the Chinese practice of footbinding (a term which conceals the horrific nature of the process, as does the clinical-sounding 'cliterodectamy' for so-called Pharaonic circumcision): the pain and frequently infection involved in achieving a small foot was thought a price worth paying in order for a girl to be in a position to marry well. There is an obvious difficulty in moving from this equilibrium to a new one, and uncoordinated individual decisions to abandon the practice are

The reason for this is that each individual in the society is faced all the time with decisions that have to be taken independently of the decisions of others. A single individual may refuse to follow or endorse the prevailing social norm governing relations between the sexes or races; but, while this gesture may be secretly admired by others who also suffer from the norm, only under very special conditions does it set off a chain reaction. The difficulty of coordinating a shift in the norms is too great. It is not simply that there is a direct cost to the individual in upsetting the expectations of others (legitimate expectations, as they will think) and gaining a reputation for behaving badly (according to the conventional norms prescribing good behaviour). There is also the consideration that even biased norms are—unless they are monstrously biased—more advantageous to everyone than the free-for-all that would arise from a breakdown of norms. The case for conformity can therefore be put to someone who is disadvantaged by the existing norms in the following terms: in the absence of some good reason for thinking that your repudiation of the existing norms constitutes an element in a shift to a new and more equal set of norms, there is a strong case for desisting that arises from reasonable fear that, if your action has any wider effects, it will be to contribute to a normative anarchy from which everyone stands to lose.

The point I have been making can be given formal expression by making use of the contrast between justice as impartiality and justice as mutual advantage. As I have said, both make an appeal to the terms of a hypothetical agreement. What divides them is the basis of the agreement. For justice as mutual advantage, the terms should reflect the balance of power between the parties, providing each with a prospect of gains over what may be expected from the absence of agreement. For justice as impartiality, the terms should be worthy of free acceptance under conditions where power relations do not play a part in the negotiations. When we observe a state of agreement in a society, we cannot safely deduce that the conditions underlying the agreement are the circumstances of impartiality because we must bear in mind the alternative possibility that the agreement rests on mutual advantage. What supports it may, in other words, be that everybody (or a large enough majority to sustain it) believes the existing terms or social cooperation to be more advantageous than a breakdown of normative order would be.[e]

not likely to be the way. However, footbinding died out quite quickly in China after it was abolished legally, despite the well-entrenched nature of the practice. This suggests that decisive government action can secure the required shift of norms.

[e] Let me insert a technical note here. It is quite in keeping with the general idea of justice as mutual advantage that there should be a range of equilibria all of which are more advantageous to everyone than the alternative of a 'state of nature'. This view of the

I began this section by making two points. The first was that the positive morality (what I called in Section 2 common-sense morality) of contemporary societies does not incorporate universal first-order impartiality. The second was that this positive morality is maintained by an informal set of sanctions, which means that at any rate in some sense it must rest upon consent. These two observations taken together constitute a prima facie case for the proposition that under the circumstances of impartiality universal first-order impartiality does not emerge. I now have to ask whether that conclusion continues to stand up once we take account of the possible ways in which the maintenance of norms by diffuse sanctions may be consistent with a violation of the circumstances of impartiality.

I see no reason for suspecting that support for common sense morality in the matter of first-order impartiality rests on false beliefs. Nor does it seem to me reasonable to suggest that the common sense conception of the demands of impartiality constitutes an unfair disadvantage of a systematic kind for any social group. It is true that, up to a certain point, increasing the stringency of first-order impartiality works to the advantage of the least advantaged groups in a society. But it is an illegitimate extension of this truth to argue that a regime of universal first order impartiality would therefore be the arrangement most advantageous to the worst-off.

Let me take the steps in turn. Consider, then, a society which regards the hiring practices of privately owned firms as purely a matter for the employer; which permits hotels and restaurants to operate a blanket

matter is not, indeed, consistent with any theory of justice as mutual advantage which presupposes (as does that of David Gauthier) that it must be possible to deduce a unique outcome from any set of initial conditions. The belief that it must be possible may well come about as a result of reckless generalization from the two-person case, where it is more plausible. (The kind of naive overconfidence in the powers of formal bargaining theory exhibited by philosophers is, significantly, much less common among game theorists themselves.) To see that the general notion of justice as mutual advantage can work perfectly well with multiple equilibria, we need look no further than the earliest and greatest systematic exponent of justice as mutual advantage, Thomas Hobbes. Not only did Hobbes allow for the possibility of alternative equilibria being consistent with a given set of underlying power relationships, it may be said that he made it the cornerstone of his political doctrine. For the burden of this doctrine was that whatever form of government is established in a society is better for everyone than the alternative being plunged back into a 'state of nature'. He thus recognized that any of a variety of different regimes might be maintained in a given society if they were once established; but he insisted that mutual advantage mandates support for the one that actually exists. It may be noted that, in his assumption that the path from one stable equilibrium to another must lie through a 'state of nature', Hobbes was invoking the same kind of consideration as I am suggesting may lie behind reluctance to upset a *status quo* in positive morality which one recognizes to be biased to one's disadvantage but still preferable to normative anarchy.

exclusion of members of certain races or ethnic groups; and, in which private clubs can exclude, say, women, blacks or Jews without fear of either general moral condemnation or legal sanction. It is surely clear that restricting the sphere of impartiality in this way works to the disadvantage of those groups in the society that are disliked or looked down upon by the kind of people who own or run firms, hotels, and restaurants, or control the affairs of golf clubs, businessmen's lunch clubs, and so on. In a Scanlonian original position, the parties would have to give due weight to the countervailing value of free association. But in any society where the result of letting people act according to their interests or inclinations was a significant degree of *de facto* discrimination, the losers from this discrimination would be able reasonably to reject the proposal that their society's common morality and laws should permit it to occur.

This is the valid step in the argument. The invalid step would be to appeal to a principle of continuity and thereby conclude that the weaker members of a society would gain the maximum amount possible if the scope of impartiality were to be universal. On this view, all the benefits of freedom of association inevitably go to the strong, while the benefits of a rule of universal impartiality are concentrated among the weak. But this is simply not so. Whatever your conception of the good, it is very unlikely that it will not include in it the ability, without incurring legal or moral sanctions, to do things with and for some people that you would not wish to do with or for other people who are (according to some impartial criterion) similarly placed to them. It is worth adding here that, unless you have a purely egoistic conception of the good, you will not regard freedom of association as valuable only to yourself. Rather, you will think that it is valuable for everybody.

Freedom of association does not cease to be a genuine value when we get to the bottom of the social scale. Think of the situation of the members of one of the Scheduled Castes (previously called 'Untouchables') in an Indian village. They will almost certainly come at the bottom of every hierarchy: landless labourers (if they can find work at all), with the lowest social status and very little political power. There is, however, absolutely no reason for supposing that freedom of association will not be valued by them—that they will not, for example, find it centrally important to their lives to be the bearers of complex rights and duties within their families that have no equivalents in their relationships to other people.

The lesson to be drawn is, I suggest, that justice as impartiality does indeed have definite implications for institutions within—and even more between—societies. It rules out practices with an unequal impact that cannot be defended against reasonable rejection on the part of those who lose from the inequality. Thus, many features of both Indian society and the international political economy that contribute to the plight of the members of the Scheduled Castes would stand condemned. But at the same time justice as impartiality does not require, and is indeed inconsistent with, a rule of universal first-order impartiality.

35. Procedural Justice

'When critics reject Rawls's theory as "too abstract" and "impartialist," they may sometimes do so because of a failure to appreciate fully the fact that it was never intended to be applied directly to concrete moral problems. Rawls, however, is quite clear on the point.'[12] In my terms, this shrewd remark by Thomas Hill translates into the claim that Rawls adheres to second-order impartiality but not universal first-order impartiality. That the theory set out in *A Theory of Justice* is one of second-order impartiality is not, I take it, in dispute. The construction of the original position guarantees that the parties cannot adopt a partial perspective, because they have no information about their own distinguishing characteristics. What I wish to focus on here is the way in which Rawls's second-order theory of justice explicitly licenses departures from universal first-order impartiality.

Robert Nozick, as is well known, attacked Rawls in *Anarchy, State, and Utopia* for advocating a distribution of goods in accordance with a patterned end-state and argued against this by saying that 'choices upset patterns'.[13] Seldom in the history of political philosophy can a criticism have been so hopelessly misdirected. In fact, Rawls insists that societies should be conceived of as a sphere in which what he calls 'pure procedural justice' operates. The basic idea of pure procedural justice is that, if the rules defining the range of legitimate choices are just, then justice can also be ascribed to the outcomes that arise when people make choices within the permissible range. 'The principles of justice apply to the basic structure and regulate how its major institutions are combined into one scheme. . . . [We] use the notion of pure procedural justice to handle the contingencies of particular situations. The social system is to be designed so that the resulting distribution is just however things turn out.'[14]

Thus, suppose the social institutions allow me to give my (justly acquired) money to anybody I choose for any reason that seems good to me. Then the outcome after I have given somebody a sum of money is just because it comes about as a result of a permissible act on my part. My act makes the new outcome just, even if it is completely arbitrary.

The point of saying that the outcome is one of pure procedural justice is that there is no way of saying what is a just distribution in advance of the decisions that people actually choose to make. Of course, Rawls stipulates that the institutions must have an overall effect of advancing the interests of the worst-off social class (i.e. must satisfy the difference principle), so the purity of pure procedural justice is qualified. But the point that Rawls is making by talking about pure procedural justice here is so important that it seems to me sensible to mark it with a special term. For what this says is that principles of justice are to be used to judge the most significant social institutions. To the extent that just institutions permit choice and chance to play a part in what happens, the outcomes are to be accounted just provided that the procedures allowing for the operation of choice and chance were followed.

If Rawls had achieved nothing else, he would be important for having taken seriously the idea that the subject of justice is what he calls 'the basic structure of society'. The idea of a social structure is of course an abstraction. What we actually see are people striving, winning and losing, getting more or less education, better or worse medical care, more or less desirable jobs, positions of more or less power in all kinds of organizations, bigger or smaller salaries and pensions, and so on. When we talk about the basic structure of a society we are concerned with the way in which institutions work systematically so as to advantage some and disadvantage others. Rawls's incorporation of this notion of a social structure into his theory represents the coming of age of liberal political philosophy. For the first time, a major figure in the broadly individualistic tradition has taken account of the legacy of Marx and Weber by recognizing explicitly that societies have patterns of inequality that persist over time and systematic ways of allocating people to positions within their hierarchies of power, status and money. It is depressing evidence of the social-scientific illiteracy of so many philosophers that someone like Nozick, who is in these terms the equivalent of a pre-Copernician astronomer, should ever have been taken seriously.

When Rawls introduces the concept of pure procedural justice in *A Theory of Justice*, he emphasizes that we can apply it only when the procedure is actually carried out. The reason for this can be seen clearly by taking up the initial illustration that Rawls offers of pure procedural justice at work, that of gambling. Let us imagine the simplest kind of lottery in which a hundred people buy a ticket for a pound and the person with the winning ticket collects the hundred pounds staked (or most of it). Whoever wins, the outcome is procedurally just (in the sense that nobody has any legitimate complaint) so long as the procedure by which the winning ticket was selected was fair and was carried out properly. There is no way of telling whether the outcome is just except by seeing how it was arrived at. There might be two situations with an identical outcome (say, ticket number thirty-four wins) but if in the first case this result arose from a fair draw and in the second case from a rigged one then the first outcome is just and the second not. 'A distinctive feature of pure procedural justice is that the procedure for determining the just result must actually be carried out; for in these cases there is no independent criterion by reference to which a definite outcome can be known to be just.'[15] Rawls writes thus in the context of gambling, and emphasizes that the whole point of gambling outcomes is that they are arbitrary. Hence we cannot say that a distribution is just in virtue of the fact that it *could* have come about as a result of gambling, because 'almost any distribution ... could have come about as a result of fair gambles'.[16] This is why the procedure has to be actually carried out: it is the procedure itself that determines what a just outcome is.[f]

The essence of pure procedural justice is, then, that there is no independent basis upon which the outcome can be criticized as unjust. I may regret the outcome of a lottery, either because I lost or because I think the winner will put the money to what I regard as a bad use. But I cannot say that the outcome is unjust so long as the lottery was entered into voluntarily and was fairly conducted. Again, if justice permits people to make whimsical choices in some matter (e.g. making bequests) no choice can be unjust however foolish or otherwise objectionable it may be. To put the point in more familiar language, let us suppose that the rules of justice establish a right to perform any of the actions x, y, or z. Then no choice from among these actions can be unjust.

[f] How can the justice of gambling be squared with Rawls's theory? The case for thinking it cannot is obvious. Are not the outcomes of gambling a perfect example of the kind of 'morally arbitrary' advantage and disadvantage that social justice is to eliminate where possible? Admittedly, Rawls allows that an unequal distribution of earnings can be justified, even though the advantages of the more productive are a matter of good luck, provided things are set up so that the worst-off class is as well of as it can be, and hence better off than it would be with a more equal distribution. This, however, is a matter of making the best of an unavoidable inequality between the developed endowments of different people. (See *Theories of Justice*, Section 28.) It is hard to see how this line of reasoning can be deployed to justify the completely gratuitous introduction of inequalities due to good and bad luck in gambling. If we ask how actual lotteries can be differentiated from what Rawls dubs the genetic lottery and the social lottery that assign people their natural endowments and upbringing, the answer surely lies in the fact that real lotteries are entered into voluntarily. Rawls himself specifies that the background fairness conditions for the outcomes of gambling to be just include the stipulation 'that the bets are made voluntarily' (*A Theory of Justice*, 86). And it is this that is, I suggest, doing the work of justifying gambling. (I shall take up the question of voluntary choice as a justification of outcomes in the next volume of this *Treatise*.)

Rawls does not, it seems to me, explain why the people in the original position would endorse pure procedural justice. However, I can see no reason why the case against universal first-order impartiality developed in Section 33 should not have as much appeal for the people in a Rawlsian original position as it would have for those in a Scanlonian original position. In particular, the people in a Rawlsian original position know that much of the value in their lives is likely to come from participation in families and other groups. (The psychology developed in Part III of *A Theory of Justice*, which is presumably included in the general information supplied to the people in the original position, makes a great deal of this.)[17] As we have seen, the integrity of groups requires that members should be permitted to do things for one another that they do not have to do for others who are similarly situated in every respect except for not being a group member. Since this kind of behaviour constitutes a violation of universal first-order impartiality, it is to be expected that Rawlsian justice will embrace institutions (the 'basic structure of society') that permit a good deal of individual discretion.

The implication of all this is, of course, that principles of justice designed for the basic structure of a society (including moral 'rules of justice' essential for coexistence) cannot be deployed directly to address other moral questions. As Thomas Hill has emphasized, we must distinguish 'the liberal aim of establishing a constitution and economic order that mutually respecting citizens can publicly affirm without judging one another's individual ways of life' from the appropriate 'moral guidelines for friendship, family, charity, personal integrity, and so forth'.[18] Here we do not 'need agreement among people of widely divergent life-styles'.[19] Hence 'one's concern for the shared values of one's community and one's best judgment regarding the most valuable ends of life may reasonably play a central role'.[20] In the next two chapters, I shall be looking at examples of the extension of impartiality to what Hill calls 'moral questions about interpersonal relations within our social structure'.[21] Chapter 10 will include an example of the direct (and inappropriate) application of Rawls's difference principle to a moral dilemma in the work of the influential social psychologist Lawrence Kohlberg.

CHAPTER 9

━━

Levels of impartiality

36. *Utilitarianism and Kantianism as Impartialist Theories*

In the previous chapter I put forward the proposition that second-order impartialist theories do not entail universal first-order impartiality. I hope that I have succeeded in showing that this is true for justice as impartiality. I believe that the same conclusion also holds for the other main varieties of impartialist theory, the Kantian and the utilitarian. What makes the position less than completely straightforward is that there have been self-proclaimed utilitarians and Kantians who have endorsed universal first-order impartiality. Contemporary anti-impartialists have exploited the existence of such people to discredit the whole idea of impartiality. But this is a cheap victory that gains nothing because the 'utilitarianism' thus destroyed is not that of Bentham or Mill, and the 'Kantianism' would have been repudiated by Kant.

In this chapter, I shall argue that Bernard Williams's criticisms of what he calls 'the impartial system' trade heavily on identifying utilitarianism and Kantianism with the eccentric variants that take them to entail universal first-order impartiality. I shall offer a parallel argument to the one in the previous chapter to make the point that, properly understood, neither utilitarianism nor Kantianism entails universal first-order impartiality and both are in fact inconsistent with it.

Let me begin, then, by saying something about Bernard Williams and utilitarianism. It is significant that Williams first developed his characteristic position in the course of attacking a crude form of utilitarian theory put forward by Jack Smart, a philosopher of science who made occasional forays into moral philosophy.[1] Williams has ever since made part of his stock-in-trade the claim that what he calls 'the impartial system' has dire implications for personal autonomy. The way in which Williams typically expresses the point is by saying that we have projects and commitments that give our lives meaning, and that these would constantly be put at risk by the operations of 'the impartial system'. This must be so, according to Williams, because the 'system' demands that we must stand ready to abandon at any moment our projects and commitments if we can discern anywhere in the world a claim on our time, attention, or money that is more urgent when assessed impartially. Now this is quite false as a general statement about the implications of second-order impartiality, but it does happen to be true of Smart's version of utilitarianism. For what Smart defended was a consequentialist theory, as I defined consequentialism in Section 4. He maintained, that is to say, that everybody has a duty to do the act at any given moment that stands to maximize total utility. It is this kind of utilitarianism—and only this kind—that is open to Williams's objection that someone with a 'ground project' that gives meaning to his life 'will be required by Utilitarianism to give up what it requires in a given case just if that conflicts with what he is required to do as an impersonal utility-maximizer when all the causally relevant considerations are in'.[2]

I shall not pursue Smart's own treatment of the topic, which is too primitive to be worth attention. Instead, I shall return to William Godwin, whom I introduced in Section 4 as an exponent of consequentialism. On Godwin's account, moral thinking is entirely forward-looking. That a promise has been made, for example, does not in itself affect the right course of action to be taken when the fulfilment of the promise falls due. Suppose that 'I have promised to bestow a sum of money upon some good and respectable purpose. In the interval between the promise and my fulfilling it, a greater and nobler purpose offers itself, and calls with an imperious voice for my cooperation.' Godwin's answer to the question 'Which ought I to prefer?' is 'That which best deserves my preference.' And this is, he assumes, the greater and nobler purpose: 'a promise can make no alteration in the case.'[3]

But what if my promise has led other people to make arrangements that they would not otherwise have made, so that my failing to carry out what I promised will inconvenience them? Godwin concedes that this is relevant, but simply because the consequences of keeping the promise and of failing to keep it have been modified as a result of the promise's having been made. 'I live in Westminster; and I engage to meet the captain of a ship from Blackwal at the Royal Exchange. My engagement is of the nature of information to him, that I shall be at the Exchange at a certain hour. He accordingly lays aside his other business and comes thither to meet me.'[4] This is, Godwin tells us, 'a reason why I should not fail him unless for some very material cause'.[5] But he adds that 'it would seem as if the reason why I should not fail him would be equally cogent, if I knew from any other source that he would be there, and that a quantity of convenience equal to the quantity upon the former supposition would accrue from my meeting him'.[6] Thus, what changes my duty from what it would otherwise have been is the fact of the captain's waiting for me at the Royal Exchange. It is immaterial how it is that he comes to be waiting there. It may be because I promised to be there; it may be because somebody mistakenly—or even maliciously —told him that I would be there and he believed it. My duty is in any case the same: to meet him if that will have the best consequences and not to meet him if there is anything more beneficent that I could do instead.

A member of a society in which everyone else acted in the way proposed by Godwin would do best (from a utilitarian point of view) to act in the same way. But a society in which everyone acted in that way would be far less effective in achieving the utilitarian end than would be one in which the norms of positive morality required the observance of appropriate rules of justice. The reasons for this are essentially those that I gave in Section 33 to explain why justice as impartiality does not entail universal first-order impartiality. This is, indeed, scarcely surprising. For the arguments that I advanced there—couched in terms of control, coordination, and compliance—were originally developed in order to explain what is wrong with Godwin's version of utilitarianism.

The Godwinian fallacy lies in looking at each calculation in isolation, and not taking adequate account of the effects on a society's capacity to function of its being known that all actions are taken on the basis of such calculations. Thus, promise-keeping needs to be given an important place in a society's positive morality because the institution of promising scores high under all three of my headings. It gives people control over their lives in that it enables them to enter voluntarily into binding commitments whose whole point is that, when the time comes to act, the parties are obliged to do what they have promised to do. Promises are instruments of autonomy because they enable us to do something—create expectations about our future behaviour—that we sometimes want to be able to do. We therefore preserve our autonomy in fulfilling our promises. Being obliged to act in order to satisfy expectations that have arisen in some other way is, in contrast, a denial of autonomy: it means that we are at the mercy of at worst deliberate manipulation by others and at best their mistakes. It is only necessary to add that autonomy is for the vast majority of people a value—something they regard as an important aspect of a satisfactory life—and the connection between control and utility is established.[a] Common-sense

---

[a] The sense of 'autonomy' relevant here is the one invoked by Williams in his criticism of Godwinian utilitarianism. Autonomy is the ability to carry out our plans and in

morality makes a sharp distinction between expectations arising from promising and expectations that have arisen in other ways. If I happened to discover that somebody was waiting for me in a certain place on the strength of bad guesswork or malicious misinformation, common-sense morality holds that it would be kind of me to go there, though it would be considered quixotic for me to put myself to any major expense or inconvenience to do so. If the other person was waiting for me as a result of my having promised to be there, however, I would be regarded as being at fault if I failed to go, unless there were some very compelling impediment. Common-sense morality corresponds here to what the utilitarian criterion, properly executed, would require.

It is easy to misidentify the problem of coordination. Often we find it suggested that the problem facing a society of Godwinians is a purely practical one. On this view, if everyone were smart enough and well-informed enough, and if time and effort were no object, rules would be unnecessary because it would be possible for everybody to calculate from first principles what would be the optimal act on each occasion. This is a delusion. The problem as posed is not merely inconceivably hard: it is strictly impossible to solve it. This is because the optimal course of action for me depends upon what I expect others to do, while the optimum course of action for others depends upon what they expect me to do. But the information that others are trying to bring about the best overall outcome is insufficient to enable me to predict what specifically they will do, and everybody else is in the same predicament. Expectations can be coordinated only by a system of rules (such as that enjoining promise-keeping) which are adhered to without regard to consequences. Only within a matrix of stable expectations created in this way does it make sense for people to make judgements about the likely consequences of acting in one way or another.

The delusion that there could be such a thing as a successfully functioning Godwinian society comes about, I believe, because philosophers commonly focus on the decision problem facing a single individual within a society in which it is implicitly assumed that the actions and reactions of the other members can be anticipated. The possibility of talking about this decision problem coherently shows only that (leaving aside all practical computational difficulties) there can be only one

---

some reasonable measure control our commitments. It should not be confused with the sense of 'autonomy' discussed in Section 20, which is concerned with the way in which conceptions of the good (and hence plans) are formed. This latter sense of 'autonomy' makes it a distinctively 'liberal individualist' value, as I have conceded. The value of autonomy in the former sense is, I suggest, far less culturally specific.

Godwinian in a group of interacting people. The fallacy lies in supposing that the conclusion can be generalized so that everybody in the group could be a Godwinian.

Considerations stemming from compliance reinforce the conclusion that keeping promises should be distinguished in positive morality from acts of beneficence of which the gratifying of expectations constitutes one class. The point here is that it is in general fairly easy to tell whether a promise has been kept or not, so promising is a norm with the characteristic that compliance with it can be relatively easily monitored.[b] In contrast, a duty to act for the best (as that appears to the actor) has the disadvantage of leaving it open to interminable dispute whether in some particular case somebody could reasonably have supposed that he was acting for the best or whether he should have done something else. I have already argued that the problem facing an agent in a Godwinian society would be insoluble. But someone trying to decide whether or not the actions of another person were worthy of censure would face the same problem and then others beside. To determine whether this person had done what he should properly have regarded as the optimific act, it would be necessary to reconstruct the process by which he reached his decision. This would entail finding out what beliefs this person had about the state of affairs and the causal relations between alternative acts and their outcomes, and then assessing the quality of these beliefs and the quality of the judgement that led to a decision based on them. It seems clear that under these conditions the whole notion of social control over action through the informal and diffused sanctions of positive morality would fall into disrepute.

Williams argues, in effect, that if people tried to follow the Godwinian prescription they would make themselves thoroughly miserable. But the implication of that is, obviously, that a society of Godwinians would score very poorly on the utilitarian criterion. There is, of course, nothing original in this observation. The classical utilitarians, Bentham and John Stuart Mill, took this line and so did David Hume, who may be regarded as a proto-utilitarian.[7] It is, therefore, disingenuous to analyse the implications of utilitarianism as if Godwin and his descendants are the genuine article and the rest are guilty of fudging it for popular consumption. The truth is, rather, that Godwin was a bad utilitarian.

[b] No doubt there is a range of variation between societies in the strictness with which the obligation to keep promises is regarded. What matters is that there should not be too large a difference between members of the same society in what they regard as an acceptable kind of excuse. For a shared convention of this kind to operate it is not, of course, necessary that anybody should be able to produce a formal definition of the general characteristics of an acceptable excuse.

37. The 'Famous Fire Cause'

Godwin's most notorious illustration of his thesis was described by
Charles Lamb as 'the famous fire cause' in which Godwin appeared as
'counsel for the Archbishop Fénelon against my mother'.[8] Godwin's
conclusion—that the bishop's life should be preferred to the mother's—
caused a good deal of scandal, which was not greatly assuaged when, in
later editions of *Political Justice*, Godwin chivalrously changed the
example so that the choice lay between Fénelon and his valet, who
might be a 'brother, father, or benefactor'. The problem—which of two
people to rescue where it is possible to rescue only one—has become a
philosophical chestnut. In this section, I shall examine Godwin's own
analysis of the 'famous fire cause' and then extend my discussion to take
in some more recent analyses of the problem.

Let me begin by setting out the context within which Godwin introduces his 'famous fire cause'. In his discussion of 'justice merely as it
exists among individuals', Godwin starts from what he archly refers to
as 'a comprehensive maxim which has been laid down upon the subject',
namely 'that we should love our neighbour as ourselves'. And this may
entail that we should love our neighbour more or less than ourselves—
or, more precisely, be prepared to do more or less for our neighbour
than for ourselves. 'In a loose and general view I and my neighbour are
both of us men; and of consequence entitled to equal attention. But, in
reality, it is probable that one of us is a being of more worth and importance than the other.' Worth and importance may arise in two ways: one
person may be 'capable of a more refined and genuine happiness' than
another; but also one person's life may be more 'conducive to the general good' than another's, because of the contribution he can make to
the welfare of others. This brings us to the 'famous fire cause'. As an
illustration of the relevance of worth, Godwin says that 'the illustrious
archbishop of Cambray was of more worth than his valet, and there are
few of us that would hesitate to pronounce, if his palace were in flames,
and the life of only one of them could be preserved, which of the two
ought to be preferred'.[9]

In principle, everyone, whatever his or her position in the business,
should be able to understand that 'the life of Fénelon was really preferable to that of the valet'. Even if I were the valet, I should have recognized this and 'have chosen to die, rather than Fénelon should have
died'.[10]

Suppose the valet had been my brother, my father or my benefactor. This
would not alter the truth of the proposition. The life of Fénelon would still be
more valuable than that of the valet; and justice, pure, unadulterated justice,

would still have preferred that which was most valuable. Justice would have taught me to save the life of Fénelon at the expense of the other. What magic is there in the pronoun 'my', that should justify us in overturning the decisions of impartial truth?[11]

In his 'Reply to Parr' (an erstwhile ally turned critic) Godwin expressed regret at his choice of Fénelon as the more worthy character: 'I perceive that I did not sufficiently take into mind the prejudices and habits of men, when I put the case of Fénelon, the writer of certain books of reasoning and invention.'[12] A man of action such as Brutus or Napoleon Bonaparte, he remarked (in 1802), might have served his purpose better. Godwin's reason for regretting the choice of Fénelon lay in the difficulty of convincing most people that it would make an immense difference whether Fénelon lived or died. Yet the argument appeals to the notion that, if Fénelon is saved, the writings that he will be able to produce in the rest of his life will bring enormous benefits to the whole human race. It seems to me that Godwin's second thoughts on the matter were good, and that the plausibility of his solution to the case as stated does indeed rest upon our inexpugnable reluctance to attach the supreme importance to the life of Fénelon that Godwin assumes for it.

In place of Brutus or Bonaparte, let me offer an example that in my view makes Godwin's case for him. Let us suppose that the person trapped in the burning building is the President of the United States and also that the Vice-President, who would succeed him if he died, is a person of notorious stupidity, incompetence, and poor judgement. (This was, it may be suggested, a scenario of more than hypothetical interest in the period 1988–92, during which the Vice-President was Dan Quayle.) Given the potentially catastrophic global implications of the President's death in these circumstances, it would be hard to deny that you really ought to rescue the President. This is so even though any criticism that was forthcoming if you rescued your parent (whichever one it was) instead of the President would no doubt be tempered by the thought that the motive that prevailed in this situation was in general an admirable one—a point that Godwin himself later conceded, as we shall see in a moment.

In truly exceptional circumstances, any second-order impartialist theory would, I believe, have to reach the same conclusion as Godwin about the right thing to do. It is an unavoidable implication of any set of moral norms that can be squared with second-order impartiality in any of its forms that people may be unlucky enough to find themselves in situations where doing the right thing entails great sacrifice. A less contrived example of the 'famous fire cause' is that of a man whose wife and child are held hostage by a terrorist organization and who is told that they will be killed unless he plants a bomb at a time and place when it will inevitably result in many deaths.[13] Perhaps none of us can be sure what we would do in such a situation, and we must all devoutly hope that we will never be put in a position that will enable us to find out. But there is, it seems to me, no question that a utilitarian, a Kantian, and a proponent of justice as impartiality would all have to say that the right thing to do is to refuse to plant the bomb.

The real objection to Godwin's system is not that it leads to the answer it gives in the case as stated (assuming that we grant the premise of the immense importance of keeping Fénelon alive) but that there is nothing in it to restrict the imperative to sacrifice your parent to a case as extreme as that. In principle, even a slight advantage in total future utility on the side of rescuing one person rather than the other should determine where your duty lies. 'So, presumably, even if we are faced with a choice as to which of two chambermaids to save from a fire, we can and should decide by first (quickly) measuring the relative worth of their lives.'[14] This is the sort of implication that enables Bernard Williams to allege that 'the impartial system' is incompatible with the pursuit of our own projects and the cultivation of special ties to certain people. But that is precisely why it is also incompatible with utilitarianism conceived of as a second-order impartialist theory.

Godwin himself was eventually struck by the force of this objection, taking a step in response to it that would, if it had been followed through, have led to the complete abandonment of his consequentialism. In response to Parr's criticism, he accepted that 'if, without pause or hesitation, I proceed to save the life of my father in preference to that of any human being, every man will respect in me the sentiment of filial affection . . . and will confess . . . that at least I have *my heart in the right place*'.[15] He then went on to make the following significant remark: 'It will come to be seriously considered, whether, in proportion to the inequality of the alternative proposed to my choice, it will contribute most to the mass of human happiness, that I should act upon the utility of the case separately taken, or should refuse to proceed in violation of a habit, which is fraught with a series of successive utilities.'[16]

Godwin is here making the crucial admission that the utilitarian end might most effectively be advanced not by our acting on 'the utility of the case separately taken' but by our cultivating habits that, when acted on consistently, are 'fraught with a series of successive utilities'. With this, act utilitarianism has given way to what has been called 'motive utilitarianism'.[17] But once it is conceded that 'the utility of the case separately taken' is not the appropriate basis on which to act, the way is clear to admitting all the considerations I have advanced in favour of defining duty as compliance with rules of justice. The concession, it has to be said, makes Godwin more impressive as a thinker but less useful as a figure on whom to pin a simple doctrine. I have often felt that, for anti-utilitarians, if Godwin had not existed he would have to have been invented. To some degree, we can now see, the 'Godwin' in philosophical currency *is* an invention. But he is too useful to dispense with, so I shall leave standing the association of Godwin with his original view that everyone has a duty to do the act that at the time holds out the prospect of having the best consequences.

Utilitarianism may be said to derive from a particular view of what the equal consideration of interests entails. We move straight from the claim that impartiality requires the equal consideration of interests to the conclusion that impartiality entails the summation of interests.[c] A possible reaction to this would be to say something along the following lines: 'This system of impartial concern for interests may be regarded as fair between *interests* but it is not fair between *people*. Equal regard for interests may, and usually will, generate unequal treatment of their bearers.' In reaction, some writers have proposed conceptions of equal treatment that are strongly anti-aggregative. However the direct and unmediated application of a principle of equal treatment can easily produce even more bizarre practical conclusions than the direct and unmediated application of the principle of utility.

An illustration is a variant of the 'famous fire cause' where the alternatives are to rescue different numbers of people. Suppose that there are a large number of people at the north end of an island and a much smaller number at the south end, and there is time only to rescue the people from one end before some catastrophe (a massive tidal wave, say) wipes out anybody still left. Utilitarian reasoning would suggest that a person with a boat large enough to rescue the larger number should go to the north end since he can thereby save more lives. 'Each

[c] Godwin quite explicitly makes this move (see *Political Justice*, 82–3). But he is not without modern successors. Thus Peter Singer makes an argument in which he moves, within the space of a single paragraph, from the idea of 'recognizing that my own interests cannot count for more, simply because they are my own, than the interests of others' to saying that we should 'adopt the course of action most likely to maximize the interests of those affected', which, as he rightly says, is 'a form of utilitarianism' (Peter Singer, *Practical Ethics* (London: Cambridge University Press, 1979), 12). Similarly, Don Locke writes that 'the function of morality, of moral principles and moral reasoning, is to provide impartial, mutually acceptable solutions to conflicts of individual interest, solutions which all the parties can accept, whatever their original position might be'. And he takes this to entail the 'principle of equal interests', which he equates with the *aggregation* of interests, that is to say Benthamite utilitarianism (Don Locke, 'The Principle of Equal Interests', *Philosophical Review*, 90 (1981), 531–59, at p. 556.)

counts for one. That is why more count for more.'[18] And common sense morality would, I believe, reach the same conclusion.

Against this, John Taurek has argued that 'when I evaluate outcomes from an impersonal perspective (perhaps we may say from a moral perspective)',[19] I 'have absolutely no reason for showing preference [to the larger number] as against [the smaller number], and no reason for showing preference to [the smaller number] as against [the larger number]. Thus I am inclined to treat each person equally by giving each an equal chance to survive'.[20] The owner of the boat should therefore flip a coin before setting out to determine which end of the island he should go to, going to the north end if the coin comes down heads and to the south end if it comes down tails. Going straight to the north end, where the larger number of people are awaiting rescue, would fail to 'reflect an equal concern for the survival of each, northerner and southerner alike'.[21]

The thought underlying this coin-tossing proposal is that simply being a member of the larger or the smaller group is a morally irrelevant basis for being rescued or not being rescued. This is true in the sense that it is brute bad luck to be one of the smaller group if the decision-rule adopted is to go straight to the end of the island where the larger number are. But we must appreciate that the real bad luck consists in not being rescued, whether this arises from the result of a coin-tossing exercise or from a decision to go straight to the northern end of the island. As Derek Parfit has commented, 'making more depend on luck will not abolish bad luck'.[22] It therefore seems reasonable to say that we should aim to minimize the number of people subject to the bad luck of not being rescued.

The ideal of equal treatment is a valid one. But the coin-tossing proposal is an abuse of it. At the second-order level, the ideal of equal treatment does indeed have universal scope: the essence of second-order impartiality is that everybody should be treated equally.[23] What that commitment to equal treatment entails will, of course, differ from one impartialist theory to another. Utilitarianism counts everybody for one in its calculus; justice as impartiality asks what rules people placed in an original position of equality would choose; and Kant assigns everyone equal citizenship in the Kingdom of Ends. What they have in common is the idea that everybody stands on the same footing. As Thomas Hill, Jr. has put it, 'All the impartiality thesis says is that, if and when one raises questions regarding fundamental moral standards, the court of appeal that one addresses is a court in which no particular individual, group, or country has *special* standing. Before that court, declaring "I like it," "It serves *my* country," and the like, is not decisive; principles must be defensible to anyone looking at the matter apart from his or her special attachments, from a larger, human perspective.'[24] We can say this, however, and still allow for the possibility that, when we look at matters from an impartial perspective, we may decide that, 'I like it' or 'It serves *my* country' should constitute morally acceptable bases for action in some circumstances. Thus, I have argued that in some areas (e.g. the choice of friends) the whole idea of treating people equally has no application. Where we have an area of legitimate personal discretion, 'I like it' is indeed an acceptable basis for action. (See Section 2.)

Much of the time, the demand that people be treated equally is a valid one to make. But we should not be so simple-minded as to confuse equal treatment with identical treatment. Let me illustrate this by asking what we mean by holding up the ideal of equality before the law. This is a demand for equal treatment, but it does not call for everybody to be treated in the same way—still less that penalties should be allocated randomly! We are demanding two things: that the laws should be administered in a non-discriminatory way and that the laws themselves should not be discriminatory. What the first demand amounts to is that decisions should be made according to law: that only those features of the situation recognized by the law should enter into the determination of the case. If the outcome can be affected by bribing the judge or intimidating the jury, if it turns on prejudice against some group of which the defendant in a criminal trial is a member, or if the outcome depends on one party's being able to hire more able counsel than the other party, the law fails to accord equal treatment to those who appear before it. The second demand, that the laws themselves should be nondiscriminatory, is satisfied to the extent that the laws do not mandate or permit differential treatment of people who are in all other respects similar (according to the legally prescribed criteria of relevance) but differ in race, gender or some other characteristic, where that characteristic should not be regarded as relevant.

The general point is that it is a fallacy to suppose that there is any free-standing concept of equal treatment at the first-order level. Before we can say whether or not people are being treated equally, we have to know how justice requires them to be treated—and to determine that we have to have recourse to second-level impartiality. Sometimes, of course, it will turn out that justice requires all the members of some large category to get the same thing. For example, it is plausibly a demand of justice in many contemporary societies that all the adult citizens, with a few carefully delimited exceptions, should have one vote apiece. And we may decide in some very rare cases that justice calls for random allocation. A case for which such a policy has been canvassed is the allocation of dialysis machines among people with kidney failure.[25]

This entails treating as irrelevant the fact that some people have better prospects of survival on an artificial kidney than others. It is by no means obvious that random allocation is the right method here.[d] Suppose that instead survival prospects are regarded as the appropriate criterion. We shall then be able to say that equal treatment means taking account of people's prospects of survival and not their race, gender, ability to pay, or any other irrelevant factor. The point is that discussion of the issue is not advanced by making a shibboleth of the concept of equal treatment. We can talk about equal treatment only after we have settled the prior issue of what should count as relevant and what should be excluded as irrelevant.

38. The 'Famous Fire Cause' Revived

I have said that Bernard Williams takes the two branches of 'the impartial system', which he also sometimes simply calls 'morality', to be utilitarianism and Kantianism. The theory that he attacks under the name of 'utilitarianism' is, as we have seen, not the theory of Bentham and Mill. Similarly, what he attacks as Kantianism has little in common with the doctrines of Kant. Indeed, in his essay 'Persons, Character and Morality', he is careful to eschew any attempt at pinning anything on to Kant himself, and instead refers vaguely to work 'of basically Kantian inspiration'[26] which, it turns out, means crude misapplications of the

---

[d] I am, with this example, dipping a toe into the much larger issue of criteria for the distribution of medical resources. The analogue of utilitarianism here is the thesis that resources should be distributed in such a way as to maximize (as far as possible) the aggregate number of 'Quality Adjusted Life Years' (QALYs). The argument is that this is a suitably impartial approach in that 'one year of healthy life is of equal value no matter who gets it' (Alan Williams 'The Value of QALYs', *Health and Social Service Journal*, 18 July 1985, 'Centre Eight', 3). Against this, it has been argued, on lines reminiscent of Taurek, that this approach fails to satisfy the requirements of equal treatment because it denies a chance of receiving medical care to people with ailments whose treatment rates a low QALY score per unit of resource expended. (See John Harris, 'More and Better Justice', 75–96 in J. M. Bell and Susan Mendus (eds.), *Philosophy and Medical Welfare* (Cambridge: Cambridge University Press, 1988), esp. p. 81.) However, the point here seems to me that, just as it is bad luck to be stranded and not be rescued, so it is bad luck to be ill and not be cured. Minimizing the amount of that bad luck is therefore a sensible objective. I can see no principle of fairness here that tells us we should visit the bad luck of not being treated on a large number of people who could be treated cheaply with highly beneficial results in order to devote the resources that would have treated them to a smaller number of people with some illness that costs more to treat and where the treatment makes less of an improvement in quality of life. The notion of somehow being fair to *diseases* by treating the same proportion of people with different diseases (or deciding whom to treat by lottery, which will tend to amount to the same thing) strikes me as utterly bizarre.

concept of equal treatment. What we get is, in fact, none other than the 'famous fire cause', presented in an even more schematic form than it was by Godwin. (Since Williams has frequently gone on record as a scathing critic of efforts to draw conclusions from radically underdescribed examples, it is perhaps surprising that he takes this one seriously.) The discussion that he lampoons occurs in a book by Charles Fried, *An Anatomy of Values.*[27]

Fried proposes a case in which 'a man could, at no risk or cost to himself, save one of two persons in equal peril', one of whom is 'say, his wife'. So long as this man 'occupies no office such as that of captain of a ship, public health official, or the like', it would, Fried says, be 'absurd to insist' that 'he must treat both equally, perhaps by flipping a coin'.[28] This is disappointing from Williams's point of view, but the sought-for absurdity emerges when Fried explains why it is all right for someone acting in a private capacity to rescue his wife rather than tossing a coin. For his answer is that the requirement of equal treatment (assumed to mean random selection) is still met, albeit in a rather esoteric way: 'The occurrence of the accident may itself stand as a sufficient randomizing event to meet the dictates of fairness, so he may prefer his friend or loved one.' Fried adds that 'where the rescuer does occupy an official position, the argument that he must overlook personal ties is not unacceptable'.[29]

This is easy to poke fun at and Williams makes the most of the opportunity. Would it be all right for someone who is in an official position to grab the nearest person? (Would proximity constitute a 'sufficient randomizing' feature?) Or must he, if he is to give everybody an equal chance of being rescued, toss coins or roll dice? And what about the case of the man who is not in an official position? If he simply rescues his own wife, the reason for thinking that the requirement of random selection has not been met is, as Williams says, that it is prima facie unfair that the other person should 'never even get a chance of being rescued'. Fried's 'answer . . . is that at another level it is sufficiently fair'. For 'although in this disaster this rescuer has a special reason for saving [his own wife]. . . , it might have been another disaster in which another rescuer had a special reason for saving [the other person].'[30] Williams's comment on this line of thought is that 'apart from anything else, that "might have been" is far too slim to sustain a reintroduction of the notion of fairness'.[31] This is surely correct. If fairness really requires equal treatment, understood as an equal chance for each of the candidates to be rescued, it really does not help matters to point out that those who 'never get a chance to be rescued' are in that position as a result of the bad luck of not being related to the potential rescuer.

The real bad luck lies in not being rescued. Whatever happens, that piece of bad luck is going to happen to one of the two 'persons in equal peril'. And we can repeat Derek Parfit's admonition that 'making more depend on luck will not abolish bad luck'. Fried's contortions in trying to square equal treatment with common sense conclusions arise solely because of his unargued assumption that equal treatment requires random selection in some shape or form. This assumption rests on the application of the notion of equal treatment at the first-order level. But the relevant conception of equal treatment here operates at the level of second-order impartiality. This rules out 'the magic of the pronoun "my"' in this sense: I cannot say 'I should rescue my wife and anybody else in a position to rescue one of two people should rescue my wife if she is one of the two.' But it does not rule out my saying: 'Everybody should rescue his own wife in such a situation.' For this does not put my wife in a specially privileged position at the second-order level. What I am prepared to do for my wife I am prepared to prescribe that anybody else should do for his wife in a similar situation—even if the consequence is that the person who is not rescued is my wife when the choice is between her and the wife of another rescuer.

The point is worth making because the general claim under consideration here is that Kantian ethics entails universal first-order impartiality. Yet it is clear from what has just been said that someone who rescues his wife can quite consistently will the maxim of his act as a universal law, and the requirement that one should be able to do this is one of Kant's formulations of the Categorical Imperative. Another formulation put forward by Kant demands that nobody should be treated as a means only. This requirement is also met if someone rescues his wife. The death of the other person is not a means to his end, which is simply to rescue his wife. The death of the other person comes about simply because he can rescue only one, so if he rescues his wife he cannot rescue the other. In the case as stated he does not wish the death of the other, either as an end in itself or as a means to the end of rescuing his wife. This can be made clear by observing that it would in no way frustrate his objectives if some other rescuer were to turn up and save the other person.[32] The third formulation of the Categorical Imperative demands that each person should be able to be conceived of as a participant in the Kingdom of Ends. This can plausibly be connected with the basic idea of justice as impartiality: that agreement is to be reached ex ante on the rules and principles for common life.[33] We can thus draw on the analysis in the previous chapter to show that this calls for second-order impartiality but not universal first-order impartiality.

I have devoted some attention to the claim that utilitarianism and

Kantianism entail universal first-order impartiality because it underlies so much of the contemporary anti-impartialist literature. It is not, however, a claim upon which Williams himself in the end rests. Having made a good deal of play with consequentialist utilitarianism and the allegedly Kantian notion of equal treatment to be found in Fried's book, Williams suddenly changes his tack towards the end of 'Persons, Character and Morality'. He now admits that, in the kind of situation specified by Fried, the rescuer has available to him a variety of 'higher-order thoughts' capable of generating a moral principle that 'can legitimate his preference, yielding the conclusion that in situations of this kind it is at least all right (morally permissible) to save one's wife'.[34] Out of this variety he mentions only one: the thought that within a utilitarian framework one might allow for a division of labour, so that there can be special obligations which are justified on the ground that things go better overall with them. However, nothing that Williams goes on to say turns on the example of an impartialist second-order theory being utilitarian, so we may extend his remarks to two-level impartialism in all its forms.

The adversary to whom Godwin replied, Dr Parr, put forward an objection to Godwin's treatment of the 'famous fire cause' that foreshadows the one made by Williams. Parr said that the question of the right person to rescue should not even be raised, to which Godwin responded (correctly, I believe) that the issue 'must be tried by the criterion of all virtue'.[35] Williams departs from Parr in as far as he does not maintain that *nobody* should ask the question. But he does say that it is inappropriate for the rescuer himself to ask the question. The two-level approach, he suggests, 'provides the agent with one thought too many: it might have been hoped by some (for instance, by his wife) that his motivating thought, fully spelled out, would be the thought that it was his wife, not that it was his wife and that in situations of this kind it is permissible to save one's wife.'[36]

I am inclined to doubt that anything very informative is to be gained by asking what is the optimal number of thoughts for a person to have in any given situation. Perhaps in general it is better to have only the number necessary for the purpose in hand but I do not think much follows from that. Consider a surgeon about to undertake a delicate operation. It might be hoped by some (for instance, the patient) that he will concentrate all his attention on making the incision in the right place rather than diverting his attention to reflections such as that, taking account of the risks inherent in the operation and the probability that it will effect a cure, the operation is on balance worth doing. But such reflections had better be available to him, even if we would not wish them to be consciously present during the operation. It would, after all, be pretty monstrous if the surgeon were able only to say that, although the operation was entirely unnecessary, performing it fitted in with his goal of perfecting his technique, or would pay for his teenage daughter's riding lessons for a few weeks.

It should be said that the 'famous fire cause', in any of its variants, is a treacherous example from which to draw any conclusions. In the nature of the case we are dealing with a decision that has to be taken amidst panic and confusion, in which haste is of the essence. As Williams says—echoing Godwin's remark that someone who rescued his nearest and dearest rather than Fénelon would be allowed to have his heart in the right place—'the consideration that it was his wife is certainly . . . an explanation which should silence comment'.[37] But beyond that, it *is*, on the basis of two-level impartialism, sufficient for him to have the thought that it was his wife.

It is, of course, true that there is a second-order justification: that in cases like this it is permissible to save one's wife. But that must be so if we are to say that in other cases 'It was his . . .' will not be available as a justification. What about 'It was his horse' or 'It was his typescript'? Suppose the horse represents years of devoted training on the part of its owner, and the typescript is the only copy of its author's life work. Perhaps Williams would say that it is all right to prefer survival of the horse or of the manuscript to the life of somebody one has never met. But surely even he must admit that at some point the legitimate priority of a personal attachment runs out. If this is conceded, Williams is faced with the embarrassment that we apparently need a general theory to tell us where this point comes. If the 'one thought too many' objection is really an objection, it now simply crops up at a different point. For we must now presumably say that, before saving his wife, the man now has to think: 'It's my wife and this is the sort of case where that thought is sufficient.'

Taken together, this chapter and the preceding one show that none of the well-established forms of impartial morality entails universal first-order impartiality. More than this, I maintain that these forms of impartial morality are actually incompatible with universal first-order impartiality. The previous chapter was devoted to demonstrating this for both the Scanlonian and the Rawlsian versions of justice as impartiality. In the present chapter, I have extended the analysis to the utilitarian and Kantian branches of impartialism. In the next chapter, I shall complete the discussion, and the book, by arguing that a characteristic line of argument against impartiality from a feminist viewpoint rests on a now familiar failure to distinguish between second-order and first-order impartiality. I shall precede this by a discussion of the work of Lawrence Kohlberg, arguing that he does genuinely exemplify the conflation between first-order and second-order impartiality of which I have accused critics of impartiality. Once we recognize that the feminist attack on impartiality takes its origins in a critique of Kohlberg, we can see how it came about that the attack itself rests on a similar confusion.

CHAPTER 10

Kohlberg and the feminist critique of impartiality

39. Introduction

Universal first-order impartiality has been advocated by very few moral philosophers. Despite this, it seems to be widely believed that morality really demands it, and that we must therefore despair of ever being able to meet its demands. This is the conclusion that emerges from James Fishkin's study of what he calls 'ordinary moral reasoners', entitled *Beyond Subjective Morality*. Its subjects were in fact fellow students or ex-students at Yale University and the University of Cambridge. Fishkin found among them a widespread belief that 'in any adequate moral system moral obligations must be determined with what might be called *strict impartiality*, that is, with no special regard for one's own interests, situation, or relations with others'.[1] Finding this demand insupportable, many of Fishkin's respondents concluded that the notion of an adequate moral system was a chimera and lapsed into various forms of subjectivism. Fishkin's study was originally carried out as part of the work for a Ph.D. dissertation supervised by Bernard Williams. And although Williams scarcely qualifies as an 'ordinary moral reasoner', it seems clear that his conception of what he calls 'morality' is the same as that found to predominate among Fishkin's subjects, and that his reaction in writing off 'morality' so conceived is also the same as theirs. Alasdair MacIntyre put his finger on this in a review essay on the book of essays including 'Persons, Character and Morality' when he wrote that 'it is not impersonality and impartiality as such that create those problems which Williams rightly stigmatizes as false problems. It is rather an impersonality and an impartiality required to hold between all persons whatsoever equally, a socially contextless impersonality and impartiality which is the source of those problems.'[2]

In the next section I shall be looking at another student of 'ordinary moral reasoners', whose subjects ranged in age from young children to adults. This is the theorist of moral development Lawrence Kohlberg. Like Fishkin, Kohlberg found that many of his subjects identified morality with universal first-order impartiality. But he was not content to report his findings. He went on to endorse this conception of morality. Kohlberg is best known for having identified six stages of moral development. The fifth and sixth stages were both described by Kohlberg as 'postconventional', by which he meant that they invite people to disregard the positive morality of their society in deciding on the right course of action in any given situation. The fifth stage is utilitarianism, in its Godwinian form. (We have already seen the 'postconventional' implications of Godwin's consequentialism in Section 37.) The sixth stage is said by Kohlberg to embody equal treatment of persons, in contrast with the equal consideration of interests represented by utilitarianism. Kohlberg calls this sixth stage indifferently Kantian or Rawlsian, but in practice he seems to envisage it in a Rawlsian way in as far as he speaks of 'contractarian respect for persons' and (as we shall see) invokes specific features of Rawls's theory such as the priority of the interests of the worst off. However, in his 'postconventional' zeal, he entirely misses out on the fact that Rawlsian impartiality operates at the second-order level and gives rise to institutions that prescribe specific obligations to people as citizens of a particular country, members of a particular family, and so on. (See above, Section 35.)

For most of his career, Kohlberg maintained that the fifth and sixth stages tend to occur in temporal sequence. Towards the end of his life, he withdrew his claim. For my purpose here, it does not make any difference whether the sixth stage actually follows the fifth stage or not. For, as Kohlberg himself conceded, to show empirically that one stage *follows* another does nothing to establish that it is a *higher* stage. So far from constituting moral development, the temporal development might constitute moral retrogression. As Kohlberg put it (in his typically confused fashion), evidence that stage six regularly follows stage five 'would not convince us of the superiority of a Kantian normative ethical position unless we were already partly convinced by Rawls's theory of justice or others like it'.[3] I am concerned here, then, with Kohlberg's claim that his stages five and six are morally superior to any others and in particular his claim that the sixth stage is the highest.

Kohlberg's conception of a moral principle is distinctly unpromising: he tells us that 'by a moral principle we mean a mode of choosing which is universal, a rule of choosing which we want all people to adopt always in all situations'.[4] This statement just might be given an acceptable reading, but Kohlberg makes it quite clear that he wants to be understood as putting forward the interpretation that gives it maximum implausibility, according to which morality is inconsistent with any notion that there can be special duties attaching to certain roles or positions. Thus, he contrasts 'principled morality', which 'defines the right for anyone in any situation', with 'conventional morality', which 'defines good behavior for a Democrat but not for a Republican, for an American but not for a Vietnamese, for a father but not for a son'.[5]

This notion of 'principled morality' is, we may note, precisely the same as the 'morality' repudiated by Williams. For, as MacIntyre wrote in the essay from which I quoted before, the 'accounts of impersonality and impartiality' that Williams takes to be entailed by utilitarianism and Kantianism 'liquidate the requirements of justice within the household or family, the requirements of justice within the political community, and the requirements of justice in a variety of other particular spheres (church and school, for instance) into some conception of the requirements of justice, as such, the imposition of which makes all or almost all social particularity irrelevant'.[6] It will therefore be no surprise that Kohlberg's 'Kantian' stage six corresponds closely to the notion of equal treatment chosen by Williams to exemplify work of 'basically Kantian inspiration' (see Section 38).

In the long run, the significance of Kohlberg's work will probably turn out to be that dissatisfaction with his six-stage sequence gave rise to an influential feminist line of criticism of impartiality. This originated with Carol Gilligan, whose 'work arose largely as a critical reaction to the studies of moral reasoning carried on by Lawrence Kohlberg and his research associates'.[7] Gilligan in fact began as one of those research assistants. She broke away from him as a result of an observation that the female subjects in his studies seemed to be more likely than the males to get stuck at stage three rather than proceeding to the 'postconventional' stages five and six. Stage three is described by Kohlberg in the following terms: 'The value of a human life is based on the empathy and affection of family members and others toward its possessor.'[8] Gilligan suggested that, sympathetically construed, the third stage represented just as high a level of moral development as did the 'impartialist' fifth and sixth stages more favoured by males, one which emphasizes the maintenance and sustenance of personal relationships rather than one concerned with abstract justice.[9]

In response to further empirical studies, Gilligan has subsequently withdrawn the claim that females tend more towards an 'ethic of caring' and males more towards an 'ethic of justice'. She 'now asserts that her aim was not to disclose a statistical gender difference in moral reasoning, but rather simply to disclose and interpret the differences in the two perspectives'.[10] But she still holds to the idea that Kohlberg's stage six represents an 'ethic of justice' and is to be contrasted with an 'ethic of caring'. It is this notion, that there are two rival approaches to moral thinking, which has been picked up by a whole school of critics of impartiality. After the next section, which is devoted to Kohlberg himself, I shall discuss the whole idea of an 'ethic of caring' supposedly in conflict with an 'ethic of justice'. I shall argue that, if the two are properly understood, there need be no conflict.

40. Two Dilemmas

Kohlberg's method of ascertaining his subjects' moral beliefs consisted of presenting them with what he called dilemmas. These were situations in which somebody had to decide what to do. The subjects were asked to say what they thought would be the right thing to do in the situation. Their answers were then coded into one of the six stages. I am interested here not in Kohlberg's data about the way in which his subjects responded to these dilemmas but in his own ideas as to what stage six— the highest stage of moral development—would say was the right response. In this section I shall set out two of Kohlberg's dilemmas and discuss his own views about them. This will, I think, be the best way of illustrating the weaknesses of Kohlberg as a moral philosopher— weaknesses that have tended to discredit the whole idea of impartiality.

I said a little earlier that Kohlberg's sixth stage had a lot in common with the notion of equal treatment that I criticized in the previous chapter. The first dilemma I want to discuss is actually a variant of the 'famous fire cause' but with the twist that the problem is not whom to save but whom to send on a suicide mission. The parallel to Fried's logic emerges clearly in the fact that Kohlberg advocates making the decision by a random procedure. The problem was called by Kohlberg 'The Captain's Dilemma', and I must begin by quoting his statement of it, which runs as follows.

In Korea, a company of ten marines was outnumbered and was retreating before the enemy. The company had crossed a bridge over a river, but the enemy were still on the other side. If someone went back to the bridge and blew it up, the company could then escape. However, the man who stayed back to blow up the bridge would not be able to escape alive. The captain asked for a volunteer, but no one offered to go. If no one went back it was virtually certain that all would die. The captain was the only person who could lead the retreat.

The captain finally decided that he had two alternatives. The first was to order the demolition man to stay behind. If this man was sent, the probability that the mission would be accomplished successfully was ·8. The second alternative was to select someone to go by drawing a name out of a hat with everyone's name on it [except the captain's name—B.B.]. If anyone other than the demolition man was selected the probability that the mission would be accomplished successfully was ·7. . . . Which of the two alternatives should the captain choose and why?[11]

I have omitted from this statement of the problem a table which purports to give the chances of survival for the expert and the non-experts under each of the two alternatives between which the captain has to choose. A whole generation of young Americans must have been thoroughly baffled by this table, since there is no way of making sense of it. And this is not the worst of it, for Kohlberg's whole analysis of the case depends on the figures in the table. It is impossible to discuss what Kohlberg says in any detail without tangling with his arithmetical blunders, so I shall content myself here with giving a general impression of Kohlberg's line of argument. I have supplied a more detailed discussion in an Appendix under the title 'The Captain's Dilemma'.

Kohlberg's approach is very similar to that of Taurek, discussed in the previous chapter (Section 37). It is the demolition expert's bad luck that more 'statistical lives' will be saved if he is sent than if the person to go is chosen by lot, just as in Taurek's example it was bad luck to be one of the people at the end of the island with fewer rather than more people waiting to be rescued. And in exactly the same way as Taurek opts for giving everybody an equal chance of survival, even though this reduces the expected number of lives saved, so Kohlberg tells us that, in demanding a lottery, the expert 'is saying he has the right to a probability of living equal to the probability the other [members of the platoon have], even if this lowers the average probability for all'.[12]

I suppose it would be possible to follow Fried's analysis of the 'famous fire cause' and say that equal treatment is not really violated by sending the expert rather than holding a lottery because the occurrence of a situation calling on the expertise of the man trained in demolition work 'may itself stand as a sufficient randomizing event to meet the dictates of fairness'. After all, the situation might instead have been one in which the best person for some suicidal mission was the tallest, the lightest, the most talented linguist, or the most skilful map-reader. However, Williams's remark that this 'might have been' is 'far too slim to sustain a reintroduction of the notion of fairness' seems apt here too.

The deeper question is, of course, why we should suppose that randomizing is called for anyway. I shall relegate a full discussion of Kohlberg's answers to the Appendix. Let me take up here (and then only briefly) the simplest, which is an appeal to Rawls's 'difference principle'. This is taken by Kohlberg to entail that the prospects of the worst-off man should be made as favourable as possible. If the expert is told by the captain to go, Kohlberg says, the expert is the worst-off man because he faces certain death. But the effect of a lottery is that nobody's prospects are as poor as that. For everybody now has a chance of surviving.[a] Since a positive prospect of survival is preferable to facing certain death, the lottery must satisfy the difference principle.[13]

There are two reasons for saying that this has nothing to do with Rawls's theory of justice. The first is that the difference principle is intended by Rawls as a principle governing the socio-economic aspects of the 'basic structure of society'. It is, in other words, a principle designed for the appraisal of social institutions. (See Section 35 above for a discussion of Rawls's repudiation of first-order impartiality.) The second is that it is absolutely central to Rawls's conception of justice that we take account of actual outcomes, and not probabilistic expectations. The worst-off position in Kohlberg's story is that of somebody who dies. The lottery does nothing to alleviate the worst outcome, which is being dead. All it does (in comparison with sending the expert) is to make it more likely that there will be more deaths than just that of the man who goes to blow up the bridge.

The correct way of looking at the situation is to say that the situation is one in which somebody has to attempt to blow up the bridge at the cost of his own life, and the choice lies between sending the man who has been specially trained for just such a contingency and sending somebody chosen by lot. This should not be a dilemma, or even present an issue that requires thinking about. The captain is an officer in a military organization. Once we insert that institutional context, we should recognize that the captain has no choice but to order the expert to go. Unless I am very mistaken about the ethos of the US Marines, a captain who had put the names in a hat instead of sending the demolition expert would be court-marshalled if he got back and this became known. He would, indeed, be equally culpable if he had asked for volunteers instead of sending the expert. Kohlberg hopelessly skews the presentation of the case by treating the captain's first asking for volunteers as if

---

[a] Kohlberg says that the lottery gives everybody an *equal* chance of survival. (I have already quoted without comment his statement that the expert, in demanding a lottery, 'is saying that he has the right to a probability of living equal to' that of the others.) This claim embodies one of Kohlberg's arithmetical errors, as I shall show in the Appendix. Nothing, however, turns for the present purpose on Kohlberg's claim about the chances being equal. The argument, such as it is, can be made by saying simply that any positive chance of survival is better than none.

it raised no issues when it is in fact just as inappropriate a move as indulging in a lottery.

There is another less subtle way in which Kohlberg gives the lottery a more favourable showing than it deserves. He stipulates that if the expert is sent he has a chance of blowing up the bridge of 0·8, and that any of the others would have a 0·7 chance of success. It is usually an objection to contrived examples that they present the alternatives as being more starkly opposed than they would be in real life. Here, in contrast, what is at stake in the 'dilemma' is fudged by making the lottery only a very slight amount less likely to result in the destruction of the bridge than sending the man who is trained for the job. An obvious objection to this is simply that it is highly implausible that someone with no specialised training would be almost as good at blowing up bridges as somebody who had been trained to do it. Given a bunch of explosives and detonators, I would rate my chances of blowing up a bridge as quite low. If we add that the job has to be done in a hurry and perhaps while under enemy fire, the chances would be vanishingly small. Reckoning the expert's prospects of success as four in five, as Kohlberg stipulates, it would surely be optimistic to put the chances of the rest even at one in ten. Substituting a figure of 0·1 for Kohlberg's 0·7 would, of course, vastly increase the expected loss of life resulting from holding a lottery instead of ordering the expert to go. (See the Appendix for further discussion of this point.)

Kohlberg's comparative odds trivialize the issue in a deeper way as well. Not only do they make little turn on the choice between the lottery and the expert, but they corrupt the basis of judgement by implying that expertise is unimportant. If an amateur is seven-eighths as likely to succeed in demolishing a bridge as an expert, the division of labour comes to seem almost an irrelevance. Yet the crux of the case is that its setting is an army, and an army is a complex organization with differentiated roles based on specific training. If the people involved had been thrown together casually as a result of some natural catastrophe, there would be some room for an issue of fairness to arise. Especially if the odds were as close as Kohlberg stipulates, the person with the best chance of success (the tallest, the strongest swimmer, or whatever) might not unreasonably propose the alternative of a lottery. But in Kohlberg's actual case—even with his preposterous comparative odds of success—the situation is already too richly structured for any issue of fairness to emerge by the time the question of whom to send arises.

Kohlberg actually quotes one of his respondents ('Philosopher 2') as making precisely this point: '[The captain] should order the expert [to go], and himself do his own job of captain in the hope of preserving the company. He should not draw lots because this would not yield as skilled and reliable a man. The expert has no right to refuse since he has undertaken to serve in the war and to be trained as a demolition man.'[14] With sublime obtuseness, Kohlberg manages to miss the point of what his respondent was saying by suggesting that 'Philosopher 2 . . . opts for aggregate utility'.[15] In fact, it is clear that the response quoted here appeals to two ideas: that the captain would be failing to do his job if he did not choose the course of action most likely to preserve his company; and that by being trained in demolition work the expert has assumed a quasi-contractual obligation to exercise his skills where they are needed. 'Philosopher 2' is thus saying that the right thing to do depends on the existence of a network of duties and obligations arising from organizational structure and from commitments created by prior actions. All this fine detail seems to lie outside Kohlberg's moral universe. Little wonder that many people have found the air in it too thin to breathe.

Before leaving Kohlberg and turning in the next section to those who have capitalized on his manifold inadequacies as a basis from which to launch a general attack on impartiality, let me extend my discussion to take in his most famous example. (Fishkin, for example, used it in the study of 'ordinary moral reasoners' to which I referred at the beginning of this chapter.) The story is about somebody named Heinz, whose wife was dying from some disease but might be saved by a certain drug, which was priced by 'the druggist' at ten times what it cost to make. Heinz could raise only half the money, and offered to pay less than the price demanded by the druggist. 'But the druggist said, "No, I discovered the drug and I'm going to make money from it." So Heinz got desperate and broke into the man's store to steal the drug for his wife.'[16] The question is: should Heinz have tried to steal the drug? Kohlberg's answer, which he claims to follow from both the utilitarian (stage five) and the Kantian/Rawlsian (stage six) varieties of 'postconventional' morality, is that Heinz did the right thing. The utilitarian calculation is that the gain to the wife (a chance of surviving) outweighs the loss to the druggist (money), while the sixth stage tells us that the right to life trumps the right to property.[17]

As with the so-called captain's dilemma, the example is rigged so that the considerations telling against Kohlberg's preferred solution are weakened to the point at which they almost disappear. The case for sending the trained demolition man was undermined by making the other members of the platoon almost as likely to succeed in blowing up the bridge as he was. Here, the case for respecting property rights is undermined by making the 'druggist' a figure out of a Victorian melodrama, who asks ten times what the drug costs to make, and refuses to accept half that sum—an amount that would still be five times the cost. Yet if the matter were really as simple as Kohlberg suggests, the villainy of the druggist is irrelevant. Suppose the drug were being sold at a little over the cost of making it (or even below cost). Kohlberg's reasoning suggests that Heinz should still break in and steal it if he couldn't afford the price, since all that is relevant is that the life of Heinz's wife is more important than the monetary loss to the druggist.

Again, if life trumps property, presumably any life trumps any property. If it were hard to break into the druggist's store and steal the drug, but easy to break into a neighbour's house and steal the money that would enable him to afford the druggist's charges, Heinz should do that. It is also irrelevant that it is Heinz's wife who is to be the beneficiary of the break-in. (There is no room for 'the magic of the pronoun "my"' in Kohlberg's fifth or sixth stages.) A well-intentioned passer-by informed of the situation would therefore be equally under an obligation to steal the drug. Indeed, Kohlberg's illustrative stage six respondent is quoted as saying that Heinz should steal the drug for someone he just knows. This respondent is quoted as explaining his view as follows: 'A human life takes precedence over any other moral or legal value, whoever it is [*sic*]. A human life has inherent value whether or not it is valued by a particular individual.'[18]

Kohlberg's failure as a moral theorist may be said to stem from his cutting off the moment of decision from both its antecedents and its consequences. In the 'captain's dilemma' this showed itself in his ignoring the institutional context and in particular the significance of the demolition expert's having undergone training to fit him for precisely the kind of contingency that has arisen when the captain has to make his decision. In the Heinz problem it emerges in his failure to think about the wider implications of stealing the drug. (Even Kohlberg's stage five 'utilitarian' is extremely myopic, and takes account only of the immediate interests of the dying woman and the druggist.) Kohlberg explicitly cites universalizability, as embodied in Kant's Categorical Imperative, as a component of stage six thinking.[19] But it seems pretty clear that the maxim of Heinz's act in stealing the drug would not withstand universalization. Conceding that life has priority over property, it is still plausible that in the long run (and not a very long run at that) lives would on balance be lost rather than saved if everyone who had a close relative with a possibility of benefiting from the drug and who could not afford to pay for it were to steal it. For it must be anticipated that the druggist would react to these constant break-ins by ceasing to manufacture the drug at all. The result would be that nobody—whether they could afford to pay for it or not—would be able to get hold of it.

We might modify Kohlberg's proposed solution, that Heinz simply makes off with a life-saving dose of the drug, and specify that he leaves behind a sum of money sufficient to reimburse the druggist for the cost of manufacture with a little bit left over as profit. This would more successfully stand up to universalization, since the druggist would still be left with an incentive to go on making the drug if everybody in a similar situation to Heinz acted likewise. But we still have to recognize that it could be endorsed only by ignoring the broader effects on the incentive to innovate that would be created by holding down anyone who discovered a life-saving drug to a small return over and above the manufacturing costs of the drug.

The rule that permits the inventor of the drug to charge what he likes for it is a crude but practical means of encouraging research. Although the druggist makes more than a normal level of profit from his discovery, his example provides an incentive for others to put time and money into trying to invent other drugs—time and money that will be lost if they are unsuccessful. Thus, his profits are in a sense not only the return on his own costs but on the costs of all unsuccessful competitors.[b] Once the discovery is made, the continued production of the drug would be worth while to the inventor so long as the price he receives more than covers the manufacturing cost. But, in the absence of some alternative way of supporting research into new drugs, we cannot expect much further innovation to come about.

The test of universalizability needs to be handled with discretion. A

[b] A more mundane example is provided by the rules governing marine salvage. Salvage is a speculative business. A ship may spend days standing by a vessel in distress and not be called upon by its captain, either because he elects to do without help or because he chooses another potential salvor. If the ship is asked for help, its efforts may be unavailing because the vessel in distress is by then unsalvageable. Either way, the owners of the ship receive no remuneration for the time lost: only successful salvage operations are rewarded. Given this institutional framework, the reward to a salvor must be sufficient to cover not only the costs incurred in a successful salvage operation but the other unremunerated costs as well. (The reward is in fact set at a fixed proportion of the salvaged value.) Otherwise, it would not be worth anybody's while to engage in salvage, and the result of that would be unnecessary loss of cargoes, ships, and lives. (See Carol Heimer, *Reactive Risk and Rational Action: Managing Moral Hazard in Insurance Contracts* (Berkeley and Los Angeles: University of California Press, 1985), esp. p. 125.) I am not committing myself to the view that the traditional (and still existing) system for paying salvors is the best or the fairest. Its obvious attraction is that it requires far less organization than, say, a scheme that would collect a levy on all international shipping and pay for the actual efforts made, whether they led to salvage or not. The point is that one cannot judge the fairness of a given award made within the existing system in abstraction from the nature of the system itself.

vulgarized version of it is to ask of any act 'What if everyone did that?' Most of the time this produces absurd conclusions. If everyone (or even every Londoner) were to go to Hyde Park, it would become horrendously crowded. But it does not, of course, follow that nobody should go to Hyde Park. There is only one context in which it is relevant to generalize from the particular act in this way. This is where the only reason for more people not performing acts of the kind in question is their recognition that there would be bad consequences for everyone if acts of this kind become widespread.

We thus have a cooperative practice creating a good (or averting a bad), and we can say that anyone who fails to join in is a 'free rider' on the efforts or forbearances of the rest—a violator of the Rawlsian 'principle of fair play' (see Section 7). The behaviour is unfair because it exploits those who comply with the demands of the practice. These people can argue against the 'free rider' as follows: 'We could each individually benefit by doing as you are doing; but we refrain because we accept that the advantages of the practice would soon be lost if many of us acted like that. You are not claiming that there is anything special about your position. Your only difference from us lies in your being prepared to act anti-socially.' The maxim of the action thus has to be formulated so as to include the free-riding context. What is ruled out is to say 'I shall do x, where it is possible to do x (or possible to benefit from doing x) only because many other people similarly placed to me are refraining from doing x on the basis of moral constraints.' For it is manifest that someone who says this cannot coherently will that the others who are similarly placed should follow his example.[c]

Does this mean that any second-order impartialist theory must lead to the condemnation of Heinz? Such a conclusion would be too hasty. For the crucial point from which we should begin is that the institutional setting presupposed in Kohlberg's story falls far short of what second-order impartiality demands. Any situation in which people will die unless they or their families can come up with the money for life-saving drugs is fundamentally unacceptable from an impartialist view-

---

[c] Kant's own illustrations of maxims that violate the Categorical Imperative in the *Groundwork* all involve some kind of free-riding. There would be no difficulty in formulating satisfactory maxims in terms that made cooperative action conditional upon the cooperative behaviour of others. It was an idiosyncrasy of Kant's, not anything inherent in the idea of the Categorical Imperative, that led him to insist that one should determine what is the right thing to do on the assumption that everybody else will do it, whether or not they actually do. As Thomas Hill points out, the problem with this is 'that acting in this world by rules designed for another can prove disastrous', Thomas E. Hill, Jr., *Dignity and Practical Reason in Kant's Moral Theory* (Ithaca and London: Cornell University Press, 1992), 66; see also pp. 249–50, where Kant and Rawls are contrasted on this point to Rawls's advantage.

point. Kohlberg specifies at the start of the story that it is set in Europe.[20] Fortunately, however, in almost all of Europe either there is a state-mandated system of medical insurance or medical services are directly provided by state agencies. Heinz's dilemma arises only as a by-product of radically defective institutions.

This is worth emphasizing because second-order impartialist theories are primarily concerned with forming judgements on institutions (counting the positive morality of a society as an institution for this purpose). Indeed, it has to be said that second-order impartialist theories have not been developed in ways that are helpful in prescribing action under conditions where the legal framework is thoroughly bad. A prominent illustration of this point is Rawls's *A Theory of Justice*, which is avowedly a contribution to 'ideal theory'. This means that it is concerned with the question of what the institutions of a just society would be. All that Rawls has to offer going beyond this is that there is a duty to bring about just institutions where they do not exist.[21] This carries him into a discussion of civil disobedience, which he understands as an open appeal to the sense of justice of other members of the society aimed at creating support for just institutions or public policies (e.g. the abandonment of an unjust war).[22] But he does not offer any thoughts about the ethics of breaking unjust laws while attempting to avoid being detected—in contrast with civil disobedience, which is, according to Rawls's definition, carried out openly. Rawls would presumably tell Heinz that he ought to campaign for a national health service. But he has nothing to contribute to the solution of Heinz's dilemma, which can hardly wait for the creation of better social institutions.

What we can do, I suggest, is take as given *pro tem* an unjust institution and ask whether, from an impartial point of view, we would wish the positive morality of a society to approve of acts contrary to its provisions. In the eighteenth century, for example, it appears that the positive morality prevalent among almost everyone except landowners saw nothing wrong in poaching, even though this was punishable with ferocious penalties. From a Scanlonian original position, it would surely not be possible to reject the proposition that food for the many should have priority over sport for the few. Second-order impartiality would therefore endorse the positive morality that accepted the legitimacy of poaching.

Where does this leave Heinz? Perhaps in a Scanlonian original position nobody could reasonably reject a rule of positive morality permitting someone in his situation to steal the drug. But this would be no more than a corollary of the major proposition that in a just society nobody would find himself in Heinz's situation. Drugs would be available as needed under some national system of health care provision, and the prices charged by drug companies would be regulated so as to leave them with enough incentive for innovation but rule out profiteering. (Alternatively, the right of patent might be restricted.) My focus in this section is not, in any case, on whether or not Heinz should steal the drug but on how we ought to think about the question. What I have been concerned to argue is that Kohlberg's error is the same as Godwin's, even though his preferred theory is not utilitarian: he too 'considers the case separately taken'.[23]

41. Justice and Caring

I now want to discuss a line of criticism of justice as impartiality that I shall refer to as feminist. Before I launch into this discussion, which will be mainly critical, I should like to make it clear that this is only one strand in recent work on justice of feminist inspiration. Thus, some writers have accepted the case for second-order impartiality but argued that in practice impartialist theories have tended to be worked out in ways that put women at a disadvantage. For example, Rawls has been criticized for treating as unproblematic the justice of the family as that institution is currently constituted in western societies and for building patriarchalist assumptions into his theory of intergenerational justice with his talk of 'heads of families' choosing the principles to govern intergenerational relations.[24] I have no quarrel with this line of analysis. Indeed, I would say that work of this sort has made for some of the most stimulating contributions to political theory in recent years. There is no question that the traditional liberal conception of a 'private sphere', where the writ of public values such as justice does not run, is a damaging myth. However, my subject in this section is not impartialist views about women but rather certain feminist views about impartiality.

Impartiality, as understood by Godwin and Kohlberg (and for his own polemical purposes by Bernard Williams), starts from an idea that is innocuous enough in itself—in fact completely vacuous. This is the claim that people who are alike in morally relevant respects should receive similar treatment. Everything then turns on what is to count as a morally relevant feature. Within the kind of common-sense morality compatible with second-order impartiality, personal preferences or personal relations are a morally acceptable basis for discrimination in certain circumstances. That I like A more than B is a good enough reason for seeing more of A than B; and 'It's my wife' is a good enough reason for rescuing my wife from a burning building instead of some (possibly more admirable) person unrelated to me. In the Godwinian or Kohlbergian conceptions of impartiality, however, the range of features of a situation accounted morally relevant is highly restricted. This is an interpretation of the demands of impartiality that leaves no room for the moral significance of prior commitments, institutionally derived obligations, or personal relations.

Marcia Baron writes of 'a pseudoversion of universalizability' according to which we are supposed to ask ' "Would I do for everyone (or just anyone) what I am doing for my friend?" . . . That is, if I am willing to do favour X for Susan, I should be willing to do the same favour for anyone.' Baron says that, although 'criticisms of impartialist ethics sometimes assume that impartialists' hold this view, she does 'not know of any impartialists who believe that our conduct should meet this test'.[25] I am inclined to think, however, that Kohlberg and Godwin both subscribe to this conception of impartialism. Thus, as we have seen, Kohlberg takes 'a moral principle' to be 'universal' in the sense that it 'defines the right for anyone in any situation',[26] the implication being that there cannot be any rule prescribing 'good behavior . . . for a father but not for a son'.[27] And Godwin 'never abandoned his claim that the truths of justice are single and uniform. If a stranger's claim is stronger than that of my own needs or my family's, I must, in justice, meet that claim if I am able.'[28] (This could be a tautology, but the strength of a claim, we must recall, is to be defined in terms of the utilitarian criterion.)

That the Kohlbergian or Godwinian conception of impartial morality should be rejected is not a proposition that is in itself distinctly feminist.[d] What can give it a feminist slant is the claim that women tend to be more sensitive than men to the poverty of any system of universal first-order impartiality and more hospitable to an 'ethic of care'. As I pointed out in Section 39, Carol Gilligan has repudiated the claim that support for Kohlberg's fifth and sixth stages is greater among males

---

[d] Two philosophers who tend to identify impartial morality with universal first-order impartiality are Samuel Scheffler and Thomas Nagel: in Scheffler's case consequentialism akin to Kohlberg's stage five; in Nagel's case an idea of 'impersonal' equality of treatment more akin to Kohlberg's stage six. They both argue for the inadequacy of impartial morality so conceived. But rather than proposing a rival 'ethic of care' that generates obligations conflicting with those generated by impartiality, they seek some grounding for individual agents to pursue their own interests or purposes even when this leads to conflicts with the demands of impartial morality. See Samuel Scheffler, *The Rejection of Consequentialism* (Oxford: Clarendon Press, 1982), and Thomas Nagel, *The View from Nowhere* (New York: Oxford University Press, 1986) and id., *Equality and Partiality* (New York: Oxford University Press, 1991). I believe that their concerns are better met by working out systematically the implications of second-order impartiality than by looking for *ad hoc* exceptions to universal first-order impartiality.

than females. Nevertheless, as Marilyn Friedman has pointed out, 'researchers who otherwise accept the disconfirming evidence [for the "different voice" hypothesis] have nevertheless noticed that many women readers of Gilligan's book find it to "resonate ... thoroughly with their own experience"'.[29] And one plausible explanation of this phenomenon is that there is a widely held perception that men and women do have different priorities. 'Men are stereotyped according to what are referred to as "agentic" norms. These norms center primarily around assertive and controlling tendencies. The paradigmatic behaviors are self-assertion, including forceful dominance, and independence from other people. Also encompassed by these norms are patterns of self-confidence, personal efficacy, and a direct, adventurous personal style.' In contrast to this, 'the gender stereotypes of women ... include: a concern for the welfare of others; the predominance of caring and nurturant traits; and, to a lesser extent, interpersonal sensitivity, emotional expressiveness, and a gentle personal style'.[30]

This, however, creates something of a puzzle, which Friedman expresses as follows: 'How could those critics who challenge Gilligan's gender hypothesis be right to suggest that women and men show no significant differences in moral reasoning, if women and men are culturally educated, trained, pressured, expected, and perceived to be so radically different?'[31] The question might, I suggest, be turned back the other way. We could ask: 'Why should a division of moral labour necessarily be associated with a differential evaluation of the two stereotypical roles?' Consider as an analogue the occupational division of labour. Suppose I think I ought to be an academic and a bricklayer thinks he ought to be a bricklayer. This is no reason for me to think that everybody should be an academic or for him to think that everybody should be a bricklayer. Nor is there any particular reason to assume that we must hold predictably divergent views about the relative importance of academics and bricklayers.

For the sake of argument, let us take it to be fact that (for whatever reason) women are more attuned to problems involved in maintaining networks of personal relationships in good working order while men are better at handling the world of 'telegrams and anger'.[32] One reaction to this would be that the members of each sex should try harder to do the things that they are stereotypically bad at: that would be quite consistent with the idea that members of both sexes should attach the same relative value to both kinds of activities (not necessarily an equal value). But it would not be inconsistent with the same idea for there to be some degree of division of labour, with women tending to specialize more in the one kind of activity and men in the other.

It may be asked whether it is compatible with justice as impartiality for a society to have differentiated expectations of this kind. My own view is that it is, though only under quite stringent conditions. (I shall take up this matter in Volume III of this *Treatise* in the context of equality of opportunity.) Provided the appropriate conditions are met, I would regard it as an issue to be argued out in terms of alternative visions of a good society rather than in terms of justice. However, what I must emphasize is that nothing turns on the answer given to the question of the justice of some kind of gender-related division of labour. The crucial point for the present purpose is that there is no reason for assuming that such a division of labour, where it exists, must give rise to different evaluations of the two sets of attributes. Why should not men and women agree about the equal value of the roles thought particularly suitable for women and those thought particularly suitable for men?

The case I wish to argue is that both of Gilligan's 'different voices'—the 'ethic of justice' and the 'ethic of care'—are valid, and should be incorporated within any satisfactory account of morality.[e] But the feasibility of this reconciliation between the two depends upon the rejection of Kohlberg's notion of justice. Gilligan and many of her followers, while reacting against Kohlberg, actually swallow a crucial element in Kohlberg's theory, the equation of justice with the kind of equal treatment that Kohlberg thought was mandated by his sixth stage of moral development.[33] Since this entails universal first-order impartiality, it fills up the whole moral space and thus leaves no room for any other basis of moral judgement to be combined with it. We can therefore easily understand how the pervasive idea of an unavoidable conflict between an 'ethic of justice' and an 'ethic of caring' comes about.

On this view of the matter, there are only two basic ways in which an 'ethic of caring' can exist alongside an 'ethic of justice' in a society. One

[e] This is the position taken by Susan Moller Okin (see *Justice, Gender and the Family*, esp. p. 15) and also by Marilyn Friedman, though I have some reservations about the terms of reconciliation that both of them propose. Friedman's own 'partial answer' to the puzzle I discussed above—that gendered stereotypes coexist with the absence of gender-linked differences within Kohlberg's schema—'depends upon showing that the care/justice dichotomy is rationally implausible and that the two concepts are conceptually compatible' (Friedman, 'Beyond Caring . . .', 97). I do not see, however, that exploding the Kohlbergian schema philosophically provides much of a solution to the puzzle. For the puzzle grows not out of what we as philosophers believe to be true, but out of what 'ordinary moral reasoners' believe to be true. And we know (from both Kohlberg's work and Fishkin's study of his 'ordinary moral reasoners') that a lot of people do mistakenly believe that impartiality corresponds to Kohlberg's stages five and six—some going on to accept it while others react by rejecting it. It therefore seems to me more sensible to query the expectation that there *should* be any connection between what Friedman calls a 'moral division of labor' based on gender and a 'different voice'.

is that each person contains within himself or herself the two warring ethics, and somehow decides how to act on each occasion according to which one comes out on top. The other is that some people are the bearers of an 'ethic of justice' and others the bearers of an 'ethic of caring'. Against this, I should like to say that *nobody* should adhere to an 'ethic of justice' if that is taken to mean the morality of Kohlberg's stage six. If it did turn out to be the case that men are more tempted to endorse Kohlberg's stage six than women, men would simply have to resign themselves to recognizing that, as well as having a shorter life expectancy than women, they also suffered the disadvantage of having to struggle harder to avoid living morally impoverished lives.

Suppose instead we say that justice is not what Kohlberg says it is but is a matter of having principles and rules that are compatible with second-order impartiality. We can still accept that an 'ethic of justice' so understood is in need of supplementation by an 'ethic of caring'. But the way in which this will work out will be very different from that envisaged by Gilligan and her allies. For we shall no longer have occasion to think of two rival 'ethics' disputing the same terrain. Instead, we shall be able to see an 'ethic of justice' and an 'ethic of caring' as complementary. I believe that, if justice is interpreted on the lines I have advocated, there is no plausible case of a genuine moral dilemma involving a clash between justice and caring. The cases that are put up seem to me to fall into two groups: those where plausible rules of justice do not determine the choice, so it is perfectly legitimate to use a 'caring' approach to decide what to do; and those where plausible rules of justice do determine the choice, so that it is a mistake to suppose that it is necessary to make a choice between the deliverances of two rival 'ethics' that both bear on the case.

An example of the first is provided by Nel Noddings in her book *Caring*.[34] She takes the case of a woman trying to decide whether to go out for the evening with her husband to some long-planned event or stay at home with her child, who is ill but not seriously or dangerously ill. Noddings is surely quite right to say that an indefinitely large number of considerations might be relevant to her decision and that none of them could be reduced to matters involving rights and duties. This is, however, simply to say that the decision is left open by the structure of rights and duties, which is why all the other considerations are free to play their part. No doubt, Godwin would say that the woman's duty is to be established by summing the utilities of the parties in the two alternative situations, and Kohlberg would maintain that his stage six would generate a uniquely right thing to do—e.g. that the woman should take whichever course of action makes the least well off out of the three people concerned as well off as possible. We can happily concede that Noddings's case tells against both of these impartialist approaches. But it does nothing to impugn the idea that caring has to fit into the structure of rights and duties.

One way of making this plain is to alter the case put by Noddings so that the woman in question is a professional nanny, who has been placed in a position of trust by the parents to look after their child while they are away and has (let us say) accepted a specific obligation to stay with it if it is ill. Suppose now that the question arises of whether she should stay in or go out for the evening with her boyfriend, as they had planned. There is, I suggest, no room here for the kinds of consideration that Noddings draws from the 'caring' perspective: how much the child wants her to stay, how long it is since the last evening out together, exactly how ill the child is, how much she herself needs a break, and so on. The decision is determined in this case by the obligation to stay and look after the child. This is not, of course, to say that it is impossible to envisage any circumstances in which that obligation might be overridden. (Suppose, for example, that the next door neighbour has to be rushed to hospital and nobody else is immediately available to do it.) The point is, however, that the circumstances must be such as to activate a duty of greater salience than that entailed by the contractual obligation to look after the child. No mere accumulation of Noddings-style considerations could do this.

The other cases are bogus dilemmas which arise from the fallacy of supposing that some generally admirable trait (loyalty, say) can somehow create a moral counterclaim to what are demonstrably the requirements of justice. A fairly typical example, which is said to be an instance 'where abstract principles clash with concrete caring', is 'the ethical dilemma for Colonel North's secretary. Ought she to have followed the nations [*sic*] laws or her loyalty to her boss? . . . In this situation, how are principles of justice and principles of caring to be related?' The answer is obvious: principles of justice win. As the author concedes, 'shredding top-secret documents and smuggling papers out of the White House are clearly illegal and violate constitutional principles'.[35] That should be sufficient to settle the issue. To regard loyalty to one's boss as a genuine moral counterweight (as this author does) is simply to display a frightening lack of moral common sense.

I have said that I do not believe it is possible to find a plausible case in which there is a legitimate conflict between an 'ethic of justice'—construed in terms of justice as impartiality—and an 'ethic of caring'. I do not wish to deny, however, that there are some partisans of an 'ethic of caring' who wish to reject not only Kohlbergian justice but justice as impartiality. The most forthright presentation of this root-and-branch opposition to impartiality is to be found in a book I have already referred to, *Caring* by Nel Noddings. This makes the usual objurgatory references to Kohlberg[36] but, far from being a useful corrective to the deficiencies of Kohlberg's fifth and sixth stages, it is nothing less than a call for a moral revolution of a far-reaching and potentially catastrophic nature.

According to Noddings, Abraham, who was prepared to sacrifice his son for a principle, is a typical father; and Ceres, who condemned the earth to barrenness for the half of each year that her daughter was away in the Underworld, is a typical mother.[37] 'The father might sacrifice his own child in fulfilling a principle; the mother might sacrifice any principle to preserve her child.'[38] On the second conception of morality, there is no room for the idea that there can be obligations imposed by the requirement that the interests of other human beings are entitled to respect simply *qua* interests of other human beings. Obligations, Noddings tells us, can arise only out of relations with other people. There 'seem to be two criteria: the existence of or potential for present relation, and the dynamic potential for growth in relation, including the potential for increased reciprocity and, perhaps, mutuality. The first criterion establishes an absolute obligation and the second serves to put our obligations into an order of priority.' The implication of this is that 'our obligation is limited and delimited by relation. We are never free, in the human domain, to abandon our preparedness to care; but, practically, if we are meeting those in our inner circles adequately as ones-caring and receiving those linked to our inner circles by formal chains of relation, we shall limit the calls upon our obligation quite naturally.'[39]

It is not clear to me whether Noddings simply wants to add Cereal morality (with women as the main bearers of it) to Abrahamic morality (with men as the main bearers of it) or whether her ideal is an entirely Cereal society. The first of these alternatives would combine two unsatisfactory moral outlooks: one characterized by a kind of rigid justice that excluded caring and the other characterized by a reckless disregard for all considerations of justice. Even if we improved its specification by substituting some more adequate notion of impartial justice for Noddings's Abrahamic ethic, the resulting society would still be very unattractive. An unavoidable feature of it would be that women would have to be excluded from all public responsibilities. For it would be impossible to trust them to carry out public duties conscientiously. Whenever a choice had to be made between adherence to principle and doing a favour for somebody with whom they had a pre-existing relation, they would sacrifice the principle.[40] In the terms set out in Section 2, it would have to be concluded that women were incapable of practising first-order impartiality in cases where that is required by holding some public office. Thus, the many leading Western political philosophers who have held precisely this view of women would have got the last laugh.[41]

Now consider the case of a society all of whose members acted exclusively on an 'ethic of caring' of the kind advocated by Noddings. Such a society would be characterized by a variant on what Edward Banfield called 'amoral familism'. This syndrome, which he claimed to be widespread in the village in Lucania (southern Italy) that he studied, expressed itself in 'the inability of the villagers to act together for the common good or, indeed, for any end transcending the immediate, material interest of the nuclear family'.[42] The villagers subscribed officially to the norms of Christianity but regarded them as hopelessly impractical as guides to conduct. In a Cereal society, people would not even pay lip-service to impartially defensible principles. Perhaps 'relation' *à la* Noddings would create a sense of obligation extending beyond the immediate family. But nobody would feel that these obligations must be subordinated to the demands of justice as impartiality.

In his book, *The Moral Basis of a Backward Society*, Banfield took as his epigraph the passage in *Leviathan* depicting 'the state men are naturally in'. It ends with the famous peroration that 'the life of man' in this state would be 'nasty, brutish, and short'.[43] A Cereal society would suffer essentially the same inconveniences as a Hobbesian state of nature. That Hobbes thought of human beings as primarily egoistic was not necessary for his conclusion. David Hume was quite prepared to concede that 'tho' it be rare to meet with one, who loves any single person better than himself; yet 'tis as rare to meet with one, in whom all the kind affections, taken together, do not over-balance all the selfish'.[44] But he still concluded, quite correctly, that 'so noble an affection' as that of people for their nearest and dearest, 'instead of fitting men for large societies, is almost as contrary to them, as the most narrow selfishness. For ... this must necessarily produce an opposition of passions, and a consequent opposition of actions....'[45] We might speculate, indeed, that people are prepared in general to act more ruthlessly in the pursuit of the interests of their nearest and dearest than in the pursuit of their own personal interests. In the absence of a sense of justice to set limits, we might conclude, 'confin'd generosity' poses an even greater threat to social order than pure egoism.

Noddings tells us that she 'emphatically' rejects as a test of a morally acceptable action that its maxim should be universalizable.[f] She is wise to do so, since the defects of the Noddings 'ethic of care' would soon be exposed by the most straightforward application of the universalizability test. Consider, for example, a disciple of Ceres determined to advance at any cost in terms of principle the interests of her daughter. Let us imagine that she is on the board of governors of the school that the daughter attends and is proposing to exploit the influence that this gives her in order to gain for her daughter some unjustified advantage— for example, special musical tuition for which some other child is much better qualified.[g] She would only have to ask herself how she would feel if she were the mother of the other child to see how morally repugnant her plan to abuse her position is.

I have said that Noddings repudiates universalizability. It remains true, however, that she is a universal prescriptivist in this sense: that she prescribes the same structure of ends to everybody.[46] (That is, at any rate, the reading that I am exploring here: I have already discussed the alternative reading according to which the prescription applies to a half of the human race.) Thus, people with nothing but the 'ethic of care' to guide their actions would inevitably find that, because of the lack of any authoritative coordinating rules, their pursuit of their ends was constantly being frustrated by others' pursuit of their (different) ends.

The people in a society governed entirely by a Cereal ethic would thus find themselves in the position of the people whose plight I discussed at the end of Chapter 1. The only difference—which would make conflict even more pervasive—is that the people in a Noddings society would be pursuing partial conceptions of the good, whereas the people considered at the end of Chapter 1 were pursuing impartialist conceptions of the good. At the beginning of Chapter 2, I widened the analysis to include partial conceptions of the good, and argued that— purely in order to pursue their ends more effectively—people with divergent ends would find it in their interests to agree on some rules of

[f] 'Many of those writing and thinking about ethics insist that any ethical judgment— by virtue of its *being* an ethical judgment—must be universalizable; that is, it must be the case that, *if* under conditions X you are required to do A, then under sufficiently similar conditions, I too am required to do A. I shall reject this emphatically' (Noddings, *Caring*, p. 5). It should be observed, however, that Noddings has an extraordinarily crude conception of what is to be universalized. Thus, she says (p. 52) that 'slogans such as "Put your husband (child) first!" are quite useless. There are times when he must come first; there are times when he cannot.'

[g] This is not a hypothetical example: I know of one school where there were four places for special musical training to be allocated, and they went to the four children whose parents were governors of the school. Since this is the kind of case where strict first-order impartiality is required, the institutional implication is (see Section 2) that parents with children attending a school should not be eligible to be governors of that school.

justice. They would thus be led to discover the idea of justice as mutual advantage. If the analysis contained in Part I of this book is correct, they would be led by the defects of justice as mutual advantage to embrace justice as reciprocity. But the lack of fit between the motive for behaving justly and the criteria of justice that is inherent in justice as reciprocity would propel them into the acceptance of justice as impartiality.

42. *Conclusion*

I have now come full circle. At the beginning of this book, back in Section 1, I denied that justice as impartiality is a 'view from nowhere', an arbitrary imposition that might appeal to 'men from Mars' but has little to offer to human beings. I have now tried to show how, starting off from the most earthy ethic imaginable, one that gave moral weight only to obligations arising from ties of affection and relation, the logic of justice as impartiality would assert itself. The triumph of an ethic of care would thus be short-lived: its own internal contradictions would lead to its transcendence.

This does not mean that the virtues of an ethic of care have to be sacrificed. Rather, it would find its proper place. 'Amoral familism' is to an appropriately conceived ethic of care as universal first-order impartiality is to an appropriately conceived ethic of impartial justice. Both are pathological overextensions of ideas that are valid within certain limits but become pernicious beyond those limits.

It should not be supposed that fitting an ethic of care into the framework of justice as impartiality entails compromising the value of care. There is an idea around, perhaps more in unreflective popular thought than among philosophers (though Bernard Williams seems to me to trade on it) that you cannot really care for somebody unless your care is completely unconditional. This should be exposed for the sentimental tosh that it is. Johnson's exhortation to Boswell, in response to a piece of conventional sententiousness on the latter's part, remains valid: 'My dear friend, clear your mind of *cant*.'[47]

The point has been made by Barbara Herman, who is both a Kantian and a mother. 'Just as I know in advance', she has written, 'that I cannot do whatever will promote my own well-being, so I know in advance and as part of my caring [for my son] that I may not be able to promote his good' in any situation in which it is 'inappropriate' to 'determin[e] the effective practical weight of interests by how much I care about them.'[48] She also makes the important point that unconditional care is not even in the long-term interests of the recipient of the care. Again speaking of her son, she says that 'his interests are not the only ones I care about (there are not only my friends, my spouse, my students, and myself, but sometimes complete strangers or causes that claim my attention and resources), and further, he will do fine, indeed he will often do better, if he relies on me less, and if my life is increasingly separate from his'.[49] The point might be put more strongly: children who grow up in an atmosphere that encourages them to believe that their parents will promote their interests at any cost are liable to develop into monsters.

The concrete demands of the moderate (i.e. non-Noddings) partisans of an ethic of care are for caring to be given greater social recognition and more financial and logistical support. They also call for the burdens of caring to be more equitably distributed. There is nothing in either of these demands that is incompatible with justice as impartiality. On the contrary, I believe (though showing it will have to await a later volume of this *Treatise*) that the principles of justice that flow from the conception of justice as impartiality will endorse both demands. If I am right about this, it provides further support for my claim that the alleged conflict between an ethic of care and an ethic of justice is a bogus one.

I have thus been carrying forward here the overall aim of Part III of this book, which is to dispel some persistent misconceptions about the nature of the theory of justice as impartiality and about its implications. Most of the problems arise from the existence of a large number of people who start foaming at the mouth the moment the word 'impartiality' is as much as mentioned. I have little hope of persuading them, since the usual red mist will presumably be summoned up by the very title of this book. I hope, however, that I may have been able to convince anyone who approaches the book with a reasonably open mind that the large and growing anti-impartialist literature leaves justice as impartiality unscathed. I argued in the previous section that it is not entirely true to say that nobody holds (or ever has held) the impartialist positions attacked by the anti-impartialists. Nevertheless, it is strange that so much passionate invective has been poured on ideas so infrequently advocated.

The trouble is that the anti-impartialists tend to proceed as if they have established more than they have by their attacks on universal first-order impartiality, in either its 'utilitarian' or 'Kantian' guises. Having dismissed that, they want to hear nothing good of impartiality. Yet, if they do not endorse a Noddings-style monolithic ethic of care (and most do not), they should accept that impartiality has a role to play. The only question ought to be exactly what that role is.

The answer that I wish to press is, of course, that the appropriate role for impartiality is supplied by the theory of justice as impartiality. In the next volume of this *Treatise*, I shall assume the correctness of that answer. Having, I hope, secured the case for justice as impartiality more firmly than I left it at the end of Volume I, I shall take up the questions originally scheduled for Volume II. I shall set out some principles that I maintain to be principles of justice, and defend them by an appeal to the theory of justice as impartiality. I shall then explore some of the problems that arise in applying them.

APPENDIX
The captain's dilemma

In Section 40, I had to discuss Kohlberg's 'captain's dilemma' in some-what vague terms because I did not want to get embroiled in a reanaly-sis of his claims about probabilities of survival under various contingencies. I shall do so here partly to fill in a gap in Section 40 and partly, I confess, because the whole business raises a question in the sociology of academia that intrigues me: how did somebody with the kind of intellect capable of producing 'Justice as Reversibility' ever get taken seriously? I assume that any adequate answer would have to shed a less than flattering light on social psychology as a scholarly discipline. But I surmise that another factor to be invoked in the explanation would have to be the so-called 'halo effect'—the presumption that a professor at Harvard University cannot be incapable of coherent thought.[a]

The table that I omitted from Kohlberg's statement of the problem is shown in Table 1.[1] A curious feature of this table is that, whereas the text has one name drawn from a hat, the second column of the table suggests that the method of selection is drawing straws. This has no sig-nificance except as setting the tone for the general daffiness to follow. The serious problem with the table is that it is impossible to give any coherent interpretation of the numbers in it.

TABLE 1: KOHLBERG'S TABLE

	Expert Goes	Draw Straws
Outcome for expert	00%	70%
Outcome for anyone else	80%	70%

The table comes without a caption and no explanation for what is in it is offered in the text. However, it is hard to see that the table can be intended to do anything other than set out the odds of survival in the two alternative scenarios. We can interpret the left hand column in this

[a] The most striking example of the halo effect (and the best example of its power) is the common finding in surveys of the reputation of American departments that Princeton's law school is among the best in the country—despite its not having one.

way so that it works out correctly, so long as we make a complete certainty out of what Kohlberg says in the text is 'virtually certain': that, if the man who is sent to blow up the bridge fails in the task, this has fatal consequences for all the rest of the company. On this assumption, we can see that the left hand column of Kohlberg's table is accurate: it tells us that if the expert is sent he has no chance of survival and the others have a chance of survival equal to the probability that the expert will succeed.

That the left hand side of the table can be given a consistent reading may give us some confidence in our surmise about the meaning of the numbers in the cells. But if that interpretation is correct the numbers on the right hand side of the table must be wrong. The upper right cell should tell us the expert's probability of surviving if some randomizing process (let us simply call it a lottery, leaving open the mechanism) is used to determine who is sent to blow up the bridge. But there is no way of making this come out at 0·7. There are two components in the calculation of the expert's odds of survival with a lottery. One is the probability that somebody other than the expert will have to go (which is 0·9). The other is the probability that this person will be successful in carrying out the mission (which is 0·7). Incidentally, Kohlberg does not make it clear whether there are ten men plus the captain or ten altogether, but since the arithmetic is simpler in the first case I am assuming that there are nine non-experts and one expert plus the captain as an eleventh man. (Nothing of significance turns on which we say.) The expert's chance of surviving is thus $0·9 \times 0·7 = 0·63$.

What can we say about the 'outcome for anyone else'? The first thing we must say is that the captain's prospects are now better than those of any of his men, since he does not participate in the lottery. This problem did not arise for the case where the expert was sent, since the captain's chances of survival were the same as those of the non-experts in the platoon. 'Everyone else' could then include the captain. With the lottery, the captain's prospects have two components: a one in ten chance of the expert's going (with an associated 0·8 probability of success) and nine chances in ten of a non-expert going (with an associated probability of success of 0·7). Thus, the probability of the captain's survival if there is a lottery among the other ten men is $(0·1 \times 0·8) + (0·9 \times 0·7) = 0·71$. For each of the others (i.e. the members of the platoon other than the expert) the probability of survival is made up of three factors. First, there is one chance in ten that he will have to go himself. Second, there is a one in ten probability that the lot will fall on the expert. And, third, there are eight chances in ten that another non-expert will have to go. The chance of survival for each non-expert is thus $(0·1 \times 0·8) + (0·8 \times 0·7) = 0·64$. If we

TABLE 2: KOHLBERG'S TABLE CORRECTED

	Expert Goes	Draw Straws
Outcome for expert	00%	63%
Outcome for anyone else	80%	64%

take it that 'everyone else' excludes the captain we get Table 2, which is the corrected version of Table 1.

I suggested in Section 40 that Kohlberg makes the dilemma artificially trivial by postulating that the other members of the platoon are almost as effective at demolition work as the man trained for it. I argued that this is implausible and in any case blunts the force of the choice between expertise and (alleged) fairness. Let us therefore recompute Table 2 for the case proposed in Section 40 in which the expert's probability of succeeding remains at 0·8 but the probability of the others succeeding falls to 0·1. This gives us Table 3.

TABLE 3: PROBABILITIES OF SURVIVAL IF NON-EXPERTS HAVE 0·1 CHANCE OF SUCCESS

	Expert Goes	Draw Straws
Outcome for expert	00%	9%
Outcome for anyone else	80%	16%

With these new figures, we can see that the lottery creates a very high cost in terms of 'statistical lives'. If the expert goes, he dies for certain and the other ten (for we must include the captain here) each have a chance of 0·8 of living. The upshot is that eight 'statistical lives' will be saved by sending the expert. Under the lottery, the expert's probability of surviving is $0·9 \times 0·1 = 0·09$; the non-experts' is $(0·1 \times 0·8) + (0·8 \times 0·1) = 0·16$; and the captain's is $(0·1 \times 0·8) + (0·9 \times 0·1) = 0·17$. The number of 'statistical lives' saved thus falls to 1·7, so we may say that making the choice by lottery instead of ordering the expert to go can be expected to cost 6·3 lives. Since there are only eleven men altogether, this is obviously a very high proportional cost. Even if we were inclined to think the lottery was fair, we might be inclined to think that fairness should give way to efficacy in this case. As I argue in Section 40, however, it is not true that any such choice is forced upon us.

Kohlberg makes a number of statements in his defence of the lottery option that are incorrect, given his own figures for the comparative likelihood of success of the expert and the non-experts. The surreal effect of this farrago is greatly enhanced by Kohlberg's suddenly talking about 'the weak man' and 'the strong man', and treating them as if they were interchangeable with the expert and one non-expert. (He does not explain what happened to the rest of the platoon.)

Kohlberg pursues two lines of argument in favour of the lottery. One is a rendering of Rawls's original position that loses one of its essential features. Rawls stipulates that the parties do not know the probability of occupying different positions, whereas Kohlberg says: 'In terms of the Rawlsian original position, we ask "What would be chosen by the captain (or the strong man or the weak man) in an original position, with an equal probability of being the weak man or the strong man (or the captain)?"' His answer is that they (or more precisely the expert and the non-expert) would opt for the lottery. He writes:

If a lottery is used the expert's probability of living is 70%; if he is ordered, the probability of living is 0%. From the standpoint of the least advantaged position—the expert's—the lottery increases his life chances 70%. How does the lottery affect the other positions? The other man's [i.e. the non-expert's] chances of life decrease only 10% by the use of the lottery, compared to the 70% decrease in life chances of the weak man [i.e. the expert] if he is ordered to go, instead of using a lottery. Both the strong man [i.e. the non-expert] and the weak man [i.e. the expert], then, choose the lottery in an original position.[2]

Kohlberg is clearly relying on the figures in Table 1 here. These were inaccurate for survival probabilities under the lottery, as we have seen, because they left out of consideration the chance of being the one who had to blow up the bridge and counted only the probability of survival if somebody else went. Even then the figures got the wrong answer for the non-experts, since they disregarded the contingency that the expert might be the one chosen by lot to go. With only one expert and one non-expert, the result of these errors is obviously magnified. For both the expert and the non-expert now have a fifty-fifty chance of having to go. Thus, the correct account (on Kohlberg's own stipulations about the chances of success if sent) will run as follows. With the lottery, the expert's survival prospects will improve from 0 to 35% ($0.5 \times 0.7 = 0.35$), and the non-expert's survival prospects will decline by 40% (from 0.8 if the expert is sent to 0.4 if there is a lottery). I have already commented that, although Kohlberg claimed that the captain would also choose the lottery, the captain was mysteriously absent when the numerical analysis was put forward. Presumably Kohlberg would assimilate him to the non-expert—which is valid only if we ignore the difference between them that arises from the captain's not taking part in the lottery. In fact, the captain does much better than either of the others from the lottery: he has a survival chance of 0·8 if the expert is sent (as does the non-expert) but still has a survival chance of 0·75 with the lottery (an equal chance of 0·8 and 0·7).

It is, of course, very odd that Kohlberg talks about the non-expert and the expert both choosing to have a lottery, since the point of the veil of ignorance (explicitly specified by Kohlberg) is that none of them knows which he actually is. One way of making sense of what he says, which would also explain some peculiarities in the way in which he sets the problem up, would be as follows. From behind the veil of ignorance, each of the two men mentioned (the expert and the non-expert) calculates that whichever of them turns out to be the expert gains a 70 per cent survival chance from the lottery rather than being ordered to go, whereas whichever of them turns out to be the non-expert loses only a 10 per cent chance of survival from the lottery instead of the expert's being ordered to go. Since the expert's gain from the lottery is far larger than the non-expert's loss, anyone with a fifty-fifty chance of being either would clearly be rational to prefer the lottery. Even if Kohlberg had remembered the captain, he would not have needed to change the general lines of this answer. For (on the basis of calculation underlying Table 1) the captain's case would be assimilated to that of the non-expert. Thus, there would now be one chance in three of gaining 70 per cent from the lottery and two chances in three of losing 10 per cent from it. Rational maximizers behind a veil of ignorance would still opt for the lottery.

If this is what Kohlberg has in mind, it is a quite amazing piece of statistical legerdemain, since it purports to prove that more 'statistical lives' will be saved if there is a lottery than if the expert goes—even though the expert is stipulated to have a higher chance of success than the non-expert! On Kohlberg's analysis, but adding in the captain, 1·6 'statistical lives' are saved if the expert is sent (0·8 for each of the other two), whereas the lottery saves 2·1 (0·7 for all three). Leaving out the captain, as Kohlberg does, makes the difference even more striking: 0·8 statistical lives saved by sending the expert versus 1·4 for the lottery.

Needless to say, if we substitute the correct figures, we get the obviously correct result that the best expectation of survival from behind the veil of ignorance specified by Kohlberg lies in ordering the expert to go. Including the captain in the calculation, we can say that the lottery saves 1·5 'statistical lives' (0·35 + 0·4 + 0·75), while sending the expert saves 1·6 'statistical lives' (0·8 + 0·8). Counting only the expert and the non-expert, as Kohlberg does, the comparable figures are 0·75 for the lottery and 0·8 for sending the expert. The differences are small, because the postulated difference in the expectation of success of the expert and the non-expert is so small. If we substituted 0·1 for 0·7 as the non-expert's probability of success, we would get (counting in the captain) 0·9 'statistical lives' saved by the lottery and—as before—1·6 saved by sending the expert. Leaving out the captain, the corresponding figures would be 0·45 and 0·8.

It is worth noticing that, on the correct analysis, the preference for sending the expert is not sensitive to the numbers of people in the different categories, or to the gap between the expected success rate of the expert(s) and non-expert(s). All we need is a structure in which the expert(s) have a higher probability of success than the non-expert(s) (and we can have any number, including zero, of people in the position of the captain). We can then immediately deduce that, whatever the proportions or the probabilities (subject to the one proviso that experts are better than non-experts), more 'statistical lives' will be saved by sending the expert (or one of them if there are more than one of them) and hence that the average probability of survival is higher if the decision is made to order the expert (or an expert) to go. In contrast, Kohlberg's analysis, as I have reconstructed it, is sensitive to both aspects of the situation. Thus, on his own contorted way of counting survival chances, attributing to the non-expert a 0·1 chance of success would mean that the expert's survival prospects rise from 0 to 10 per cent with the lottery, while those of the non-expert (or the non-expert and the captain) fall from 80 to 10 per cent.[b] It supports my reconstruction that this could explain why the non-experts are stipulated to be almost as good as the expert.

As far as the numbers are concerned, we may observe that, with Kohlberg's stipulated success rates, the lottery would not be so attractive if we brought back the rest of the platoon that so mysteriously disappeared at this point. For then, on Kohlberg's way of analysing it, the expert would gain a 70 per cent chance of survival from the lottery but nine non-experts and the captain would all lose 10%. The conclusion would therefore have to be that more 'statistical lives' are saved by sending the expert than by the lottery. If Kohlberg's line of reasoning takes the form I have suggested, this feature could explain the otherwise unexplained disappearance of the rest of the platoon at just this point in the discussion.

Kohlberg assumes that the parties in the original position are trying to do the best for themselves. On that assumption, maximizing the

---

[b] These numbers will no doubt seem bizarre—and they are. But they are simply what we arrive at if we substitute 10% for 70% in the passage quoted above from Kohlberg. If the absurdity is more apparent now, this again illustrates the way in which Kohlberg's stipulation that the non-experts are almost as good at demolition as the expert fudges the issues.

number of 'statistical lives' saved would, in my view, be the rational decision rule. The interpretation of Kohlberg's argument that I have offered implies this decision rule and is at least to that extent valid. All that is wrong with it is the analysis of what conclusion the decision rule leads to. Moreover, I have been able to show that two odd features of Kohlberg's account—the small difference in expected success rates between the expert and the non-experts and the reduction of the non-experts to one man—can be explained if we suppose that this is the line of argument he has in mind.

Nevertheless, there are two grounds for thinking that (as well as or instead of this one) he has another line of argument in mind. One of these grounds lies in the reference to the expert as occupying 'the least advantaged position'. The other is (as we shall see below) that he apparently believes that the analysis of choice from behind a 'veil of ignorance' is equivalent to the direct application to the case of Rawls's difference principle, which required that the least advantaged position should be as good as possible. Both of these points suggest an alternative line of analysis that Kohlberg may have in mind. According to this, we attribute the parties extreme risk aversion. This leads them to adopt a maximin decision rule, according to which the option to be chosen is the one that maximizes the advantage of the least advantaged. Rawls himself says in *A Theory of Justice* that we should not attribute any special psychology to the people in the original position but then (as we saw in Section 9) has to rely on a maximin decision rule to get the difference principle out of the choice in the original position. We could therefore say that Kohlberg would be following Rawls if he were adopting a maximin decision rule for his own analysis.

How would this go? I take it that the reasoning would have to run as follows. If the decision prescribed from the original position is to send the expert, that gives him a zero chance of survival while the other man's (or men's) probability of surviving is 80 per cent. But if the lottery is chosen they all (on Kohlberg's analysis) have a probability of surviving of 70 per cent. Therefore, the worst off position goes up from a 0 to a 70 per cent chance of survival. The lottery thus clearly accords with a maximin decision rule. This conclusion would still stand up if we substituted the correct figures for those supplied by Kohlberg. For we could still conclude that maximin is better satisfied by the lottery, which gives the expert a 35 per cent chance of survival and the non-expert a 40 per cent chance, than by a decision to send the expert, which gives him no chance of survival.

I wish to insist, however, that the use of expectations of survival here is ill-founded. If what we are concerned with is the worst that can happen, this means the worst actual outcome. It is true that, when they step out from behind the 'veil of ignorance,' the expert and the non-expert both have some positive expectation of living if they have chosen the lottery. But that positive expectation lasts only until the moment at which the lottery is carried out. Then one faces certain death while the survival chance of the other has doubled.

From the point of view of somebody who is extremely risk-averse, the crucial feature of the situation is that somebody is going to die whatever happens. (Recall that if nobody is sent to blow up the bridge it is 'virtually certain' that they all die.) From behind the veil of ignorance, the participants can see that there is a one in two chance of being the one who has to blow up the bridge (or one in three if we include the captain), and nothing that is decided about the way in which the person is selected will change that fact. All that the method of selection can have any effect on is the survival prospects of the man (or the two men) who are not selected. This is higher if the expert is told to go than with a lottery (under which there is only a 50 per cent chance that the expert goes). Anybody who is extremely risk averse must surely in this situation—given that the worst outcome is death, whatever is decided—opt for the solution that minimizes the risk of death. And that means deciding that the expert must be told to go.

I have already mentioned that Kohlberg regards the analysis of choice in an original position as equivalent to the direct application of the difference principle. 'Alternatively stated,' he says, the parties 'would choose to apply the difference principle, stating that no inequalities in life chances are justified unless they are of benefit from the point of view of the least advantaged, here the weak man [i.e. the expert].'[3] As I mentioned in Section 40, Kohlberg assumes that this must lead to the lottery: he apparently regards it as so obvious that he does not bother to argue in favour of it. But it is in fact a false inference. The point is the one I have just been making. The difference principle deals in real outcomes, not in statistical expectations prior to lotteries. The worst thing that can happen to anyone (within the range of alternatives offered by the example) is dying. Anyone who dies is the worst off, or one of the worst off if there are more than one. Since somebody is bound to die, the worst outcome is the same under either method of selecting the person to go. The difference principle is therefore silent on the choice between the two methods of selecting the person who is to try to blow up the bridge.

An extension of the difference principle ('leximin') specifies that, if the worst-off person is equally badly off under two alternative scenarios, we look at the next person up the rankings, and so on. On the strength of this, we can say that it is preferable to send the expert. Since one person dies anyway, we look at the situation of the other man (or two men) under the two alternatives. There is, obviously, more chance that he (or they) will survive if the expert goes than if the choice is made to depend on a lottery. The conclusion is, therefore, that either the difference principle is agnostic or (in the extended form of leximin) it recommends sending the expert.

The real lesson to be drawn is, of course, the one argued for in Section 40. It is inappropriate in a situation such as that of the 'captain's dilemma' either to deploy a Rawlsian original position or to make use of Rawls's difference principle. Doing either is to fail to distinguish between what is appropriate for the design of major social institutions and what is appropriate for deciding about particular problems that arise within them. In particular, impartiality is crucial at the second-order stage at which principles for institutions are proposed. How far it is required at the first-order level is something to be determined at the second-order level.

NOTES

PREFACE

1. Brian Barry, *Theories of Justice* (Hemel Hempstead: Harvester-Wheatsheaf and Berkeley and Los Angeles: University of California Press, 1989).
2. Ibid. p. xiii.
3. Ibid.
4. A preliminary statement of two principles may be found in id., 'Chance, Choice, and Justice', in *Liberty and Justice: Essays in Political Theory*, vol. II (Oxford: Clarendon Press, 1991), 142–58.
5. Id., 'The Welfare State and the Relief of Poverty', *Ethics*, 100 (1990), 503–29.
6. John Rawls, *A Theory of Justice* (Cambridge, Mass: Harvard University Press, 1971).
7. See Barry, *Theories of Justice*, 6–8.
8. Robert Nozick, *Anarchy, State and Utopia* (New York: Basic Books, 1974).
9. The differences are conveniently summarized in the Preface that Rawls contributed to the French translation, which was based on the same text as the German translation. In this, Rawls lists the articles that, he says, state more amply and satisfactorily the points that are new in the revised text. See 'Préface de l'édition française', 9–14 of John Rawls, *Théorie de la Justice*, trans. Catherine Audard (Paris: Editions du Seuil, 1987).
10. Two recent authors talk about 'the slightly strange situation whereby other theorists seek to defend Rawls's theory in versions apparently stronger than those to which he himself is happy to subscribe', Stephen Mulhall and Adam Swift, *Liberals and Communitarians* (Oxford: Blackwell, 1992), 21. I find it slightly strange that they find this situation slightly strange.
11. Some people have said in print that they think the treatment of the concept of the public interest in my *Political Argument* is inferior to that contained in an earlier article. They may well be right. (See *Political Argument* [Hemel Hempstead and Berkeley and Los Angeles: Harvester-Wheatsheaf and University of California Press, 1990, originally published 1965], 190–202.)
12. John Rawls, 'The Basic Structure as Subject', in Alvin Goldman and Jaegwon Kim (eds.), *Values and Morals: Essays in Honor of William Frankena, Charles Stevenson, and Richard B. Brandt* (Dordrecht, Holland: D. Reidel Publishing Company, 1978.)
13. Stanislaw Lem, *Imaginary Magnitude*, trans. Marc E. Heine (New York: Harcourt Brace Jovanovich, 1984) and *A Perfect Vacuum*, trans. Michael Kandel, in *Solaris, The Chain of Chance, and A Perfect Vacuum* (Harmondsworth, Middx: Penguin Books, 1981).

14. Henry Beard and Christopher Cerf, *The Official Politically Correct Dictionary and Handbook* (London: Grafton, 1992).

CHAPTER 1

1. K. R. Popper, *The Open Society and Its Enemies* (London: Routledge & Kegan Paul, 4th edn. 1962), vol. II, pp. 234 and 236.
2. Ibid., vol. I, p. ix.
3. Ibid.
4. The standard works in this genre are Robert E. Lane, *Political Ideology* (New York: Free Press, 1962) and Jennifer Hochschild, *What's Fair: American Beliefs about Distributive Justice* (Cambridge, Mass: Harvard University Press, 1981).
5. See Amy Gutmann, 'The Challenge of Multiculturalism in Political Ethics', *Philosophy & Public Affairs*, 22 (1993), 171–206, esp. pp. 173–8.
6. I am referring here particularly to Michael Walzer, whose views are discussed in my 'Social Criticism and Political Philosophy'. This was first published in *Philosophy & Public Affairs*, 19 (1990), 360–73, and is reprinted (with a page of introductory material) in my *Liberty and Justice: Essays in Political Theory*, vol. II (Oxford: Clarendon Press, 1991), 9–22. I discuss Alasdair MacIntyre's version in Chapter 5 below.
7. John Rawls, *A Theory of Justice* (Cambridge, Mass: Harvard University Press, 1971).
8. See T. M. Scanlon, 'Contractualism and Utilitarianism', in Amartya Sen and Bernard Williams (eds.), *Utilitarianism and Beyond* (Cambridge: Cambridge University Press, 1982).
9. Jeremy Bentham, *Rationale of Judicial Evidence* in *The Works of Jeremy Bentham*, vol. VI, ed. J. Bowring (Edinburgh: William Tait, 1843), 350.
10. Thomas Hobbes, *Leviathan*, ed. with an introduction by C. B. Macpherson (Harmondsworth, Middx: Penguin, 1968), chap. 15, p. 212, italics suppressed. (See *Theories of Justice*, section 6 for a discussion of Hobbes and 'acception of persons'.)
11. Max Weber, *Economy and Society*, edited by Guenther Roth and Claus Wittich (Berkeley and Los Angeles: University of California Press, 1978), vol. I, p. 225.
12. Ibid., vol. II, p. 975.
13. Henry Fielding, *Tom Jones* (New York: W. W. Norton & Co, 1973), Book XVI, ch. VI, p. 660.
14. Mark Sagoff, *The Economy of the Earth: Philosophy, Law, and the Environment* (Cambridge: Cambridge University Press, 1988), p. 149.
15. J. Baird Callicot, 'Animal Liberation: A Triangular Affair', *Environmental Ethics* 2 (1980), 311–38 at p. 320, repr. in J. Baird Callicott, *In Defense of the Land Ethic: Essays in Environmental Philosophy* (Albany, NY: State University of New York Press, 1989), 21.

16. The words quoted are those of Aldo Leopold, a pioneer of ecocentrism: *A Sand County Almanac* (New York: Oxford University Press, 1966), 420. For recent statements of the ecocentric perspective, see (in addition to Callicott) Lawrence E. Johnson, *A Morally Deep World: An Essay on Moral Significance and Environmental Ethics* (Cambridge: Cambridge University Press, 1991), Peter S. Wenz, *Environmental Justice* (Albany, NY: State University of New York Press, 1988), and Paul Taylor, *Respect for Nature* (Princeton, NJ: Princeton University Press, 1986). A general survey can be found in Robyn Eckersley, *Environmentalism and Political Theory: Towards an Ecocentric Approach* (Albany, NY: State University of New York Press, 1992).
17. Peter Singer, 'All Animals are Equal', in Singer (ed.), *Applied Ethics* (Oxford: Oxford University Press, 1986), 215–28. See also id., *Animal Liberation* (2nd edn. London: Jonathan Cape, 1990), ch. 1 (pp. 1–23), and *Practical Ethics* (Cambridge: Cambridge University Press, 1979), ch. 3 (pp. 48–71).
18. Sagoff, *Economy of the Earth*, 157.
19. See Callicott, 'Animal Liberation', who makes this point in some detail.
20. William Godwin, *An Enquiry Concerning Political Justice and its Influence on Modern Morals and Happiness*, ed. Isaac Kramnick (Harmondsworth, Middx.: Penguin, 1976), 175.
21. Shelly Kagan, *The Limits of Morality* (Oxford: Clarendon Press, 1989), p. 1.
22. Ibid., 2.
23. Max Beerbohm, *A Christmas Garland* (London: William Heinemann, 1950), 41–2.
24. Kagan, *Limits of Morality*, 2.
25. Godwin 'to elucidate the term duty' says that it 'is that mode of action on the part of the individual which constitutes the best possible application of his capacity to the general benefit', *Political Justice*, 190.
26. 'The assertion "I am morally bound to perform this action" is identical with the assertion "This action will produce the greatest possible amount of good in the Universe"', G. E. Moore, *Principia Ethica* (Cambridge: Cambridge University Press, 1903), 147.
27. I have argued for this conclusion at some length elsewhere. See 'Epilogue' in Brian Barry and Russell Hardin (eds.), *Rational Man and Irrational Society? An Introduction and Sourcebook* (Beverly Hills, Calif.: Sage Publications, 1982), 367–86.
28. Kagan, *Limits of Morality*, 15–19 and 46–80.
29. Alasdair MacIntyre, *After Virtue: A Study in Moral Theory* (2nd edn. Notre Dame, Ind.: University of Notre Dame Press, 1984), 15.
30. J. M. Keynes, *Two Memoirs: Dr. Melchior: A Defeated Enemy and My Early Beliefs* (London: Rupert Hart-Davis, 1949), 85, quoted (slightly inaccurately) on p. 16 of MacIntyre, *After Virtue*.

CHAPTER 2

1. Thomas Nagel, *Equality and Partiality* (New York: Oxford University Press, 1991), 164.
2. Ibid. 162.
3. Ibid. 163–4.
4. Joseph Cardinal Bernadin, quoted (without citation) by Ronald Dworkin in *Life's Dominion: An Argument about Abortion and Euthanasia* (London: Harper Collins, 1993), 49–50.
5. See for example John Rawls, *A Theory of Justice* (Cambridge, Mass.: Harvard University Press, 1971), 327, where 'religious interests' are included in 'conceptions of the good'.
6. Nagel, *Equality and Partiality*, 164.
7. Thomas Hobbes, *Leviathan*, ed. with an introduction by C. B. Macpherson (Harmondsworth, England: Penguin 1968), ch. 13, p. 188.
8. Rawls, *A Theory of Justice*, 343. An almost identical passage occurs on p. 112.
9. See H. L. A. Hart, *Law, Liberty and Morality* (Stanford, Calif.: Stanford University Press, 1963), 20. The usage originated within utilitarian theory, where it was contrasted with 'critical morality' based on the utilitarian criterion.
10. See Michael Taylor, *Community, Anarchy and Liberty* (Cambridge: Cambridge University Press, 1982) for a discussion of the conditions necessary for informal sanctions to be effective.
11. Hart, *Law, Liberty and Morality*, 20.
12. Hobbes, *Leviathan*, ch. 15, p. 203.
13. See David Gauthier, *Morals by Agreement* (Oxford: Clarendon Press, 1986), ch. IV. This aspect of Gauthier's theory is ably criticized by Alan Nelson in 'Economic Rationality and Morality', *Philosophy & Public Affairs*, 17 (1988), 149–66, esp. pp. 156–61.
14. Ashutosh Varshney, 'Contested Meanings: India's National Identity, Hindu Nationalism, and the Politics of Anxiety', in *Daedalus* 122 (1993), 227–61, quotation on pp. 252–3; a more extended account, on which I draw below, is on p. 249.
15. Ibid. 246.
16. Plato, *The Republic*, 338c. Quotation on p. 13 of the edition translated and edited by Raymond Larson (Arlington Heights, Ill.: AHM Publishing Corp., 1979).
17. Dee Brown, *Bury My Heart at Wounded Knee: An Indian History of the American West* (London: Barrie and Jenkins, 1971), 368.
18. Gauthier, *Morals by Agreement*, p. 294.
19. Ibid. 294–7.
20. Ibid. 268.
21. Ibid. 18 n. 30. The inhuman implications of Gauthier's theory are discussed in Allen Buchanan, 'Justice as Reciprocity versus Subject-Centred Justice', *Philosophy & Public Affairs*, 19 (1990), 227–52 at pp. 230–2.

Notes to Pages 43–53 271

22. Brown, *Bury My Heart at Wounded Knee*, 189.
23. Thrasymachus' statement of his case is ambiguous between saying that justice is the content of the laws or obedience to them. But in Socrates' restatement, which Thrasymachus accepts, justice is equated with doing what is laid down in legislation. And this fits in better with the subsequent development of the argument. See Plato, 339 c and d (p. 14 in the Larson edn.).
24. Ibid. 338 e (pp. 13 and 14 in the Larson edn.).
25. I discuss the rather complex problem of Hume's usage of 'justice' in a note on p. 153 of *Theories of Justice*.
26. David Hume, *A Treatise of Human Nature*, ed. L. A. Selby-Bigge, 2nd edn., ed. P. H. Nidditch (Oxford: Clarendon Press, 1978), 492.
27. Gauthier, *Morals by Agreement*, 2.
28. Ibid.
29. I used the term myself fifteen years ago in Brian Barry, 'Justice as Reciprocity', in Eugene Kamenka and Alice Erh-Soon Tay (eds.), *Justice* (London: Edward Arnold, 1979), 50–78; repr. in Barry, *Liberty and Justice: Essays in Political Theory*, vol. II (Oxford: Clarendon Press, 1991), 211–41.
30. Allan Gibbard, 'Constructing Justice', *Philosophy & Public Affairs*, 20 (1991), 264–79 and id., *Wise Choices, Apt Feelings: A Theory of Normative Judgment* (Oxford: Clarendon Press, 1990), esp. pp. 261–4.
31. Ibid. 261.
32. Ibid. 262.
33. Ibid. 262–3. For Hume's similar idea that property rules (his rules of justice) solve disputes by appealing to the imagination, see *Theories of Justice*, p. 171.
34. Gibbard, 'Constructing Justice', 272.
35. See Ian Macneil, *The New Social Contract* (New Haven, Conn.: Yale University Press, 1980) and Hugh Collins, 'Distributive Justice through Contracts', *Current Legal Problems*, 45 (1992), Part 2: *Collected Papers*, ed. R. W. Rideout and B. A. Hepple (Oxford: Oxford University Press, 1992), 49–67.
36. An excellent analysis of game forms and their relevance to the morality of institutions may be found in Russell Hardin, *Morality within the Limits of Reason* (Chicago: Chicago University Press, 1988).

CHAPTER 3

1. H. L. A. Hart, 'Utilitarianism and Natural Rights,' in Hart, *Essays in Jurisprudence and Philosophy* (Oxford: Clarendon Press, 1983), 181–97 at p. 195.
2. John Rawls, *A Theory of Justice* (Cambridge, Mass.: Harvard University Press, 1971), 121.
3. Ibid.

4. Ibid. 17.
5. Ibid.
6. John Rawls, 'Justice as Fairness: Political not Metaphysical', *Philosophy & Public Affairs*, 223–51 at 237, n. 20.
7. Ibid.
8. On page 16 of *A Theory of Justice*, the comment about the theory of justice being part of the theory of rational choice immediately follows the statement that 'principles of justice may be conceived as principles that would be chosen by rational persons'. And at the other end of the book, on p. 583, the paragraph in question is entirely about the specification of the original position.
9. Ibid. 120.
10. Rawls, 'Justice as Fairness . . .,' 237, n. 20.
11. Id., *A Theory of Justice*, 18.
12. Ibid.
13. Ibid.
14. Ibid. 20.
15. Ibid.
16. Ibid., 20–1.
17. Ibid. 20.
18. Ibid. 21.
19. Kingsley Amis, *Memoirs* (London: Hutchinson, 1991), 156.
20. Henry Phelps Brown, *Egalitarianism and the Generation of Inequality* (Oxford: Clarendon Press, 1988), 440–500.
21. Ibid. 444.
22. Ibid.
23. Ibid. 500.
24. An argument to this effect may be found in Shelly Kagan, *The Limits of Morality* (Oxford: Clarendon Press, 1989), 39–46. I argued along the same lines in *Theories of Justice* (section 41), and refer the reader to that place for a more extended discussion than that contained in the text.
25. Rawls, *A Theory of Justice*, 29.
26. Id., *Political Liberalism* (New York: Columbia University Press, 1993), 15–18.
27. 'As understood in justice as fairness, reciprocity is a relation between citizens expressed by principles of justice that regulate a social world in which everyone benefits judged with respect to an appropriate benchmark of equality defined with respect to that world', ibid. 17.
28. I discussed this issue in relation to *A Theory of Justice* in my *Theories of Justice* (section 30). In *Political Liberalism*, Rawls says that among the problems left over by his theory, which assumes that 'persons are normal and fully cooperating members of society over a complete life' is 'the question of what is owed to those who fail to meet this condition, either temporarily (from illness and accident) or permanently' (p. 21). He adds that he thinks the theory 'yields reasonable answers . . . to part of [this question], to the problem of providing for what we may call normal health care'

(ibid.) No doubt any sort of social insurance notion will cover medical care and earnings replacement for those who are normally contributing members of society. But the implicit admission is that Rawls cannot, any more than could Gauthier (see section 7), accommodate the idea that justice demands support of the congenitally disabled.

29. I think that Rawls's intentions have been correctly stated by Peter de Marneffe in 'Liberalism, Liberty, and Neutrality', *Philosophy & Public Affairs*, 19 (1990), 253–74. He suggests that the maximin decision rule in the original position, which leads to exclusive concern with the worst possible outcomes under alternative principles of justice, should not be regarded 'as rising out of the general problem of rational choice under uncertainty. Rather, the maximin principle represents in a rational choice idiom our convictions about fairness and the separateness of persons (in contrast to the principle of expected utility maximization, which would represent in a rational choice idiom the utilitarian principle of aggregate maximization)' (p. 257 n. 4). In other words, Rawls starts with the conviction (rendered by him as the 'separateness of persons') that an institution that makes one person more wretched than anyone need be can never be justified on the ground that it makes other people better off than they would otherwise be. He then seeks to represent this conviction in the original position by stipulating that the parties will operate with a maximin decision rule in choosing principles of justice.

30. Rawls, *A Theory of Justice*, 176.

31. 'Of course, under normal conditions public knowledge and confidence are always imperfect. So even in a just society it is reasonable to admit certain constraining arrangements to insure compliance, but their main purpose is to underwrite citizens' trust in one another', ibid. 577.

32. Rawls, *Political Liberalism*, 142.

33. Ibid.

34. Ibid. 143.

35. Id., *A Theory of Justice*, 497.

36. Ibid., 454.

37. Ibid. 455.

38. Thus, Rawls says in *A Theory of Justice* (p. 182) 'that utilitarianism, as I have defined it, is the view that the principle of utility is the correct principle for society's public conception of justice'.

39. Rawls, *A Theory of Justice*, 145.

40. Ibid.

41. Ibid. 576.

42. Ibid. 573. I recommend the rest of this eloquent paragraph, incidentally, to anybody still inclined to think that *A Theory of Justice* is all about rational calculation.

43. Ibid., pp. vii–viii.

44. The two versions come apart in their treatment of issues involving population size. Nothing turns on the choice between these two variants of utilitarianism for the purposes of this book.

45. Rawls, *A Theory of Justice*, 183. The statement in the text is my interpretation of Rawls's observation 'that the conditions of generality of principle, universality of application, and limited information as to natural and social status are not enough by themselves to characterize the original position of justice as fairness. The reasoning for the average principle of utility shows this. These conditions are necessary but not sufficient' (ibid.). What has to be added to clinch the derivation of the two principles of justice is the requirement that the parties in the original position must take account of 'the strains of commitment'.

46. Ibid. 178.

47. Ibid. 177.

48. Rawls himself sometimes puts forward the invalid form of the argument in *A Theory of Justice*, though much that he says about the rationale of the difference principle is consistent with the valid form. In *Political Liberalism*, however, he says (without explaining its significance in the theory) that 'the least advantaged members of society are given by description and not by a rigid designator' (7 n. 5).

49. T. M. Scanlon 'Contractualism and Utilitarianism' in Amartya Sen and Bernard Williams (eds.), *Utilitarianism and Beyond* (Cambridge: Cambridge University Press, 1982), 103–28, quotation on p. 115 n. 10.

50. Id., 'Levels of Moral Thinking', in Douglas Seanor and N. Fotion (eds.), *Hare and Critics* (Oxford: Clarendon Press, 1988), 129–46, quotation from pp. 137–8.

51. Id., 'Contractualism and Utilitarianism', 110.

52. Ibid. 112.

53. Ibid. 111.

54. Ibid.

55. Ibid. 112.

56. Rawls, *A Theory of Justice*, 211.

57. Ibid. 231.

58. Ibid.

59. P. J. Kelly, *Utilitarianism and Distributive Justice: Jeremy Bentham and the Civil Law* (Oxford: Clarendon Press, 1990), 68–9.

60. John Stuart Mill, 'Utilitarianism' in *Collected Works of John Stuart Mill* vol. X: *Essays on Ethics, Religion and Society*, ed. J. M. Robson (Toronto: University of Toronto Press, 1969), 255.

61. Alasdair MacIntyre, *Whose Justice? Which Rationality?* (Notre Dame, Ind: University of Notre Dame Press, 1988), 403.

62. Ibid.

63. MacIntyre summarizes Aquinas' view by saying that 'the Pope has legitimate authority over secular rulers'. He adds, perhaps redundantly, that this is 'a position strikingly at odds with that of liberal, secular modernity', ibid., 201.

64. Quoted by Kelly, *Utilitarianism and Distributive Justice*, 73.

65. See ibid., chs. 4–7, for a discussion of these principles.

66. MacIntyre, *Whose Justice? Which Nationality*, 199.

67. Ibid. 200.
68. Ibid. 201.
69. Ibid. 2.
70. Bernard Williams, *Ethics and the Limits of Philosophy* (Cambridge, Mass: Harvard University Press, 1985), 1.
71. The object of Williams's criticism is something that he calls 'morality' or 'the morality system'. (See ibid. 174–96.) This is taken to be exemplified by two moral systems that may be described as impartialist: utilitarianism or Kantianism. (See below, Chapter 9, for a discussion of these as impartialist theories.) Justice as impartiality would clearly fall within the scope of Williams's criticism of 'morality'.
72. 'Some religions distinguish between universal principles that bind all, and principles that bind only believers in the right faith', Joseph Raz, 'Facing Diversity: The Case of Epistemic Abstinence', *Philosophy & Public Affairs*, 19 (1990), 3–46, quotation from p. 25.

CHAPTER 4

1. *Utilitarian Logic and Politics: James Mill's 'Essay on Government', Macaulay's Critique and the Ensuing Debate*, edited and introduced by J. Lively and J. Rees (Oxford: Clarendon Press, 1978).
2. John Stuart Mill, 'Bentham' in *Collected Works* vol. X: *Essays on Ethics, Religion and Society*, ed. J. M. Robson (Toronto: University of Toronto Press, 1969), 108. See especially Jeremy Bentham, *Constitutional Code* vol. I, ed. F. Rosen and J. H. Burns (Oxford: Clarendon Press, 1983).
3. Article 8 of the Convention, under which the decision fell, says: 'Everyone has the right to respect for his private life and family life, his home and his correspondence.' There then follow a number of qualifications, none of which was held to apply. See Mary Ann Glendon, *Rights Talk: The Impoverishment of Political Discourse* (New York: The Free Press, 1991), 146–51.
4. For the opinions in this case, Bowers v. Hardwick (1986), see Gerald Dworkin (ed.), *Morality, Harm, and the Law* (Boulder, Col.: Westview Press, 1994), 93–104. For discussions see Glendon, *Rights Talk*, 151–8 and Stephen Macedo, *Liberal Values: Citizenship, Virtue and Community in Liberal Constitutionalism* (Oxford: Clarendon Press, 1990), 193–7.
5. Thomas Nagel, *Equality and Partiality* (New York: Oxford University Press, 1991), 162.
6. Macedo, *Liberal Values*, 195–6.
7. *Report of the Committee on Homosexual Offences and Prostitution*, 1957, Cmnd 247 (known as the Wolfenden Report). The similarity between the Committee's rationale and Mill's 'simple principle' is pointed out by H. L. A. Hart in *Law, Liberty and Morality* (Stanford, Calif.: Stanford University Press, 1963), 14–15.

8. John Stuart Mill, *On Liberty*, in *Essays on Politics and Society*, ed. J. M. Robson (Toronto: University of Toronto Press, 1977), *Collected Works* vol. XIX/1, pp. 213–310, quotation from p. 223.
9. Ibid. 224.
10. Ibid.
11. Ibid. 282.
12. Ibid. 224–5.
13. See Thomas Scanlon, 'Preference and Urgency', *The Journal of Philosophy*, 72 (1975), 655–69.
14. The phrase is from Nagel, *Equality and Partiality* 156.
15. Ibid.
16. Ibid. 165
17. Ibid. See for a similar view Roger Wertheimer, 'Understanding the Abortion Argument', in J. M. Finnis, M. Cohen, T. Nagel, T. Scanlon (eds.), *The Rights and Wrongs of Abortion* (Princeton, NJ: Princeton University Press, 1974), 23–51.
18. See Amy Gutmann and Dennis Thompson, 'Moral Conflict and Political Consensus' in R. Bruce Douglass, Gerald M. Mara, and Henry S. Richardson (eds.), *Liberalism and the Good* (New York and London: Routledge, 1990), 125–47. I agree in broad terms with their critique. Where I differ from them is that I do not believe that justice as impartiality entails a principle of preclusion.
19. Nagel, *Equality and Partiality*, 164–5.
20. Mill, *On Liberty*, 224–5. See also David O. Brink, 'Mill's Deliberative Utilitarianism', *Philosophy & Public Affairs*, 21 (1992), 67–103, esp. pp. 89–90.
21. Quoted from Macaulay, 'Speech on Gates of Somnanth' on pp. 916–17 of Henry Yule and A. C. Burnell, *Hobson-Jobson*, new edn. by William Crooke, (London: Linguasia, 1989 [1886]).
22. Quoted in Yule and Burnell from W. Newman in *Fortnightly Review*, NS, 15 (1874), 181.
23. It is significant that one of the bodies working against the continuation of female genital mutilation is a United Nations Working Group on Harmful Traditional Practices. See Efua Dorkenoo and Scilla Elworthy 'A Cry in the Dark', *Guardian*, 21 April 1992, p. 31. See also Amy Gutmann, 'The Challenge of Multiculturalism in Political Ethics', *Philosophy & Public Affairs*, 22 (1993), 171–206, esp. p. 195, where she suggests that 'as typically practiced, cliterodectamy may qualify as a form of torture' and thus be 'morally indefensible even in a context where most men and women . . . support it'.
24. In their critique of Wertheimer's argument for the preclusion principle, Gutmann and Thompson write: 'Wertheimer's argument depends on giving decisive weight to the fact that the government need not act to make abortion legal [i.e. that government inaction is possible]. But there is no decisive reason to favor government inaction under conditions in which human life is arguably at stake', 132.

25. Kristin Luker, *Abortion and the Politics of Motherhood* (Berkeley and Los Angeles: University of California Press 1984).
26. See for an example Amy Gutmann, *Liberal Equality* (Cambridge: Cambridge University Press, 1980).
27. Cass R. Sunstein, 'Something Old, Something New', *East European Constitutional Review* 1 (1992), 18–21, quotation from p. 20.
28. Id., 'Against Positive Rights', *East European Constitutional Review*, 2 (1993), 35–8, quotation from pp. 36 and 37.
29. Will Kymlicka and Wayne J. Norman, 'The Social Charter Debate: Should Social Justice Be Constitutionalized?' Network Analyses: Analysis No. 2 (January 1992), published by Network on the Constitution, Ottowa, Canada, pp. 1–2. They report (ibid.) that a charter along these lines was supported by 85 per cent of Canadians (88 per cent in Quebec).
30. Sunstein, 'Against Positive Rights', 37.
31. Kymlicka and Norman, 'The Social Charter Debate' 5.
32. Sunstein, 'Against Positive Rights', 36.
33. I have discussed this concept, with a number of illustrations from public policy, in ch. 9 of *Political Argument* (London: Routledge & Kegan Paul, 1965; Hemel Hempstead: Harvester Wheatsheaf and Berkeley and Los Angeles: University of California Press, reissue with new Introduction, 1990).
34. Kymlicka and Norman, 'The Social Charter Debate' 10.
35. Malcolm Dean, 'Can Britain Digest a Bill of Rights?' *Guardian*, 16 May 1992, p. 20.
36. This idea may be found in William Nelson, *On Justifying Democracy* (London: Routledge & Kegan Paul, 1980), 100–21, and in Joshua Cohen 'Democratic Equality', *Ethics*, 99 (1989), 727–51.
37. The expression comes from the title of Arend Lijphart's book about Dutch politics, *The Politics of Accommodation* (Berkeley, Calif.: University of California Press, 1968; 2nd edn. 1975). It should be said, however, that the divisions within Dutch society based on religion that were the subject of the accommodation Lijphart discusses probably never entailed the systematic discounting of the claims of one group by the members of another. The form in which such sentiments did turn out to be widespread in the Netherlands was anti-Semitism, which led during the Second World War to a good deal of gratuitous cooperation with the extermination programme of the Nazi occupation forces.
38. Michael Walzer, 'Philosophy and Democracy', *Political Theory*, 9 (1981), 379–99, quotation from p. 383.
39. The expression is that of Macedo, *Liberal Values*, 69.
40. Walzer, 'Philosophy and Democracy', 383.
41. See for a stimulating analysis Jane J. Mansbridge, *Beyond Adversary Democracy* (New York: Basic Books, 1980) and ead., 'Motivating Deliberation in Congress', in Sarah Baumgartner Thurow (ed.)., *Constitutionalism in America*, vol. II (New York: University Press of America, 1988), 59–86.

42. During the last Labour government in Britain (1974–9) there was a good deal of talk about the political system's being too 'adversarial'. The fundamental dishonesty of this movement was dramatically demonstrated by the complete silence that the main publicists fell into once the Thatcher government—which was an infinitely more ruthless and offensive practitioner of 'adversarial politics'—came into power. See for example S. E. Finer (ed.), *Adversarial Politics and Electoral Reform* (London: Anthony Wigram, 1975); Nevil Johnson *In Search of the Constitution: Reflections on State and Society in Britain* (Oxford: Pergamon, 1977).

43. The relevant literature here is on so-called consociational democracy. I have discussed this in my essay 'Political Accommodation and Consociational Democracy', repr. in *Democracy and Power: Essays in Political Theory*, vol. I (Oxford: Clarendon Press, 1991), 100–35.

44. I have explored this in a game-theoretical analysis in *Political Argument*, 243–50.

45. See Dennis Thompson, *The Democratic Citizen* (Cambridge: Cambridge University Press, 1970).

46. See Charles R. Beitz, *Political Equality* (Princeton, NJ: Princeton University Press, 1989), 209–13.

47. See Ken Newton, 'Neutrality and the media,' in *Liberal Neutrality*, eds. Robert E. Goodin and Andrew Reeve (London: Routledge, 1989), 130–56.

48. Thus, it has repeatedly been found that somebody who is made redundant by his employer is less aggrieved about it (holding all other factors constant) if he feels that his case was handled fairly—if, for example, he was able to present his own arguments and had a sense that they were being taken seriously rather than as part of a pro forma process of consultation. For the application of the same idea to the law of the land, see Tom Tyler, *Why People Obey the Law* (New Haven, Conn.: Yale University Press, 1990).

49. See especially T. M. Scanlon, 'The Aims and Authority of Moral Theory', *Oxford Journal of Legal Studies*, 12 (1992), 1–23.

50. G. A. Cohen, 'Incentives, Inequality, and Community', *The Tanner Lectures on Human Values*, vol. XIII ed. Grethe B. Peterson (Salt Lake City, Utah: University of Utah Press, 1992) 263–329, quotation on p. 302. Cohen adds in a footnote (ibid. 302 n. 25): 'I have always thought that the right reply to a white South African who says, to an anti-Apartheid advocate, "You would see things differently if you were in my position", is: "Quite: I'm sure it does blind one's vision." '.

51. Claus Offe, 'Strong Causes, Weak Cures: Some Preliminary Notes on the Intransigence of Ethnic Politics', *East European Constitutional Review*, 1 (1992), 21–3, quotation on p. 23.

CHAPTER 5

1. Alasdair MacIntyre, *Whose Justice? Which Rationality?* (Notre Dame, Ind.: University of Notre Dame Press, 1988), 3.
2. I have discussed MacIntyre's ideas about the 'Enlightenment project' in a review of *Whose Justice? Which Rationality?* which originally appeared in *Ethics*, 100 (1989), 160–8 and was reprinted in my *Liberty and Justice: Essays in Political Theory*, vol. II (Oxford: Clarendon Press, 1991), 110–22.
3. MacIntyre, *Whose Justice? Which Rationality?*, 3–4.
4. See Charles Taylor, 'Atomism' in Alkis Kontos (ed.), *Powers, Possessions, and Freedom* (Toronto: University of Toronto Press, 1979), 39–61; reprinted in his *Philosophy and the Human Sciences: Philosophical Papers*, vol. II (Cambridge: Cambridge University Press, 1985), 187–210. Taylor says at the beginning of this paper (p. 39) that 'atomism' is a term used only by those hostile to the doctrine he describes and that its supporters 'tend to prefer others, like "individualism" '.
5. John Rawls, *A Theory of Justice* (Cambridge, Mass: Harvard University Press, 1971), 137.
6. Robert Nozick, *Anarchy, State, and Utopia* (Oxford: Blackwell, 1974), p. ix.
7. See MacIntyre, *Whose Justice? Which Rationality?*, 326–48.
8. Ibid. 335–6.
9. Ibid. 336.
10. Ibid.
11. Ibid. 345.
12. Ibid.
13. J. S. Mill, *On Liberty*, in *Essays on Politics and Society*, ed. J. M. Robson (Toronto: University of Toronto, 1977), *Collected Works* vol. XIX/1, 213–310.
14. Quotations from p. 13 of Will Kymlicka, *Liberalism, Community and Culture* (Oxford: Clarendon Press, 1989). The paragraph from which these quotations are drawn is repeated *verbatim* in id., *Contemporary Political Philosophy: An Introduction* (Oxford: Clarendon Press, 1990), 204. I should mention that Kymlicka does not appear to recognize that, in putting forward an ideal of self-determination, he is advancing a second-order conception of the good. Nothing, however, turns on this as far as my own discussion is concerned.
15. I have already suggested that most famous liberals in the past would have dissociated themselves from neutrality if the idea had been explained to them. An example of a contemporary liberal (defined by his support for liberal institutions of the kind mentioned in the text) who explicitly rejects neutrality is Joseph Raz, *The Morality of Freedom* (Oxford: Clarendon Press, 1986).
16. Kymlicka, *Contemporary Political Philosophy*, 207. I should say that Kymlicka goes on (pp. 207–30) to defend this against two lines of attack, but he does not consider the argument that I make here.

17. Bruce A. Ackerman, *Social Justice in the Liberal State* (New Haven, Conn.: Yale University Press, 1980), 11, italics in original.
18. Kymlicka, *Liberalism, Community and Culture*, 18.
19. Ibid. 12; id., *Contemporary Political Theory*, 204.
20. See Michael Freeden, *The New Liberalism* (Oxford: Clarendon Press, 1978).
21. MacIntyre, *Whose Justice? Which Rationality?*, 337.
22. Ibid. 336.
23. Ibid. 343.
24. Ibid.
25. Ibid.
26. Ibid. 336.
27. Ibid. 342.
28. Ibid.
29. It has been suggested that Bentham himself postulated such 'stylized facts' about preferences: 'given Bentham's characterization of human nature as purposive, the configuration of rights and titles prescribed by the principle of right will be one that maximizes social well-being by extending to each agent as wide a sphere of personal inviolability as possible', P. J. Kelly, *Utilitarianism and Distributive Justice: Jeremy Bentham and the Civil Law* (Oxford: Clarendon Press, 1990), 74.
30. Ibid. 95 n. 57. See also Neal Patrick, 'A Liberal Theory of the Good', *Canadian Journal of Philosophy* 17 (1987), 567–81.

CHAPTER 6

1. Jeremy Bentham, *An Introduction to the Principles of Morals and Legislation* (1789), ed. J. H. Burns and H. L. A. Hart (London: Methuen, 1982).
2. P. J. Kelly, *Utilitarianism and Distributive Justice: Jeremy Bentham and the Civil Law* (Oxford: Clarendon, 1990), 59.
3. Richard Arneson, 'Property Rights in Persons,' *Social Philosophy & Policy*, 9 (1992), 201–30, quotation from p. 216.
4. Id., 'Neutrality and Utility', *Canadian Journal of Philosophy*, 20 (1990) 215–40, quotation from p. 240.
5. Ibid. 232.
6. See Ronald Dworkin, 'Liberalism', in his *A Matter of Principle* (Cambridge, Mass.: Harvard University Press, 1985), 191–204.
7. See, for example, Joseph Raz, *The Morality of Freedom* (Oxford: Clarendon Press, 1986), 110–62.
8. See, for example, Jeremy Waldron, 'Legislation and Moral Neutrality', in Robert E. Goodin and Andrew Reeve (eds.), *Liberal Neutrality* (London: Routledge, 1989), 61–83, and Stephen Mulhall and Adam Swift, *Liberals and Communitarians* (Oxford: Blackwell, 1992), esp. pp. 29–32.

9. Ronald Dworkin, 'What Is Equality?', *Philosophy & Public Affairs*, 10 (1981), 185–246 and 283–345.

10. Dworkin says that 'normally it is a sufficient justification, even for an act that limits liberty, that the act is calculated to increase what the philosophers call general utility—that it is calculated to produce more over-all benefit than harm', id., *Taking Rights Seriously* (Cambridge Mass.: Harvard University Press, 1977), 191. For 'external preferences', see pp. 223–39.

11. John Rawls, *Political Liberalism* (New York: Columbia University Press, 1993), 214.

12. Ibid. See also id., 'The Domain of the Political and Overlapping Consensus', *New York University Law Review*, 64 (1989), 233–55, p. 241, where Rawls says that justice as fairness 'may have little specific to say about innumerable economic and social issues that legislative bodies must regularly decide'. What I take to be essentially Rawls's views on this matter have been elaborated by one of his students, Peter De Marneffe. See his 'Liberalism, Liberty, and Neutrality', *Philosophy & Public Affairs*, 19 (1990), 253–74, esp. p. 259.

13. See Amartya Sen, 'Equality of What?' in his *Choice, Welfare and Measurement* (Oxford: Clarendon Press, 1982), 353–69, and 'Rights and Capabilities', in *Resources, Values and Development* (Cambridge, Mass.: Harvard University Press, 1984), 307–24; Richard Arneson, 'Equality and Equal Opportunity of Welfare', *Philosophical Studies*, 56 (1989), 77–93; and G. A. Cohen, 'On the Currency of Egalitarian Justice,' *Ethics*, 99 (1989), 906–44.

14. See on this point Jon Elster, *Local Justice: How Institutions Allocate Scarce Goods and Necessary Benefits* (New York: Russell Sage Foundation, 1992).

15. Allan Gibbard, 'Manipulation of Voting Schemes: A General Result' in Brian Barry and Russell Hardin (eds.), *Rational Man and Irrational Society? An Introduction and Sourcebook* (Beverly Hills, Calif.: Sage Publications, 1982), 355–66.

16. Kenneth J. Arrow, *Social Choice and Individual Values* (2nd edn., New York: Wiley, 1963).

17. This originated in the heyday of logical positivism with Lionel Robbins's *An Essay on the Nature and Significance of Economic Science* (3rd edn., New York: New York University Press, 1984).

18. Michael Dummett, *Voting Procedures* (Oxford: Clarendon Press, 1984).

19. Ibid. 142.

20. Ibid.

21. David Miller, 'Deliberative Democracy and Social Choice', in David Held (ed.), *Prospects for Democracy: North, South, East, West* (Cambridge: Polity Press, 1993), 74–92, quotation from p. 87.

22. Ibid. 87. See also Joseph Raz, 'Liberalism, Skepticism, and Democracy', *Iowa Law Review*, 74 (1989), 761–82, where the same distinction is made (on p. 778) between views about what is right and wrong on one hand and 'tastes and inclinations' on the other. (Raz's example is football versus baseball.) The rationale for voting in matters of right and wrong that is put forward by Raz is, however, Rousseauan (see next paragraph but one in the text).

23. Ibid.
24. There is a remarkably stupid idea in the literature of political philosophy to the effect that there is some sort of 'paradox' involved in affirming the legitimacy of some procedure for taking a decision (voting is the example usually discussed, but decision by a political authority would do equally well) and at the same time holding a view of one's own about what the outcome ought to be. See Richard Wollheim, 'A Paradox in the Theory of Democracy', in Peter Laslett and W. G. Runciman (eds.), *Philosophy, Politics and Society* (Oxford: Blackwell, 1962), 71–87. I have pointed out the absurdity of this idea in 'Wollheim's Paradox: Comment', *Political Theory*, 1 (1973), 317–22.
25. Douglas Rae, 'Decision-Rules and Individual Values in Constitutional Choice', in Barry and Hardin (eds.), *Rational Man and Irrational Society?*, 305–312.
26. Alasdair MacIntyre, *Whose Justice? Which Rationality?* (Notre Dame, Ind.: University of Notre Dame Press, 1988), 343.
27. It may be noted that MacIntyre had already treated cost–benefit analysis as an attempt to apply the utilitarian criterion in Ch. 6 (pp. 62–78) of his previous *After Virtue* (Notre Dame, Ind.: University of Notre Dame Press, 2nd edn., 1984).
28. Aaron Wildavsky, *Speaking Truth to Power: The Art and Craft of Policy Making* (New York: Macmillan, 1979), 202. Quoted in Mark Sagoff, *The Economy of the Earth: Philosophy, Law and the Environment* (Cambridge: Cambridge University Press, 1988), 97.
29. 'Participants are prone to respond with indignation to questions about the compensation they would require to accept pollution of the Grand Canyon National Park, or of an unspoiled beach in a remote region. The indignation is expressed by the rejection of the offered transaction as illegitimate, or by absurdly high bids', Daniel Kahneman and Jack L. Knetsch, 'Valuing Public Goods: The Purchase of Moral Satisfaction', *Journal of Environmental Economics and Management*, 22 (1992), 57–70, quotation from p. 69.
30. See *Valuing Environmental Goods: An Assessment of the Contingent Valuation Method*, R. G. Cummings, D. S. Brooksire and W. D. Schultze (eds.), (Totowa, NJ: Rowman and Allanheld, 1986), where it is said (p. 36) that 'large differences between WTA and WTP measures derived from applications of the CVM persist and remain unexplained'. Table 3.2 on p. 35 contains a summary of results in fifteen studies, showing ratios of average WTA to average WTP. These mostly lie in the range between 3 : 1 and 6 : 1 but three studies show ratios of over 10 : 1.
31. Robert Cameron Mitchell and Richard T. Carson, 'Appendix: Some Comments on the State of the Arts Assessment of the Contingent Valuation Method Draft Report', in ibid. 237–45, quotation on p. 243.
32. 'Comments by Professor Daniel Kahneman', 185–94 of ibid., quotation on p. 192.

33. See fig. 12.2 on p. 191 of ibid. For a more extended analysis of 'embedding', see Kahneman and Knetsch, 'Valuing Public Goods: . . .'.
34. Ibid. 191–2.
35. Sagoff, *The Economy of the Earth*, 95.

CHAPTER 7

1. T. M. Scanlon, 'Contractualism and Utilitarianism', in Amartya Sen and Bernard Williams (eds.), *Utilitarianism and Beyond* (Cambridge: Cambridge University Press, 1982), 103–28, quotation from p. 116. (I endorsed this answer in *Theories of Justice*, 284–9.)
2. Ibid. 117.
3. Rawls, *A Theory of Justice* (Cambridge, Mass.: Harvard University Press, 1971), 517.
4. Ibid.
5. Ibid.
6. Charles E. Larmore, *Patterns of Moral Complexity* (Cambridge: Cambridge University Press, 1987).
7. Ibid. 50, italics in original.
8. Ibid. 54.
9. Ibid.
10. Ibid.
11. Ibid. 67.
12. Ibid. 68.
13. Ibid.
14. Ibid. 55. For a brief discussion of Habermas, see note b on page 196.
15. Scanlon, 'Contractualism and Utilitarianism', 121.
16. Alasdair MacIntyre, *Whose Justice? Which Rationality?* (Notre Dame, Ind.: University of Notre Dame Press, 1988); Peter Singer, *Animal Liberation* (2nd edn. London: Cape, 1988).
17. Larmore says of the argument from scepticism (along with two others that I mention in the next paragraph but one) that 'such justifications are fine for those persuaded by them' (Larmore, *Patterns of Moral Complexity*, 60). Though this sounds rather dismissive, I read him as saying that they are good arguments once the premises are granted. This interpretation is supported by his later remark (p. 68): 'I must insist once again that I do not hold a neutral justification [i.e. one not involving a conception of the good] to be the only justification for neutrality.' I take this to refer to these three arguments.
18. Ibid. 51.
19. Ibid. 51.
20. Ibid., italics suppressed.
21. Ibid. 53.

22. I believe that Larmore is wrong to maintain that the only objection to the argument from autonomy to neutrality is that it rests on a controversial conceptions of the good. I argued in Section 20 above that autonomy does not generate neutrality.
23. Ibid. 59.
24. Ibid. 60.
25. Ibid.
26. Ibid.
27. Ibid.
28. Ibid.
29. Ibid. 61, italics in original.
30. Ibid. 62.
31. Ibid. 64–5, italics suppressed.
32. Ibid. 68.
33. It appears on p. 227 of Thomas Nagel, 'Moral Conflict and Political Legitimacy', *Philosophy & Public Affairs*, 16 (1987), 215–40. The quotation containing the expression appears below in the text.
34. Larmore, *Patterns of Moral Complexity*, 53.
35. Nagel 'Moral Conflict and Political Legitimacy', 229.
36. Ibid.
37. Ibid.
38. Ibid.
39. Ibid.
40. Ibid. 230.
41. Ibid.
42. Thomas Hobbes, *Leviathan*, ch. 32. This passage occurs on p. 411 of C. B. Macpherson (ed.), *Leviathan* (Harmondsworth, Middx: Penguin Books, 1968), but omits the words 'may err' (added here from other editions) without which the passage is unintelligible.
43. Nagel, 'Moral Conflict and Political Legitimacy', 232.
44. Ibid.
45. Ibid. 230.
46. Joseph Raz, 'Facing Diversity: the Case of Epistemic Abstinence', *Philosophy & Public Affairs*, 19 (1990), 3–46, quotation on p. 39.
47. See id., *The Morality of Freedom* (Oxford: Clarendon Press, 1986).
48. Thomas Nagel, *Equality and Partiality* (New York: Oxford University Press, 1991), 163 n. 49.
49. Ibid. 168.
50. Ibid.
51. Susan Mendus, *Toleration and the Limits of Liberalism* (London: Macmillan, 1989), 77.
52. '[Rawls] intends to put forward not a skeptical position about religious knowledge but a restriction on the sorts of convictions that can be appealed to in political argument', Nagel, 'Moral Conflict and Political Legitimacy', p. 228.
53. Ibid., citing Rawls, *A Theory of Justice*, 217–18. This passage in Rawls's

book says that we might concede that everybody should follow the will of God but deny that any particular view about what the will of God demands can properly be enforced. This is to state the conclusion, but does nothing to settle the nature of the premise from which that conclusion is to be derived.

54. Rawls, *A Theory of Justice*, 214.
55. Id., 'Justice as Fairness: Political not Metaphysical', *Philosophy & Public Affairs*, 14 (1985), 223–51, quotation from p. 250, emphasis supplied.
56. Id., *A Theory of Justice*, 213.
57. Ibid.
58. Ibid. 215.
59. Ibid. 213.
60. Ibid.
61. Ibid.
62. Ibid. 208.
63. Ibid.
64. Ibid.
65. Ibid.
66. Ibid.
67. Ibid. 212.
68. Ibid. 213.
69. Id., *Political Liberalism* (New York: Columbia University Press, 1993), 224.
70. Ibid. 224, 225.
71. Ibid. 224–5.
72. Ibid. 138. Nagel, in his article advocating 'epistemological restraint', claims that Rawls's later views definitely commit him to this doctrine. But, as with his supporting quotation from *A Theory of Justice*, the one he offers from 'Justice as Fairness ...' states the conclusion but no distinctive premise from which it is to be derived: the passage cited simply says that certain views 'are not to be introduced into political discussion' but does not say why (Nagel, 228–9, citing Rawls, 'Justice as Fairness ...', 231).
73. Rawls, *Political Liberalism*, 63.
74. Ibid. 61 n. 15.

CHAPTER 8

1. See especially Thomas E. Hill, Jr., *Dignity and Practical Reason in Kant's Moral Theory* (Ithaca, NY and London: Cornell University Press, 1992).
2. Alasdair MacIntyre, *After Virtue: A Study in Moral Theory* (2nd edn., Notre Dame, Ind.: University of Notre Dame Press, 1984), 257–8, quotation from F. Nietzsche, *The Will to Power*, trans. R. J. Hollingsworth and Walter Kaufmann (New York: Random House, 1967), 505.
3. The underlying phenomenon here is one of cognitive dissonance reduction: see Leon Festinger, *A Theory of Cognitive Dissonance* (Evanston, Ill.: Row,

Peterson, 1957). The social psychologist Melvin Lerner has argued that there is a pervasive psychological need to believe that the world is a just place: see M. J. Lerner, *The Belief in a Just World: A Fundamental Delusion* (New York: Plenum, 1980).

4. What follows is inevitably somewhat speculative, but the participant-observer studies of Michael Buroway are relevant. See his *Manufacturing Consent* (Chicago: University of Chicago Press, 1979) and *The Politics of Production* (London: Verso, 1985). See also, for a general statement, Michael Mann, 'The Social Cohesion of Liberal Democracy', *American Sociological Review*, 35 (1970), 423–39.

5. The process of party competition analysed by Anthony Downs takes the policy preferences of the voters as exogenous, it may be noted: see Anthony Downs, *An Economic Theory of Democracy* (New York: Harper and Row, 1958).

6. See Adam Przeworski and John Sprague, *Paper Stones: A History of Electoral Socialism* (Chicago: Chicago University Press, 1986). Their argument is, in brief, that the homogeneous working class on which Marx pinned his hopes never became a clear majority and has been declining in size over most of this century.

7. For a succinct statement of the reasons, see Nicholas Barr, *The Economics of the Welfare State* (London: Weidenfeld & Nicolson, 1987), 192–4.

8. I have discussed the concepts of liability and vulnerability to non-compliance elsewhere. See 'Can States be Moral? International Morality and the Compliance Problem', which can be found in my *Democracy, Power and Justice: Essays in Political Theory* (Oxford: Clarendon Press, 1989), 411–33, and in the second volume of the two-volume version, *Liberty and Justice* (Oxford: Clarendon Press, 1991), 159–81.

9. Aristotle, *Politics*, Book II, in Jonathan Barnes (ed.), *Complete Works of Aristotle* (Princeton, NJ: Princeton University Press, 1984), vol. II, pp. 2000–23.

10. The topic of unequal norms (what she calls 'norms of partiality') is addressed in chapter 4 of Edna Ullman-Margalit, *The Emergence of Norms* (Oxford: Clarendon Press, 1977).

11. The 'Great Ape Project', with which Singer is centrally involved, seeks to extend certain basic human rights to our closest cousins among the species. These rights include freedom from imprisonment and torture. The objectives seem to me admirable, but the point made in the text still remains: the rights demanded are essentially rights of recipience rather than rights of participation. See Paola Cavalieri and Peter Singer (eds.), *The Great Ape Project: Equality beyond Humanity* (London: Fourth Estate, 1993).

12. Hill, *Dignity and Practical Reason . . .* , 235.

13. Robert Nozick, *Anarchy, State and Utopia* (New York: Basic Books, 1974), Pt II.

14. John Rawls, *A Theory of Justice* (Cambridge, Mass.: Harvard University Press, 1971), 274–5.

15. Ibid. 86.
16. Ibid.
17. See esp. ibid. 475–6.
18. Hill, *Dignity and Practical Reason* . . . , 238.
19. Ibid.
20. Ibid. 238–9.
21. Ibid. 238.

CHAPTER 9

1. See J. J. C. Smart and Bernard Williams, *Utilitarianism: For and Against* (London: Cambridge University Press, 1973).
2. 'Persons, Character and Morality', in Bernard Williams, *Moral Luck: Philosophical Papers 1973–1980* (Cambridge: Cambridge University Press, 1981), 1–19, quotation from p. 14.
3. William Godwin, *An Enquiry Concerning Political Justice and Its Influence on General Virtue and Happiness* (London: Printed for G. G. and J. Robinson, 1793 in two volumes continuously paginated), vol. I, p. 151.
4. Ibid.
5. Ibid.
6. Ibid.
7. I have discussed Hume's analysis of rules of justice in Section 20 of *Theories of Justice*. The significance of rules for Bentham is emphasized by P. J. Kelly in his *Utilitarianism and Distributive Justice* (Oxford: Clarendon Press, 1990). As far as Mill is concerned, ch. 5 of *Utilitarianism* is completely explicit in distinguishing justice from beneficence and insisting that promise-keeping is a duty while beneficence is not. See J. S. Mill *Utilitarianism* in *Essays on Ethics, Religion and Society*, ed. by J. M. Robson, in *Collected Works*, vol. X (Toronto: University of Toronto Press, 1969).
8. Don Locke, *A Fantasy of Reason: The Life and Thought of William Godwin* (London: Routledge & Kegan Paul, 1980), 168. (There is an account of the whole 'cause' in ch. 14 of Locke's book, pp. 167–79. Godwin's subsequent thoughts on the topic are discussed on pp. 197–200.)
9 Quotations in this paragraph all from William Godwin *Political Justice*, ed. Isaac Kramnick (Harmondsworth, Middx.: Penguin Books, 1985), 169–70.
10. Ibid.
11. Ibid.
12. The official title of Godwin's 'Reply to Parr' is *Thoughts Occasioned by the Perusal of Dr Parr's Spital Sermon* (London: G. G. and J. Robinson, 1801). The quotation is from p. 42. Reprinted in Mark Philp (ed.), *Political and Philosophical Writings of William Godwin*, vol. II (London: Pickering & Chatto, 1993), 165–208, quotation on p. 187.

13. This is the crux of Brian Moore's novel, *Lies of Silence* (London: Bloomsbury, 1990).
14. Marcia Baron, 'Impartiality and Friendship', *Ethics*, 101 (1991), 836–57, quotation from p. 840.
15. Godwin, 'Reply to Parr', 40–1, italics in original. (Philp (ed.), *Political and Philosophical Writings of William Godwin*, 187.)
16. Ibid. 41 (Philp (ed.), 187).
17. R. M. Adams, 'Motive Utilitarianism', *Journal of Philosophy*, 73 (1976), 467–81. See also Peter Railton, 'Alienation, Consequentialism, and the Demands of Morality', *Philosophy & Public Affairs*, 13 (1989), 134–71.
18. Derek Parfit, 'Innumerate Ethics', *Philosophy & Public Affairs*, 7 (1978), 285–301, at p. 301.
19. John Taurek, 'Should the Numbers Count?', *Philosophy & Public Affairs*, 6 (1977), 293–316, at p. 304.
20. Ibid. 306.
21. Ibid. 316.
22. Parfit, 'Innumerate Ethics', 300–1 n. 17.
23. For a similar claim, see Will Kymlicka, *Contemporary Political Philosophy: An Introduction* (Oxford: Clarendon Press, 1990), esp. p. 4.
24. Thomas E. Hill, Jr., 'The Importance of Autonomy', in *Women and Moral Theory*, ed. Eva Kittay and Diane Meyers (Totowa, NJ: Rowman and Allanheld, 1987), 132.
25. See, for example, Guido Calabresi and Philip Bobbitt, *Tragic Choices* (New York: W. W. Norton, 1978) and Jon Elster, *Local Justice: How Institutions Allocate Scarce Goods and Necessary Burdens* (New York: Russell Sage Foundation, 1992).
26. Williams, *Moral Luck*, 1.
27. Charles Fried, *An Anatomy of Values* (Cambridge, Mass.: Harvard University Press, 1970).
28. Ibid. 227.
29. Ibid.
30. Williams, *Moral Luck*, 17–18.
31. Ibid. 18.
32. The importance of this from a Kantian point of view is brought out well in Alan Donagan, *The Theory of Morality* (Chicago: University of Chicago Press, 1977).
33. The connection is argued for by Thomas E. Hill, Jr., in his *Dignity and Practical Reason in Kant's Moral Theory* (Ithaca, NY and London: Cornell University Press, 1992). See ch. 11, 'Kantian Constructivism in Ethics', 226–50.
34. Williams, *Moral Luck*, 18.
35. Godwin, 'Reply to Parr', 39 (Philp (ed.), 186).
36. Williams, *Moral Luck*, 18.
37. Ibid.

CHAPTER 10

1. James Fishkin, *Beyond Subjective Morality: Ethical Reasoning and Political Philosophy* (New Haven, Conn.: Yale University Press, 1984), 79.

2. Alasdair MacIntyre, 'The Magic in the Pronoun "My" ', *Ethics*, 94 (1983), 113–25, at p. 123.

3. See Lawrence Kohlberg, 'A Reply to Owen Flanagan and Some Comments on the Puka-Goodpaster Exchange', *Ethics*, 92 (1982), 513–28, quotation from p. 525.

4. Id., 'Education for Justice', in J. Gustafson (ed.), *Moral Education* (Cambridge, Mass.: Harvard University Press, 1970), 57–83, quotation from p. 69.

5. Id., 'From Is to Ought: How to Commit the Naturalistic Fallacy and Get Away with It in the Study of Moral Development', in T. Mischel (ed.), *Cognitive Development and Epistemology* (New York: Academic Press, 1971), 151–235, quotation from p. 185.

6. MacIntyre, 'The Magic in the Pronoun', 123. It should be borne in mind that this is precisely the conception of impartiality that MacIntyre himself attacks. In addition to the quotation from *Whose Justice? Which Rationality?* at the beginning of Chapter 5, consider a passage from his lecture 'Is Patriotism a Virtue?' Here he writes that impartialist morality requires that 'we assume an abstract and artificial—perhaps even an impossible—stance, that of a rational being as such, responding to the requirements of morality not *qua* peasant or farmer or quarterback, but *qua* rational agent who has abstracted him or herself from all social particularity', The Lindley Lecture (Lawrence, Kansas: The University of Kansas, 1984), 12.

7. Marilyn Friedman in 'Beyond Caring: The De-Moralization of Gender', in Marsha Hanen and Kai Nielsen (eds.), *Science, Morality and Feminist Theory* (Calgary, Alb.: The University of Calgary Press, 1987), *Canadian Journal of Philosophy*, supp. vol. 13 (1987), 87–110, quotation from p. 92 n. 10.

8. Lawrence Kohlberg, 'Justice as Reversibility', in Peter Laslett and James Fishkin (eds.), *Philosophy, Politics and Society*, 5th ser. (New Haven, Conn.: Yale University Press, 1979), 257–72. The passage quoted occurs on p. 260.

9. Carol Gilligan, *In a Different Voice: Psychological Theory and Women's Development* (Cambridge, Mass: Harvard University Press, 1982; repr. with 'Letter to Readers', 1993). For a list of subsequent papers by her see n. 1 on p. 87 of Friedman, 'Beyond Caring . . .'.

10. Friedman, 'Beyond Caring . . .', 92, citing Carol Gilligan, 'Reply', *Signs*, 11 (1986), 324–33, at p. 326.

11. Originally presented in 'From Is to Ought'. I am following the later discussion in 'Justice as Reversibility', 269.

12. Kohlberg, 'Justice as Reversibility', 271.

13. Ibid. 272.

14. Ibid. 270.

15. Ibid.
16. Ibid. 259.
17. Ibid. 261–4.
18. Ibid. 261.
19. 'Universalizability is exemplified in Kant's maxim of the categorical imper-
    ative, "So act that the outcome of your conduct could be the universal
    will", or "act as you would want all human beings to act in a similar situa-
    tion" ', ibid. 257–8.
20. The story begins: 'In Europe, a woman was near death . . .', ibid. 259.
21. Rawls's view of this duty is not a very demanding one: 'we are to assist in
    the establishment of just arrangements when they do not exist, at least
    when this can be done with little cost to ourselves', John Rawls, *A Theory
    of Justice* (Cambridge, Mass: Harvard University Press, 1971), 334.
22. Rawls is explicit about the limitations of his discussion—see esp. ibid. 351.
23. William Godwin, 'Reply to Parr', *Thoughts Occasioned by the Perusal of
    Dr Parr's Spital Sermon* (London: G. G. and J. Robinson, 1801), 41.
    Reprinted in Mark Philp (ed.), *Political and Philosophical Writings of
    William Godwin*, vol. II (London: Pickering & Chatto, 1993), 165–208,
    quotation on p. 187.
24. A good example of this line of analysis is provided by the work of Susan
    Moller Okin. See especially her *Justice, Gender and the Family* (New York:
    Basic Books, 1989), ch. 5.
25. Marcia Baron, 'Impartiality and Friendship', *Ethics*, 101 (1991), 836–57,
    quotation from p. 851.
26. Kohlberg, 'Education for Justice', 69.
27. Id., 'From Is to Ought', 185.
28. Mark Philp, *Godwin's Political Justice* (London: Duckworth, 1986), 210.
29. Friedman, 'Beyond Caring . . .', 93; internal quotation from Catherine G.
    Green and Eleanor E. Maccoby, 'How Different is the "Different Voice"?',
    Signs, 11 (1986), 310–16 at pp. 314–15.
30. Ibid. 95–6.
31. Ibid. 97.
32. Friedman (pp. 95–6 n. 6) suggests that a contrast between the priorities of
    men and women along these lines is popularly held to exist. The expression
    'telegrams and anger' is borrowed from Margaret Schlegel in *Howards
    End*. Talking to her sister, she says: 'The truth is that there is a great outer
    life that you and I have never touched—a life in which telegrams and anger
    count. Personal relations, that we think supreme, are not supreme there',
    E. M. Forster, *Howards End*, ed. Oliver Stallybrass (Harmondsworth,
    Middx: Penguin Books, 1975), 41.
33. A good example of this is Iris Marion Young, who writes in *Justice and the
    Politics of Difference* (Princeton, NJ: Princeton University Press, 1990) that
    'modern ethics establishes impartiality as the hallmark of moral reason'
    (p. 99) and explains that 'the moral point of view' is to be arrived at 'by
    abstracting from all the particularities of the circumstances on which moral
    reason reflects', including 'feelings, desires, interests, and commitments that

he or she may have regarding the situation, or that others may have' (p. 100).

34. Nel Noddings, *Caring: A Feminine Approach to Ethics and Moral Education* (Berkeley and Los Angeles: University of California Press, 1984), 52–3.
35. Joseph de Rivera, 'Love, Fear and Justice: Transforming Selves for the New World', *Social Justice Research*, 3 (1989), 387–426, quotation from pp. 396–7.
36. See esp. Noddings, *Caring . . .* , 95–7.
37. Ibid. 40–43.
38. Ibid. 37.
39. Ibid. 86. (This is, incidentally, a fair sample of the Noddings prose style.)
40. Friedman points out (p. 103) that the ethic of care 'degenerates precipitously' if it results in officials caring for their relatives by making nepotistic appointments.
41. See Carole Pateman, ' "The Disorder of Women": Women, Love, and the Sense of Justice', *Ethics*, 91 (1980), 20–34 (repr. in Carole Pateman, *The Disorder of Women: Democracy, Feminism and Political Theory* (Cambridge: Polity Press, 1989), 17–32) and Susan Moller Okin, *Women in Western Political Thought* (London: Virago, 1980).
42. Edward C. Banfield, *The Moral Basis of a Backward Society* (New York: The Free Press, 1958), 9–10.
43. Thomas Hobbes, *Leviathan*, ed. with an introduction by C. B. Macpherson (Harmondsworth, Middx.: Penguin, 1968), 186.
44. David Hume, *A Treatise of Human Nature*, ed. L. A. Selby-Bigge, 2nd edn. ed. P. H. Nidditch (Oxford: Clarendon Press, 1978), 487.
45. Ibid.
46. For 'universal prescriptivism' of a sort that makes it equivalent to universalizability, see R. M. Hare, *The Language of Morals* (Oxford: Clarendon Press, 1952) and id., *Freedom and Reason* (Oxford: Clarendon Press, 1963).
47. James Boswell, *Life of Boswell*, ed. R. W. Chapman (London: Oxford University Press, 1970), 1235 (15 May 1783).
48. Barbara Herman, 'Agency, Attachment, and Difference', *Ethics*, 101 (1991), 775–97, quotation from p. 784.
49. Ibid. 782.

APPENDIX

1. Lawrence Kohlberg, 'Justice as Reversibility', in Peter Laslett and James Fishkin (eds.), *Philosophy, Politics and Society*, 5th ser. (New Haven, Conn.: Yale University Press, 1979), 257–72, table on p. 269.
2. Ibid. 272.
3. Ibid.

INDEX

11; and empirical approach, 207–13; and equal treatment, 7–8, 226–7, 246–7, 249; Godwin and, 218–28, 250; Hume and, 221, 287 n. 7; and inequality, 211–13; and justice as impartiality, 120, 194–216, 217; and Kantian theory, 12, 217, 228–32, 235, 236, 241, 242–4, 256; Kohlberg on, 233, 235, 249, 266; maximization of good as, 12; Mill and, 217, 221, 287 n. 7; Nagel on, 247 n.; and positive morality, 205, 207–13; and promises, 218–21; Rawls and, 216; Scanlonian theory and, 195–213; Scheffler on, 247 n.; second-order impartiality, relation to, 11–12, 194–5, 233, 256–7; utilitarian (Godwinian) form of, 12, 194, 217–28, 235, 246–7, 250, 256, 287 n. 7. *See also* Second-order impartiality

First principle of justice (Rawls), 70–2

Fishkin, James S., 234, 241

Footbinding in China, 209 n.

Forster, E. M., 290 n. 32

Free riders, 203, 244

Freedom. *See* Liberty, as a conception of the good; Rights

Freedom of speech, 70, 85, 96

Freedom of worship: autonomy as a conception of the good, derivable from, 129–31; as a basic right, 70; conceptions of the good, derivable from some, 84–5; constitutional guarantee of, 83–4, 93–4, 96; as equal treatment of religions, 83–4, 93–4; evaluation of from viewpoint of conceptions of the good, 82; and justice as impartiality, 82–5, 142, 143, 163–4; and justice as mutual advantage, 163–4; importance of, 87, 165 n.; Rawls on, 83, 184–7; religious conflict, as origin of, 169–70; and utilitarianism, 85, 134–6, 142

French Declaration of the Rights of Man and of the Citizen, 8

Fried, Charles, 229, 230, 237, 238

Friedman, Marilyn, 248, 249 n., 291 n. 40

Friends, choice of, 15, 23, 246

Fundamental equality: in American and French Declarations, 8; and circumstances of impartiality, 100, 102–3; equal respect as, 176–7, 182; and impartiality, 7; and reasonable agreement, 8; and Scanlonian theory, 113

Gambling, 214–15

Game laws, and positive morality, 245

Game theory: bargaining games, 210 n.; and justice, theories of, 51, 271 n. 36; and veto, 278 n. 44. *See also* Rational choice theory

Gandhi, Rajiv, 38

Gauthier, David, 42–5, 210 n., 270 nn. 13, 21, 272 n. 28

Gender. *See* Sexual equality and inequality

General Will (Rousseau), 148 n.

Geneva, Calvinism in, 208

Genital mutilation, female, 90, 91, 209 n., 276 n. 23

Geometry, moral (Rawls), 53, 54

Germany: conversion of Jews in, 170; economic policy in, 198 n.; welfare policy in, 97

Gibbard, Allan, 48–50, 59, 60 n.

Gilligan, Carol, 236–7, 247–8, 249–50

Glendon, Mary Ann, 275 nn. 3, 4

Godwin, William, 246; 'duty' defined by, 24–5, 269 n. 25; as consequentialist, 23–4, 218; on 'famous fire cause', 222–5, 231, 232, 247, 287 n. 8; and impartiality, 120, 194, 201, 217–28, 235, 246–7, 250; as motive utilitarian, 224–5, 232; on promises, 218–19

Good, as a non-natural property, 26. *See also* Conceptions of the good; Maximization of good

Goodin, Robert E., 21 n., 150 n.
Great Ape Project, 286 n. 11
Green, Thomas Hill, 126, 131
Green theory of value (Goodin), 21 n., 150 n.
Gutmann, Amy, 276 nn. 18, 23, 24, 277 n. 26

Habermas, Jürgen, 168, 196 n.
Hardin, Russell, 271 n. 36
Hare, R. M., 291 n. 46
Harm: concept of, and positive harm principle, 87–8; as locus of agreement among conceptions of good, 25, 87–8, 141–2; and rules of justice, 34; utilitarianism, component in calculus of, 141; and welfare, 140 n.
Harm principle. *See* Negative harm principle; Positive harm principle
Harris, John, 228 n.
Hart, H. L. A., 53, 58, 275 n. 7
Health care. *See* Medical care
Heimer, Carol, 243 n.
Heinz's dilemma (Kohlberg), 241–6
Herder, Johann Gottfried von, 5
Herman, Barbara, 255–6
Hill, Thomas, Jr., 213, 216, 226, 244 n., 288 n. 33
Hindu religion, 38, 209
Hitler, Adolf, 115
Hobbes, Thomas: on 'acception of persons', 13; Banfield cites, 253; justice as mutual advantage, exponent of, 31, 60 n., 194, 210 n.; on multiple equilibria, 206 n.; reply to 'foole', 37; on revelation, 179; and stability, 63; and state of nature, 46 n., 253; and violent death, avoidance of, 31–2
Hobhouse, L. T., 126
Hochschild, Jennifer, 268 n. 4
Hoggart, Simon, 181
Holmes, Stephen, 161 n.
Homosexual rights: conceptions of

the good, derivable from some, 84–5; constitutional guarantee of, 83, 94; as equal treatment, 84; European Court of Human Rights and, 83, 275 n. 3; justice as impartiality and, 83–5, 142, 143, 163–4; justice as mutual advantage and, 163–4; United States Supreme Court and, 83, 275 n. 4; utilitarianism and, 135, 136, 142
Horse, rescue of, 232
House of Commons, 105, 106
Human rights, 4, 83, 275 n. 3
Hume, David: and circumstances of justice, 45 n.; conventionalist conception of fairness of, 49, 271 n. 33; and first order impartiality, 221, 287 n. 7; justice, defined by, 44, 271 n. 25; and justice as mutual advantage, 42, 44; as proto-utilitarian, 221; on selfishness, 253
Hungary, constitution of, 96

Ideals, personal, 78–9
Ideology, and legitimation of inequality, 198–9, 285 n. 3, 286 n. 4
Impartial spectator theory, 59
Impartiality: anti-impartialists and, 191–5, 247 n., 256–7; bureaucrats and, 13–14, 17–18; and children, 14–15, 18–19, 99, 194, 254; and club membership, 15–17, 19, 211–12; common-sense idea of, 11–12, 13–19, 194, 207–13, 219–20, 234; and conceptions of the good, 20–2, 42–3, 111; consequentialist, 23–7; and equal treatment, 7–8, 226–7, 246–7, 249; and families, 14–15, 18–19; and fundamental equality, 7; Godwin and, 120, 194, 201, 217–18, 235, 246–7, 250; impartial spectator theory as, 59; judges and, 13, 17, 18; and justice as impartiality, 191–2, 256–7; and Kantian theory, 191–2; Kohlberg and, 246–8; MacIntyre

on, 119–20, 234, 236, 289 n. 6;
parents and, 14–15, 18–19, 194;
Rawls on, 60 n.; in schools, 14, 18,
99, 254; two kinds of, 11–12;
utilitarianism as expression of,
191–2; Williams on, 191, 217, 228,
231, 234, 236, 246, 275 n. 71. *See
also* Circumstances of impartiality;
Feminist critique of impartiality;
First-order impartiality; Justice as
impartiality; Second-order impartiality
India: ban on *The Satanic Verses* in, 88;
Hindu religion in, 38, 209; inequality in, 209, 212; quotas for stigmatized groups in, 100, 101 n.;
scheduled castes in, 107, 212–13;
Shah Bano case in, 38; Thugs, in, 89;
Westminster model unsuited to, 106
Indians, American, 41–3, 45 n., 50
Inequality: and beliefs, 208–9; in
Britain, 198 n., 207; and common-
sense morality, 207–13; ethnic, in
Eastern (post-Soviet) Europe,
114–15; and first-order impartiality,
211–13; in India, 209, 212; legitimation of, 198–9, 285 n. 3, 286 n. 4;
and positive morality, 10, 207–10,
286 n. 10; Rawls and, 54–5, 66–7,
71; and reasonable agreement, 7–8,
67, 70; of rights, 71, 72, 208–9; in
South Africa, 209; in Third World
countries, 198 n.; in United States,
198 n., 207. *See also* Power,
inequality of; Racial equality and
inequality; Sexual equality and
inequality
Information: and acceptance of
inequality, 208–9; and circumstances of impartiality, 107–8; in
Rawlsian original position, 124,
184–5, 187, 213, 216; in Scanlonian
original position, 68–9, 208–9
Intensity of preferences, 146–7, 149,
153, 281 n. 17

Interest rates, 122
Intergenerational justice, 246
International Monetary Fund, 198 n.
'Interpretative' political philosophy,
3–7, 9, 10–11
Islam, 4 n., 122, 171
Islanders, rescue of, 225–6
Israel, 66 n.

Japan, 198 n.
Jefferson, Thomas, 126
Jews: conversion among, 170;
deportation of, 18, 277 n. 37;
exclusion of from club, 15–17; and
Nazis, 194. *See also* Judaism
Johnson, Neville, 278 n. 42
Johnson, Samuel, 255
Judaism, 78, 275 n. 72
Judges: activism in United States by,
99; impartiality required of, 13, 17,
18; in Nozickean society, 202;
political decisions, unsuited to,
96–7. *See also* Courts
Justice: circumstances of, 45 n.; courts
and, 93–9; currency of, 145, 281 n.
14; duty to promote, 245, 290 n. 21;
ethic of, in feminist theory, 249–53;
as fairness (Rawls), x, 8, 54, 272 n.
27; of families, 246, 290 n. 24;
game-theoretical analysis of, 51,
271 n. 36; Hume's definition of, 44,
271 n. 25; intergenerational, 246; of
laws and policies, and circumstances of impartiality, 100–8, 277
n. 36; Mill on, 73; morality, relation
to, 68, 72–9; stability of, 62–3, 64–5,
198–9, 285 n. 3, 286 n. 4;
Thrasymachus on, 39, 43–4, 271 n.
23. *See also* Justice as impartiality;
Justice as mutual advantage; Justice
as reciprocity; Motive for being
just; Principles of justice;
Procedural justice; Rules of Justice
Justice as impartiality: and a priori
method, 195–207; and abstraction,

Liberal individualism (*cont.*):
preferences, 134, 146, 154; as
presocial rights theory, 125; want-
satisfaction and, 128, 133–7
Liberal institutions: autonomy as
basis of, 129, 279 n. 14; utilitarianism as basis of, 134–6. *See also* Civil
rights; Democracy
Liberal paradox (Sen), 135 n.
Liberalism: Larmore on, 177; Nagel
on, 177, 178. *See also* Liberal
individualism; Liberal institutions
Liberty, as a conception of the good,
87
Lijphart, Arend, 277 n. 37
Locke, Don, 225 n., 287 n. 8
Locke, John, 46 n., 125
Lottery, and first-order impartiality:
in Captain's Dilemma, 237–41,
258–66; and medical treatment,
227–8; and rescue, 226, 229
Lucania (Italy), 253
Luce, Edward, 41 n.
Luck, bad. *See* Bad luck
Luker, Kristin, 92–3
Lutheran Church, 165 n.

Macaulay, Thomas Babington (Baron
Macaulay), 89
Macedo, Stephen, 275 n. 4
MacIntyre, Alasdair: on Aristotle,
193–4; and cost–benefit analysis,
154, 282 n. 27; on the Enlightenment, 74 n. f, 121, 170 n.; on
impartiality, 119–20, 234, 236,
289 n. 6; and justice as impartiality,
13, 73, 119–38, 139–40, 162, 183,
234; on liberal individualism, 119,
122, 123–4, 125–8, 134, 136–7; on
neo-Thomism, 74 n. g; on neutrality between conceptions of the
good, 13, 73, 119–21, 125–8, 137–8,
139–40; on Nietzsche, 193; on
preferences, 134, 146, 154; on
rationality, as basis of justice as

impartiality, 53, 74 n. f, 119, 121–2,
170 n.; on Thomism, 73–5, 122, 123,
126, 171, 274 n. 63; on traditions,
73–4; on utilitarianism, 139–40,
154–5, 161; on voting, 134, 146,
154; on want-satisfaction, as a
conception of the good, 133–7,
139–40, 154, 282 n. 27; on Williams,
234
Majority: abuse of, 104; one-party,
106; voting system, 146–8, 282 n. 24
Mann, Michael, 286 n. 4
Mansbridge, Jane J., 277 n. 41
Marine salvage, 243 n.
Marines, United States, 238
Marriage laws in India, 38
Mars, men from, 7, 255
Marx, Karl, 286 n. 6
Maximin decision rule, 61, 163, 264–5,
273 n. 29
Maximization of good: as consequentialist impartiality, 23–7; and
constitutional rules, 81; as a duty,
23–5; as form of first-order impartiality, 12; justice as impartiality,
contrasted with, 76–7; and problem
of disputes about the good, 12,
26–7; as rational, 25, 76; in
Rawlsian original position, 58–9,
72; and rules of justice, 72–6. *See
also* Consequentialism
Media of mass communication, bias
in, 108, 198
Medical care: constitutional guarantees of, 96; distribution by lottery
of, 227–8; in Europe, 245; Gauthier
on, 42; justice as impartiality
requires system of, 244–6; QALYs
and, 228 n.; Rawls on, 272 n. 28
Mendus, Susan, 172 n.
Menu, voting on, 147
Mill, James, 81
Mill, John Stuart: on acceptability of
utilitarianism, 192; and autonomy
as a conception of the good, 129; on

310 *Index*

Rescue (*cont.*):
Categorical Imperative and, 230;
common-sense morality and, 15,
226, 246–7; of Fénelon ('famous fire
cause') 222–5, 231, 232; lottery and,
226, 229; second-order impartiality
and, 11–12, 194–5, 233; and
universalizability, 230
Resources, and utility, 149
Revelation: of preferences, 146;
religious, 179–80
Rights: American Bill of, 83;
American Declaration of
Independence, 8; of animals, 208,
286 n. 11; European Convention on
Human Rights, 83, 275 n. 4; French
Declaration of, 8; human, 4, 83, 275
n. 4; moral, 79; political, 109, 110;
presocial, 125; rules of justice
assign, 72; social, 96–9, 277 n. 29;
unequal, 71, 72, 208–9; to vote, 208.
See also Civil rights
Robbins, Lionel, 281 n. 17
Roman Catholics: and Albigensians,
176; Counter-Reformation, 170;
discrimination against in Britain,
165 n.; and natural law thinking,
169; and neo-Thomism, 74; and
religious toleration, 163–4; in wars
of religion, 169–70. *See also*
Thomism
Roman republic, 89–90
Romania, corruption in, 18 n.
Rousseau, Jean-Jacques, 148
Rules. *See* Constitutional rules; Rules
of justice
Rules of justice: and circumstances of
impartiality, 100–11; defined, 12, 72;
and first-order impartiality, 204–7;
and harm, 34; and justice as impartiality, 12, 52, 72–9; and justice as
mutual advantage, 33–7; legal and
moral rules included in, 34, 100, 201,
206; and maximization of good,
72–6; principles of justice, relation

to, 75–6; and private property, 201;
rights assigned by, 72; in a theory of
justice, 46; in a Thomist society,
74–5; in a utilitarian society, 72–3,
160, 287 n. 7. *See also* Legal sanctions; Moral sanctions
Rushdie, Salman, 4 n., 88

Safety net, 203
Sagoff, Mark, 158
Salvage, marine, 243 n.
Salvation, religious, 28–9
Sanctions. *See* Legal sanctions; Moral
sanctions
Scandinavia, 108
Scanlon, T. M., 10, 52, 111, 113, 165.
See also Scanlonian original
position; Scanlonian theory
Scanlonian original position: and a
priori approach, 195, 200; and
bureaucracy, 204; and circumstances of impartiality, 99–100, 196,
207–9; exposition of, 67–72; and
fairness, 68, 113; and first-order
impartiality, 200, 205, 206–9,
212–13; information held by people
in, 68–9, 107, 124; and institutions,
justifications of, 68, 165; motives of
people in, 67, 108, 121; and neutrality between conceptions of the
good, 120; and presocial rights, 125;
Rawlsian original position, comparison with, 10, 67, 120–1; reasonable
agreement and, 10, 168; restrictions
on arguments in, 167, 168; and
Thomism, 122; veto in, 106–7
Scanlonian theory: and abstraction,
120–1; and circumstances of
impartiality, 100, 113, 197–8, 207;
civil rights derived within, 70–2;
contractual, 67, 165; exposition of,
67–70; first-order impartiality and,
195–213; freedom of worship
derived within, 83–4; and fundamental equality, 113; and motiva-

314

Author's note

To avoid redundancy and keep to one level of subhead only, headings that are subdivided do not appear elsewhere as subheads. Instead, they are listed under '*See*' or '*See also*'. It should therefore be borne in mind that '*See also*' items may be at least as central to the topic of the main heading as any of the subheads under that heading. Among the endnotes, only substantive notes are indexed, and the only names indexed are those that are quoted or discussed in substantive notes.